Multinational
Corporations

Multinational Corporations

The Political Economy of Foreign Direct Investment

Edited by
Theodore H. Moran
Georgetown University

Lexington Books
D.C. Heath and Company/Lexington, Massachusetts/Toronto

Library of Congress Cataloging in Publication Data
Main entry under title:

Multinational corporations.

    Includes index.
    1. International business enterprises—Developing countries—Addresses, essays,
lectures. 2. Investments, Foreign—Developing countries—Addresses, essays, lectures.
I. Moran, Theodore H., 1943–
HD2932.M84   1985   338.8′ 88′ 724   85-45293
ISBN 0-669-11241-0 (alk. paper)
ISBN 0-669-11242-9 (pbk. : alk. paper)

Published simultaneously in Canada
Printed in the United States of America
Casebound International Standard Book Number: 0-669-11241-0
Paperbound International Standard Book Number: 0-669-11242-9
Library of Congress Catalog Card Number: 85-45293

The paper used in this publication meets the minimum requirements of American National
Standard for Information Sciences—Permanence of Paper for Printed Library Materials,
ANSI Z39.48-1984.

Contents

Preface

The understanding of multinational corporate behavior, and its implications for home and host countries, has advanced substantially over the past decade on three levels: the analysis of corporate strategy, the assessment of the impact of international firms on the societies where they are located, and the design of appropriate public policies toward inward or outward investment. At the same time the struggle to influence or control multinational corporate activities so as to generate jobs, expand exports, secure resources, penetrate markets, and create technology has intensified. This book gathers the best of the new generation of research on multinational corporations and places it in the context of the debates that will decide whether the liberal international economic order that has sustained the West since the end of World War II will survive into the future.

The book is divided into three parts, the last of which offers conclusions on the book as a whole. The first two parts are described below. Chapters 1 and 7 contain analytical overviews of parts I and II, respectively. Short summaries, written by the editor, appear at the head of those chapters not written by the editor himself.

Part I deals with the impact of foreign direct investment on the Third World. The aggregate data on economic growth, income distribution, political autonomy and social welfare, surveyed in chapter 1, underscore the need for individual case studies that differentiate between sector and type of country. This part examines the determinants of bargaining power between international companies and host countries and the opportunities, constraints, and dangers in natural resource industries, mature technology manufacturing industries, and high technology manufacturing industries. It contrasts cases in which the host governments were able to utilize competition among the multinationals to play one off against another for better terms (as in the computer industry in India) with cases in which the host governments did not (as in the pharmaceutical industry in Mexico). And it looks at the counter-risk strategies of the multinationals themselves, including the attempt to use political pressure and influence within the developing countries where they operate. Finally, it focuses on the special issue of appropriate technology with a novel selection on the growing phenomenon of investment by multinationals from Third World country origins.

Turning to the developed countries, part II asks whether the growing power of some Third World governments to harness multinationals (albeit modest and selective) constitutes a threat to the industrial strength of the First World. It examines the controversy about whether international competition is leading to the deindustrialization of the United States by both imports from abroad and outward investment by U.S. multinationals (a controversy that has a long tradition in European literature as well). It concentrates specifically on the debate about whether the movement of corporate operations out of the home country constitutes a contemporary version of the runaway plant phenomenon. And to put these controversies and debates into a setting that allows an understanding of current policy outcomes, it surveys the political economy of the policymaking process for trade as well as investment in the developed countries. It examines new transnational alliances that international companies have been building to evade conventional pressures toward cloture and ensure access to markets and technology that might otherwise be closed to them. Finally, it focuses on the increasingly tense cases (such as the Soviet gas pipeline case) in which the multinationals have conflicting sovereign directives placed directly upon them.

In part III, the book turns to the policy implications of these studies for both home and host countries. It extracts the lessons from these cases about how the Third World can best gain the benefits and avoid the costs of foreign direct investment. It also looks at the policy alternatives posed to developed countries: whether it is necessary to meet the challenge of international competition through slowing the pace of change or wise to construct a special industrial policy of firm-specific or sector-specific interventions to match the emergence of other multinational companies around the world. Finally, it examines the evolving structure of the international system and the prospects for further change: whether the liberal principles of the postwar era could exist only as long as the United States was a hegemonic power and are now bankrupt and whether the international system is likely to evolve toward cloture, toward a structure of competing mercantilisms, or toward a new era of sovereignty at bay as the multinationals pursue their own self-interested strategies around the globe.

This book is designed for corporate strategists and governmental policymakers, as well as for upper-level undergraduate and graduate classes in political science, political economy, economics, business administration, and management. It should be a useful supplement to texts on development, trade, and finance, as well as on corporate strategy and investment behavior.

The book draws on formative inspirations at Harvard University and to modestly more mature reflections at Georgetown University. It is the direct outgrowth of the opportunity to teach in the Karl F. Landegger Chair of International Business Diplomacy at the Georgetown School of Foreign Service. It reflects the support of, and is dedicated to, my family, changing and evolving, during difficult and troubled times.

Part I
Multinational Corporations and the Developing Countries

1

Multinational Corporations and the Developing Countries: An Analytical Overview

Theodore H. Moran

W hat is the impact of foreign direct investment on the development of countries in the Third World? This is one of the oldest and most fiercely debated questions in the literature on multinational corporations.

The conventional tradition of development economics has consistently viewed the impact of foreign direct investment on the Third World benignly, a perspective that springs directly from prevailing neoclassical assumptions about the conditions of market behavior.[1] Foreign investors bring new, scarce resources—capital, technology, management, and marketing skill—to the host country. Their presence increases competition, improves efficiency, adds jobs, and improves the distribution of income (by lowering the returns to capital while bidding up wages). Within this framework, it is difficult not to arrive at favorable conclusions about the contribution of multinational corporations to the process of development. Increasingly, however, as the principal assumptions of the neoclassical perspective have been tested as hypotheses rather than merely accepted as givens, they have been found lacking, and the results have rendered the assessment of how international companies may affect the development process much more complex.

The first challenge arose from exploring the relationship between international investment and the competitiveness of the markets in which it occurs. In a pathbreaking shift away from the neoclassical vision, Stephen Hymer and Charles Kindleberger were the first to propose that foreign direct investment was in fact logically incompatible with competitive markets.[2] Without some kind of market imperfections, they argued, the disadvantages of operating in a foreign environment would favor local entrepreneurs over international competitors. The importance of market imperfections in motivating foreign investment was extended in the product cycle model of Raymond Vernon, who traced the decision to invest abroad as a corporate strategy of following up exports before technological and managerial advantages became diffused in overseas markets.[3] More recently the role of imperfect competition has been formalized in Richard Caves's idea of sector-specific capital, which accounts for the phenomenon of cross-investment in industries where the parent corporations sit on opposite sides of national borders while profit rates remain differentiated between sectors within each country.[4] Since the mid-1970s, then, the dynamics of foreign direct investment have increasingly been explained as corporate strategies to defend barriers to entry into an industry and extend the ability of the parent company to extract oligopoly rents.

To buttress the theoretical perspective of foreign investment as necessarily having to embody important elements of oligopoly power, the empirical examination of the phenomenon has shown that it does tend to take place in industries in which concentration ratios are high rather than low. Fishwick and Pugel, for example, have demonstrated, in separate studies, a high correlation between industry concentration and outward investment in the United States, United Kingdom, France, and Germany.[5] Conversely, viewed from the perspective of a recipient country in the Third World, Brazil and Mexico, for example, have received 83 percent and 84 percent (respectively) of foreign investment in sectors in which the four-firm concentration ratio exceeded 50 percent.[6]

Further upsetting the neoclassical paradigm, multinational firms frequently do not bring in much, if any, new capital from outside when they invest.[7] Rather, to establish themselves, they appropriate local capital for their own use. At the same time, they tend to utilize capital-intensive technology developed in response to the factor proportions in their home economies where wages are higher.[8] And they seek host country protection from competitive forces that might drive them to develop new, least-cost, labor-intensive production methods more appropriate to a Third World locale. In such circumstances the possibilities for creating distortions in the local environment abound. In the extreme, foreign companies might capture the commanding heights of the host economy, soak up indigenous sources of capital as they drive local firms out of business, create a small labor elite for themselves while transferring the bulk of the workers into the ranks of the unemployed, and siphon off oligopoly profits for repatriation to corporate headquarters. This could hardly be favorable for the rate of growth or the structure of the development process. It opens the debate about the impact of multinational corporations to some of the more sophisticated Marxist and *dependencia* writings.[9]

Whether such dire results are the predominant, let alone inevitable, consequence of the impact of multinational corporations or whether the outcome might be expected to be much more favorable cannot be determined from the aggregate studies that have been attempted. Reuber demonstrated that the stock of foreign investment per capita is positively correlated with gross national product (GNP) per capita across the Third World, but by itself this discovery does not necessarily establish a causative linkage.[10] Chase-Dunn and

Bornschier attempted to show a negative relationship between the stock of foreign direct investment and the rate of growth of the recipient countries, but flaws in their statistical methodology have undermined the results.[11] Dolan and Tomlin did find a negative relationship between foreign investment stocks and rates of growth, but they simultaneously discovered a positive link between foreign investment flows and rates of growth.[12] The fact that the flow variable measured a more recent period than the stock variable might suggest, among other things, that the contribution of multinational corporations to the development process has been changing over time.

To come to grips with the question of how much of a contribution multinational companies make to development, it is necessary to shift from the macro perspective to the micro and examine case studies of how individual host countries have in fact been affected, sector by sector, by foreign investors in their midst. A static perspective has proved particularly inappropriate as host governments have taken a more and more active part in shaping the course of corporate operations in their countries.

Foreign Investor–Host Country Bargaining: Opportunities and Dangers in the Extractive Sector

In terms of theory, the predominant model that economists have used when looking at the relations between foreign investors and host countries has been one of bilateral monopoly: the foreign investor has control over the capital, technology, management, and marketing skills needed to launch the project successfully; the host country has control over access before the investment is made and over the conditions for operation afterward.[13] While the interaction need not necessarily be zero-sum, there is likely to be a struggle over the structuring of the project and the distribution of the benefits.

What will determine the outcome of that struggle? How are the benefits likely to be divided? Edith Penrose was one of the first to attempt to set a standard by arguing that the foreign company should receive just what is necessary to induce it (and others) to commit itself to invest in the first place and prevent it from withdrawing afterward.[14] Others, including Charles Kindleberger, challenged this formulation.[15] The Penrose standard, Kindleberger argued, might constitute the lower limit of the amount one should expect the foreigner to receive. The upper limit, however, would be the scarcity value to the host country of the services the foreign company had to offer, that is, the price at which the country would rather forgo those services and do without the investment. The distance between these two extremes, the upper and the lower limits, might be very wide.

The early attempts to look at foreign investor–host country relations within the framework of bilateral monopoly suffered from being too static and too indeterminant. To add more dynamism to the analysis, Raymond Vernon introduced the idea of what he called the "obsolescing bargaining."[16] Central to Vernon's formulation was the role of risk and uncertainty. Before the investment was made, the production costs determined, and the market established, risk and uncertainty would be high for the foreign company. To induce the latter to invest, the agreement would have to be structured to reward the company handsomely if the project proved successful. At the same time, the host government faced the choice of signing a generous investment contract and getting some benefit in return or refusing to allow a generous investment contract and receiving no benefit at all. Within this incentive structure, the rational solution would be to grant an investment agreement that was steeply tilted to favor the foreigner at the outset.

The dynamism in the obsolescing bargain that accounts for a shift in power from the foreign investor to the host country springs from the dissipation of risk and uncertainty if the project proves successful. It may also come from a kind of hostage effect, where the company cannot easily threaten to withdraw, credibly, once its investment has been sunk. Finally, it can be fed by the augmentation of host capabilities as the country moves up a learning curve of bargaining and managerial skills, the better to drive a hard bargain with the foreigner and/or to threaten to replace him if he balks at renegotiating the initial contract. (The renegotiation of investment contracts can also be speeded by competition, when a second investor tries to underbid the first in an attempt to take away the concession.) Whatever the combination of specific causes, the obsolescing bargain model predicts that the initially favorable investment agreement for the foreigner is likely to be subsequently renegotiated in favor of the host country.

The obsolescing bargain framework constituted a breakthrough in several respects. Not only did it provide a dynamic understanding of the evolution of bargaining relations between a host country and foreign company over the life of a project, it also offered a model of economic nationalism based on rational self-interest rather than on otherwise popular interpretations about machinations of leftists or waves of antiforeign emotions. Furthermore it provided, on the one hand, a realistic expectation about how favorable to the foreigner new investment concessions would have to be to attract investment. On the other hand, it provided a hopeful perspective about the eventual strengthening of the hand of Third World authorities in renegotiating the initial agreement to capture more and more of the benefits from foreign investment. And it explained the otherwise counterintuitive outcome of having some of the world's largest (and presumably most powerful) corporations suddenly become quite vulnerable to host country authorities.

The idea of the obsolescing bargain was tested first in case studies in the extractive sector, such as copper and petroleum, in which there was a definite pattern of tightening the early beneficial terms of the concession agreements after the operation came successfully on-line.[17] Host country demands included higher taxes, greater processing, joint marketing, more employment of nationals in managerial positions, and shared ownership.[18] The swing in tax rates ran as high as thirty percentage points (38 percent to 68 percent effective rate) in copper and forty-two percentage points (50 percent to 92 percent effective rate) in petroleum. Local refinery capacity was pushed up from a very low figure in 1960 to 38 percent of Third World copper output and 52 percent of Third World petroleum output in 1980. The drive for the placement of nationals in supervisory and management positions had varied success. When Kennecott was nationalized in Chile in 1971, only two of the ten thousand employees were U.S. citizens. In Zaire in 1979, twelve years after the formal nationalization of Union Minière, at least two hundred foreign technicians were still required in key positions to operate the mines.

The first selection in this book, Michael Shafer's study of the mining sector in Zaire and Zambia, grows out of the tradition of obsolescing bargain analysis. He shows exclusive fifty-year concessions with minimal tax rates giving way to 51 percent host-owned joint ventures with tax rates as high as 87 percent. But Shafer takes this perspective an important step forward. Whereas the early research highlighted the gains host authorities could achieve from successful brinksmanship with foreign companies that could be maneuvered to stay and expand local operations, Shafer focuses on what may happen when governments push the obsolescing bargain to its extreme: full nationalization. He argues that nationalization of mineral production in vertically integrated industries may have negative consequences for most Third World economies. The principal reason for this is a loss of the insulation provided by the international mining companies. This insulation provides a buffer between the state and an often volatile commodity market, between the state and other vertically integrated companies, between the state and self-serving officials, and between the state and the demands of special interest groups, such as labor.

Shafer's analysis divides the negative ramifications of this loss of insulation into international and domestic aspects. At the international level, the Zambian and Zairian governments overlooked the fact that vertical integration ensured the multinationals' outlets for their production in times of glut and a degree of control over the violent price swings that characterize most commodity markets. This was supplemented by informal vertical integration, or long-term sales contracts with major buyers, which were also forgone once the Zairian and Zambian industries were nationalized. In its place the nationalized copper companies attempted to form a copper producers' cartel, the Intergovernmental Council Exporting Countries (CIPEC).

But the cartel did not provide a mechanism for price control by the producer governments because, Shafer argues, there is an inherent contradiction between nationalization and cartelization. State-owned enterprises, with their multiple and divergent goals and constituencies, find it much more difficult than companies to focus in concert on the common objective of high and stable profits. Cartels with state-owned companies as the primary actors tend to have the effect of undermining oligopoly control if they try to maintain output (and employment) in the weak as well as the strong side of the business cycle.

Furthermore, the reaction of the rest of the copper industry to a producer's cartel, coming at the same time as the Organization of Petroleum Exporting Countries (OPEC), was such that the risk to the nationalized industries was magnified. Investment shifted to the high-cost, lower-grade safe countries and away from higher-quality, less expensive Third World sites. The scramble for new, secure sources of supply thus resulted in a misallocation of the industry's scarce resources and an exacerbation of the problem of excess capacity throughout the entire international copper industry. The consequent overproduction and lower prices naturally had a negative impact on the performance of the nationalized companies.

At the domestic level, Shafer argues that insulation is essential because of the weakness of most newly independent Third World states: they do not possess strong institutions that can run the industry autonomously in the face of local pressures. Rather, nationalization has the effect of magnifying the economic and political consequences of state weakness. In the case of Zaire, rampant corruption and greedy officials meant that state financing could not be sustained at levels that allowed for maintenance of the industry and/or for new investment. In Zambia, the loss of insulation between the state and labor ironically resulted in less, rather than more, satisfaction of labor's demands. Without the buffer of the multinationals, the government was compelled by union leaders to increase the number of semiskilled jobs. The wage gap between skilled and unskilled workers widened, and the government, once a champion of the workers against the foreign corporations, became an ally of the nationalized company against the union.

Finally Shafer asks whether the experiences of Zaire and Zambia can be generalized to all cases of nationalization in the extractive sector. He concludes that nationalization always incurs costs but that its extent varies with the strength, resources, and autonomy of the state. Since most Third World governments do not have the institutional framework, the technocratic skills and expertise, or the incentive structure that allows officials to avoid making business decisions based on short-term economic and political gain, the costs associated with nationalization may therefore be inordinately high.

Shafer's analysis shows that the obsolescing bargain can hold dangers as well as opportunities. He suggests that the government's goal of realizing broader economic benefits from the copper multinationals could have been achieved while stopping short of nationalization.

Foreign Investor–Host Country Bargaining: The Manufacturing Sector in Mature and High Technology Industries

The most dramatic cases of the obsolescing bargain took place first in natural resources, but the phenomenon has been present for at least two decades in the manufacturing sector as well. Here host country objectives have been more complex. They included higher taxes and joint ownership, as in the extractive industries, but have come to center on the goal of harnessing the manufacturing multinationals more directly to the process of industrial development. Host country demands clustered around *performance requirements* in two areas: (1) pressuring the multinationals to produce more value-added domestically, provide more local content in their finished product, and expand the linkages into the indigenous economy and (2) pushing the multinationals to use their worldwide marketing networks to export more products and components out of the host economy.

Past research in this area has focused on foreign investment in sectors with mature, relatively stable technology, which have been central targets for the nationalism of the more advanced of the Third World countries.[19] Among these, the automotive industry has figured most prominently.[20] In 1957 local content in the automobile industry in Latin America, for example, was 30 percent; in 1980, local content had been pushed to approximately 70 percent, with requirements imposed by Argentina set at 95 percent, by Mexico set at 60 percent, and by Brazil set at 100 percent. At the same time Mexico tied the importation of components, dollar for dollar, to the value of exports. And Brazil limited expansion in the domestic market to foreign companies willing to undertake an export program of $400 million over a ten-year period. Competition from Volkswagen, Fiat, Toyota and Datsun placed GM, Ford, and Chrysler under strong pressure to comply.

The studies that have been done in this area do not record a pattern of unambiguous success. Bennett and Sharpe have pointed out in the case of the Mexican automobile assembly, for example, that there are demand rigidities and enforcement difficulties in trying to use multinationals for export promotion. Similarly, Coronil and Skurski have shown the problems of pursuing a strategy of industrial expansion by the multinational car companies in a small and inefficient market like Venezuela.[21] Still, the evidence of host country advances in forcing international corporations in mature technology industries to create more value-added locally and to expand the export of indigenously produced products and components is clear. In Mexico, for example, foreign automobile firms employed approximately 9,000 workers in 1962; in 1977 they employed more than 39,000, with supplier industries and distributors employing 109,000 more. Rhys Jenkins and Peter West argue that the tractor industry may be following the pattern set in the automotive sector, with the addition of Japanese and Socialist-bloc companies as competitors to the traditional U.S., Canadian, and European multinationals.[22] (For the reaction on the part of organized labor in the developed world about losing jobs as a result of Third World attempts to extend the obsolescing bargain to manufacturing multinationals, see p. 124.)[23]

But what about high technology industries? Do the same dynamics apply? Can host authorities use leverage to harness high technology multinationals as well as mature technology companies? Here the study of the evolution of the computer industry in India by Joseph Grieco (chapter 3) is particularly valuable.

Grieco examines the computer industry in India during three consecutive periods (1967–1972, 1973–1977, 1978–1980) as an explicit test case of the extent to which host countries can control and benefit from multinationals in high technology industries. In the first period Grieco looks at (1967–1972), India found itself in a very weak position. Despite vigorous host country representations, IBM rebuffed its central demand by refusing categorically to share ownership with the Indian government. The British firm, ICL, did allow India a 40 percent ownership stake in its manufacturing unit, but the parent kept corporate decision making that affected activities in India out of India's reach. Almost all of the computer systems installed in India in this early period were controlled by foreign suppliers. And India's computer policy institutions were fragmented and enjoyed little authority or control over the industry. There existed, in effect, a stalemate between the two ministries in charge of policy affecting the computer industry.

In the second period Grieco examines (1973–1977), the stalemate was broken, but policies aimed at control of the multinationals were, in his judgment, misdirected. Two new agencies, the Electronics Commission and the Department of Electronics, made the promotion of an indigenous computer industry a priority through the creation of a national champion state company, ECIL (Electronics Corporation of India, Ltd.). However, rather than fostering the development of the private local firms that were just beginning to multiply in this period, Grieco notes that the computer bureaucracy instead chose to protect the government enterprise, ECIL, by restricting any imports that could conceivably compete with it. This reinforced the adverse consequences of another policy adopted by the bureaucracy: encouragement for procuring the largest and most advanced systems that only IBM and ICL could provide. Thus, during this period India was giving preference to the importation of large systems while limiting access to alternative foreign systems, in effect perpetuating the country's own weakness while playing to the multinationals' strength.

India's bargaining position did not improve, Grieco argues, until technological advances and changes in the structure of the international computer industry widened India's available policy options. First, the number of foreign computer firms with activities in developing countries such as India expanded from nine to more than sixteen firms. Second, computer systems and components became less expensive and more diverse. Innovations in the industry led to small systems architectures (the minicomputer and the microcomputer), which were easier for developing countries to duplicate and more appropriate to their needs. At the same time, the international industry became less concentrated and offered India alternative sources of supply for computer components. These components became the building blocks that India could acquire for use in conjunction with the newly available smaller systems.

These international developments coincided with institutional changes and shifts in policy within India's data processing industry that enabled the country to exploit these opportunities. India's previous approach of encouraging the intensive use of a small number of large systems was replaced by regulations that instead allowed the importation of a large number of smaller systems that India could more easily reproduce. And the country adopted a strategy of actively trying to attract other firms to India, Burroughs being the most prominent example. As a consequence, in contrast to the 1960s when the government had no choice but to accept IBM's refusal to share ownership, the 1970s were marked by India's pursuance of its policies even at the cost of losing the leading firm in computer technology. By 1977 IBM withdrew entirely from the Indian market, but Burroughs and ICL remained under the government's terms.

India's objective of strengthening the indigenous computer industry was not fully realized until the final period Grieco examines (1978–1980). A new director, appointed to head both the Department of Electronics and the Electronics Commission, lifted what institutionalized roadblocks remained. He further relaxed restrictions on computer imports. The national firm's (ECIL's) market share was rapidly overtaken by more efficient, privately owned indigenous firms that built their own links to international suppliers. India's technological lag—the difference in years between a system's introduction in the advanced countries and its adoption in a developing country—decreased. Technological sophistication—measured by Grieco as the cost per bit of main memory—also advanced.

Thus India met its twin objectives of greater control over the computer multinationals and development of an indigenous computer industry by a roundabout way. The early efforts to take control directly by limiting foreign penetration backfired. But rapid technological change in the international industry increased the options available to the country. It was not until India took advantage of this source of strength by outward-looking development policies, whereby imports increased and other firms entered the country, that the computer sector came close to its full potential.

Grieco uses his study of the computer industry in India to test whether the Marxist *dependencia* school or the bargaining school serves better as a predictor of relations between high technology multinationals and developing countries. In his characterization, the Marxist *dependencia* school asserts that multinationals will never bestow advantages on less developed economies because their power will always lie outside the control of the state. Bargaining between the country and the corporation, when it occurs, is over marginal issues that do not result in a shift of power over corporate activities affecting the state. Proponents of the bargaining school, in contrast, argue that negotiations can result in significant changes in the degree of control and distribution of benefits between the state and the multinational enterprise. On the basis of his case, Grieco sides with the bargaining school argument that progress for the less developed economies can come through active engagement with, not detachment from, the international economy and the multinational corporate community.

Is Grieco's argument valid for all high technology industries that multinationals invest in in the Third World? The conclusion Grieco arrives at rests on the proposition that host authorities will be able to take advantage of competitive pressures within international industries to reduce their dependence on any one corporation and ultimately to play potential investors and technology suppliers off against one another. This has been one of the most hotly debated propositions in the literature on multinational corporations.

One side argues that the product cycle ensures the gradual diffusion of tightly held technologies and production processes, allowing the entry of new actors into the marketplace. Raymond Vernon, for example, traces the steady erosion of concentration ratios in the automobile, aluminum, petroleum, lead, pulp and paper, zinc, copper, and petrochemical (styrene monomer) industries between 1950 and 1975 as evidence that oligopoly power can seldom be maintained over time.[24] Dunning and Pierce similarly found a decline in the share of the top three firms in twelve of fourteen industries in the Fortune 500 between 1962 and 1972.[25]

The other side fears that a conglomeratization of international firms may mean that multinationals meet in several product and national markets, reinforcing their shared appreciation of interdependence. This could lead to a live-and-let-live philosophy.[26] In this situation host countries would have difficulty provoking rivalry among foreign companies because that could trigger reprisals elsewhere. Even worse than this, according to Newfarmer, is the possibility that global concentration could be increasing, at least at the level of the largest fifty to two hundred firms.

The case study of the India computer industry tends to support the more optimistic product-cycle perspective rather than the more pessimistic reconcentration perspective, but clearly there can be no definitive answer on the basis of one case. Grieco's study suggests another point, however: that Third World countries are likely to have to do more than merely take competition among potential international investors for granted. Rather, whether through public or through private efforts, Third World countries will have to play an active role in *stimulating* rivalries within the international corporate sectors in which they are seeking investment.

This idea has a well-documented history in extractive industries and some support in manufacturing industries as well. In petroleum, copper, and nickel, there is evidence that the dangling of concessions in front of independents is an effective strategy to make the majors fearful about an upset in the oligopoly equilibrium.[27] The resulting anxiety about market shares has produced competitive bidding to enter a given country and lock up new sources of supply.

In manufacturing industries, Third World governments may have similar possibilities of playing one investor off against another. There is evidence that international companies play what Knickerbocker has called "follow the leader" in making investments in the Third World.[28] He has found a statistical burst phenomenon in which once the first company establishes itself in a country, several more corporations invest in rapid succession in the same industry.

As both the computer and the automobile cases illustrate, this competition among multinational corporations can be a powerful tool in the hand of Third World authorities. Whereas the *dependencia* school worries about the growing number of multinationals, the bargaining school argues that the multiplication of subsidiaries can strengthen rather than weaken the position of Third World governments. Raymond Vernon has found that the number of foreign subsidiaries in agricultural chemicals in Brazil, for example, grew from two to ten between 1960 and 1970, in Mexico from four to seven, in Colombia from one to eight, in India from one to seven; in plastics materials and synthetics in Brazil from seven to fifteen, in Mexico from twelve to nineteen, in Colombia from two to eight, in India from four to sixteen; in general industrial machinery in Brazil from three to seven, in Mexico from three to eleven, in Colombia from one to one, in India from one to four.[29]

But, as the next section indicates, bargaining with multinationals has limits, limits in part determined by counterstrategies on the part of the foreign companies themselves.

Limits to Host Country Power: Foreign Control of Technology and the Exercise of Political Influence

In the preceding case, dynamic changes in computer technology gave India new alternatives to strengthen its position in relation to the international computer industry. In the next case presented in this book (chapter 4), Gary Gereffi's study of the pharmaceutical industry in Mexico between 1975 and 1982, the ability of foreign firms to maintain control over the technology of producing steroid hormones (and consequently over the distribution and marketing of the final product) limited Mexico's ability to exact benefits from the industry. But control over technology was not the only factor that led to this outcome. It was also due to the fact that the political counterstrategies of the multinationals within the Mexican governmental and bureaucratic apparatus worked.

Mexico possesses one of the world's largest sources of barbasco, the principal ingredient for natural steroid hormones, and hoped to convert this, with the participation of international drug companies with a state-owned firm, Proquivemex, into a flourishing industry that would benefit peasant growers, produce finished products to serve domestic needs, and generate foreign exchange with a dynamic penetration of external markets. But Mexico's success in harnessing the international companies to achieve these goals was much more modest than originally hoped. Ultimately the state managed to achieve only a higher price for the raw material and greater payments to the peasants. Thus, a forceful program was converted into mild reform.

In the study there are case-specific reasons why Proquivemex faltered in its effort to mold the foreign corporations' private international goals to serve the social needs of the state. The peso's devaluation, the internal scarcity of the raw material, and the increasing use of substitute products contributed to Proquivemex's mixed success. There was also a conflict of goals, both within the Mexican bureaucracy and between the central government and Proquivemex. National economic goals, such as the promotion of exports, for example, conflicted with the state firm's social goals of obtaining higher raw materials prices for the peasants.

Beyond these factors, however, Gereffi argues that continuing domination of technology by the foreign firms kept many of the potential benefits from the steroid hormone industry beyond the grasp of the host country. And Mexico did not try, or was not successful at playing one international drug company off against another, as happened in the case of computers in India. As a consequence, Gereffi concludes, until developing countries gain access to major barriers of entry such as technological know-how within certain manufacturing industries, strategies to increase state autonomy will necessarily be limited.

Gereffi's contribution goes beyond identifying control over technology as a source of strength for foreign investors. Rather, that strength is also due to the effectiveness of the political counterstrategies of the pharmaceutical multinationals in Mexico. Here Gereffi makes an important contribution to the question of how multinational investors can exercise political influence within Third World countries, and his analysis is more subtle than most of the other literature in this field.

Dependencia writers have tended to assert that multinational firms have solid local political alliances and great local political influence, with the margin for autonomous domestic policy action extremely thin. International business writers, in contrast, tend to argue that foreign companies are continuously buffeted by hostile local forces, discriminated against on a regular basis, and left to operate almost totally without domestic political clout.

In the complex and murky area of domestic political linkages, what does the evidence about multinationals indicate? First, it suggests that ideology alone is not a very strong binding element, as conservative political groups have shown themselves quite willing to participate in and even to lead the attack against foreign investors when this can divert efforts at reform from themselves or gain them legitimacy and popular support.[30]

Second, it suggests that alliances or rivalries on the basis of self-interest are extremely diverse. On the one hand, local business groups may, in some instances, constitute a national bourgeoisie opposed to foreign penetration because of the concrete economic threat posed by the multinationals. Public opinion surveys in Argentina, Brazil, Chile, Peru, Colombia, Mexico, and Venezuela, for example, have shown that domestic businessmen, especially smaller businessmen, are frequently even stronger in their support for national controls over foreign firms than labor unions, student groups, or the intelligentsia.[31] On the other hand, there may be, in other instances, a *comprador* elite eager to ally with foreign companies and identify their own interests with the foreigners' welfare. In an aggregate survey, Stephen Kobrin has found that the choice of local capitalists as partners is likely, statistically, to shield foreign investors against the prospect of nationalization.[32] In a case study in Brazil, Peter Evans found international companies, domestic companies, and state enterprises similarly forming a comfortable ensemble.[33] Evans's analysis shows the indigenous companies gaining a competitive edge through their alliances with foreign firms and at the same time reaping a disproportionate share of the benefits from the relationship. Going a step further, Richard Newfarmer found the manufacturer's association of the electrical and electronics industry in Brazil gradually taken over by representatives of foreign firms (from 35 percent of official positions in 1962 to 60 percent in 1975).[34]

Third, the interplay of domestic politics adds an independent periodicity to nationalistic pressures on foreign investors. Attacks on international companies, condemnations of past investment agreements, and demands for more benefits from them appear to convey legitimacy and build popular support.[35]

Finally, the data suggest that multinational corporations do not do well in head-to-head public confrontations with host authorities. Studies from Latin America and Canada show that the more politicized an investment dispute with a foreign company becomes, the greater the likelihood of an outcome considered favorable by the host country.[36]

In the context of these findings, Gereffi shows how the international pharmaceutical companies sought to redefine the nature of their battle with the state company from a foreign-national conflict to a generalized struggle against the policies of the central government. Their strategy was to reduce their own profile, arouse the rest of the private sector against a broad common threat, exacerbate the conflict of goals within the bureaucracy, and gain allies against elements of the government that were suddenly portrayed as being too interventionist in the local private economy.

Thus Gereffi helps keep earlier assertions about the growth of Third World power and the weakening of multinational corporations in perspective. The outcome of any bargaining relationship between host authorities and foreign investors may be substantially shaped by the ability of the latter to form political alliances, and exercise political influence, within the host society itself.

Managing Political Risk: Multinational Corporate Strategies to Limit Vulnerability to Economic Nationalism

Chapter 4 introduces the theme of counterstrategies adopted by international investors to minimize their exposure to economic nationalism in the Third World. The effort to play on internal differences within the host country and to construct local political alliances, however, is only one of several counterstrategies that multinational companies have been experimenting with.

The preeminent impetus to include political risk management as one of the elements of corporate strategic planning was the fall of the shah of Iran in 1979.[37] As Theodore Moran points out in chapter 5, the initial focus of attention on the part of corporate managers was political risk appraisal, or the effort to predict the likelihood of social upheaval of the kind that overthrew the shah. This reflected a realistic assessment that broad-based revolutions constituted the greatest threat to investments in the Third World. But the effort in this direction was tempered in three ways. First, there has been no reliable system of indicators for forecasting revolution. Overprediction has been as much a problem as underprediction. (General Pinochet in Chile, for example, was asserted to be on his way out more than a dozen times between 1980 and 1985; eventually some analyst may be right.) Second, corporate strategists came to recognize that although social revolution is a threat, it is nowhere as important in overall terms as contending with the less dramatic pressures of everyday economic nationalism. Third, corporations have needed to find ways to continue to operate even in the face of political risk.

Consequently there has been a growing search for methods to assess the vulnerability of investment projects to risks associated with nonrevolutionary situations and for techniques to help mitigate those risks. Clearly, then, as Moran points out, the investment characteristics identified in the previous studies in this book as conveying strength or weakness to host government authorities can be turned on their head to form the basis for *project vulnerability assessment*: large fixed investment, mature technology, undifferentiated marketing, and increasing competition point to vulnerability; smaller investments, tightly held technology, control over marketing, and lack of competition point to relative invulnerability.

Beyond this, the study identifies four strategies that corporations have been adopting to operate despite the presence of risk and vulnerability. First, some corporations have begun to rethink the pure engineering approach to project design. Instead of the biggest, best, world-scale-sized facility built all at once, they have started to sequence the investment process in a way that may provide a series of bargaining chips to play to satisfy nationalistic pressures over a long payback period. Second, they have created arrangements to obtain materials for local operations and to dispose of the output of local operations elsewhere in the corporate system that provide protection against the ability of one host country to nationalize a complete operation. Third, they have attempted to construct loan structures that function as a financial deterrent to a fundamental abrogation of the investment agreement. Finally, they have shown a new interest in selecting local partners who might provide an umbrella of protection under all foreseeable contingencies of political change in the domestic environment.

How much of a constraint are these corporate strategies likely to impose on the behavior of Third World national governments? Although Moran surveys some data on the effectiveness of these strategies, the experience is too brief and the evidence from the industries in which they are found is thus far too scant to permit a thorough evaluation. Nevertheless, some preliminary prognoses are offered in the conclusion to this book (chapter 13).

New Sources of Foreign Investment: Third World Multinationals and Appropriate Technology

The question of appropriate technology has always occupied a special place in the literature on multinational corporations, and the analysis of this issue presents something of an intellectual puzzle. On the one hand, one would expect international companies to want to maximize their profits by employing labor-intensive processes more suited to the factor proportions in the less developed world. On the other hand, the evidence indicates that international companies from the advanced economies tend to bring with them and use the production techniques from their home countries that are designed to conserve on labor. How does the literature explain this apparent contradiction?[38]

Part of the discrepancy in choosing capital-intensive technologies in labor-abundant economies is explained by hidden subsidies to capital, such as government loans in a highly inflationary environment with low or negative real rates of interest. Part is explained by a desire for managerial flexibility in adjusting output to cyclical market conditions in the face of labor laws that make it difficult to lay off workers or by hidden costs to the corporation in terms of managing a large work force. Some is explained by host country regulations that are unmistakably counterproductive with regard to the importation of labor-intensive technology, such as discrimination against second-hand equipment (second hand does not necessarily mean second best, although there must be a certainty that replacement parts for the equipment are readily available).

Beyond these explanations, a major reason for the utilization of inappropriate technology is the fact that multinational corporations seek, and host governments grant, protection against competitive pressures in the marketplace. Yeoman found, for example, that the less the price competition faced by the firm, the greater the propensity of the multinational to utilize the production techniques used in the home country without adaptation. In contrast, the stimulus of competition pushed the foreign corporation to modify operating procedures so as to employ more labor.[39]

Louis T. Wells's "Small Scale Manufacturing as a Competitive Advantage" (chapter 6) comes at the issue from a new angle by focusing not on multinational corporations from the developed world but on the growing number of multinationals from Third World countries themselves.[40] He argues that the investor in less developed countries (LDCs) has several unique attributes that give it a competitive edge over the multinational from the advanced economies and contribute to the overall development process of most LDCs. International companies from the industrialized economies, driven by the strategies of their parent, tend to focus their efforts on technological innovation and marketing rather than on cost minimization or the adaptation of production processes and product lines to Third World markets. As a result, there is a niche for Third World investors who offer investment projects suited for efficient, small-scale manufacture and for less expensive, labor-intensive technology.

First, Wells shows that Third World multinationals possess an advantage over their industrialized country counterparts in most small-scale manufacturing industries because they are generally small themselves. Despite the shortcomings in the data, there is a strong likelihood that the average subsidiary of a developing country investor is significantly smaller than its industrialized country competitor. Plants owned by industrialized country parents are on the average twice the size of plants owned by developing country parents, and capacity utilization is much higher (and production therefore more cost-efficient) in plants provided by LDC investors. This translates into a competitive edge for the Third World multinationals because the markets for most manufactured goods in Third World economies are small. Economies of scale are less often advantageous, and larger size can actually result in redundant capacity and higher costs.

A second area Wells points to where LDC multinationals are more than competitive with other international companies is in the adaptation of Western technology to the needs of Third World markets. Wells compares capital-to-labor ratios for subsidiaries of parents from developed and less developed countries to discover whether plants of LDC origin are in fact more labor intensive. The data indicate that both the average and median capital-to-labor ratio of LDC international firms is almost half that of industrialized country subsidiaries. Wells is uncertain whether this is due to labor-intensive techniques or merely results from the smaller plant size and lesser amount of working capital of LDC investors. Ambiguous data prevent an unqualified answer, but Wells notes that the general conclusion regarding the higher labor intensity of LDC multinational technology is also supported by a case study of the evidence from Thailand.

Wells observes that LDC entrepreneurs have also demonstrated an ability to scale down Western technology to fit host country requirements, at the same time increasing their own profits. This skill in technological adaptation is an important know-how, which only LDC investors appear able to offer developing economies, a technology neither advanced country multinationals nor indigenous firms provide.

In addition, the operations of LDC multinationals are also more flexible in responding to Third World country needs. Management in large corporations in the advanced countries tends to devote much attention to marketing and to product improvement, reflecting the nature of consumer markets. As a result, Wells suggests that advanced country multinationals focus their efforts on convincing Third World consumers to accept a given number of products. LDC multinationals, in contrast, devote their activities to responding to existing market gaps, offering a wide variety of goods to fill those gaps.

Lower overhead enables multinationals from LDCs to offer less expensive products in what Wells notes is a more price-sensitive market. They devote lower expenditures to buildings, capital and equipment, and salaries paid to managers and technicians. The attention of LDC firm management is far more focused on cost minimization than is the case for advanced country subsidiaries. LDC multinationals therefore gain an edge in industries where cost competition is severe.

There are other advantages to Third World economic planners from dealing with LDC multinationals. The fact that LDC subsidiaries are more independent from their Third World parent than are their industrialized country counterparts often means more host country control over the project and less conflict with the investor. Third World multinationals thus have extra appeal because a major source of contention—trying to make the global strategy of the company mesh with the economic priorities of the state—is less prominent. And because their capital resources are often less, LDC firms are more likely to seek out local partners and more likely to obtain inputs locally without the need for a push from the government.

The benefits of investment by LDC multinationals in Third World economies are therefore various: they present more opportunity for local control, their technology is more labor intensive and suited to LDC markets, their focus is primarily on cost reduction and price competitiveness, and the overall expense to the local economy is less.

Still there may be some disadvantages in comparison to advanced country multinationals. LDC investors are less likely to provide the host country with a continuing stream of technology that could result in product innovation or increased productivity. Moreover, although the output of LDC firms may be more suitable to LDC markets, the firms are often less successful as exporters. And although subsidiaries of multinationals from LDCs are more likely to form joint ventures with local partners and obtain inputs locally, they are also more likely to pay lower wages to local workers. Finally, LDC firms can arouse political or ethnic sensitivities when they contribute to the strength of an unpopular minority, such as the Chinese in Indonesia or the Indians in East Africa.

Notes

1. For a survey of the traditional neoclassical approach supporting foreign direct investment, see Michael P. Todaro, *Economic Development in the Third World* (New York: Longman, 1981), pp. 402–404. Also, Arthur McCormack, *Multinational Investment: Boon or Burden for the Developing Countries?* (New York: W.R. Grace & Co., 1980), and Orville L. Freeman, *The Multinational Company: Investment for World Growth* (New York: Praeger, 1981).

2. Stephen H. Hymer, *The International Operations of National Firms: A Study of Direct Foreign Investment* (Cambridge, Mass.: MIT Press, 1976); Charles P. Kindleberger, *American Business Abroad: Six Lectures on Direct Investment* (New Haven, Conn.: Yale University Press, 1969).

3. Raymond Vernon, "International Investment and International Trade in the Product Cycle," *Quarterly Journal of Economics* 80 (May 1966); Louis T. Wells, Jr., ed., *The Product Life Cycle and International Trade* (Boston: Division of Research, Graduate School of Business Administration, Harvard University, 1972).

4. Richard E. Caves, "International Corporations: The Industrial Economics of Foreign Investment," *Economia* 38 (February 1971) and *Multinational Enterprise and Economic Analysis* (Cambridge: Cambridge University Press, 1982).

5. F. Fishwick, *Multinational Companies and Economic Concentration in Europe* (Paris: Institute for Research and Information on Multinationals, 1981); T.A. Pugel,

International Market Linkages and U.S. Manufacturing: Prices, Profits, and Patterns (Cambridge, Mass.: Ballinger, 1978).

6. J.M. Connor, *The Market Power of Multinationals: A Quantitative Analysis of U.S. Corporations in Brazil and Mexico* (New York: Praeger, 1977).

7. S. Lall and P. Streeten, *Foreign Investment, Transnationals and Developing Countries* (London: Macmillan, 1977); L.D. Westphal, Y.W. Ree, and G. Pursell, "Foreign Influences on Korean Industrial Development," *Oxford Bulletin of Economics and Statistics* 41 (November 1979).

8. For the debate about multinationals and appropriate technology, see p. 17.

9. For Marxist and dependency perspectives on multinational corporations and development, see Fernando Henrique Cardoso and Enzo Faletto, *Dependencia and Development in Latin America* (Berkeley: University of California Press, 1979); Ernest Mandel, *Marxist Economic Theory* (Monthly Review Press, New York, 1968), vol. 2; Thomas J. Biersteker, *Distortion or Development: Contending Perspectives on the Multinational Corporation* (Cambridge, Mass.: MIT Press, 1978); and Theodore H. Moran, "Multinational Corporations and Dependency: A Dialogue for Dependentistas and Non-Dependentistas," *International Organization* 32, no. 1 (Winter 1978).

10. G.L. Reuber, with H. Crookell, M. Emerson, and G. Gallais-Hammond, *Private Foreign Investment in Development* (Oxford: Clarendon Press, 1973).

11. C. Chase-Dunn, "The Effects of International Economic Dependence on Development and Inequality: A Cross-National Study," *American Sociological Review* 40 (December 1975); V. Bornschier, "Multinational Corporations and Economic Growth: A Cross-National Test of the Decapitalization Thesis," *Journal of Development Economics* 7 (June 1980). The methodologies employed would produce a negative relationship between the rates of growth of host country per capita income and the stock of foreign direct investment even if there were no behavioral impact at all.

12. Michael B. Dolan and Brian Tomlin, "First World-Third World Linkages: External Relations and Economic Development," *International Organization* (Winter 1980). They also found that income inequalities within countries are unrelated to patterns of foreign investment.

13. Cf. Raymond F. Mikesell, ed., *Foreign Investment in the Petroleum and Mineral Industries: Case Studies of Investor-Host Country Relations* (Baltimore: Johns Hopkins Press for Resources for the Future, 1971).

14. Edith T. Penrose, "Profit Sharing between Producing Countries and Oil Companies in the Middle East," *Economic Journal* (June 1959); "International Economic Relations and the Large International Firm," in E.F. Penrose, Peter Lyon, and Edith T. Penrose, eds., *New Orientations: Essays in International Relations* (New York: Humanities Press, 1970); and *The Large International Firm in Developing Countries: The International Petroleum Industry* (London: Allen and Unwin, 1968).

15. Charles P. Kindleberger, *Economic Development*, 2d ed. (New York: McGraw-Hill, 1965), p. 334.

16. Raymond Vernon, *Sovereignty at Bay: The Multinational Spread of U.S. Enterprises* (New York: Basic Books, 1971); Theodore H. Moran, *Multinational Corporations and the Politics of Dependence: Copper in Chile* (Princeton: Princeton University Press, 1974); David N. Smith and Louis T. Wells, Jr., *Negotiating Third World Mineral Agreements* (Cambridge, Mass.: Ballinger, 1975).

17. Moran, *Multinational Corporations;* Franklin Tugwell, *The Politics of Oil in Venezuela* (Stanford, Calif.: Stanford University Press, 1975); Adalberto S. Pinelo, *The Multinational Corporation as a Force in Latin American Politics: A Case Study of the International Petroleum Corporation in Peru* (New York: Praeger, 1973); Richard L. Sklar, *Corporate Power in an African State: The Political Impact of Multinational Mining Companies in Zambia* (Berkeley: University of California Press, 1975).

18. Details of investment agreements can be found in Rex Bosson and Bension Varon, *The Mining Industry and Developing Countries* (New York: Oxford University Press, for the World Bank, 1977); Raymond Mikesell, *Foreign Investment in Copper Mining: Case Studies of Mines in Peru and Papua New Guinea* (Washington, D.C.: Resources for the Future, 1975); S.K.B. Asante, "Restructuring Transnational Mineral Agreements," *American Journal of International Law* 73 (1979); S. Sideri and S. Johns, eds., *Mining for Development in the Third World: Multinational Corporations, State Enterprise and the International Economy* (New York: Pergamon, 1980); and *Structure and Strategy in the International Copper Industry* (New York: U.N. Centre on Transnational Corporations, 1981).

19. Richard D. Robinson, *National Control of Foreign Business Entry: A Survey of Fifteen Countries* (New York: Praeger, 1976); C. Fred Bergsten, Thomas Horst, and Theodore H. Moran, *American Multinationals and American Interests* (Washington, D.C.: Brookings, 1978), ch. 10; Isaiah Frank, *Foreign Enterprise in Developing Countries* (Baltimore: Johns Hopkins University Press, 1980).

20. Organization of American States, *Regulation Policies toward Multinational Corporations for Host Countries within the Organization of American States: Generalizations from the Analysis of Issues in the Automotive Sector* (Washington, D.C.: OAS, 1974); Ronald Muller and David Moore, *Brazilian Bargaining Success in Befiex Export Promotion Program with the Transnational Automotive Industry* (New York: U.N. Centre on Transnational Corporations, 1978); and Douglas C. Bennett and Kenneth E. Sharpe, "The World Automobile Industry and Its Implications," in Richard Newfarmer, ed., *Profits, Progress, and Poverty: Case Studies of International Industries in Latin America* (Notre Dame, Ind.: University of Notre Dame Press, 1985).

21. Douglas Bennett and Kenneth E. Sharpe, "Transnational Corporations and the Political Economy of Export Promotion: The Case of the Mexican Automobile Industry," *International Organization* (Spring 1979), and "Agenda Setting and Bargaining Power: The Mexican State vs. Transnational Automobile Corporations," *World Politics* 32 (1979); Fernando Coronil and Julie Skurski, "Reproducing Dependency: Auto Industry Policy and Petrodollar Circulation in Venezuela," *International Organization* (Winter 1982). Having a home-grown firm of equal production efficiency and marketing ability might avoid these difficulties. Westphal et al. show that the bulk of Korea's export growth has been accomplished by indigenous firms. And Helleiner and Jenkins point out that there are some sectors in which local firms have a superior export performance in comparison to multinationals. Still, for many industries, the utilization of the international marketing channels of foreign corporations may be the best available option in the short or medium term. L.E. Westphal, Y.W. Rhee, and G. Prusell, "Foreign Influence on Korean Industrial Development," *Oxford Bulletin of Economics and Statistics* 41, no. 4 (November 1979); G.K. Helleiner, "Manufactured Exports from Less-Developed Countries and Multinational Firms," *Economic Journal*

83 (1973); Rhys Jenkins, "The Export Performance of Multinational Corporations in Mexican Industry," *Journal of Development Studies* 15 (1979).

22. Bennett and Sharpe, *Transnational Corporations*; Rhys Jenkins and Peter J. West, "The International Tractor Industry and Its Impact in Latin America," in Newfarmer, *Profits*. Bargaining with multinationals need not be confined to direct equity investment, of course. When Cessna refused Brazilian demands to begin local production, the government created a state enterprise by a licensing agreement with Piper. Jack Baranson, *North-South Technology Transfer: Financing and Institution Building* (Mt. Airy, Md.: Lomond Publications, 1982).

23. Third World use of performance requirements to create employment and boost exports leads to an interesting dichotomy of perception. Critics from the less developed world complain that key decisions are still being made in the boardrooms of Detroit, Tokyo, and Milan. Organized labor representatives from the developed world complain that those key decisions are being made in a way that favors Brazil, Mexico, and Argentina at the expense of Detroit, Tokyo, and Milan.

24. Raymond Vernon, *Storm over the Multinationals: The Real Issues* (Cambridge, Mass.: Harvard University Press, 1977).

25. John H. Dunning and R. Pierce, "Profitability and Performance of the World's Largest Industrial Companies," *Financial Times* Advisory Group, 1975, cited by Newfarmer, *Profits*.

26. Newfarmer, *Profits*.

27. The stimulation of competition among multinationals as a strategy to strengthen the bargaining power of host authorities is not in contradiction with the observation that most foreign investment takes place in concentrated industries. Rather, anxiety about the loss of market share can be a strong motivator of competitive behavior within even relatively tight oligopolies. For the strategy of creating oligopoly anxiety between majors and independents in the petroleum and mineral sectors, see Theodore H. Moran, "The International Political Economy of Cuban Nickel Development," in Cole Blasier and Carmelo Mesa-Lago, eds., *Cuba in the World* (Pittsburgh: University of Pittsburgh Press, 1979).

28. Fred T. Knickerbocker, *Oligopolistic Reaction and Multinational Enterprise* (Boston: Division of Research, Graduate School of Business Administration, Harvard University, 1973).

29. Vernon; *Storm over the Multinationals*, p. 78. Beyond the issue of stimulating rivalry among foreign investors to enter the national market, there is the question of whether multinational corporations lead to a decrease or an increase in concentration ratios in the local market as they acquire, or destroy, local firms. Vernon suggests that foreign investment decreases local concentration ratios. Lall, in contrast, finds that foreign investment raised the level of concentration in Malaysia. Evidence from Brazil and Mexico shows both increasing and decreasing concentration in different sectors. For the studies of Brazil and Mexico, see Newfarmer, *Profits*, pp. 34–36. For Malaysia, see Sanjaya Lall, "Multinationals and Market Structure in an Open Developing Economy: The Case of Malaysia," *Weltwirtschaft Archiv* (June 1979).

30. Moran, "Multinational Corporations." See also Alfred Stepan, *The State and Society* (Princeton: Princeton University Press, 1978), and David G. Becker, *The New Bourgeoisie and the Limits of Dependency: Mining, Class, and Power in "Revolutionary" Peru* (Princeton: Princeton University Press, 1983).

31. Jorge I. Dominguez, "Business Nationalism: Latin American National Business Attitudes and Behavior towards Multinational Enterprises," in *Economic Issues and Political Conflict: U.S.-Latin American Relations* (London: Butterworth, 1982).

32. Stephen J. Kobrin, "The Forced Divestment of Foreign Enterprise in the LDCs," *International Organization* (Winter 1980).

33. Peter Evans, *Dependent Development: The Alliance of Multinational, State, and Local Capital in Brazil* (Princeton: Princeton University Press, 1979).

34. Richard Newfarmer, "Multinationals and Marketplace Magic," in Charles P. Kindleberger and David B. Audretsch, *The Multinational Corporation in the 1980s* (Cambridge, Mass.: MIT Press, 1983).

35. Thomas A. Poynter, *Multinational Enterprises and Government Intervention* (London: Croom Helm, 1985). For a systematic attempt to construct behavioral models of government policy toward foreign investors, see Richard E. Caves, *Multinational Enterprises and Economic Analysis* (Cambridge: Cambridge University Press, 1983), ch. 10.

36. David Leyton-Brown, "The Multinational Enterprise and Conflict in Canadian-American Relations," *International Organization* 28, no. 4 (Autumn 1974); Joseph S. Nye, Jr., "Transnational Relations and Interstate Conflicts: An Empirical Analysis," *International Organization* 28, no. 4 (Autumn 1974).

37. William Ascher and William H. Overholt, *Strategic Planning & Forecasting: Political Risk and Economic Opportunity* (New York: Wiley, 1983); and Stephen J. Kobrin, *Managing Political Risk Assessment: Strategic Response to Environmental Change* (Berkeley: University of California Press, 1982).

38. Walter A. Chudson and Louis T. Wells, Jr., *The Acquisition of Technology from Multinational Corporations by Developing Countries* (New York: United Nations, 1974); D.J.C. Forsyth and R.F. Solomon, "Choice of Technology and Nationality of Ownership in Manufacturing in a Developing Country," *Oxford Economic Papers* 29 (July 1977); S. Lall, "Transnationals, Domestic Enterprises, and Industrial Structure in Host LDCs: A Survey," *Oxford Economic Papers* 30 (July 1978); Lynn K. Mytelka, *Regional Development in a Global Economy: The Multinational Corporation, Technology, and Andean Integration* (New Haven: Yale University Press, 1979); B.S. Chung and C.H. Lee, "The Choice of Production Techniques by Foreign and Local Firms in Korea," *Economic Development and Cultural Change* 29 (October 1980); Steven W. Langdon, *Multinational Corporations in the Political Economy of Kenya* (London: Macmillan, 1981).

39. Wayne A. Yeoman, *Selection of Production Processes for the Manufacturing Subsidiaries of U.S.-Based Multinational Corporations* (New York: Arno Press, 1976). One might explain multinational corporate behavior as a strategy of sticking with production practices that are familiar until pushed by competition to take a chance on experimenting with something new. Or one might hypothesize that the investor compares the marginal cost of the known technique with the total cost of designing a new process to incorporate local factor availability. Wells has argued that in an absence of market competition, "engineering man" who prizes technological sophistication for its own sake can take precedence over "economic man" who would minimize production costs. Louis T. Wells "Economic Man and Engineering Man: Choice in a Low-Wage Country," *Public Policy* 21 (Summer 1973).

40. See also T. Agmon and C.P. Kindleberger, eds., *Multinationals from Small Countries* (Cambridge, Mass.: MIT Press, 1977).

2

Capturing the Mineral Multinationals: Advantage or Disadvantage?

Michael Shafer

Michael Shafer's study of the copper industry in Zaire and Zambia represents a new wave of increasingly sophisticated case studies of the relationship between multinational corporations and host countries in the Third World. It examines the shift in bargaining strength from foreign investor to host authorities that has proceeded further in natural resources than in other industry sectors, with many substantial gains for the host.

In Zaire and Zambia the pressures of economic nationalism pushed the governments to full nationalization of the foreign-owned mines. According to Shafer, however, nationalization did not bring the expected benefits but rather inflicted unexpected costs on both countries' national economies. The primary reason for the difficulties of nationalization as a state strategy, in Shafer's analysis, was the loss of insulation previously provided by the international mining corporations. This loss of insulation has both domestic and international dimensions, from resisting excessive union demands to obtaining new mining capital.

The extent of the impact of the loss of insulation depends on the strength of the state. In general, Shafer concludes that most mineral-producing countries in the Third World are too politically weak to avoid the negative economic consequences of nationalization.

Chapter 1 places Shafer's analysis of opportunities and dangers in the extractive sector within the context of emerging theories of multinational investor-host government bargaining strength.

This chapter was prepared under the auspices of the African Study Group at the Center for International Affairs, Harvard University, and was presented in an earlier version at the 8th annual Third World Conference, Chicago, Illinois. The author would like to thank Jorge Dominguez, Brian Levy, Joseph Nye, Dov Ronen, Robert Rotberg, Raymond Vernon, and Louis Wells for their kind words and helpful criticism.

n the early 1960s, Third World leaders followed Kwame Nkrumah's advice and sought first the political kingdom. It was not enough, however, and in the late 1960s they turned their attention to the "economic kingdom" in search of the "full permanent sovereignty of every state over its natural resources and all economic activities." Nationalization and the subsequent formation of "producer associations" (or cartels of national producers) were the preferred tools; indeed, the U.N. General Assembly declared nationalization itself to be "an expression of the full permanent sovereignty of the State."[1] This quest for permanent sovereignty through nationalization and cartelization may be seen most clearly in the wave of nationalizations in natural resource industries that swept the Third World in the late 1960s and early 1970s.

Through nationalization, Third World governments hoped to make major gains on a variety of fronts. In the international realm, nationalization, particularly when combined with cartelization, seemed an excellent weapon with which to attack a world economic system perceived to be operated by the rich, for the rich. Third World countries hoped to free themselves from the position of captive producers in vertically integrated companies and to wrest control over key—sometimes unique—national resources from foreigners. They wanted, too, a larger share of the economic rents and, in conjunction with other national producers, higher, more stable prices for their production. In the domestic realm, the nationalizers aspired to replace the corporate profit motive with a national "social welfare motive." Nationalization, they thought, would make rational economic planning possible for the economy as a whole and enhance the government's financial position sufficiently to make economic diversification and the promotion of balanced economic growth attainable. They also wished to generate greater employment opportunities and, particularly, the more rapid advancement of their citizens to all levels of company management. No less important, governments sought to silence domestic critics and rally supporters by taking over the most obvious symbols of "foreign exploitation": the subsidiaries of large multinational corporations.

Zaire and Zambia each seemed the model of the Third World country for which nationalization promised these many benefits. Indeed, at independence foreign copper mining operations were, to all intents and purposes, the national economies of these two countries. Nationalization thus appeared to offer Zaire and Zambia the chance to capture the very fulcrum of their domestic economies and a long lever with which to lift themselves internationally. Between 1965 and 1975, for example, copper generated on average 35 percent of Zambia's GDP, accounted for 95 percent of the total value of exports, and contributed 45 percent of total government revenues.[2] In Zaire, copper has traditionally accounted for 60 to 70 percent of total export earnings, and export taxes—of which 90 percent derive from mineral exports—generate 70 percent of the national budget. Moreover, both countries possess substantial reserves of extraordinarily rich copper ores and currently account for 12 and 7 percent of total world production respectively.[3] Their nationalized mining operations, NCCM-RCM and Gecamines, rank second and third respectively among world copper producers, far ahead of such private giants as Kennecott, Rio Tinto Zinc, and Ananconda. Similarly, they rank first and fourth in total copper smelting capacity; and Zambia, showing far more downstream integration than the typical Third World mineral producer, is also the world's largest refiner of copper.[4]

But a decade and a half after nationalization, none of the anticipated benefits has materialized. In Zambia, for example, government revenues from mining have fallen sharply since nationalization. Even in 1974, despite a boom in copper prices, the mining sector contributed just 39 percent of total government revenues, 6 percent less than the annual average of the preceding decade. This figure then declined dismally through 1975 and 1976 to 13.3 and then 2.6 percent, and finally came to rest at zero percent in 1977 and 1978.[5] At the same time, the new tax structure that accompanied nationalization actually "made net revenue from copper more variable with price without substantially reducing dependence."[6] Although the figures are less reliable, Zaire seems to have suffered similarly.[7] In both countries much mining, smelting, and refining capacity stands idle; maintenance of equipment is poor, plant and facilities are falling into disrepair; and new investment is almost nonexistent. Moreover, despite efforts to reduce dependence on the mining sector and diversify exports, both countries have *increased* their dependence to extraordinary levels.[8] At the same time, gross domestic investment fell through the 1970s at an *annual* average rate of 5.0 percent in Zaire and 5.6 percent in Zambia.[9] Labor discontent and the threat of urban political violence are rife in both countries; strikes seriously disrupted copper production in Zambia three times in 1981 alone. And, although their copper industries were debt-free and entirely self-financing until shortly after nationalization, both Zaire and Zambia have since accumulated staggering foreign debts, largely in support of the nationalized mining companies.[10]

Nationalization of Zaire's and Zambia's copper mining industries failed to deliver "permanent sovereignty" over their economic futures or any other of the sought-after goals. Nationalization had unanticipated *costs* that either nullified its benefits or actually turned it against the interests of the nationalizers.

To understand why these two major nationalizations came to grief requires an examination of both the international and the domestic dimensions of the problem. High expectations of nationalization as a tool for redefining the relationship between Third World copper producers and the international economy resulted from a misunderstanding of the world copper industry, an underestimation of the vulnerability of non-vertically integrated national producers, and an overestimation of the possible strength of a copper producers' cartel. High expectations for the beneficial domestic impact of nationalization foundered on the unwarranted assumption that the nationalizing governments either truly represented the interests of "the nation" or were interested in and capable of using the newly nationalized assets to attain the declared goals of nationalization.

At each level, the key to failure is the *loss of insulation*; that is, the ways in which nationalization, by removing the buffer that private mining corporations once provided, has increased the exposure of these fragile governments and their citizens' welfare to direct international and domestic pressures, economic and political. The notion of "insulation" summarizes a wide range of unperceived risk management and custodial functions that the multinational mining corporations fulfilled, which in effect protected these two governments, their copper industries, and their citizens.[11] With nationalization, these various forms of insulation were lost. With the unexpected costs this loss entailed went the possibility that these two countries, at least, would be able to achieve the declared goals of nationalization.

At the international level, the mining companies attempted to defend the market for copper and the producer's place in it, thus buffering Zaire and Zambia against its inevitable ups and downs. The mining companies pursued upstream oligopoly and market risk management through vertical integration in order to raise rents and control the costs of market volatility, policies of equal benefit to companies and countries. Nationalization, however, contributed to the demise of upstream oligopoly, made market risk more difficult to manage, and left national producers at a disadvantage to the remaining vertically integrated, multinational mining companies. Similarly, prior to nationalization, the mining companies guaranteed access to international capital markets and sufficient investment funds. Since nationalization this buffer has been lost, leaving Zaire and Zambia to find their own financing and tying the availability and cost of funds for their copper industries directly to their governments' shaky credit ratings.

At the domestic level, the mining companies' buffering role spared Zaire, Zambia, and their citizens certain consequences of their political systems' weakness and lack of autonomy. The financial and managerial autonomy of the private mining companies served to insulate Zaire's and Zambia's copper industries from exploitation for short-run economic and political gain and, conversely, to insulate these governments against union demands for excessive wages and benefits. Since the loss of this insulation, however, the nationalized copper companies have been systematically abused and the regimes have faced rapidly growing overloads of often conflicting demands.

Loss of insulation by itself does not, of course, provide a full explanation for the failure of nationalization in Zaire and Zambia. Three additional factors must be taken into account. First, the market dilution of the copper industry in the postwar period, the widespread availability of copper ores (particularly with newly improved extraction technologies), and the serious threat of substitution all mitigate against the success of any effort to win enduring gains solely through control at the production stage. Second, both Zaire and Zambia possess extremely weak political and economic systems, and at the time of nationalization had almost no trained mining managers or technicians.[12] Thus, in neither case were the nationalizers ready and able to take over the operation of huge, complex industries without some losses. Finally, both countries have suffered the disruptive effects of the struggle against white Rhodesia, chronic transportation bottlenecks, the oil price surge, soft demand for copper, high international interest and inflation rates, and declining terms of trade.

These factors should not be allowed to overshadow the importance of insulation loss. To the contrary, their very importance accounts for the centrality of loss of insulation in understanding the failure of nationalization. At the international level, it is precisely because of increasing risk and the need for some form of vertical integration in the copper industry that the loss of insulation is critical. At the domestic level, it is precisely because they do not possess strong, autonomous state institutions nor sufficient cadres of trained managers and technicians that Zaire and Zambia need worry about insulation. And since transportation problems have not worsened, Rhodesia has now successfully become Zimbabwe, and all other copper producers face similar oil prices, interest rates, depressed demand, and so on, loss of insulation offers a useful explanation of Zaire's and Zambia's peculiarly bad showings. Moreover, to argue that if oil were still $2.00 a barrel and copper $1.00 a pound insulation would be a nonissue and Zaire's and Zambia's nationalizations would be successful is simply to mistake the short term for forever. Like any insurance policy, insulation may appear unnecessary or even onerous in boom times. Those who cancel then, however, regret having done so when the bad times strike—and in as volatile a market as that for copper, the bad times are never far away.

The International Dimension

The Myth of Nationalization

At the heart of the heroic mythology of nationalization is the notion that the contest of Third World country and transnational mining corporation is one of David and Goliath. It seldom is. In fact, relations between the two tend instead to be marked by a steady shift of power from corporation to country. The initial preponderance of the mining company reflects its near monopoly on technical know-how, managerial resources, and capacity to raise large capital investments. Since they alone can tap a country's resources the mining companies can demand high returns, low taxes, few if any regulations about foreign exchange and profits repatriation, and other such concessions. Once the investment is sunk, however, the balance of power shifts rapidly in favor of the host country. As it does, the host country's ability to demand a greater share of the economic rents, more say in management, and, if it likes, equity in the mining operations also increases. What is more, there is little, if anything, the company can do to maintain its privileged position.[13]

This pattern of shifting power is evident in Zaire's nationalization of the Société Générale de Belgique, parent company of Union Minière de Haute Katanga, and Zambia's successful demand for 51 percent (now 60%) equity in what were Zamanglo (Zambian Anglo-American, Ltd.) and Roan Selection Trust. In 1960, the Société Générale de Belgique (SGB) owned or controlled most of what was worth owning in the Belgian Congo. Directly or indirectly SGB operations accounted for 70 percent of the economy including, most importantly, control of the Union Minière de Haute Katanga (UMHK). Through UMHK, SGB also controlled virtually all Congolese copper, cobalt, diamond, and uranium mining (22% of the GDP, 60% of exports), and exclusive rights to Katangan mining through 1990.[14] On 31 December 1966, just six turbulent years after independence, however, Joseph Mobutu issued a "declaration of economic independence," expropriated UMHK's assets, and transferred them to the Société Générale Congolaise de Minerais (Gecomin, later Gecamines).

The balance of power had not yet shifted fully in favor of the Congo, however. Because UMHK held five months' supply of copper in Belgium, was sole marketing agent in Katangan production, could threaten other, needed investments, supplied nearly all technical and managerial personnel, and knew that the financially strapped Congo derived 70 percent of its desperately needed foreign exchange from copper sales, the company was able to demand concessions. After six weeks of wrangling, Société Générale de Minerais (SGM, a UMHK subsidiary) signed a new, quite favorable agreement with the government. The agreement left ownership in government hands while SGM undertook to manage mining and metallurgical facilities and to market all production for cost plus a percentage of sales. Gecomin was to supervise all operations and to preside over the training of Zairians to move into management and administrative positions. In 1973, Zaire established a state marketing agency to supervise and eventually to take over foreign sales of Zairian mineral production.

A similar pattern can be seen in Zambia's step-by-step move to take majority control of its mining industry.[15] In 1964, two large international mining groups, the Anglo-America Corporation of South Africa (Zamanglo) and Roan Selection Trust, a subsidiary of American Metal Climax, controlled the Zambian copper industry and held the major mining concessions in perpetuity. In an effort to retain more copper earnings, Kenneth Kaunda in 1968 limited company remittances to 50 percent of after-tax profits. A year later, the Mines and Minerals Act declared all mineral rights to belong to the state. Finally, on 1 January 1970 the government took over 51 percent of each of the two mining groups.[16] Tax provisions passed at the same time ultimately gave the government 87 percent of all company profits.[17]

Under the new arrangements, Roan Selection Trust became Roan Consolidated Mines (RCM) and Zamanglo became Nchanga Consolidated Copper Mines (NCCM), both under the government industrial holding company, ZIMCO. Bonds were issued for the book value of nationalized shares, and a ten-year management and sales agreement left the mining corporations effective control of those operations. In 1973, however, Zambia redeemed the bonds (borrowing heavily in international capital markets to do so) and formed the Metal Marketing Corporation of Zambia to be sole agent for Zambian metal production. And finally, between 1974 and 1975, the management contracts were paid off, leaving the Zambian mining industry self-managing.[18]

Oligopoly and Risk Management

With the conclusion of the new agreements, Zaire and Zambia seemed to have gained all the goals of nationalization. They soon proved hollow. The formal assertion of sovereignty proved small recompense for the major negative consequences, both direct and indirect, of nationalization. Thinking to nationalize and exploit their market positions, Zaire and Zambia instead helped to undermine the value of their copper asset, made efforts to exercise it for purposes of development more difficult, and added to the barriers against future expansion of their mining industries. The problem was that neither understood the weakness of the copper oligopoly and the distinct limits it placed on them as producers, nor the variety of critical protective functions that the companies fulfilled. Zambia and Zaire failed to realize that, while they might have legitimate differences with the companies over the *division* of economic rents, they and the companies were still in the same boat: the structure and nature of the international copper industry determined their prospects equally, and damage done to the industry was damage done to both companies and countries.

Two mistaken assumptions underpinned Zaire's and Zambia's initial decisions to nationalize copper production: first, that the mining companies were underpricing their copper; and second, that without the companies their market power was sufficient to get more for it. The two are inextricably linked, and both derive from a fundamental misunderstanding of the international copper industry.

The first assumption resulted from mistaking a short-term price surge for a long-term price trend, and thus misreading corporate producers' efforts to defend the industry. The origins of the problem date to 1957 when, faced with a serious supply glut, the private mining companies agreed to reduce African copper production by 10 percent. This proved insufficient, and in 1960 production was cut a further 5 percent and the three largest copper companies began to purchase copper aggressively on the London Metals Exchange (LME). The program worked well and stabilized prices at an acceptable level through 1963, despite a weak market. In 1964, however, the market improved and prices rose sharply. Fearing that high prices would provoke substitution (thus reducing future demand), the corporate producers then attempted to cap the rise by holding prices at a level below the LME price. The effort lasted until mid 1966, when the temptation of soaring prices finally proved too much to resist. One by one, all the major producers returned to contracts based on LME prices.[19] In the interim, however, both Zairian and Zambian officials had concluded that the restraints denied them a fair price for their copper. Moreover, as copper prices continued to climb, they became convinced that control of the copper industry would mean control of an ever more valuable asset. Instead, nationalization has seriously undermined that asset and its owners. To understand why requires an examination of the industry.

Two clearly related strategic goals have dominated corporate planning in the copper industry: the creation and maintenance of an upstream oligopoly, and the containment of catastrophic risk. Through restricted competition, oligopoly offers producers higher than "normal" rents plus greater market control and predictability. Key to this restricted competition are high barriers to entry into the industry, relative unavailability of substitutes, and the ability of a limited number of producers to cooperate to fend off new entrants and control prices or production (or both) to prevent the development of substitutes. Over the years, the major corporate producers attempted a variety of methods to maintain the oligopoly: they tried to keep new ore bodies "on ice" until sustained demand favored exploitation;[20] they sought industry agreements to control existing production; and on various occasions they endeavored to institute a more stable producers' price system to replace the volatile LME as a price-setting mechanism.

Simple upstream oligopoly was not enough in the copper industry, however, where the burden of huge fixed investments and high price volatility form a potentially deadly mix. The difficulty, as Theodore Moran notes, is that "inelasticities of supply and demand in the short run tend to shift market power abruptly from producer to consumer and back again."[21] Unpredictable strikes or mining disasters may result in shortages and price surges overnight; the need to service high fixed costs constrains reductions of production at the margin during periods of soft demand and so produces gluts and price slumps. The major copper mining corporations have thus long sought protection through vertical integration in order to assure themselves outlets for their production in time of glut and to make possible a degree of internal control over the copper market's violent price swings. To complement formal integration, the major producers have also attempted to establish a sort of "informal" vertical integration through mutually beneficial long-term sales contracts with major buyers. They agree with the buyer, in effect, to forgo the extreme high prices of periods of shortage and to guarantee that they will not shift the consumers' copper supply to a higher bidder. In return, consumers agree to forgo rock-bottom prices in times of glut and instead to continue to take the suppliers' copper at the somewhat higher, agreed price. Informal vertical integration is, in other words, a shared insurance policy.[22]

Unfortunately for the copper industry, neither strategic goal was ever fully grasped for long; and nationalization may have pushed both beyond reach forever. Even before the wave of nationalizations in the late 1960s and early 1970s, the copper oligopoly was in serious decline. Technological development and the spread of mining and management know-how have brought vast new reserves of ore within the reach of many new producers around the world, thus undermining the barriers to entry; the ready availability and low, comparatively stable cost of aluminum have led to considerable, permanent substitution; and the major copper producers have proved incapable of regulating production or prices in any sustained way. The spread of nationalization simply contributed to this process by markedly increasing the horizontal dilution of the oligopoly. The resulting proliferation of mining operations under different, competing management reduced still further the possibilities for price control and so further encouraged both substitution and the boom-bust cycle in copper. Thus, while by no means the sole cause of the copper oligopoly's demise, nationalization was certainly a contributing factor. The nationalizers, no less than the remaining private producers, face a riskier world for it.

Considered in terms of the traditional risk management mechanisms employed in the copper industry, nationalization poses special problems. As national producers, nationalized copper mining operations cannot easily seek downstream protection through vertical integration, especially across borders. Nor can they protect themselves against the substitution threat by buying into the aluminum industry (as many of the private copper companies have done). National producers are thus reduced to dependence upon informal integration through long-term marketing contracts. But as research by Raymond Vernon and Brian Levy indicates,

> experience over the past two decades points to the conclusion that the family of contracts described earlier provides nothing like the stability and predictability . . . that is ordinarily associated with ownership. Despite the existence of such contracts, buyers commonly back away from their commitments when ore is in very easy supply. . . .[23]

In short, because of nationalization, national producers deprive themselves of the best available means for managing risk and put themselves at a marked disadvantage to vertically integrated multinational producers.

Neither Zambia nor Zaire perceived these costs of nationalization when they joined other Third World producers in a three-pronged strategy, a strategy that amounted, in effect, to an all-out attack on both oligopoly and risk management in the copper industry. First, they took control of their mining industries in order to guarantee themselves the lion's share of the economic rents. Second, they sought what the tight copper market of the late 1960s and early 1970s would bear for their production. And third, they attempted to use a national producers' cartel, the Intergovernmental Council of Copper Exporting Countries (CIPEC), to control production in times of glut and thus maintain prices. They sought, in other words, the consumers' nightmare: the full exercise of market power at both top and bottom of the business cycle. Although they never achieved their goal, the CIPEC effort had a real impact. Coming as they did at the same time as OPEC's *coup,* shortages of a variety of nonfuel minerals, and a renewal of scare scenarios about strategic mineral vulnerability, CIPEC's declarations and its members' actions struck a raw nerve. The result was a sharp and devastating backlash.

In the face of nationalization and soaring prices, both the traditional corporate producers and many consumers began a concerted effort to develop new mines in politically "secure" areas, even if it meant mining higher-cost, poorer ores.[24] Roan Selection Trust, for example, undertook operations in Iran, Botswana, Indonesia, and Australia; both Anglo-American and Union Minière shifted to Australia and Canada. Other giants like Kennecott and Anaconda, nationalized in Chile, devoted their attentions to new endeavors in the United States or such "safe" countries as Australia, Canada, and South Africa. Major copper consumers like Germany's Norddeutsche Affinerie of Hamburg and Metallgesellschaft A.G. began to integrate backwards, often with the assistance of their governments, and again in "safe" countries. One major study finds, for example, that although investment is down in general, "developing countries have experienced a *disproportionate reduction* in new capital formation in the copper industry."[25] Similarly, John Tilton's figures indicate that the countries for which average annual growth in copper production *exceeded* the Western average (3.16% per annum) over the last few years were the Philippines, South Africa-Namibia, Australia, and Canada (11.26, 7.43, 4.89, and 4.49% per annum respectively), all of which are considered "safe areas for investment."[26]

The effects of the scramble for new, secure sources of copper have been negative for everybody concerned. Major investment in comparatively high-cost, low-grade ore production and away from high-quality Third World ores represents a misallocation of economic resources with long-term consequences, since the size and costliness of copper mining operations make them long-term propositions. In the nearer term, the development of new production capacity led to the further dilution of the copper oligopoly and an exaggeration of the earlier trend toward excess capacity. This weakened the industry's ability to shape prices and production at the same time it brought on line new supplies and so made such control critical—particularly as worldwide recession lowered demand. As a result, concludes one major study of the copper industry's future, "the industry as a whole may adjust less rapidly to price signals triggered by demand shifts, with over-production reflected in prolonged periods of relatively low prices."[27]

Zaire, Zambia, and other national producers suffered the consequences—glut and depressed prices—along with the rest of the industry. Indeed, they may have suffered more severely, bearing a disproportionate share of the reduction in world consumption versus production. This seems to have happened because at least initially both countries' marketing agencies ignored, indeed dismembered, the informal network of buyer-seller links tying their production to markets in Europe and Japan. At the same time, traditional corporate producers were able to secure new supplies with which to keep their old networks open and new, backwardly integrating consumers *cum* producers stressed security of supply through such mechanisms as loan paybacks through production. Any such contention is difficult to support without extensive field research or dependence on anecdotal sources. Still, the fact that between 1974 and 1978, for example, total Western copper production rose by 4 percent per year while Zaire's production fell an average 6 percent per year and Zambia's 8 percent per year suggests some degree of exclusion from the market.[28] A World Bank study reporting that "Africa's" (read Zaire's and Zambia's) share of total world copper exports fell from 28.2 percent in 1970–72 to 19.2 percent in 1976–78 hints at a similar conclusion.[29]

CIPEC Constrained

CIPEC is not, nor is it likely to be, sufficient insulation against the ill winds that now sweep the copper industry. Ironically, the two-part U.N. strategy for the promotion of a permanent sovereignty, nationalization with cartelization, contains an unexpected internal contradiction with serious consequences. Nationalization makes a cartelization extremely difficult, while nationalization without cartelization provides no compensation for lost insulation. It thus leaves the nationalizer in a weaker position vis-à-vis the international market than before.

CIPEC's weakness can be explained both by the factors that have led to the failure of all past efforts to cartelize copper and by others peculiar to the new situation in which state-owned enterprises and not private corporations are the primary actors. Traditionally, successful cartels have required that producers share common goals, cost structures, and marketing arrangements.

They require, moreover, limited scrap recycling, high barriers to substitution, and low elasticity of demand. In the case of copper, however, none of these conditions has held for long. Furthermore, as Raymond Vernon suggests, the increasing role of state-owned enterprises actually increases the volatility of commodity markets both because they dilute the oligopoly and because,

> Instead of being able to concentrate on the common objectives of high and stable profits, as a group of private oligopolists from different countries are often in a position to do, the state-owned enterprises are likely to find their ability to cooperate affected by the differing situations of their respective governments.[30]

These difficulties are aggravated by the greater general difficulties of state-to-state, as opposed to company-to-company, negotiations.

The situations of Zaire and Zambia highlight the weakness of CIPEC and the vulnerability of its members. Zaire's and Zambia's production costs are among the highest in the world;[31] a major recycling threat exists; aluminum substitution continues; many alternative suppliers have excess capacity; and a World Bank study indicates that even the short-run elasticity of CIPEC copper is so close to one (1) that members' ability to increase earnings by increasing prices are negligible.[32] Because of extreme dependence on revenues from mineral production, neither Zaire nor Zambia is in a position to cut back production or hold prices in times of glut,[33] nor could either afford to withhold any substantial portion of their production from the market, particularly if in the short run it might jeopardize debt servicing. Moreover, already faced by serious labor unrest in the mines, Zambia's fragile government could ill afford to close even those mines that incur substantial losses. Thus, precisely because the copper industries are state-owned, decisions necessary for successful cartel action are impossible. The governments of Zaire and Zambia are too weak to run the economic and political risks of acting like rational oligopolists.

Realizing CIPEC's limitations and the difficulties they face as isolated producers, both Zaire and Zambia have attempted to act more like multinational producers. Both have attempted to promote further downstream integration at home. Neither country, however, possesses a sufficiently large domestic market to support a domestic fabrication industry. Moreover, the tariff structures of those industrialized countries that possess markets discriminate against wrought copper products.[34] To circumvent these limitations and to develop secure outlets for their production, both Zambia and Zaire have recently pursued a policy of downstream integration in Europe and made efforts to reestablish the network of formal and informal marketing ties they originally cast off. Marian Radetski notes that in 1978, for example, Zambia acquired a 50 percent interest in a French continuous casting rod plant with a 140,000 ton per year capacity for which Zambia will supply all the copper.[35] Gecamines and Union Minière may soon collaborate in a similar project. While economically sound, such policies reflect a rather marked shift of approach from that embodied in the earlier declarations concerning nationalization.

Mining Finance

In addition to reducing their insulation in the international copper market, nationalization unexpectedly reduced Zaire's and Zambia's insulation in international capital markets. Nationalization seemed to promise greater freedom of choice among sources of investment capital and greater control over them. In fact, however, its consequences threaten Zaire and Zambia with new and tighter restrictions, possible curtailment of investment in their mining sectors, and hence in their future development.

Historically, mining projects in the Third World depended almost exclusively on foreign equity investment for new operations or internal generation of capital by ongoing ones. The multinational mining corporations were able to borrow the huge sums necessary on the strength of their solid credit ratings and the existence of onshore assets that could serve as collateral for large lenders. Private equity investment dried up in the late 1960s, however, as the mining corporations' sensitivity to political risk rose sharply with the rash of Third World nationalizations. The nationalization of Zaire's and Zambia's copper industries of course contributed to the demise of traditional mining finance and, like all the others concerned, companies and countries, Zaire and Zambia were forced to turn to new methods.

The period of nationalization coincided with the beginning of a period of rapidly rising costs and sharp growth in the capital needs of the copper industry. In 1951, new copper production capacity (mine, smelter, refinery) cost $1,300 per annual ton and the expansion of existing capacity $900 per annual ton; by 1979, major projects (mine, concentration plant, smelter, refinery, and infrastructure) cost between $6,000 and $8,000 per ton annual capacity.[36] To pay off, such projects require copper prices between $0.90 to $1.00 per pound. Such prices would be high in historical terms and are far above the $0.70 per pound that has prevailed in the latter half of the 1970s and the early 1980s. At these costs, the World Bank estimates that African producers will have to attract one billion dollars per year in the 1980s if they are to rehabilitate and expand existing facilities, begin new ones, and undertake needed exploration. The Bank also estimates that fully 75 percent of the needed investment will necessarily be from foreign sources. Neither Zambia's nor Zaire's mining industry, for instance, is capable of generating sufficient internal cash to finance the needed rehabilitation of existing facilities, let alone significant new ones.[37] But finding the necessary outside funds, particularly on politically and economically acceptable terms, will be difficult.

Corporate reaction to nationalization, big future capacity requirements, and much bigger capital requirements to meet them have produced two distinctly negative outcomes for Third World copper producers such as Zaire and Zambia: a marked shift in the location of investment and a change in the investment mechanism itself. Despite large capital needs, sufficient funds will indeed be available for copper investment. The problem is one of *distribution:* the lion's share of all mining investment is today oriented toward the industrialized countries. In the words of one expert, "trends suggest that the conflict between host governments and mining corporations has significantly redirected the geographic location of new copper capacity."[38] It seems likely that this trend will continue. With the curtailment of equity investment, the mining sector has come to depend on "project financing." Project financing emphasizes anticipated cash flow from an operation rather than the creditworthiness of the sponsoring company; on the assembling of a variety of different sources of capital; and, most important, on as wide a sharing (or "syndication") of the risk involved as possible.

In and of itself, of course, project financing is not a bad thing. Indeed, it often makes available financing that would have been impossible to find if it had been necessary to depend upon private equity investment. But project financing also imposes important costs for national producers, costs that greatly reduce the hoped for benefits of nationalization. The practical effect of the shift to project financing is to increase the risk incurred by national producers and often simply to put them out of the running for new investments. Project financing agreements, for example, often require that prospective borrowers be able to assure markets for the output of new projects.[39] Such a requirement emphasizes the weakness of national producers competing in a partially vertically integrated market. Similarly, the involvement in new projects of several companies and banks, often of different nationalities, reduces host countries' bargaining power. Moreover, under project financing agreements both banks and mining companies insist that host countries accept an important part of project risk. Countries that will not—or cannot—may be unable to find financing. Even when extended, loans may also require specific cash flow targets be met, such that "until the financial results of a mining project are satisfactory [i.e., match the predictions used to justify the original loan] the sponsors, both mining companies and host country governments, are held directly liable for the debt service."[40] Thus, for example, when world copper prices failed to maintain the projected level used in financing calculations for a Gecamines expansion project, the government of Zaire was obligated to make up the difference between expected and actual cash flow to the World Bank and other lenders.[41]

Nationalization *per se* has had two distinct consequences for Zambia's and Zaire's efforts to finance the expansion of their mining industries: it has raised the cost and lowered the ceiling on available funds. Nationalization effectively removed the "insulation" between the general economic condition of the country (and particularly of the government) and that of the copper companies. As Obidegwu and Nziramasanga note, "As part of the 1970 takeover agreement, the government of Zambia accepted the responsibility of guaranteeing all loans raised abroad by the industry, thus tying the financing of copper development to the overall health of the Zambian economy."[42] Zaire is in a similar position. Thus, as Zaire and Zambia have sunk further into debt, the rate at which they can borrow to rehabilitate and strengthen their one viable economic sector has risen. Since 1973, for example, Zambia's mining companies have found it extremely difficult to borrow, and have been limited to short maturity loans (five years) at very high rates, possibly as much as 20 percent higher than prime industrial borrowers would pay.[43]

Pushed far enough—as in the cases of both Zaire and Zambia—the problem becomes one of getting loan funds at all. In part the difficulty arises from commercial banks' awareness that "countries are not companies." There are distinct limits to the banks' ability to shape countries' policies sufficiently to guarantee the security of loans made to governments with shaky economies. More important, however, are "industry limits" and "country limits," levels of indebtedness for industries or countries beyond which a commercial bank will not lend. Moreover, the concentration of lending to the Third World in a handful of major banks (in the United States six banks account for more than two-thirds of the total) means that "the effect on a developing country can be very severe if even a few banks determine that the exposure limit has been reached."[44]

The cumulative effect of these difficulties has been to erode the position of many Third World copper producers and to reduce "permanent sovereignty." The size of project stretches the capacity of the system to finance them and leaves would-be host countries to bid against one another by offering better and better conditions to would-be investors.[45] As a result, concludes a U.N. review of the current status of the effort to achieve permanent sovereignty over natural resources, "in many cases, in order to obtain the necessary financing, managerial capacities, and marketing abilities for projects, developing countries have to propose conditions which [are] attractive to mining companies and financing institutions."[46] Put more bluntly by the World Bank, the key question for Third World producers in need of mining finance is simple: at what terms?[47] For Zaire and Zambia, the question is and may remain: at any terms?

The Domestic Dimension

The international dimension of nationalization cannot be studied on its own. Arguments that do so stand on two equally unwarranted and naive assumptions:

first, that "Zaire" and "Zambia" are unitary actors in the international economy, easily and correctly identifiable with their official declarations on economic independence; and second, that their governments are simple, efficient, and autonomous "black boxes" for translating public needs into national policy. They assume, in other words, the existence of regimes committed *in practice* to converting the assets won through nationalization into the declared goals of nationalization and, in fact, capable of doing so.

But clearly neither regime functions to promote the interests and preferences of all citizens or "the nation." Neither the Zairian nor the Zambian state is sufficiently secure or autonomous to attempt the effort. Rather, each is more accurately characterized as the allocator of national resources among those few with access to political power. First among these, of course, are the countries' leaders, whose foremost interests are regime maintenance and benefits for themselves and their own. They are, however, very little more than first among equals. For the very weakness of the states over which these leaders preside and the strength of other politically potent groups severely constrain their ability actually to transform Zaire and Zambia. Thus, the cautionary logic of regime maintenance argues for the furtherance of the current distribution of power, although the long-run consequences may be bad for the country as a whole and even the short-run consequences may mean reduced government ability to control resources and demands upon them.

From this perspective, nationalization offered Zaire and Zambia slimmer opportunities and higher risks than initially claimed. Domestic gains anticipated from nationalization never materialized because nationalization did not, and could not, address the domestic *political* difficulties that affected the actual use to which the newly nationalized assets were to be put. Nationalization *per se* could do nothing to reduce the political constraints Zaire's and Zambia's regimes faced because of their weakness and lack of autonomy vis-à-vis politically potent interest groups. Nationalization, therefore, offered no prospect of enhancing their capacity to promote truly national social welfare goals, economic diversification, and more rational, national economic planning over and against the interests of others with access to political power. To the contrary, nationalization and the attendant loss of insulation have exaggerated the problems of state weakness and imposed heavy unanticipated costs on both citizens and governments.

Political Exploitation of the Copper Asset

Any explanation of insulation's importance in Zaire and Zambia—or conversely, the unanticipated domestic costs of nationalization—must begin with the singular political weakness of these two regimes. There are, of course, important differences between President Mobutu's predatory, personalist style of politics and Kenneth Kaunda's "Humanism." But Zaire and Zambia are similar in their fundamental fragility. Both governments sit precariously on fragmented political societies, lacking the means to confront opponents. Both are faced with the constant need to steady a shaky coalition of the politically potent, to placate its key members, and, where necessary, to buy off the potentially threatening. The task requires money: money in the form of investment, services, salaries, patronage; and money forgone in the form of tax concessions, subsidized loans, etc. These requirements are exaggerated by the very size of the countries' public sectors and the regimes' efforts to create inclusive coalitions of politically significant groups, both ethnic and economic.

In Zambia, Kenneth Kaunda rules as a central balancing figure in a fragmented political system recently described as "the variable and inherently unstable structural framework erected on the endemic sectional foundation of Zambian politics."[48] Kaunda has strengthened his position by carefully establishing himself as arbiter among contending forces and by the practice of systematic, arbitrary political and administrative manipulation. (The latter point is best seen in Zambia's ongoing game of musical ministries.) In doing so, Kaunda also presided over the establishment of a pattern of income and consumption, revenue and expenditure, that has become "a necessary condition for the existing alignment of political forces."[49] This pattern shows clearly in the continued skewing of government expenditure in favor of the politically potent copperbelt and line-of-rail provinces, and the growth of the equally potent, extremely costly bureaucracy.[50] As their numbers and importance have grown, public sector employees have succeeded in extracting higher salaries, housing rent cuts, unrealistically low food prices, higher housing allowances, increased loans, and other new privileges even in the face of copper's price collapse in 1975. To maintain this "existing alignment," Kaunda required increasing revenues. These, after an early windfall immediately after the end of the Federation, necessarily depended on higher returns from the copper industry.

In the case of Zaire, Mobutu's manipulation of the political and economic systems is still clearer. Mobutu holds the fragmented state together by use of a complex system of officially sanctioned, even encouraged, corruption and payoff. René Lemarchand observes that "what little legitimacy the state can claim for itself is rooted in the opportunities for self-enrichment offered through political office."[51] Mobutu himself minces no words on the subject, telling bureaucrats on 26 May 1976, "If you want to steal, steal a little cleverly, in a nice way. Only if you steal so much as to become rich overnight, will you be caught."[52]

From the beginning, Mobutu has depended upon copper revenues. Faced early on with outside suspicion, a stagnant economy, and near-total political fragmentation, Mobutu saw in nationalization of the copper industry a trio of benefits. It offered the means to prove his Third World credentials and to enhance his bargaining power with the mineral-hungry West. Most important, nationalization hugely expanded the financial resources of Mobutu's regime, giving him the means to buy allegiances and a degree of political stability. The IMF added to this by recommending in its 1967 economic stabilization plan both sharply increased mineral production and sharply increased export taxes on mineral exports. The combination markedly increased government revenues and foreign exchange earnings, both necessary to support a rapidly growing government "establishment," formal and informal.

Nationalization did more, however, than offer Zaire's and Zambia's regimes readier access to company profits. By eliminating the insulation between the companies' and the countries' treasuries, it jeopardized the funds needed by the industry for maintenance, depreciation, and future investment. Even the private mining companies faced heavy pressures to pay over to the government their operating surpluses and the funds set aside for future investment. As government corporations, the nationalized industries are less able to resist these pressures, particularly as the primary allegiance of state-appointed directors is to the regime, not the company. As a result, when nationalization failed to produce the high, steady stream of funds anticipated and instead government revenues from mining actually began to decline, both Zaire and Zambia drew on these monies to meet their current needs—to the future detriment of their copper industries, national economies, and the welfare of all citizens.

While Zaire and Zambia have been siphoning off internally generated operating and investment capital, government equity in the industry has brought government responsibility for future investment. Thus, in Zambia the government's 51 percent share brought with it responsibility for 51 percent of new capital requirements in the mining sector, while in Zaire nationalization led to complete government responsibility for those of Gecamines. Nationalization, in other words, placed the maintenance and expansion of the mining sector in direct competition with all other sectors and interest groups, at a time when rapidly increasing recurrent expenditure needs were progressively reducing the portion of total revenues available for public capital investment.[53]

The removal of insulation between the industry's capital needs and the treasury has led both Zaire and Zambia to rob Peter to pay Paul. The "trade-off" shows particularly clearly in the areas of foreign exchange allocation and foreign debt. In Zambia, for example, 20 percent of export earnings goes to debt service, another 60 percent to the costs of mining (equipment, spare parts, raw materials), and just 20 percent remains for all other needs.[54] Because that last 20 percent is insufficient to meet the capital needs of development and diversification, funds for these purposes can come only from further borrowing or from a reduction in mining's share of foreign earnings. The latter has prevailed, particularly in the face of mounting deficits. Zambia has simply failed to purchase needed parts, equipment, and raw materials, and has allowed production to stagnate for lack of the foreign exchange necessary to carry out expansion projects.[55] In Zaire, likewise, Gecamines and other mining companies have been denied sufficient foreign exchange to maintain stocks of spare parts and raw materials.[56] Government investment in mining has stagnated, and efforts are under way to "reprivatize" the industry by attracting direct foreign equity investment. Conversely, the huge capital needs of the mining industry and the huge debts incurred as a result have also severely reduced the funds available for other development projects and restricted the possibility of borrowing to finance them.[57]

Government-Labor Conflict

One final unanticipated cost of nationalization requires elucidation: the poisoning of state-labor relations. One of the primary aims of nationalization is to solidify support for the regime among key labor groups, for whom nationalization supposedly promises higher wages, better benefits, access to skilled and administrative positions, and more generally sympathetic management. However, the long-term effects of nationalization are likely to be negative for both parties.

Because of their markedly different pasts, Zaire and Zambia differ substantially on this score. In Zaire, mining developed on the basis of migrant labor recruited from villages at often great distances from the mines. As a result of ethnic differences with the local population, the temporary nature of their sojourn at the mines, and the maintenance of family ties with their home villages, Zairian miners never developed an identity as miners to supplant or even complement their ethnic identities. Like the Belgian colonial administration before it, the Mobutu regime has carefully cultivated these ethnic divisions, prohibited or controlled union activity, and limited any form of political organization among the miners. Consequently, ever since nationalization government-labor relations in Zaire have not been an issue of major or continuing political importance, nor have miners been able to mobilize effectively to press economic demands on the government.

In contrast, Zambia has long had a relatively stable mining population, has an even longer history of mine unionization, and currently has the highest percentage of its population in wage labor of any Black African country. Unionized mine labor played a key role in the struggle for independence and in the winning coalition of Kaunda's United National Independence Party (UNIP), which, in turn, championed miners' demands for better wages and an end to racial job reservation. Later, union allegiance to his leadership proved critical to Kaunda in UNIP's factional struggles of the late 1960s and early 1970s. Indeed, although hard to prove, it seems likely that one of Kaunda's political motives for nationalization was the desire to outflank the more radical wing of UNIP, led by Simon Kapwepwe. Still, the miners' union has fought to maintain its independence. As the saying goes on the copperbelt, "UNIP to UNIP and Union to Union."[58] This, and the political threat posed by the existence of such an autonomous, influential, well-organized, and financially secure body at the heart of the country's sole major industry, laid the groundwork for union-regime conflicts.

Nationalization transformed the Zambian government from champion of the mineworkers against the companies into an ally of the companies against the union. Indeed, since the takeover of the copper industry, Kaunda has declared that "for a union to push a claim against the State is to push a claim against the people."[59] Union and government have come to loggerheads, government seemingly devoted to union-busting and labor risking accusation as traitor for defending workers' interests. Put another way, nationalization transformed industrial relations into an intensely political issue and drove a wedge between the regime and a vital, potent, long-term ally. Simultaneously, nationalization eliminated the foreign mining companies as convenient scapegoats for union anger and buffer for regime protection against it.

The Zambian government has attempted a fist and glove strategy to deal with the mineworkers and promote two key governmental goals inimical to the union's definition of workers' interests: wage control and increased labor productivity. Shortly after nationalization, the government enacted the tough Industrial Relations Act of 1971. This *inter alia* outlawed strikes in the copper industry and established an Industrial Relations Court, thus giving the regime effective control over the resolution of all union demands.[60] At the same time, government officials attempted to get the union leadership to abandon worker advocacy for a management-like productivity orientation by appointing top officials to sit on the boards of various relevant state holding companies and on "work councils" responsible for hiring, firing, and promotion. The government also sought to control access to union office, by cajolery where possible but by force if necessary.

Neither coercion nor cooptation has worked very well, and both have had important negative consequences. Indeed, there is an ironic, almost tragic, twist to the problem—another unanticipated cost of nationalization. At the heart of the government's complaints against the miners' union is the fulfillment of one of nationalization's primary goals: increased, "Zambianized," mine employment. Thus, on the one hand, government attacks on the union for productivity problems have been misplaced while they have provoked considerable ill will. On the other, government efforts to coopt union leadership have been equally inappropriate and have served only to divide the union, reducing leadership control and promoting wildcat strikes.

Zambianization surfaced as a major political issue with independence in 1964 and the companies moved with alacrity to accommodate government demands. They were in a particularly good position to do so: major capital investments in the 1950s had sharply increased output per worker and the cost-price ratio for Zambian production allowed considerable flexibility in reshaping the manning and wage structures of the industry without seriously threatening profits.[61] The new manning structure, initiated to move Africans into once "white," skilled jobs, turned on job fragmentation, however; it ultimately "led to a proliferation of semi-skilled, supervisory and bureaucratic occupations. . . ."[62] Following nationalization, the government also used Zambianization as a convenient means of offering prestigious, lucrative patronage to persons of power. The long-term effect, as Philip Daniel notes, was overmanning and "unsuitable levels of labor costs per ton of copper."[63] Initially, this seemed to make little difference because of buoyant copper prices and the low cost of mining Zambia's high-grade ores. As ore grades declined, and particularly when prices collapsed in 1975, the hidden impact of the new manning structure and political featherbedding became painfully obvious. But by this time the system was in place and the Zambian government, not the companies, faced the consequences.

The problem is most pronounced not at the blue-collar end of the labor force, where union strength was traditionally greatest, but at the upper technical and managerial levels. Here both the numbers of Zambians (and expatriates) employed and the wages paid them have increased faster than at the lower levels, particularly since nationalization.[64] In addition, there has been a progressive shift in the allocation of mining sector labor away from production and into nonproductive, but highly paid, bureaucratic employment. Nowhere is this more evident than in the nearly 100 percent increase between nationalization (1970) and 1974 in the size of the central services divisions of the two nationalized mining groups—although no new functions were added to either operation.[65] A certain portion of this must be explained by the presence of Zambian "shadows," learning jobs by sharing them with their current expatriate occupants. But much of the increase clearly results from adding considerable numbers of political "appointees" to otherwise quite sufficient staffs.

These changes have had two important consequences and point to a number of equally important conclusions. First, there has been a marked redistribution of the wage bill to the advantage of the new "skilled" and "junior supervisory" personnel and at the expense of the union rank and file.[66] Second, the cost of high salaries and generous benefits for a large and growing cadre of white-collar mining bureaucrats has been added to the labor costs of Zambian copper production without any compensatory increase in productivity. Consequently, if Zambia has a labor-related productivity problem, it arises not from union activity but rather from an inordinate growth in the number of white-collar mining bureaucrats who are unlikely to be union members. By virtue of their political potency, however, these individuals are precisely those the government is least likely to be able to control.[67] Thus, for example, even when the industry was still staggering under the impact of the 1975 price collapse and production workers were still being laid off in large numbers at the lower end of the skill scale, 1,700 new white-collar workers were added to the upper end with "the proportionate increase . . . greatest in the highest categories."[68] Moreover, because they are middle class, demand luxury housing, cars, and so on, these white-collar mining bureaucrats have an additional economic impact far beyond the copper industry.

These trends also have important consequences for government-union relations directly. Through cooptation, election control, and judicious coercion, the government has by and large been able to coopt the union's national leadership and so to stop major, official union strikes. But the victory has been pyrrhic. Workers, particularly at the lower end of the wage scale, have come to distrust both the union leadership and the government as much as they once distrusted white mining management. Moreover, as the wage gap has widened between unskilled and part-skilled workers and those above, the union itself has begun to show signs of severe strain. A yawning gap now exists between officials and the rank and file, control of the union is increasingly decentralized and beyond the reach of the national leadership (and thus the government), and wildcat strikes have come to plague the industry. The government is stuck, on the one hand, with inflated labor costs due to concessions made to white-collar mining bureaucrats over whom it can exercise little control, and, on the other, with wage demands and strike threats by the union rank and file over whom it possesses rapidly waning control that can be exercised only at great political cost.

A brief examination of nationalization's impact on state-labor relations in Chile and Peru indicates that the Zambian experience is by no means unique. In Chile, mine unionization dates from the late 19th and early 20th centuries, and mine unions have for more than fifty years been the backbone of the Communist and Socialist Parties of Chile. The unions and parties worked together effectively to win comparatively good wages and benefits for the miners and to champion the cause of nationalization in the political arena. Thus in 1971, consistent with declared Socialist Party policy, Salvador Allende extended Chile's 51 percent control of the copper industry to 100 percent nationalization. Equally consistently, the copper miners almost immediately pressed for—and then struck for—major wage increases from their old ally.

So began a struggle that continued until Allende's overthrow in 1973. It seriously undermined the Socialist government's power and prestige. Allende found it extremely difficult, ultimately impossible, to cap the miners' wage demands despite the country's critical financial situation and increasing pressure from labor groups in other sectors for wage increases that would bring their wages up to a par with miners'. At the same time, however, as a result of the government's efforts to hold down wages in the copper industry, the Christian Democrats began to make their first important inroads into the traditionally Socialist and Communist ranks of the copper miners. Finally, in 1973, just months before the coup, protesting copper miners actually marched into Santiago to demonstrate their dissatisfaction with the government. Since taking power, the Pinochet government has maintained 100 percent control of the copper industry and has contained labor demands. But it has done so only because it owes nothing to the miners politically and has been willing to employ extremely repressive measures against the unions.

Peru differs markedly from Zambia and Chile in certain ways, but confirms the central importance of the unanticipated cost of nationalization to state-labor relations. Peru, too, has a long history of mine unionization, dating from the early organizational efforts of the APRA party. In Peru, however, nationalization occurred in 1969 not as a result of union-party action, but rather by fiat of the newly installed military junta of General Velasco. Indeed, the military's aim in nationalizing the mines was to overcome traditional worker distrust of the military and to break the miners' union-APRA link. The effort failed. In fact, nationalization made the military government itself the direct target of worker demands and worker organizations. Continuing state-labor clashes, bloodshed, and even suggestions that reprivatization be considered indicate that Peruvian governments are still paying a high price for the Velasco regime's failure to perceive this particular cost of nationalization.

Conclusion

It is important to note the explanatory limitations of loss of insulation. Arguing the negative consequences of insulation loss does *not* suggest that without nationalization Zaire and Zambia would have flourished; nor that left to themselves Union Minière, Zamanglo, and Roan Selection Trust would have avoided the many pitfalls described above. Given worldwide recession, inflation, and high interest rates, no ownership arrangement could have saved entirely from harm two countries so dependent upon copper revenues; nor could it have miraculously guaranteed sufficient markets or investment funds. By the same token, no ownership scheme could have avoided inevitable tensions among the companies, regimes, miners, and middle classes over pricing, production levels, taxation, investment, wages, and employment. But if the argument for insulation is correct, there is reason to believe that the short- and long-term impacts of copper's price collapse might be less severe, mining finance might be somewhat easier to find and less expensive, the trade-offs between the mining sector and other development-related investments might be less stark, and the governments of Zaire and Zambia might be less subject to direct political and economic pressures from miners and the middle classes. The maintenance of insulation, in other words, might have kept a bad situation from getting worse; loss of insulation certainly contributed to its worsening.

It remains, finally, to ask whether any generalizations are possible from these two, admittedly extreme, examples. To what extent are the negative consequences of loss of insulation suffered by Zaire and Zambia inevitable and universal or, conversely, contingent upon the peculiarities of these two neighboring countries? The cases of Zaire and Zambia seem to suggest an equivocal answer: loss of insulation imposes near-inevitable costs for Third World nationalizers of natural resource industries, but the size and manageability of the costs may vary from country to country. This variability seems to depend, in turn, on the strength and autonomy of the nationalizer's political system. Let us briefly explore the question of costs and their manageability by examining, first, the general consequences of loss of insulation in international commodity markets, international capital markets, and relation to organized labor; and, second, the mechanisms used by nationalizers to minimize those consequences.

The loss of insulation in international commodity markets appears to have high costs for all nationalizers. Because the mining industry in general is characterized by high fixed costs, large economies of scale, and limited numbers of participants, control of market risk is the critical objective of major mining firms. The single best means available for achieving such control is internalization of the market through vertical integration. Consequently, all national producers (except the very few with the prospect of vertical integration at home) will be at a disadvantage—that is, will face higher risk with less control—as a result of losing the insulation once provided by vertical integration within the displaced multinational mining corporation. Some national producers will be able to achieve very limited market risk management through long-term contracts with consumers beyond their borders. However, such contracts provide very little security when needed most. Furthermore, and here enters an important element of variability, states such as Zaire, Zambia, Botswana, Niger, and Papua New Guinea that possess very limited trained manpower will simply be unable to mount the sophisticated marketing efforts necessary to achieve even limited market risk management without the benefits of vertical integration.

The loss of insulation vis-à-vis international capital markets seems to pose a less intractable problem, but again the size of the cost imposed varies directly with the political strength of the nationalizer. Clearly the relatively successful examples of Third World state-owned enterprises in natural resource industries are precisely those whose organization *recreates* insulation. Thus, for example, both Venezuela's C.V.G. Ferrominera Orinoco and Brazil's Companhia Vale do Rio Doce have maintained financial autonomy from the state, retain profits for operating expenses, investment, etc., and pay taxes in much the same way as would private mining companies. As a result, neither suffers the disabilities that afflict Zaire's and Zambia's state mining corporations because of close identification with their near-bankrupt governments. Here, as before, the real variable is political—whether the state possesses the trained personnel to run such operations and the strength to deny the temptation to manipulate them for short-run economic and political gains. In this regard, however, Zaire and Zambia seem far closer to the Third World norm than Brazil and Venezuela.

Lastly, the diverse cases of Zambia, Chile, and Peru seem to indicate that a widespread incidence of strained government-labor relations results from the loss of insulation. Yet again, the key variable in determining the impact of the loss of insulation seems to be the strength of the state. Thus, the Pinochet regime in Chile and a string of Brazilian regimes since 1964 have proven themselves to be both willing and able to counter increased labor demands on government with authoritarian regimentation and, where necessary, brutal repression. On the other hand, in Venezuela the conflict seems to be dampened by Ferrominera's autonomy and the relative openness of the democratic system of government. But in Zambia and Peru, as in Chile under Allende and presumably in other potential nationalizers, the weakness of the state and its lack of the means either to coerce or to cajole the sustained support of workers in nationalized industries makes the loss of insulation a critical problem.

In conclusion, certain natural resource producing countries may be able to control the negative consequences of insulation loss sufficiently to realize at least some of the hoped for benefits of nationalization. But they will be few in number. For most Third World producers, political weakness makes the necessary damage control measures impossible. As a result, it may, ironically, be better for these states and their citizens to endure what otherwise seems to be a demeaning relationship of subservience and to seek the goals of nationalization by means that do not threaten insulation.

Notes

1. U.N. General Assembly, "Declaration and Action Programme on the Establishment of a New International Economic Order," 6 May 1974(e).

2. *Zambia: A Country Study,* American University Foreign Area Studies (Washington, D.C., 1979), p. 189.

3. U.S. House, Committee on Interior and Insular Affairs, Subcommittee on Mines and Mining, *Sub-Saharan Africa: Its Role in Critical Mineral Needs of the Western World* (July 1980), pp. 5–6.

4. Marian Radetski, *Mineral Processing in Developing Countries* (New York: U.N. Industrial Development Organization, 1980), pp. 23–24.

5. See *Zambia: A Country Study,* pp. 188–89, and Dorothea Mezger, *Copper in the World Economy* (New York: Monthly Review Press, 1980), p. 231.

6. James Cobbe, *Governments and Mining Companies in Developing Countries* (Boulder, Col.: Westview, 1979), p. 237.

7. See, for example, *Zaire: A Country Study,* American University Foreign Area Studies (Washington, D.C., 1979), p. 187.

8. World Bank figures, for instance, indicate that between 1961 and 1976–78 (average) the percentage share of total exports accounted for by Zaire's top three exports (all minerals, topped by copper) increased from 52.0% to 91.1%. In Zambia, the increase was from 93.9% to 96.2%. World Bank *Accelerated Development in Sub-Saharan Africa: An Agenda for Action* (Washington, D.C., 1981), p. 156.

9. Ibid., p. 146.

10. Marian Radetski and Stephen Zorn, *Financing Mining Projects in Developing Countries: A United Nations Study* (London: Mining Journal Books, 1979), pp. 36–37.

11. This is not to suggest that the mining companies fulfilled these functions for reasons of charity. Indeed, in many ways the insulation provided was quite incidental to the corporations' interests. The issue here, however, is one of consequences.

12. World Bank, *Accelerated Development*, p. 9.

13. Raymond Vernon refers to this process as the "obsolescing bargain." For a full exposition, see *Sovereignty at Bay: The Multinational Spread of U.S. Enterprises* (New York: Basic Books, 1971).

14. Guy Gran, ed., *Zaire: The Political Economy of Underdevelopment* (New York: Praeger, 1979), pp. 264–65.

15. For an excellent study of the "obsolescing bargain" in Chile, see Theodore Moran, *Multinational Corporations and the Politics of Dependence: Copper in Chile* (Princeton: Princeton University Press, 1974).

16. Government holdings increased to 60% in 1978.

17. C. Fred Bergsten, Thomas Horst, and Theodore Moran, *American Multinationals and American Interests* (Washington, D.C.: Brookings, 1978), p. 136.

18. Chukwuma Obidegwu and Mudziviri Nziramasango, *Copper and Zambia: An Econometric Analysis* (Lexington, Mass.: Lexington Books, 1981), p. 5.

19. Wolfgang Glusche et al., *Copper: The Next Fifteen Years* (Boston: D. Reidel, 1979), p. 12; Robert Bowen and Ananda Gunatilaka, *Copper: Its Geology and Economics* (New York: Wiley, 1977), p. 299; Richard Sklar, *Corporate Power in an African State: The Political Impact of Multinational Mining Companies in Zambia* (Los Angeles: University of California Press, 1975), pp. 52–53.

20. Sir Ronald Prain, cited in John Tilton, *The Future of Nonfuel Minerals* (Washington, D.C.: Brookings, 1977), p. 52.

21. Moran, *Multinational Corporations*, p. 50.

22. For discussion of informal vertical integration, see Walter Labys, "The Role of State Trading in Mineral Commodity Markets: Copper, Tin, Bauxite and Iron Ore," *Les Cahiers du CETAI* no. 79–06, April 1979; Moran, *Multinational Corporations,* Dani Rodrik, "Managing Resource Dependency: The U.S. and Japan in the Markets for Copper, Iron Ore, and Bauxite," Harvard Program on US-Japanese Relations, Center for International Affairs, Working Paper no. 81-3, August 1981; and Raymond Vernon and Brian Levy, "State-Owned Enterprises in the World Economy: The Case of Iron Ore," in Leroy P. Jones et al., *Public Enterprise in Less-Developed Countries* (Cambridge: Cambridge University Press, 1983).

23. Vernon and Levy, "State-Owned Enterprises," p. 22.

24. In 1977, for example, C. Fred Bergsten, then Assistant Secretary of Treasury, testified to the Senate Committee on Foreign Relations that American companies preferred to invest in American deposits one-half as rich as those in LDCs and promising

only one-half the return because of the political risk factors: U.S. Senate, Committee on Foreign Relations, Subcommittee on Foreign Assistance, "OPIC Authorization," *Hearings*, 95th Cong., 1st Sess., 27, 29 July and 4 August 1977, p. 11.

25. Glusche et al., *The Next Fifteen*, p. xxix. Emphasis in original.

26. Tilton, *Future*, p. 44.

27. Glusche et al., *The Next Fifteen*, p. xxvi.

28. Mezger, *Copper*, pp. 216–17.

29. World Bank, *Accelerated Development*, p. 21. These figures clearly understate the size of the decline in Zaire's and Zambia's market share since they include South African-Namibian production, which increased rapidly throughout this period. Still, such figures are obviously open to alternative explanations, the simplest of which is that due to mismanagement, underinvestment, and deterioration of facilities, Zambian and Zairian mines were simply unable to maintain, let alone expand, production.

30. Raymond Vernon, "State-owned Enterprises in Latin American Exports," *Quarterly Review of Economics and Business* 21 (Summer 1981), p. 106.

31. See, for example, Bowen and Gunatilaka, *Geology and Economics*, p. 12; Mezger, *Copper*, p. 229; and Sklar, *Corporate Power*, pp. 65–66.

32. John Markakis and Robert Curry Jr., "The Global Economy's Impact on Recent Budgetary Politics in Zambia," *Journal of African Studies* 3 (Winter 1976–77), p. 413.

33. Klaus Billerbeck, *On Negotiating a New Order of the World Copper Market*, Occasional Paper of the German Development Institute no. 33 (Berlin, 1975), p. 15.

34. World Bank, *Accelerated Development*, p. 158.

35. Radetski and Zorn, *Financing*, pp. 92, 115.

36. U.N. Center on Transnational Corporations, *Transnational Corporations in the Copper Industry* (New York, 1981), p. 18.

37. Radetski and Zorn, *Financing*, pp. 73–74, 36–37.

38. Tilton, *Future*, p. 45. See, too, Bergsten, "OPIC Authorization," pp. 14–15; OECD, *Interfutures* (Brussels: OECD, 1979), pp. 153–57; and Amos Jordan and Robert Kilmarx, *Strategic Mineral Dependence*, Washington Papers 7:70 (Beverly Hills, Cal.: Sage, 1979), pp. 30–31.

39. U.N. Economic and Social Council, Committee on Natural Resources, *Permanent Sovereignty over Natural Resources*, E/C.7/119, 7 May 1981, p. 17.

40. Radetski and Zorn, *Financing*, p. 85.

41. Ibid., p. 41.

42. Obidegwu and Nziramasanga, *Copper and Zambia*, p. 18.

43. See Radetski and Zorn, *Financing*, pp. 36–37, and Metzger, *Copper*, p. 220.

44. Radetski and Zorn, *Financing*, p. 74.

45. See, for example, U.N. Center on Transnational Corporations, *Transnational*, p. 62.

46. U.N., *Permanent Sovereignty*, p. 21.

47. World Bank, *Accelerated Development*, p. 99.

48. *Zambia: A Country Study*, p. 40.

49. Markakis and Curry, "Budgetary Politics," p. 403.

50. In fact, between 1966 and 1973 public sector employment accounted for 55% of all new employment in Zambia and by 1976 constituted fully 71% of all

formal employment in the country, or 14.2% of the working age population: World Bank, *Accelerated Development*, pp. 17, 40–41. Thus, recurrent expenditure rose 39% from 405.8 million Kwacha in 1974 to 564.4 million Kwacha in 1977: *Zambia: A Country Study*, p. 263.

51. Cited in David Gould, *Bureaucratic Corruption and Underdevelopment in the Third World: The Case of Zaire* (New York: Pergamon, 1980), pp. 32–33.

52. Cited in ibid., p. xiii. This is Mobutu's own personal version of Proverbs 28:20: "He that maketh haste to be rich shall not be innocent."

53. Even during the copper price boom years of 1970–74, public capital investment fared badly against competitors. While overall public spending during the period maintained an average level of 34% of GDP, public capital outlays declined steadily from 11% of GDP in 1970 to just 5.6% in 1974. Recurrent expenditures figures show the opposite trend: Markakis and Curry, "Budgetary Politics," p. 411.

54. Mezger, *Copper*, p. 232.

55. *Zambia: A Country Study*, p. 190.

56. U.S. House, *Sub-Saharan Africa*, pp. 11–12.

57. Gecamines' financial woes have forced the government of Zaire to offer tax relief to the state mining company. "This tax relief," note Radetski and Zorn, "in turn accounts for a substantial portion of the government's own deficit since that time." *Financing*, pp. 40–41.

58. Cherry Gertzel, "Labour and the State: The Case of Zambia's Mineworkers' Union," *Journal of Commonwealth and Comparative Politics* 13 (November 1975), p. 293.

59. Sklar, *Corporate Power*, p. 124.

60. Ibid., pp. 122–23 and Gertzel, "Labour and the State," p. 293.

61. Philip Daniel, *Africanization, Nationalization, and Inequality: Mining Labor and the Copperbelt in Zambian Development* (Cambridge: Cambridge University Press, 1979), p. 94.

62. Ibid., p. 167.

63. Ibid. A similar pattern can be observed in the case of Zairianization. Ilunga Ilunkamba reports, for instance, that " 'Zairianization' of the staff following nationalization dealt with administrative functions, without leading to any appreciable reduction in the total number of technicals. Thus the total complement of employees was increased, without regard to the efficiency of the operation." "Copper, Technology and Dependence in Zaire: Towards the Demystification of the New White Magic," *Natural Resources Forum* 4 (April 1980), p. 149.

64. Between August 1972 and June 1976, for example, the proportion of "unskilled" and "part skilled" workers in the mine labor force declined from 69.2% to 51.6% while that of "officials" and "skilled and junior supervisory personnel" increased from 10% to 15%. Daniel, *Africanization*, p. 113.

65. Ibid., p. 116.

66. In just 29 months, between August 1972 and January 1975, the Gini coefficient for wage distribution among copper industry workers (excluding senior staff) increased from 0.222 to 0.246. Ibid., p. 160.

67. Markakis and Curry note that "localization will undoubtedly resolve some issues. But it may also reinforce the constraint posed by the Zambian middle class, which is the primary beneficiary of this process." Expatriates have been replaced by

Zambians with political clout who have been able to demand the continuation of many of the perquisites once used to induce expatriates to stay, such as near-free luxury housing, cars, insurance and pension plans, loans, personal servants, and even a "scarcity allowance." "Budgetary Politics," pp. 419–20.

    68. Daniel, *Africanization,* p. 165.

3

Between Dependency and Autonomy: India's Experience with the International Computer Industry

Joseph M. Grieco

Do the shifts in bargaining power in favor of Third World governments that are apparent in the natural resource sector extend to the manufacturing sector as well? Do they extend even to high technology manufacturing? Joseph Grieco's study of India's experience with the international computer industry represents a rare look at whether, and how, Third World governments can take advantage of multinationals in high technology industries.

Grieco shows that India's initial attempts to build and protect a state computer company had a counterproductive result in terms of the national objective of limiting and controlling the foreign computer multinationals and of fostering the growth of an indigenous computer industry. He argues that developments in technology altered the structure of the international computer industry by the 1980s so as to multiply the options available to India, allowing the host authorities to reconstitute their relations with foreign companies in a more favorable way. In contrast to some other international industries, Grieco shows that technological change was a source of state rather than corporate power in the case of the computer sector in India.

Grieco's study highlights the importance of the host country's ability to take advantage of competition among foreign companies to improve its own position. Chapter 1 analyzes this case from the perspective of the larger debate about whether competition among multinationals is increasing and how Third World governments may be able to stimulate it when it does not readily exist.

The author thanks Duncan L. Clarke, Jack Donnelly, Glenn Fong, Peter J. Katzenstein, Michael Mastanduno, John J. Mearsheimer, Richard N. Rosecrance, and Louis T. Wells for their valuable comments on various drafts of this chapter. The author is grateful to the following institutions for their generous support of the research reported here: at Cornell University, the Center for International Studies, the Peace Studies Program, and the South Asia Program; at Princeton University, the Center of International Studies; at Harvard University, the Division of Research in the Graduate School of Business Administration; the Institute for the Study of World Politics; and the American Institute of Indian Studies. Of course, all statements of fact and opinion are the sole responsibility of the author.

Two major schools of thought contend today on whether developing host countries can increase their power over multinational enterprises. India's experience with the international computer industry serves here as an important test of these two schools. This section summarizes the basic arguments of the "bargaining school" and the "Marxist-dependencia school" on relations between developing countries and multinational enterprises. It also evaluates the usefulness of India's experience as a test case.

Three propositions constitute the bargaining school's understanding of relations between developing countries and multinationals.[1] First, the terms by which an enterprise operates in a country, and the distribution of benefits between the parties, result from negotiations and the balance of bargaining power between the country and the company. Second, in early interactions the balance of power and benefits often favors the multinational. The developing country may control access to its markets and resources, but the enterprise has more important bargaining assets through its control of capital, technology, and managerial expertise. Third, and most important, over time the host country is likely to gain access to the various sources of bargaining power earlier controlled by the enterprise. As the country attains greater bargaining power, it forces the balance of benefits to shift in its favor. In sum, according to the bargaining school, prolonged contacts with foreign enterprises afford developing countries the experience needed to manage these relations more effectively and to their greater benefit.

In recent years certain Marxist-dependencia writers have introduced into their analyses the recognition that multinationals do contribute to the "growth" of economic capabilities of several advanced developing countries. Moreover, very recent Marxist-dependencia scholarship recognizes the phenomenon of bargaining between developing countries and multinationals in which the former may extract some concessions from the latter. However, compared to the bargaining school the Marxist-dependencia school maintains that what bargaining takes place is over marginal issues. The major decisions about the evolution of industries in developing countries continue to be made by multinationals and therefore the extent, timing, and form of growth in developing countries depend fundamentally upon loci of power outside the developing countries. Moreover, compared to the bargaining school the Marxist-dependencia school sees very little chance of developing countries' being able or willing to try to attain fundamentally greater control over multinationals operating in their economies. Therefore, industries in developing countries may grow due to the presence of multinationals, but these industries remain outside the control of their hosts. In essence, Marxist-dependentistas, even those employing recent complex formulations, consider the multinational enterprise to be the instrument by which advanced capitalist societies place developing countries in a basically subordinate and dependent position in the international economy.[2]

Recent commentary on the case study method points to the utility of India's computer experience as a test of the relative strength of these two schools of thought. If the most extreme phenomena predicted by a theory (i.e., "hard cases") are observed, then strong support is given to the theory.[3] Involving both a developing country and a technologically dynamic industry, the present case is just such a "hard case" for the bargaining school.[4] The school holds that developing countries can, in general, cause the balance of bargaining power to shift in their favor. However, causing this shift in power is most difficult for developing countries, according to the school, in bargaining that involves high technology multinationals.[5] If a developing country like India is successful with high technology enterprises in an industry like data processing, this would give strong support to the school.

On the other hand, the Indian case constitutes an "easy case" for the Marxist-dependencia school. According to this school, developing countries are generally unable or unwilling fundamentally to change their relations with multinationals; this is especially true in cases involving high technology multinationals.[6] In such cases developing countries are supposed to be at their very weakest. They should be without meaningful success if they dare to try to reformulate their ties with high technology enterprises. Hence a country like India should clearly fail, according to the Marxist-dependencia school, in bargaining about major issues with computer multinationals. Indian success in computers would therefore cast severe doubt on the adequacy of the Marxist-dependencia school's line of argument.

The next section presents a descriptive review of India's improving performance from 1960 to 1980 in dealing with the international computer industry. Two subsequent sections offer an explanation of this improved Indian experience. At the international level, changes in data-processing technology and in the structure of the industry created new opportunities for India to become more self-directed in computing. At the domestic level, India developed the institutions needed to exploit these international changes in a way favorable to the country. The final section argues that India's computer experience illustrates the general analytical superiority of the bargaining school over the Marxist-dependencia school. At the same time, it proposes a modest revision of the bargaining school's understanding of the capability of some developing countries to negotiate with high technology multinationals.

India's Changing Fortunes in Computing, 1960–1980

By the mid 1960s the Indian government had three stated goals concerning ties between India and the international computing industry. First, India should participate in the ownership and control of foreign computer subsidiaries in the country. Second, by the late 1960s, wholly Indian producers should satisfy most of the country's computer needs, with foreign units temporarily supplying only very exotic technologies and large systems. Third, India should have access to and participate in the manufacture of the most advanced systems available internationally.[7]

These were the concrete goals of Indian policy, and they may be used as a yardstick to measure both India's performance in computers and changes in that performance over time. This section focuses on the degree to which these goals were met during three periods: 1967–72, 1973–77, and 1978–80. (The rationale for this choice of periods is clarified below, in a section on Indian institutions and politics in the area of computer policy.) In general, the evidence suggests that India's performance in the second and third periods improved substantially over the first. However, as a result of political-economic developments within India the domestic institutions that led Indian computing during 1978–80 were quite different in identity and orientation from the local institutions that were responsible for the country's initial computer progress during 1973–77.

Corporate Organization

In 1966, two foreign computer firms had substantial sales and manufacturing activities in India: International Business Machines (IBM), and Britain's International Computers and Tabulators (ICT), which in 1968 became a part of International Computers Limited (ICL). The Indian government advised IBM in 1966 and 1968 that the company should share ownership of its local activities with Indian nationals. In both instances the firm responded that its highly internationalized and interdependent operations required centralized coordination and control. This precluded sharing ownership of any particular international subsidiary with individuals of the country in which the firm's unit was operating. Indeed, in 1968 IBM advised the government that it would terminate its operations in India rather than share ownership of its Indian subsidiary. The government decided not to press the matter, and IBM was permitted to retain full control over its Indian operations.[8]

ICT/ICL experienced a slightly more complicated situation in India: it had split its operations into two units, one for manufacturing and one for sales. The manufacturing unit involved 40 percent Indian ownership, thus giving the impression that ICT/ICL was sensitive to Indian policy concerns. However, the sales unit was appointed the sole distributor of the manufacturing unit's products (this was in fact a provision of the manufacturing unit's statement of incorporation), and, furthermore, made all of the decisions about the activities it would undertake. This relationship rendered irrelevant Indian partial ownership of the manufacturing unit, which could not affect the activities of ICT/ICL in India.[9]

The Indian government in the late 1960s was unable to ensure effective Indian participation in the ownership and direction of the local units of foreign computer firms. The experience of the government in the 1970s, however, was markedly different. For example, after intense negotiations ICL agreed to merge its two units and to own only 40 percent of the successor corporation in India, thus ensuring Indian participation in both the marketing and the manufacturing activities of ICL in India. Moreover, after the Indian government resisted Burroughs's efforts to establish a wholly owned subsidiary, the company announced in 1977 that it would establish a subsidiary in India as a joint venture with Tata Enterprises. Each would own 50 percent of the new company. Finally, the government began anew in 1973–1974 to urge IBM to share equity of its local unit with Indian nationals. The company responded by offering new and quite high levels of manufacturing activities that would be useful to the government in terms of foreign exchange earnings and the transfer of technology, as well as direct technical assistance to India's data-processing programs, to be exchanged for an exemption from the Indian policy that the company share equity. But IBM again indicated that it would withdraw from India rather than be compelled to share ownership and to submit to other controls on its Indian operations. In contrast to 1966 and 1968, the government decided to press its maximum demands on equity. IBM announced in November 1977 that it would withdraw from India by June 1978—as in fact it did.[10] Thus, in contrast to the 1960s, the government had decided by the mid 1970s that it could afford to pursue its policy even at the cost of losing the world's premier computer enterprise.

During the late 1970s Burroughs and ICL consolidated their operations in India, and IBM completed its withdrawal from the country. The major new development within the Indian computer industry during this period was the emergence of several wholly Indian systems-engineering firms, firms that were not under the direct control of the central government. For most of the 1970s, the only wholly Indian computer enterprise had been the central government's Electronics Corporation of India Limited (ECIL). By the end of the decade, however, three other Indian firms were designing and assembling systems: Hindustan Computers Limited (HCL), a joint venture between a private Indian firm and the Uttar Pradesh state government; DCM Dataproducts (DCM), a subsidiary of Delhi Cloth Mills; and Operations Research Group (ORG), a subsidiary of Sarabhai Enterprises. A fourth Indian enterprise, International Data Machines (IDM, founded by former IBM employees with the assistance of IBM), marketed and serviced a microsystem designed and assembled by the Indian firm National Radio and Electronics Company, a subsidiary of Tata Enterprises.[11] (National Radio and Tata-Burroughs are two entirely separate operations.) By 1980 ECIL's Computer Division had about 1000 employees; together, Burroughs and ICL had roughly 600 employees; and the new Indian entrants had about 1900 employees.[12]

Table 3–1
Computer Market Structure of India, 1960–1980
(systems installed, by source and by period, in absolute numbers and percentage shares of total)

| | 1960–1966 | | 1967–1972 | | | |
| | Estimate I | | Estimate I | | Estimate IA | |
Source	No.	(%)	No.	(%)	No.	(%)
ECIL	0	0	5	3.4	13	8.5
HCL	0	0	0	0	0	0
DCM	0	0	0	0	0	0
IDM	0	0	0	0	0	0
ORG	0	0	0	0	0	0
IBM	31	73.8	106	73.0	106	69.3
ICL	2	4.7	17	11.7	17	11.1
Burroughs	0	0	0	0	0	0
Computer Automation	0	0	0	0	0	0
Data General	0	0	0	0	0	0
Digital Equipment	0	0	1	0.7	1	0.6
Hewlett-Packard	0	0	1	0.7	1	0.6
Honeywell-CII	0	0	12	8.2	12	7.6
Univac-Varian	0	0	0	0	0	0
Soviet	2	4.7	1	0.7	1	0.6
Other Indian	2	4.7	0	0	0	0
Other foreign	5	11.9	2	1.4	2	1.2
Total	42	99.8%	145	99.8%	153	99.7%

Sources: Estimate I for 1960–1966 and 1967–1972 is based on data in Om Vikas and L. Ravichandran, "Computerization in India: A Statistical Review," *Electronics: Information and Planning* 6 (December 1978):318–51. Estimate 1A in 1967–1972 contains a report of 13 ECIL system installations by the end of 1972. This is based on a report of a total of 18 ECIL installations as of the end of fiscal year 1972–1973 in India (Republic), Lok Sabha, Estimates Committee, *Sixty-Sixth Report: Department of Electronics* (New Delhi: Lok Sabha, April 1974), p. 101, subtracting 5 TDC-12s reported to have been installed during January–March 1973 in P. Gopalakrishnan and N.S. Narayanan, *Computers in India: An Overview* (Bombay: Popular Prakashan, 1975), pp. 133–42. Estimate II non-ECIL installations for 1973–1977 adds to each source systems that, according to Vikas and Ravichandran, were installed by 1977 but whose recipients did not report to the

Market Structure

India's second computer goal was the fostering of indigenous sources of supply for most of the country's computer needs. India's performance in this regard is summarized in table 3–1, which reports on the country's computer market structure between 1960 and 1980. The data consist of the absolute numbers, and the percentage shares of the total, of all systems installed during each

| 1973–1977 | | | | 1978–1980 | |
| Estimate I | | Estimate II | | Estimate III | |
No.	(%)	No.	(%)	No.	(%)
77	40.3	167	52.7	98	10.2
0	0	0	0	390	40.5
0	0	0	0	265	27.5
0	0	0	0	17	1.8
0	0	0	0	70	7.3
6	3.1	19	6.0	0	0
19	9.9	21	6.6	20	2.0
5	2.6	6	1.9	25	2.6
5	2.6	19	6.0	1	.1
0	0	0	0	7	.72
48	25.1	48	15.1	35	3.6
10	5.2	10	3.1	6	.62
2	1.0	2	0.6	2	.20
4	2.1	6	1.9	18	1.9
9	4.7	9	2.8	0	0
0	0	0	0	0	0
6	3.1	10	3.1	8	.83
191	99.7%	317	99.8%	962	99.87%

government the exact dates of system deliveries. ECIL installations in Estimate II for 1973–1977 and Estimate III for 1978–1980 are from "Growth of Indigenous Effort," in "Special Section on Computers in the 1980's," *Commerce,* 31 May 1980, p. 925. Figures for HCL, DCM, IDM, and ORG installations during 1978–1980 (and listed in Estimate III) were collected by the author in interviews with officers of these firms. Data for most of the actual installations of foreign systems during 1978–1980 are unavailable (except for 10 systems from Hewlett-Packard, Burroughs, and Digital Equipment reported by Vikas and Ravichandran as delivered during January–March 1978), and therefore most foreign system figures in Estimate III represent the number of systems approved for import by the Indian government during this period. These import approvals are reported in the *Annual Report of the Department of Electronics* (New Delhi, 1978, 1979, and 1980).

period by the various sources. Three major observations can be made on the basis of these data. First, in the six years after India announced its computer goals the country made virtually no progress toward encouragement of an indigenous computer supplier. At the very most, ECIL was the source of 8.5 percent of all systems installed between 1967 and 1972, and its portion of the market may have been as low as 3.4 percent. In contrast, IBM was the source of almost three-fourths of all systems installed during the same period, a market share not less than that it had enjoyed from 1960 to 1966, that is, the period before India began its national computer policy. A second major observation is that between 1973 and 1977 ECIL surged ahead and became the single largest systems supplier in India, while at the same time IBM's market share collapsed.

Finally, during the last years of the decade wholly Indian enterprises as a group continued to grow as an important force in the Indian computer market. Within the indigenous computer industry what was remarkable about the 1978–80 period was the extremely important role taken on so rapidly by Indian enterprises other than ECIL. During this period the four new suppliers almost immediately outpaced ECIL. This was a noteworthy development because the new firms had made deliveries for no more than three years, while ECIL had done so for almost ten years. Moreover, while in mid-decade ECIL's market share by number of installations was greater than that of foreign suppliers, during 1978 to 1980 it fell behind both enterprises not fostered by the central government and foreign suppliers active in India.

Technology of Systems

Two measures are employed here to assess India's changing ability to acquire and to fabricate technologically sophisticated computer systems. The first measure is based on the proposition that the data-processing industry is technologically so dynamic that the introduction of new families of systems results in dramatic increases in performance and efficiency. (Concrete evidence of this relationship can be observed below, in table 3–4.) This suggests that a valid indicator of the technological status of a developing country's computer base is the average difference in years between a computer model's introduction in the advanced countries (which can serve as a baseline since these countries are the first to be exposed to new models) and the same model's introduction in the developing country. This information on temporal (and probably technological) lags for the foreign-origin portion of India's computer base is presented in table 3–2.

As table 3–2 shows, India's temporal (and probably technological) lag increased in the 1967–1972 period compared to the prepolicy period of 1960 to 1967, but this technological regression was reversed during the 1973–1977 period and the technological gap continued to narrow at the end of the decade. The jump in the lag during the 1967–1972 period was the result of manufacturing efforts undertaken in India during these years by IBM and ICL; their efforts consisted of importing previously used systems for refurbishment at their respective local facilities and then renting these systems to Indian customers. However, by returning in the mid and late 1970s to imports as the major form of access to foreign-origin systems, India obtained computers of greater technological sophistication more rapidly, thereby cutting the technological lag.

Table 3–2
Lag of Foreign Computers in India, 1960–1980

	1960–66	1967–72	1973–77	Estimated 1978–80
Number of systems	33	126	95	87
Total lag (years)	145	1049	351	231
Average lag (years)	4.4	8.3	3.7	2.6
Foreign systems in survey (percent)	82.5	90.0	83.0 [a] / 67.0	84.0

Sources: The entry-dates for systems into India during 1960–66 and 1967–72 are from Om Vikas and L. Ravichandran, "Computerization in India: A Statistical Review," *Electronics: Information and Planning* 6 (December 1979):318–51. The introduction dates of IBM systems into the advanced countries are from Montgomery Phister Jr., *Data Processing Technology and Economics* (Santa Monica: Santa Monica Pub. Co., 1976), pp. 338–46; for the Burroughs and Digital Equipment systems, their respective annual reports, various years; for Soviet systems, Bohdan O. Szuprowicz, "Soviet Bloc's RIAD Computer Systems," *Datamation* 19 (September 1973):80–85; for the ICL-1901A, *Meet ICL* (Bombay, n.d.); and the annual surveys of small computer systems in *Datamation* 20 (July 1974):50–61; 22 (October 1976):91–105; 23 (September 1977):189–214; and 24 (August 1978):113–26. For the late 1978–80 period it was assumed (on the basis of interviews) that systems approved for import by the government during a fiscal year were installed within the same calendar year as the last quarter of the fiscal year during which approval had been granted. As a result, the shortest delivery period was assumed to be 9 months, the longest 21 months. Approval dates were taken from Department of Electronics, *Annual Report* (New Delhi, various years). Additional introduction dates for foreign systems into advanced countries were located for the 1978–80 period in *Auerbach Computer Technology Reports, Electronic News,* and *Computer Review* (1975 and 1981).

Note: As an illustration of the measure, suppose that India in 1965 received only two computers from American sources and assume that the first system had been introduced in the U.S. in 1960, the second in 1962. The lag of the first unit (time between its introduction in the U.S. and in India) would be 5 years; for the second unit, the lag would be 3 years. The total lag would be 8 years, or an average lag of 4 years for foreign-origin systems installed in India during 1965.

[a]83% from Estimate I, 67% from Estimate II. As explained in the sources for table 3–1, Estimate II for the 1973–1977 period includes several foreign systems that were installed by 1977 but for which exact installation dates (which would be needed for their inclusion in the figures presented in table 3–2 are unavailable. The exclusion of these systems from table 3–2 thus lowers the percentage-coverage of foreign systems in the survey for Estimate II, 1973–1977, compared to Estimate I.

To examine the technological sophistication of systems fabricated in India (by both foreign and indigenous companies), the second measure employed in this study is the cost-per-bit of main memory used by the central processor (the unit that performs computations and controls the computer system as a whole) of only those systems fabricated in the country; a lower cost-per-bit of main memory indicates technological advances over a main memory with a higher cost-per-bit. The data are presented in table 3–3, and compared using this measure are the major systems fabricated in India during 1967 to 1972 (the IBM-1401), the systems that IBM hoped would succeed the

Table 3–3

Per-bit Costs of Selected IBM, ECIL, and DCM Main Memories

Company	IBM			ECIL		DCM
System	1401	360/30	360/40	TDC-312	TDC-316	Galaxy 11
Year introduced	1960	1965	1965	1974	1975	1978
Cost-per-bit ($ current)	.93	.32	.21	.25	.14	.06

Sources: The data for IBM systems are from Phister, *Data Processing Technology,* pp. 339, 342; data on the TDC-312 and 316 are from Vikas and Ravichandran, "Computerization in India," p. 327, and Om Vikas, "Indigenous Development of Computer Systems, Peripherals, and Computer Communication Facilities," *Electronics: Information and Planning 5* (August 1978)), pp. 793, 807, 811; and the Galaxy 11 data are from an interview conducted at DCM Dataproducts (January 1981).

Note: Indian costs are translated from rupees at an exchange rate of 8 rupees per dollar.

1401 in India during the early 1970s (the 360/30 and 360/40), two systems fabricated during the mid and late 1970s by ECIL (the TDC-312 and TDC-316), and a system fabricated at the end of the decade by DCM (the Galaxy 11).

The main memories of both the TDC-312 and the 316 have a better cost performance than the 1401, the 360/30, and the 360/40, suggesting that these Indian systems, fabricated between 1973 and 1977, were more advanced technologically than those fabricated by IBM between 1967 and 1972. The Indian systems were also more advanced than the 360s IBM proposed to follow the 1401. It should be noted that in 1971 IBM proposed to follow its 360 program with the assembly of some new and the refurbishment of previously utilized IBM-370s (probably models 115, 125, or 135). Any of these systems would have been superior to the ECIL systems, thus raising the question of whether India suffered by its refusal to accept IBM's offer. However, ICL agreed in 1977 to assemble new ICL-2904s, and these compare quite favorably with the 370 models IBM was likely to have fabricated in India. In any event, the 370 proposal faded in 1974 when IBM, aware that the proposal would not be accepted by the government, withdrew it in favor of an offer to manufacture line printers at the company's Indian facility.[13]

Finally, systems fabricated in India at the end of the decade continued to improve technologically. Again notable, however, was the leading role taken by the non-ECIL domestic industry. For example, in 1978 the per-bit cost of main memory of an ECIL TDC-316 was the rupee equivalent of about $.14; in contrast, the per-bit cost of main memory for the DCM Galaxy 11 (which is roughly comparable to the TDC-316 in the functions it can perform) was the rupee equivalent of approximately $.06, under one-half of the ECIL cost. India was making further gains at the end of the 1970s in meeting its goal of acquiring and producing data-processing equipment of greater technological sophistication, but regarding domestic technological development the most impressive gains were achieved by the new Indian computer firms rather than by the government's own computer enterprise.

In sum, India made very little progress in the years just after it articulated its computer goals regarding corporate organization, market structure, and technology transfer; but it achieved significant progress in later years. A second feature of Indian computing was the replacement of the central government's firm by several nongovernment enterprises in leading the country's indigenous computer industry. The challenge, of course, is to explain these developments.

The International Creation of Opportunities for India

Described in the following paragraphs are developments in computer technology and in the structure of the international computer industry. These developments widened the range of policy opportunities available to India to the extent that, when it became capable of exploiting these internationally derived opportunities, India did in fact reform its relations with foreign computer firms and made significant progress toward its policy goals in data processing. Two technological developments are examined from the perspective of their impact on India: the evolution of prices and performance of computer components, and the emergence of minicomputer and microcomputer architectures. These technological developments were made more readily available to India as a result of the final development in computing to be discussed in this section, namely the expansion of greater numbers of foreign computer firms into the developing world.

To give a sense of the improvements that have taken place in data processing, table 3–4 reports the time and cost required between 1955 and 1976 to

Table 3–4
Processing Times and Costs of Computer Systems, 1955–1976

Year	Processing Time, 1700 Operations (seconds)	Cost of Operations ($)	Cost of Million-Bit Main Memory ($ thousands)
1955	375	14.54	8500
1960	47	2.48	6000
1965	37	.59	1600
1974	5	.28	150
1976	3	.11	90

Sources: Erich Bloch and Dom Galage, "Component Progress: Its Effect on High Speed Computer Architecture and Machine Organization," *Computer* 11 (April 1978), p. 71; and Thomas Comella, "Business Machines: Harnessing the Information Explosion," *Machine Design,* 21 June 1979, p. 48.

execute 1700 operations by and to store one million bits of information in the main memory of representative computer systems. Computer hardware developments clearly have allowed staggering increases in the speed and efficiency of data processing. As the table indicates, in twenty years the speed of systems has increased by a factor of one hundred, while costs have decreased by factors of 132 for overall processing and 94 for main memory.

These improvements can, in turn, be related to changes in the components used as the building blocks for computer systems. Two classes of innovations have led to more powerful and less expensive components: changes in the characteristics of a given type of component or its manufacturing process, and innovations that have led to wholly new types of components and fabrication procedures. An example of the first type of innovation is the move from germanium point-contact transistors, manufactured in the 1950s, to silicon planar transistors, manufactured in the late 1950s through the early 1970s. The move in the 1950s from vacuum tubes to transistors and another move from transistors to integrated circuits in the 1960s are examples of the second type of technological transformation. Also, advances in fabrication have been extremely important in the case of integrated circuits. Improvements such as learning to decrease the average sizes of components within an integrated circuit and decreasing the number of circuit-destroying impurities in production facilities have increased the rate at which integrated-circuit "chips" can be produced. They have also increased the density of components that can be embedded within a chip. All of these factors, in turn, lead to higher performance and lower per-component costs for an integrated circuit.[14]

In the 1960s and early 1970s, small systems architectures—the minicomputer and the microcomputer—emerged internationally, and the development of such systems also affected India's range of computer opportunities. Minicomputers soon developed cost-to-performance improvements that matched the experience of mainframe systems. In 1965, for instance, a Digital Equipment PDP-8 central processor (4,000-word main memory and 1.5 microsecond cycle time) cost $17,000 in current dollars; by 1975 the PDP-8 (with an improved cycle time) cost about $2,500 in current dollars.[15] Appearing in 1971, microprocessors were soon using 4, 8, and 16 bit "words," and some micros had main memories of 8 million bytes (or 1 million 8 bit "words").[16] A "word" here is a block of bits—the basic medium in which a computer system operates internally—and larger numbers of bits per word are associated with more capable systems.

Overall, by the end of the decade some inexpensive minicomputers could perform the functions previously executed by mainframes, and microcomputers could execute the functions previously handled by minicomputers. Improvements were also taking place in peripheral units used in small systems: for example, in 1971 IBM introduced the "floppy disk," a flexible magnetic disk that offers high levels of auxiliary storage at low cost. These floppy disks have themselves evolved, so that a 3.2 million bit system costing in current dollars about $400 in 1972 could be purchased for about $275 in 1978; alternatively, $400 in 1978 could purchase a floppy-disk system storing 12 million bits of information.[17]

While these technological innovations in components and new architectural configurations for small systems have increased the range of options theoretically available to any data-processing consumer, the evolution of the international computer industry has perhaps facilitated their actual availability to at least several developing countries. For example, while only nine American computer firms appear to have been active in the developing world in the mid 1960s (with a total of 76 sales units and 13 manufacturing units), in the mid 1970s no fewer than sixteen American firms were active in developing countries (with a total of 134 sales units and 30 manufacturing units). Moreover, a larger number of firms accounted for the majority of units in the later period: while four firms accounted for 80 percent of both sales and manufacturing units in the 1960s, respectively seven and eight firms were needed to account for 80 percent of sales and manufacturing units in the 1970s. This suggests that the growth of units cannot be ascribed to only one or two firms and this, in turn, suggests that the availability of products from alternative suppliers increased for the developing world in the 1970s.[18]

Other new competitors from Japan and Europe may also have enhanced the bargaining opportunities of several of these countries in the 1970s. For example, Japan exported about $48 million in computer equipment to Asian countries in 1977, rivaling the presence of many American firms. Also, Britain's ICL created an extensive marketing presence in the developing world: by 1977, the company had sales activities in over forty developing countries (including all of the members of the "assertive" upper tier) and sales to these countries contributed 12 percent to 15 percent of the total revenue of ICL in 1977. These and other non-American firms such as Siemens and Nixdorf of Germany, CII (with Honeywell) in France, and Olivetti of Italy began by the 1970s to compete with American firms not only in developing countries but in some cases in the American market itself.[19]

Finally, during the late 1960s and early to mid 1970s several new American, Japanese, and European semiconductor enterprises were founded and began to compete in the field of integrated circuits: in the United States alone, thirty such firms commenced operations between 1966 and 1976. Many of these firms soon became active in international markets for computer components. In 1976, for example, Fairchild and Motorola each sold over $130 million in components to international buyers, National Semiconductor had international revenues of $29 million, and Mostek and Intersil each had over $15 million in foreign sales of electronic components. These and other American firms (especially the leaders, Texas Instruments and

Intel), Japanese firms such as Nippon Electronics, and European firms such as Siemens were the major suppliers of components to the computer industry of the advanced capitalist societies. They could also be used by firms in developing countries.[20]

In sum, by the 1970s many features of data processing potentially worked to the advantage of a developing country seeking to establish its own course of action in the area of computers. First, the minicomputer and microcomputer emerged; built with increasingly powerful components, these systems were becoming very inexpensive. A developing country might therefore follow the lead of the majority of firms in the advanced societies and simply purchase these components, using them as inputs for their own uniquely designed small systems. Moreover, these components were becoming available from an increasing number of suppliers that were primarily in the business of selling components, not full systems. These suppliers were more than willing to make available these computer building blocks to customers from developing countries. Third, if a country wished to continue linkages with the international computer industry even as it established its own national sector, its range of alternative foreign firms was very much greater in the 1970s than in the 1960s. This greater range increased the possibility that at least one or two firms could be found that would establish relations on terms favorable to the developing country concerned. Of course, a developing country still needed to recognize and to exploit these opportunities. It is to India's developing sense and subsequent actual exploitation of the new opportunities from abroad that we now direct our attention.

India's Exploitation of International Opportunities

Developments in the technology and industrial structure of international computing created new opportunities for India to become more self-directed in data processing. However, India's progress in computing resulted not only from international developments but also from an increasing domestic capacity to exploit external developments. This section reviews the shifts in strategy and policy that enabled India to improve its situation in computing; these shifts are then linked to the evolution of Indian institutions active in computing; and, finally, the institutional changes are shown to have been a reflection of political struggles within the Indian data-processing industry as it developed during the 1960s and 1970s.

Changes in Strategy and Policies

India's computer failings during the late 1960s and early 1970s were the result of a combination of an ill-conceived computer strategy and an application of general industrial policies that unintentionally detracted from achievement of the country's computer goals. In terms of strategy, throughout the 1960s India sought to move toward the efficient (i.e., intensive) use of a small number of large systems.[21] This interest in large systems through the end of the 1960s (when in the developed countries consumers were switching to small systems) led India to use computers that the country was least able to fabricate domestically.

The government was eager for some sort of computer manufacturing in India. It turned to IBM and ICL; both were already manufacturing other types of business equipment in India. As an incentive, the government told the firms they could retain and control most of their foreign earnings from the export of noncomputer products in order to import the capital equipment, parts, and components needed for their computer manufacturing programs. This policy, of course, meant that only IBM (and ICL to a lesser extent) could be highly active as computer suppliers in India, since only they had the export capabilities that India had made a prerequisite to the importing of items needed for the local supply of systems.[22] IBM believed that the only rational path for the long-term development of a computer industry in India was an evolutionary one that led to the gradual production of increasingly advanced systems: first IBM-1401s, then IBM-360s, and then IBM-370s.[23] This opposed the corporate strategy preferred by the government, and it resulted in India's having a large number of 1401s while the rest of the world used 360s and even 370s. Finally, not only did Indian policies contribute to this situation in India; at the end of the 1960s they also made it seem unlikely that a different computer strategy could be undertaken.

This was the situation from 1966 and 1967 through 1970 or 1971. However, in 1971 and 1972 the government altered both its computer strategy and its supporting policies. Rather than focusing on large systems, the government's strategy henceforth would be to encourage the use and manufacture of small systems. The government, having discovered that these systems could be designed and assembled in India on the basis of imported components and peripherals,[24] developed a variety of policies to support its new strategy. These policies included the funding of ECIL's computer development efforts and the establishment of an export-processing zone whose occupants—foreign electronics firms—generated foreign exchange earnings that were more tightly controlled by the government than had been the practice with IBM in the 1960s, and were usable in part to import the hardware needed for the indigenous assembly of computers. The government also instituted several administrative policies designed to make foreign systems less available, thereby compelling the use of ECIL products. Finally, by attracting Burroughs to India, retaining ICL, and setting in motion the small systems strategy, the government lowered the costs of pushing IBM on the equity issue and on other issues relating to the control over IBM's operations in India. The company felt compelled to withdraw.

India's plans for its computer industry were clear by 1975 or 1976. ECIL was to be India's "national champion" in computers. ICL, according to the government, was to fabricate (with increasing levels of local value added) minisystems—in particular the ICL-2904—with capabilities beyond the range of systems provided by ECIL. ECIL and ICL minicomputers were to satisfy the bulk of India's computer requirements, and they were to be different enough so that ECIL would have a protected market. Burroughs was expected to provide a few very large (and very expensive) mainframe systems per year, to cover computing requirements beyond the capabilities of minicomputers. From a foreign exchange viewpoint Burroughs would finance these imports through its export of software and dot-matrix printers, and India was to acquire additional foreign exchange funding from international bodies like the United Nations Development Program. The remaining foreign exchange costs of the industry (i.e., those of ECIL and, to a lesser extent, ICL) were to be offset by the earnings of foreign electronics firms at the export zone. To ensure ECIL's viability, the government expected strictly to control minisystem imports after a certain number had become available and had made the Indian computer community aware of the capabilities of minicomputer technology.

For about two years the government controlled the Indian computer community in accordance with these expectations. But in 1978 the government announced a change in strategy: new, wholly indigenous entrants were to be permitted to engage in systems engineering.[25] The government attempted to restrict the new enterprises to microcomputers so that they could not compete with ECIL, but this proved a miscalculation. Many Indian users apparently believed that the less expensive microcomputers provided by the new firms could substitute for the much more expensive small minicomputers provided by ECIL. As consumers chose the former over the latter, ECIL's market share rapidly narrowed. Moreover, in 1978 and 1979 the government clearly relaxed its efforts to restrict computer imports. As imports increased, ECIL's market share continued to deteriorate. The Indian government had been able to gain control of the computer community in the early 1970s and was able to lead it in the mid 1970s. But by the end of the decade the government had given way to new, wholly indigenous systems engineering firms and to the preference of Indian computer users for easier access to a wider range of foreign systems.

Computer Institutions and Political Struggles

These developments reflected the evolution of capable Indian computer institutions as well as changes in the balance of power among these institutions as they vied for control over Indian computing. During the late 1960s India's computer policy institutions were fragmented and enjoyed little authority. For example, the policy unit assigned during the 1960s with the procurement of computers for the government—the Computer Centre in the Planning Commission's Department of Statistics—had no authority over a governmental office's actual choice of a computer system. There was no policy unit responsible for ensuring the acquisition by Indian users of modern systems, and no single unit had the responsibility or the power needed to support an indigenous supplier. Research and development relating to a small minicomputer was underway at the end of the 1960s at the Bhabha Atomic Research Centre (under the Atomic Energy Commission).[26] However, this effort did not affect the decisions of the policy unit responsible for granting the industrial licenses needed to manufacture systems, the Department of Defence Supplies (in the Ministry of Defence). Indeed, it was the Department of Defence Supplies that granted to IBM and ICL licenses to undertake the refurbishment of used equipment.

This fragmentation of authority over computers was the direct result of a clash during the late 1960s between the Ministry of Defence and the Atomic Energy Commission for control over Indian electronics.[27] Both bureaucratic organizations had equal control over the policy body established in 1966 to guide Indian electronics, the Electronics Committee of India. However, while neither Defence nor Atomic Energy had sufficient power in the late 1960s to overrule the other and take charge of electronics in the country, each had enough power to block the full execution of the other's policy efforts. The stalemate allowed both organizations (as well as others) to undertake to some extent their respective programs in electronics: ECIL was under Atomic Energy, while Defence controlled an enterprise named Bharat Electronics Limited, which served as a subcontractor to ICL. Defence, furthermore, thought IBM's activities a step in the right direction. However, the cost of this jurisdictional confusion was an immobilized Indian computer industry.

During the 1960s, as noted above, Defence controlled industrial licensing for computers and other electronics equipment. Using this power, it sought to hamper ECIL's entry into the electronics industry. This gave the atomic energy policy "network" a strong incentive to break its stalemate with Defence and, building upon national dissatisfaction over the country's progress in electronics, this network waged a campaign in 1969 and 1970 that led to a victory over Defence for control of national electronics policy. New policy units were created—the Electronics Commission and the Department of Electronics—which were supposed to be neutral but which were, in fact, heavily staffed by key members of the atomic energy network.[28] These new policy units (not surprisingly) soon made promotion of ECIL computers a high priority. Over 80 percent of all funding committed by the Commission and Department during the 1970s to computer research and development (totaling about $8 million) went to ECIL and the Tata Institute for Fundamental Research (which is under the Atomic Energy Commission; it carried out software research and development for the ECIL computer effort). It was also the Commission and Department that obtained the authority in 1975 to block the import of computers if ECIL systems could substitute for them.[29] The minicomputers developed by ECIL, the TDC-312 and TDC-316, were based on the architectures of Digital Equipment's PDP-8 and PDP-16. ECIL products reflected India's increasing access in the mid 1970s to several international suppliers of components and peripherals. Different ECIL systems contained components from Intersil and Motorola, floppy-disk drives from Shugart, Pertec, and BASF, hard-disk drives from Memorex, Pertec, and BASF, and printers from BASF and Dataproducts.[30]

Finally, the Commission and Department formulated the new linkages of the mid 1970s between India and the international computer industry. With the cooperation of the Trade Development Corporation, the Commission studied the possibility of establishing the export-processing zone that eventually was to attract Burroughs to India.[31] The Commission and Department also froze the operations of, and carried on the negotiations concerning new operations with, IBM and ICL, and they established the terms under which Burroughs gained entry into India. Also, they believed that one of the major unspoken bargaining advantages enjoyed by IBM was the fact that so many systems in India were from this one source. Withdrawal of service for these systems, should IBM leave the country as a result of government pressure, was a major potential problem for the country and had served in the past to limit the degree to which the government had pressed the firm. For this reason, and to lessen the attractiveness of foreign systems generally after ECIL products became available, the Commission established the Computer Maintenance Corporation (CMC).[32] With IBM's exit, Burroughs's entry, the retention of ICL under the government's terms, and the promotion of ECIL and CMC, the new policy units appeared to be clearly in charge of the Indian computer industry by 1976 or 1977.

However, during 1978 through 1980 this policy hegemony was successfully challenged by computer users and by wholly indigenous enterprises that wanted to enter the systems-engineering industry. One key problem for the Commission and Department was that, since ECIL was receiving so much apparent protection, it was not developing very efficient computer systems. Also, while the policy units had the authority to delay imports as a way of protecting ECIL and could delay the entry of new wholly indigenous enterprises into the industry, they did not have absolute power over Indian computing.

For example, they could not compel a user to choose ECIL, and they could not forbid the importation of a foreign system if the applicant for the import could show that such a system was necessary to perform computing functions beyond the capabilities of ECIL products. Given the extreme costliness of ECIL systems and their very long delivery delays (18 to 24 months), many

Indian users were willing to go through the tedious and time-consuming procedures needed to show the policy units that an import was required. Moreover, many users learned to formulate their requests for imported systems such that ECIL products did not seem to be realistic alternatives.[33] The gap in prices between ECIL and international products was so great that a foreign system much larger than actually needed was still less expensive than an ECIL product (and of vastly superior performance), and therefore a user rationally could skew the proposal toward a larger system. Also, several Indian enterprises took advantage of the government's interest in generating foreign exchange earnings in such a way that a "software export scheme" announced in 1976 was turned into a mechanism to bypass restrictions on computer imports.[34] These efforts to avoid ECIL and to obtain imported computers were made by public and private enterprises alike. In addition, users such as Air India and the Ministry of Steel, and representatives of users such as the Ministries of Commerce and Industrial Development, all complained directly to the Commission and Department that they should have easier access to foreign systems.[35]

While these problems concerning imports were becoming acute in 1977 and 1978, the computer policy units were also challenged on the issue of the entry of new, wholly indigenous firms into the systems engineering industry. This challenge was mounted directly by the enterprises seeking entry and, to a lesser extent, their governmental sponsor, the Ministry of Industrial Development. On the one hand, the firms lobbied directly with policy officials from the Department and Commission. Perhaps more important, the firms waged a campaign against the two policy units through the use of articles published in newspapers sympathetic to the enterprises, and especially the *Economic Times* and *Financial Express*.[36] Charges made in a number of articles appearing in early 1978 included the delay of the growth of the indigenous computer industry, the squandering of foreign exchange resources since users did everything possible to avoid ECIL, and, perhaps most seriously, possible "collusion between a section of powers-that-be [i.e., the Commission and Department] and powerful foreign interests to keep at bay the emergence of a vibrant nationally based minicomputer industry."[37]

From early 1978, critical questions began to be put to Prime Minister Desai in Parliament about the delays of the policy units in licensing new computer enterprises. In July, the Chairman of the National Committee on Science and Technology called for a government investigation of the Commission and Department, and Desai was called upon to respond to this recommendation. And Desai was asked why the Electronics Commission Chairman and Department Secretary, M.G.K. Menon, was holding two additional high-level positions in government; Desai responded that Menon had given up his electronics position ten days earlier.[38] Menon, former director of the Atomic Energy Commission's Tata Institute, thus lost responsibility for Indian electronics.

The new head of the Commission and Department, B. Nag, had no ties to the atomic energy network. Nag moved quickly to permit the entry of new, wholly indigenous firms into the computer industry. Four of these new entrants (HCL, ORG, DCM, and IDM/NELCO) actually made deliveries in 1978 and 1979, and became extremely successful competitors with ECIL. The new firms were very capable of locating international supplies of components and peripherals: for example, DCM Dataproducts incorporated in its systems Kennedy magnetic tape and hard-disk drives, Shugart floppy-disk drives, and printers manufactured by Centronics; HCL's systems incorporated microprocessors from Intel and peripherals manufactured by Centronics and Shugart.[39]

As the Indian computer industry was undergoing this transformation, the policy framework for the electronics industry was also changed. An investigation of the Commission and Department began in December 1978, and Prime Minister Desai appointed a strong critic of the two units as chairman of the investigating committee: Secretary in the Ministry of Steel, A. Sondhi.[40] The Sondhi Committee suggested in its final report that the Commission be abolished. Prime Minister Desai rejected this, but pressures on the Commission and Department were such that Electronics Commissioner Nag thought it prudent to accept another Sondhi Committee recommendation: the establishment (in November 1979) of an interdepartmental committee to oversee and direct India's future computer policies, thus undercutting the authority of the Commission and Department in this area.[41] At the end of the decade, India's wholly indigenous small systems firms were thriving, and advanced technology systems were entering the country from abroad. This progress was, however, made possible by removing or side-stepping those individuals who were responsible for India's first steps during the early to mid 1970s toward greater national self-direction in computing.

Conclusion

Over time, India significantly increased its ability to manage and to benefit from its relations with members of the international computer industry. In terms of corporate organization, market structure, and transfers of technology, India at first was unsuccessful in its attempts to mold the local activities of multinational computer firms in accordance with the data-processing objectives established by government. Over time, government and wholly indigenous enterprises were able to take advantage of developments in international computing in such a way as to reconstruct relations with the international industry on terms more favorable to India. As a result, the country's data-processing industry was growing at the end of the 1970s in a much more self-directed fashion than it had been in the late 1960s.

These "hard case" findings lend strong support to the bargaining school's basic hypothesis that developing countries enhance their power over multinationals over time. From the perspective of the Marxist-dependencia school, on the other hand, India should have failed in its negotiations with the international computer industry; but this "easy case" did not evolve as expected. The case therefore offers strong grounds to question the validity of Marxist-dependencia arguments.

While the Indian case shows the general analytical superiority of the bargaining school over the Marxist-dependencia school, it also suggests a modest reformulation of elements of the school's analysis. According to the bargaining school, international technological change is likely to inhibit or constrain the increase in developing countries' bargaining power as they negotiate with high technology multinationals. The Indian case suggests instead that international innovations in computer technology combined with changes in the industry's international structure in such a way as to expand the country's computer opportunities and therefore its potential bargaining power. Second, and equally significant, the bargaining school suggests that developing countries are often unable to mobilize domestic resources to bargain effectively with high technology multinationals. However, the case of India and computers makes clear that at least the more powerful developing countries do possess a formidable ability to organize themselves in order to exploit international industrial and technological changes in such a way as to improve their relations with multinational enterprises. Other technology-intensive industries should be examined to determine if they are tending to display data processing's key characteristics of lower input-prices and increasing international competition. If other high-technology industries are in fact evolving along these dimensions in a manner similar to that in data processing, then the bargaining school's basic thesis will capture events with increasing ease and frequency in what has been to date its most difficult cases.

Our focus on India has permitted an examination of one important developing country. Of course, most other developing countries have not attained the level of national power reached by India, and therefore India's experiences with computer multinationals may not be indicative of the levels of success to which most developing countries can aspire as they negotiate with high technology enterprises. On the other hand, India's industrial structure is similar to Brazil's and Mexico's. In terms of scientific manpower productively employed Brazil is close to India, and Brazil and Mexico match or exceed India in terms of financial resources available per science and technology worker. Hence, India's bargaining success with multinationals might also be achieved by Brazil and Mexico at present. In addition, Colombia and Venezuela may soon catch up to India in terms of potential bargaining power, and Nigeria and Indonesia may do so over the longer term. India's successes with multinationals suggest a realistic standard to which these countries might aspire.[42]

India, Brazil, and Mexico at present, together with Colombia, Indonesia, Nigeria, and Venezuela over the longer term, constitute most of what might be termed the emerging assertive upper tier of the developing world. These important and increasingly advanced countries have contacts with a wide variety of multinational enterprises, in contrast to upper-tier countries such as Saudi Arabia, which thus far have interacted mostly with oil multinationals. At the same time, these assertive upper-tier countries are extremely sensitive about possible threats by multinationals to their national autonomy, and they seek to control and to compel an improvement in the terms of their relations with foreign enterprises through the employment of stringent legal and administrative regimes on foreign capital. (This "assertive" strategy on foreign firms contrasts with that followed by newly industrializing developing countries such as Hong Kong, Taiwan, and South Korea, which seek foreign-enterprise-assisted growth through relatively accommodating regimes.)

Assertive upper-tier developing countries have much to gain through study of the Indian experience with computers and the basic argument of the bargaining school. These countries cannot expect to enjoy both *complete* national autonomy and extensive, productive economic ties with advanced capitalist societies. At the same time, however, the Indian experience suggests that assertive developing countries do not face a stark choice between autonomy and dependency. Assertive developing countries may become "dependent" as a result of contacts with advanced capitalist societies for the acquisition of particular goods, services, technology or flows of capital. However, these countries can also expect to learn, over time, how to manage (and to increase their benefits resulting from) these "dependent" relationships. Hence, these countries do not need to equate being "dependent" on specific ties with advanced capitalist societies with a general situation of "dependency" on advanced capitalism. Assertive upper-tier developing countries need not feel compelled to follow strategies of "delinkage" from international capitalism.[43] Instead, they can be increasingly confident of their ability to achieve national self-direction and economic development within the context of active participation in the international economy.

Notes

1. Important statements by Raymond Vernon include "Foreign-Owned Enterprises in the Developing Countries," *Public Policy* 15 (Boston: Graduate School of Business Administration, Harvard University, 1966), pp. 361–80; "Long-Run Trends in Concession Agreements," *Proceedings of the American Society of International Law,* April 1967, pp. 85–89; "The Power of Multinational Enterprises in Developing Countries," in Carl Madden, ed., *The Case for the Multinational Corporation* (New York: Praeger, 1975), pp. 151–83; *Sovereignty at Bay: The Multinational Spread of U.S. Enterprises* (New York: Basic Books, 1971), pp. 46–59, 105–6,

256–57; *Storm Over the Multinationals: The Real Issues* (Cambridge: Harvard University Press, 1977), pp. 139–74, 194–99. Important discussions by Theodore Moran include *Multinational Corporations and the Politics of Dependence: Copper in Chile* (Princeton: Princeton University Press, 1974); and "Multinational Corporations and Dependency: A Dialogue for Dependentistas and Non-Dependentistas," in James A. Caporaso, ed., *Dependence and Dependency in the Global System,* special issue of *International Organization* 32 (Winter 1978), pp. 170–200. Also see Charles Kindleberger, *American Business Abroad: Six Lectures on Direct Investment* (New Haven: Yale University Press, 1969), pp. 147–59; Raymond F. Mikesell, "Conflict in Foreign Investor–Host Country Relations: A Preliminary Analysis," in Mikesell, ed., *Foreign Investments in the Petroleum and Mining Industries* (Baltimore: Johns Hopkins Press [for Resources for the Future, Inc.], 1971), pp. 29–55; C. Fred Bergsten, "Coming Investment Wars?", *Foreign Affairs* 53 (October 1974), pp. 135–52; and Bergsten, Thomas Horst, and Moran, *American Multinationals and American Interests* (Washington, D.C.: Brookings, 1978), pp. 369–81.

2. Important Marxist-dependencia analyses of the multinational corporation include Fernando Henrique Cardoso, "Associated-Dependent Development: Theoretical and Practical Implications," in Alfred Stepan, ed., *Authoritarian Brazil: Origins, Policies, and Future* (New Haven: Yale University Press, 1973), pp. 142–76; Cardoso and Enzo Faletto, *Dependency and Development in Latin America,* 2d ed. (Berkeley: University of California Press, 1979), pp. 159–64; Arghiri Emmanuel, "The Multinational Corporations and the Inequality of Development," *International Social Science Journal* 28 (1976), pp. 760–64; Peter Evans, *Dependent Development: The Alliance of Multinational, State, and Local Capital in Brazil* (Princeton: Princeton University Press, 1979); and Stephen Hymer, "The Multinational Corporation and the Law of Uneven Development," in J. Bhagwati, ed., *Economics and World Order: From the 1970s to the 1990s* (New York: Free Press, 1972), pp. 113–40. Finally, see Theotonio Dos Santos, "The Structure of Dependency," and Celso Furtado, "The Concept of External Dependence in the Stages of Underdevelopment," both in Charles K. Wilbur, ed., *The Political Economy of Development and Underdevelopment* (New York: Random House, 1973).

3. See Harry Eckstein, "Case Study and Theory in Political Science," in Fred I. Greenstein and Nelson W. Polsby, eds., *Strategies of Inquiry,* vol. 7 of the *Handbook of Political Science,* edited by Greenstein and Polsby (Reading, Mass.: Addison-Wesley, 1975), pp. 79–137. India's experience with computers does not constitute an Ecksteinian "critical case" for either the bargaining or the Marxist-dependencia school. Such a case would involve the most powerful multinational enterprises (which could be those firms in the computer industry, according to both schools) and the weakest developing country (which is certainly not India). Yet within the developing world "strong" multinationals (i.e., those in high technology manufacturing industries) have extensive operations only in relatively advanced developing countries. Hence, for the foreseeable future most instances of significant bargaining between "strong" multinationals and developing countries are likely to involve the more advanced countries.

4. According to one important standard for comparing technological intensiveness of manufacturing industries—annual research and development expenditures as a percentage of total yearly revenue—data processing is technologically the most

dynamic industry at present. For a discussion of the measure, see Raymond Vernon, William Gruber, and Dileep Mehta, "The R&D Factor of International Trade and in International Investment of the United States," in Louis T. Wells Jr., ed., *The Product Life-Cycle and International Trade* (Boston: Graduate School of Business Administration, Harvard University, 1972), pp. 114–15. For a comparison of 31 manufacturing industries, see the annual survey of research and development in American industry, *Business Week,* 27 June 1977, pp. 62–84; 3 July 1978, pp. 48–77; and 2 July 1979, pp. 52–72. Also, see U.S., National Science Foundation, *Research and Development in Industry: Technical Notes and Statistical Tables* (Washington: NSF, 1978), p. 34.

5. For these arguments see Vernon, *Sovereignty at Bay,* pp. 105–6, 256–57; "Power of Multinational Enterprises," pp. 167–68; *Storm,* pp. 71–72. Also see Bergsten, "Coming Investment Wars," p. 139; and Bergsten, Horst, and Moran, *American Multinationals,* pp. 377–80.

6. Evans, *Dependent Development,* pp. 199–212, gives the fullest account from the Marxist-dependencia viewpoint of the inhibiting effects of technology on host country bargaining power. Cardoso and Faletto, *Dependency and Development,* pp. 161–62, see the technology problem as existing not only between a specific enterprise and the government but also between the advanced capitalist society from which the firm originates and the developing country represented by the government.

7. On these expectations, see India (Republic), Electronics Committee of India, *Electronics in India* (New Delhi, 1966); India (Republic), Lok Sabha, *Parliamentary Debates,* 3rd Series (3 March 1966), pp. 3885–3886; and India (Republic), Indian Investment Centre, *India Invites Foreign Capital* (New Delhi: Caxton Press, 1965).

8. Jack Baranson, "Technology Transfer Through the International Firm," *American Economic Review* 670 (May 1970), p. 439; and IBM Interview Materials (February 1979). Interviewees were granted anonymity by the author, but interviewees understood that notes of conversations were available to the author's dissertation committee at Cornell University. Interviews were conducted in North Tarrytown, New York (June and September 1978); London (July–August 1978, and January 1979); Paris (July 1978 and January 1979); Detroit (October 1978); New Delhi (January-February 1979 and January 1981); and Bombay (February 1979). For the results of the thesis research, see Joseph Morris Grieco, "Between Dependence and Autonomy: India's Experiences with the International Computer Industry," (Ph.D. diss., Cornell University, 1982).

9. International Computers and Tabulators Manufacturing Company, *Prospectus* (Bombay, 24 January 1964), pp. 1, 6; and *First Annual Report and Accounts* (Bombay, 8 May 1964), p. 6.

10. ICL/London (July 1978) and ICL/India (February 1979) Interview Materials; Burroughs/Detroit (October 1978) and Tata-Burroughs/Bombay (February 1979) Interview Materials; and IBM Interview Materials (June–July 1978, February 1979).

11. ORG, DCM, IDM, and HCL Interview Materials (January 1981); and IBM Interview Materials (June–July 1978, September 1978, February 1979).

12. Ibid., and Tata-Burroughs Interview Materials (February 1979) and "Growth of Indigenous Effort," *Commerce* (Bombay), 31 May 1980, p. 925; and International Computers India Manufactures, *Annual Report and Accounts, 1979–1980* (Bombay, December 1980), pp. 17–32.

13. IBM Interview Materials (June–July 1978, and telephone interview, April 1980); and "ICL Asked to Make 100 Medium-Range Computers," *Economic Times* (Bombay), 19 November 1977, p. 6.

14. For a discussion of the invention and evolution of the transistor, see "The Solid State Era," chap. 5 of *Fifty Years of Achievement: A History,* special issue of *Electronics,* 17 April 1980, pp. 216–73. Also see A.A. Shepherd, "Semiconductor Device Developments in the 1960's," *Radio and Electronic Engineer* 42 (January–February 1973), pp. 11–12. Also see Charles Weiner, "How the Transistor Emerged," *IEEE Spectrum* 10 (January 1973), pp. 24–33; and Ernest Braun and Stuart MacDonald, *Revolution in Miniature: History and Impact of Semiconductor Electronics* (Cambridge: Cambridge University Press, 1978), pp. 11–66, 83–86. On the integrated circuit see Braun and MacDonald, pp. 101–120, and M. Wolff, "The Genesis of the Integrated Circuit," *IEEE Spectrum* 13 (August 1976):44–53. On process improvements for integrated circuits see the articles by Robert N. Noyce, William C. Holton, and William G. Oldham in the special issue on microelectronics, *Scientific American* 237 (September 1977).

15. Digital Equipment Corporation, *Annual Report 1975* (Maynard, Mass., 1975), p. 11.

16. On the microcomputer see Dwight H. Savin, *Microprocessors and Microcomputer Systems* (Lexington, Mass.: Lexington Books, 1977); Gene Bylinsky, "Here Comes the Second Computer Revolution," *Fortune,* November 1975, pp. 134–39; Kenneth Rose, "The Microcomputer Revolution," *Modern Materials Handling* 34 (August 1979), pp. 178–85; and Charles J. Sippl, *Microcomputer Handbook* (New York: Petrocelli/Charter, 1977).

17. See Bruce Minaldi, "A Guide to Data Storage for Micros and Minis," *Instrument and Control Systems* 50 (August 1977), pp. 41–43; also see Len Yencharis, "Micro/Mini Storage Peripherals Driven by Disk, Tape Advances," *Electronic Design,* 25 October 1979, p. 62, and J. Egil Juliessen, "Where Bubble Memories Will Find a Niche," *Mini-Micro Systems* 12 (July 1979), p. 60.

18. These data were gathered from the annual reports, 10-K Forms, and prospectuses of 21 U.S. computer manufacturing enterprises, including the top 10 firms in the industry.

19. International Computers Ltd., *Annual Report and Accounts 1977* (London, December 1977), p. 11; and Marilyn Rurak, *The American Computer Industry in Its Competitive Environment* (Washington: U.S. Department of Commerce, 1976).

20. Figures are taken from the annual reports and 10-K Forms of the respective firms. On the integrated circuit industry, see U.S. Congress, Senate, Committee on Commerce, Science, and Transportation, *Industrial Technology* (Washington, D.C.), 30 October 1978, and I.M. Mackintosh, "Integrated Circuits: The Coming Battle," *Long Range Planning* 12 (June 1979):28–37.

21. See R. Narasimhan, "Meaningful Goals in Computer Development, Production, and Use," in India (Republic), Electronics Committee of India, *Electronics* (Bombay: Electronics Commission, 1971), pp. 372–74.

22. On the entitlement program see India (Republic), Lok Sabha, Public Accounts Committee, *Two-Hundred and Twenty-First Report: Computerization in Government Departments* (New Delhi: Lok Sabha Secretariat, April 1976), pp. 196–98.

23. IBM Interview Materials (July 1978).

24. See India (Republic), Technical Panel on Minicomputers, "Report of the Panel on Minicomputers," *Electronics: Information and Planning* (Bombay) 1 (February 1974), pp. 478–517; see also the various annual reports of the Department of Electronics.

25. On the "New Strategy" to allow wholly indigenous entrants into the microcomputer sector, see statement of Prime Minister Moraji Desai in India (Republic), Lok Sabha, *Lok Sabha Debates,* 6th Series, 11 (15 March 1978), pp. 186–90, and 24 (28 March 1979), pp. 233–36. Also see "Licensing and Development of Computer Industry—Government Policy," *Electronics for You* (New Delhi) 12 (March 1980), p. 12; and Department of Electronics, Annual Report, 1977–1978 (New Delhi, 1978), p. 102.

26. For a discussion of this policy fragmentation, see the Public Accounts Committee, *221st Report: Computerization.*

27. For several references to the struggle see Electronics Committee of India, *Electronics.*

28. In 1971, the individual selected to head both the Commission and the Department was M.G.K. Menon, who was until then director of the Tata Institute for Fundamental Research, which is under the Atomic Energy Commission. His key deputy in the Department was A. Parthasarathi, who had been a principal officer in the AEC. An important analyst for the AEC, N. Seshagiri, was chosen to head the Electronics Commission's intelligence gathering and analysis unit.

29. On funding for ECIL, see Om Vikas, "Indigenous Development of Computer Systems, Peripherals, and Computer Communications Facilities," *Electronics: Information and Planning* 5 (August 1978):773–842; and annual reports of the Department of Electronics. It should be noted that the 1975 grant of authority over computer imports to the Department formalized practices the Department had begun in 1971 and 1972.

30. ECIL Interview Materials (January 1981).

31. India (Republic), Department of Electronics, *Annual Report, 1971–1972* (New Delhi, 1972), pp. 23–24.

32. Interview, former official in Department and Commission (January 1981).

33. Interview, Manager, Data Processing Department, India Public Sector Enterprise (January 1981).

34. See "New Import Policy for Software Exports," *Times of India* (New Delhi), 3 January 1981, and India (Republic), Lok Sabha, *Lok Sabha Debates,* 7th Series, 2 (8 March 1980), p. 191.

35. In an interview with the author (January 1981), an official in the electronics policy area indicated that the newspaper articles, together with parliamentary questions, letters, telephone calls, and meetings, were the main means of attack on the Commission and Department in 1977–1978.

36. Ibid.

37. See "Computer Output Checked," *Financial Express* (Bombay), 20 February 1978; "Policy on Small Computers Soon," *Economic Times,* 12 January 1978; "All Free to Make Minicomputers," *Economic Times,* 18 February 1978; "Minicomputer Policy Ready," *Economic Times,* 6 March 1978; "Decision Soon on Minicomputers,"

Economic Times, 14 August 1978. The charge of "collusion" was made in the 12 January *Economic Times* article.

38. India (Republic), Lok Sabha, *Lok Sabha Debates,* 6th Series, 11 (15 March 1978), p. 190; 17 (2 August 1978), p. 98; and 20 (13 December 1978), pp. 63–64.

39. DCM and HCL Interview Materials (January 1981).

40. "Electronics Policy to be Reviewed," *Economic Times,* 11 December 1978.

41. "Licensing, Growth Policy Drawn Up," *Economic Times,* 14 November 1979. Also, see "Development of Computers," *Commerce,* 1 December 1979, pp. 1085–86.

42. For comparisons of general economic statistics, see International Bank for Reconstruction and Development, *World Development Report 1979* (Washington: IBRD, 1979), pp. 126–27, 136–37; J.W. Wilke, *Statistical Abstract of Latin America* vol. 20 (Los Angeles: UCLA, 1980), pp. 267, 282; Central Intelligence Agency, *National Basic Intelligence Factbook* (Washington, D.C.: GPO, January 1979 and January 1980); and IBRD, *World Tables 1976* (Washington: IBRD, 1976), pp. 61, 79, 121, 169, 179, 243. For comparisons of national scientific capabilities, see United Nations Educational Scientific and Cultural Organisation, *Statistical Yearbook* (Paris: UNESCO, 1979), pp. 755–61.

43. For a "critical but sympathetic" discussion of the delinkage strategy, see Carlos F. Diaz-Alejandro, "Delinking North and South: Unshackled or Unhinged," in Albert Fishlow et al., *Rich and Poor Nations in the World Economy* (New York: McGraw-Hill for the Council on Foreign Relations, 1980s Project, 1977). For a recent analysis of the strategy and its applications to Tanzanian trade policy, see Thomas J. Biersteker, "Self-Reliance in Theory and Practice in Tanzanian Trade Relations," *International Organization* 34 (Spring 1980):229–64. As Biersteker notes, most dependency writers, and other critics of international capitalism such as Johan Galtung, Immanuel Wallerstein, and Arghiri Emmanuel, advise developing countries that they should delink from and, perhaps later, "restructure" their relations with advanced capitalist societies.

4

The Renegotiation of Dependency and the Limits of State Autonomy in Mexico (1975–1982)

Gary Gereffi

Foreign investors continue to possess important sources of strength in maintaining their position in relation to the demands of economic nationalists in the Third World. High among these sources of strength may be control over technology and over the distribution and marketing of the final product. The pharmaceutical industry in Mexico provides a valuable contrast to the computer industry in India.

Gary Gereffi argues that the pharmaceutical industry in Mexico is an example of the limits of reformist nationalism, or a strategy of expanding state autonomy and bargaining power short of nationalization while remaining within a capitalist development. Until Third World countries can duplicate many of the technological and managerial capabilities of the multinationals, Gereffi concludes, their ability to develop an industry in an autonomous fashion will be limited. In addition, multinational corporations can build domestic political linkages to try to counter nationalistic pressures. In the Mexican case, the multinationals portrayed their conflict with the state in a way that enabled them to arouse the Mexican private sector against a perceived common threat and drew the latter to their side.

Chapter 1 places this case study of the pharmaceutical companies' political strategy in Mexico within a broader examination of the ability of multinationals to build political alliances in the Third World countries where they have invested.

I n January 1975 Productos Químicos Vegetales Mexicanos S.A. de C.V. (Proquivemex) was created by the Mexican state to control all transactions related to the gathering, processing, and sale of barbasco.[1] Proquivemex bought "green" barbasco from the peasants, put it through a drying process (in which it loses 80 percent of its volume by weight), and then resold the barbasco to the six TNCs in the industry at a price fixed by Proquivemex. Thus, the TNCs no longer had any direct contact with the peasants; all business was mediated by the state-owned firm. Proquivemex was created largely in response to barbasco's declining share in the world production of steroid hormones and to internal pressure stemming from the exploitation of the peasants in the industry. The TNCs were labeled the cause of both problems and were also chosen as the main mechanisms for financing solutions.

The efforts by the state to try to establish new priorities in Mexico's steroid hormone industry via Proquivemex will be analyzed as a case of "reformist nationalism" in which the Echeverría government was not trying to make a total break with the dominant powers in the capitalist system, nor was it abandoning a capitalist path to internal development. Rather, it was proposing "a redefinition of dependency that, at the same time it [was] accelerating the development process, [was] also expanding the margin of autonomy and the bargaining power of the internal power centers" (Labastida, 1975:33).

In carrying out this analysis I will first discuss the problem of Mexico's barbasco in both a world industry and national context. Second, I will outline the state's strategy for using barbasco as a lever to increase its autonomy vis-à-vis the TNCs in order to get them to contribute more to national goals of internal growth and welfare. Finally, I will show how the TNCs defended their interests by broadening their base of private sector support in Mexico, thus converting Proquivemex's forceful program into mild reforms.

Barbasco

The fundamental problem faced by Mexican barbasco in the world market is that it was losing ground rapidly to alternative source materials for steroid hormones. Whereas in the late 1950s diosgenin from Mexico's barbasco accounted for 80 to 90 percent of the world production of steroids, by the early 1970s this percentage had dropped to 40 to 45 percent. To make matters worse, the rate of Mexico's decline as a supplier of steroid source materials appeared to be accelerating. From 1963 to 1968 the world demand for steroid raw materials nearly doubled, while Mexico only upped its diosgenin output by 33 percent; from 1968 to 1973 world demand rose by another 50 percent, by the production of Mexican diosgenin increased by only 10 percent—from 500 metric tons to 550 (see table 4–1).

There are both external and internal reasons for the declining share of Mexican barbasco in world steroid production. Clearly there was an effort on the part of the pharmaceutical buyers of steroid intermediate materials to lessen their dependence on Mexico (a near-monopoly supplier in the 1950s) by developing alternate source materials. In particular there has been a sharp

Table 4–1
World Steroid Raw Material Sources

Country	Material	Production[a]		
		1963	*1968*	*1973*
Mexico	Diosgenin	375	500	550
	Smilagenin	—	10	—
United States	Stigmasterol	60	150	280
	Total synthesis	—	—	30
Guatemala	Diosgenin	10	30	—
Puerto Rico	Diosgenin	—	20	—
France	Bile acids	20	50	50
	Total synthesis	—	50	50
Germany and Netherlands	Cholesterol and bile acids	5	10	—
Germany	Total synthesis	—	—	70
Africa	Hecogenin	20	40	40
India	Diosgenin	10	30	—
China	Diosgenin	—	80	250
Canada	Conjugated estrogens	—	—	100
Total		500	970	1,420
Mexico's production as a percentage of total world production		75%	53%	39%

Sources: Applezweig, 1969:64; Bremer et al., 1976:12.
[a]Production figures expressed as tons of diosgenin.

increase in the percentage of politically "safe" raw materials coming from the home countries of the TNCs—the United States, Germany, and France. Nevertheless, in and of itself the external challenge to barbasco is not decisive in explaining Mexico's decline as a raw material supplier in the industry. With the exception of stigmasterol, used by Upjohn in the United States, no other raw material approaches diosgenin's quantitative importance as a steroid source material.[2] One reason is that diosgenin is still more versatile than most of its rivals. Another is that the TNCs with producing subsidiaries in Mexico have a vested interest in using diosgenin rather than its substitutes.

There is an internal reason that helps explain why the Mexican production of steroids has not kept pace with world demand: barbasco appears to be growing scarce. The cause is that more and more of the land where wild barbasco grows is being cleared for agriculture and livestock use. Of the 7.6 million hectares in Mexico that are suitable for barbasco growth, 80 percent has already been converted to other uses, leaving only 1.5 million hectares from which barbasco can still be gathered.[3] Complicating this problem is the fact that the average yield of diosgenin from barbasco has dropped (from 6 percent to 4 percent).[4]

Mexico was not facing an acute shortage of barbasco in the mid-1970s. Yet these two trends—external substitutes for barbasco and its potential internal scarcity—created a fear that Mexico's steroid hormone industry could become internationally marginalized and that as a result the six TNCs almost surely would decide to leave the country for better prospects elsewhere.[5] Mexico would thus suddenly lose a major source of foreign exchange, and twenty-five thousand peasants would lose an important source of income.[6] Politically, therefore, the steroid hormone industry suddenly became much more strategic to the Mexican state during the 1970s. In addition, Mexico's dependence on the foreign manufacturers of finished steroid products remained as strong as ever since the country had to continue importing costly quantities of steroid drugs and oral contraceptives. After thirty years of producing for the rest of the world, a national industry that could supply the Mexican population still did not exist.[7]

The Strategy of the Mexican State

Confronted with these circumstances, the state adopted a strategy in which it could use its sovereignty over barbasco to force a negotiation with the TNCs regarding new contributions they would be expected to make to promote greater national development of the steroid hormone industry. The key to this strategy lay in the state's ability to impose upon the TNCs *new conditions of access to barbasco*. There were three conditions, two formal and one informal, that were eventually proposed by the state.

The two formal conditions were: 1) that the TNCs pay a much higher price for the processed barbasco (which they would now be receiving from Proquivemex) than they had in the past, and 2) that the TNCs devote a certain percentage of their installed capacity to produce finished steroid hormones for Proquivemex (to be used either as exports or for sale to the internal market). Although the exact amounts with respect to price and the installed capacity requirement later became negotiable, it was made clear that if an agreement satisfactory to the state was not reached on both counts the TNCs would not receive any barbasco. A third condition emerged out of the direct negotiations between the state and the TNCs. Although not made a formal requirement of access, it did appear that the Echeverría government strongly desired the Mexicanization of the six TNC subsidiaries in the industry, all of which were 100 percent foreign owned.[8] The state plan was to be implemented by Proquivemex since the state-owned firm controlled all the buying (from the peasants) and the selling (to the TNCs) of barbasco.

In April 1975 Proquivemex began selling its dry (i.e., processed) bar-basco to the TNCs at a price of P $20 (20 Mexican pesos) per kilogram;[9] before Proquivemex, the same material had cost the foreign firms P $10 to $12 per kilogram. Then at its January 1976 board of directors meeting the state company made two major changes: it raised the price of dry barbasco from P $20 to P $70 a kilogram, and it required that the six TNC subsidiaries turn over 20 percent of their installed capacity to "toll manufacture" the products selected by Proquivemex.[10]

In order to understand the purpose of these demands, it is necessary to take a closer look at the goals and assumptions of the state strategy, which were different in kind, not just degree, from those of the TNCs. Proquivemex saw its goals as social and national in nature; the objectives of the TNCs, on the other hand, were eminently private and global.[11] This is the fundamental reason that the conflict between the two sides became so prolonged and bitter.

Proquivemex had two primary goals: to improve the welfare of the peasants, and to defend Mexico's rural natural resources. The peasant policy makes clear the social nature of the state firm's goals. One of the main factors leading to the creation of Proquivemex was social protest. It came especially from student groups in the barbasco-producing states who felt that the peasants were being exploited by the TNCs because they were paid too little for the barbasco they gathered.[12] Before the panic-buying characteristic of 1974 when TNC prices rose as high as P $2.00 (due at least in part to the transnationals' anticipation of Proquivemex), the top price paid the peasants was alleged to have been around P $0.60 per kilogram of collected root.

In reality, however, the TNC pricing policy was a reflection of the extremely low standard of living characteristic of rural Mexico in general. For example, in 1970 the price of P $0.60 per kilogram of collected barbasco was equal to, and in some cases even double, the average daily income of the peasants in all five of the barbasco-growing states.[13] In addition, setting a low price for barbasco was made even easier because gathering the plant was a complementary economic activity; the peasants' main source of income came from cultivating their traditional crops (such as corn, beans, rice, coffee, and fruit). In short, the TNCs took advantage of the fact that the peasants in Mexico have consistently paid more of the costs and received less of the benefits from Mexican development than has any other sector of the population (see Hansen, 1971). Proquivemex was much more concerned about this general problem than it was about giving the individual collectors of barbasco more money; in fact, in 1974 the state firm paid the gatherers approximately the same as the TNCs did.[14]

The real aim of Proquivemex was to improve the basic structure of the peasant economy in the barbasco-growing regions of Mexico. The general means used to achieve this end were: 1) to increase peasant resources at the level of the *ejido* (an area of land collectively owned by peasants in rural Mexico) in order to undercut the power of rural middlemen and *caciques* (local political bosses), and 2) to develop new rural industries using vegetable or plant resources other than barbasco. With respect to the *ejidos,* Proquivemex designed programs to give them more autonomy in three areas usually controlled by the *caciques*: transportation, the sale of basic foods, and credit. First, the state firm provided the *ejidos* with freight trucks that were used to transport both barbasco and the peasants' traditional crops (since the two harvest periods do not overlap). This allowed for reductions of up to 75 percent in the freight charges previously set by the *caciques.* These same trucks also served a second major function: they helped lower the price for basic foods. A program was established with Conasupo (the state firm controlling basic food supplies) whereby, rather than returning empty, the freight trucks would come back to the countryside filled with basic foods at official prices after delivering their load in Mexico City. The price the peasants were paying for corn, for example, was cut by nearly 60 percent by this program—from P $4.50 per kilogram (in rural stores, often owned by the *caciques*) to the official price of P $1.95 per kilogram. A similar program was set up with the state fertilizer company, Guanos y Fertilizantes de México (now known as Fertimex). Finally, the stable price set by Proquivemex for collected barbasco relieved the onerous dilemma that confronted the peasants when prices were much lower: since they were often short of cash, they either had to harvest their crops early or go to the *caciques* for short-term credit. With respect to new rural industries, Proquivemex's projects included the production of quinine from cichona tree bark and the production of citric concentrates used in the manufacture of Vitamin C products.

The national emphasis of Proquivemex's program can be seen in its ideas for defending natural resources. Whereas a foreign subsidiary in Latin America usually thinks of a natural resource as a raw material to be exported, Proquivemex adopted the increasingly common posture of resource-rich developing countries: natural resources are best protected by industrializing them in their country of origin. This point of view was repeatedly expounded by Proquivemex's general director: "For us to remain at the level of exploiting raw materials would be to accept technological and economic dependency" (*Excelsior,* Oct. 11, 1975).

> What we want is to compete on equal terms with [the TNCs], within the regime of the mixed economy. We are the owners of barbasco; they, of the technology, and each must defend himself as he can. . . . We are looking for the vindication of a natural resource, and in that respect we will not take one step backward. We are unable to accept being mere providers of raw material. We want to participate in research and industrialization. (*Excelsior,* Aug. 19, 1976).

In an effort to develop a Mexican owned and operated productive capacity for basic steroid hormones, Proquivemex announced early in 1976 its plans to build three diosgenin manufacturing plants. It also decided to formulate basic pharmaceutical products and its own birth control pill (Mestril). And in order to assure the future supply of barbasco, it began to rationalize the collection of the natural resource.[15]

The big catch in Proquivemex's whole plan was that the TNCs had to finance it. The state hoped that the TNCs were still dependent enough on Mexico as a source of supply to make them vulnerable, at least in the short run, to increased demands. It also hoped that because the subsidiaries in Mexico were vertically integrated to parent companies that produced final steroid hormone products, the raw material price in Mexico could be raised above what the international market would bear for an "independent" intermediate goods manufacturer since the raw material costs could be paid out of accumulated profits further along the integrated production line. What the state plan did not anticipate was the possibility that the TNCs would find local political allies to help them build a strong defense.

The Transnational Corporations' Defense

In January 1976 Proquivemex raised its price for dry barbasco from P $20 to P $70 per kilogram. The state firm insisted that the price was not arbitrary. Rather, it tried to capture the greatest quantity of resources possible from the raw material with the condition that the price of dry barbasco to the TNCs, plus the costs of transforming it, plus reasonable profit margins (which were left undefined) would not surpass the price of the products obtained from barbasco.[16] The TNCs vehemently claimed that at a price of P $70 per kilogram of raw material Mexican steroid hormone exports could not remain internationally competitive and that in fact Mexico's share of the world market had been declining at the pre-Proquivemex costs of P $12 per kilogram or less due to the strong competition from alternative source materials.[17]

Faced with the new P $70 price, the front-line defense of the TNCs was not to buy any barbasco from Proquivemex. This strategy was made viable because most of the TNCs had built up an inventory of barbasco sufficient to carry them through 1976. The possibility that the TNCs could refuse to buy from Proquivemex for one year represented a series of dangers to the state firm's plan. First of all, the end of 1976 corresponded with the end of a sexennial administration in Mexico; if the TNCs could hold out until Echeverría left office there was a chance the incoming president would not allow Proquivemex to play such an active role in the industry. Second, Mexico's steroid exports would drop drastically, thus creating economic pressures to arrive at a settlement. Third, with Proquivemex's warehouses already full, it would not be able to continue buying from the peasants at a normal rate, thus aggravating rather than improving their situation in the countryside.

Proquivemex therefore decided to rely on strong mass support from the peasants to try to break the stalemate with the TNCs. This time, however, the demands were not for payment of the higher barbasco price; they were for nationalization. Spurred on by reports that the TNCs were threatening Proquivemex with a boycott as a result of the new price increase,[18] the state firm helped organize a mass assembly of peasants in the state of Veracruz calling for President Echeverría to nationalize the steroid hormone industry.[19] In August another mass meeting of one thousand *ejidal* leaders representing more than one hundred thousand peasants was held, this time in Mexico City.[20] Nationalization was again called for since the TNCs (with one exception[21]) had still not bought a gram of barbasco from Proquivemex in 1976.

Echeverría did not respond to either request for nationalization. It is quite likely that the outbursts by both sides in the press as well as the ability of Proquivemex to mobilize the peasants took top government officials by surprise (especially the Veracruz meeting in March). On both occasions, however, the results were the same: the idea of nationalization were discarded, the conflict was quickly pushed up between the six TNCs and the government. Significantly, Proquivemex was not invited to participate in these negotiations. The probable reason is that the state firm had overstepped its boundaries for autonomous action as determined by top officials in the state bureaucracy. After the March protest the vehicle for these negotiations was a joint government/private sector study commission; three government members (one each from the ministries of National Patrimony, Industry and Commerce, and the Presidency) and three industry members represented each side. Between March and August this commission only met twice, however, perhaps hoping that the interest shown by the government and the at least implicit reprimand given Proquivemex would improve relations between the two sides. Such was not the case.

Whereas the March meeting of peasants against the TNCs presented a generalized demand for nationalization, in August Proquivemex's directors supported this demand with two specific offenses charged against the foreign firms. The first was that they owed the peasants P $470 million for neglecting to pay "*derechos de monte*" to the *ejidos* over the past twenty-five years.[22] The second charge was that the TNCs had defrauded the federal treasury in Mexico at a rate of P $1 billion per year. The charge of tax fraud refers to the TNC practice of transfer pricing and will be commented on in some detail.

When transfer pricing is used to try to reduce a TNC's global tax burden, exports to an affiliated company are often undervalued, whereas imports from an affiliate have a higher than normal price. The objective is to transfer funds out of a given country without paying taxes on them. According to Proquivemex's director, the real value of the TNCs' steroid hormone exports from Mexico should have been P $1.4 billion annually (based on world market prices for their products) instead of the P $400 million they were charging. This represented an annual loss to Mexico of P $1 billion of taxable income. At current tax rates this meant the Mexican government was losing P $420 million (42 percent corporate earnings tax) and the workers in the industry were losing P $80 million that should have been distributed to them as shared profits (*El sol de México*, Aug. 17, 1976).

The mechanism that accounts for such a big difference can be seen in the following examples in which the export price for a given product is compared with the price at which the same product was imported into Mexico. (It makes no difference from the point of view of national taxable income whether the exporting and importing are done by the same firm or by two different ones.) In 1972 one of the TNCs in Mexico imported the hormone progesterone at a price of P $30,000 a kilogram, while the value given to progesterone as an export by a second TNC in the same year was P $1,365 a kilogram. The case of estradiol is particularly dramatic. Whereas it was exported by Syntex for slightly over P $11,000 a kilogram, astradiol was imported into Mexico by another company for P $1 million a kilogram, 88 times the export value given by Syntex.[23]

Actually, the overpricing of steroid hormone imports into Mexico was neither new nor was the information needed to demonstrate it hidden. Detailed product and country-specific data on steroid hormone imports have been published by Mexico's Ministry of Industry and Commerce since 1965. In each year significant overpricing of imports is evident. Table 4–2 summarizes this published information for five well-known steroid hormone products imported into Mexico in 1974. The rate of overpricing was not estimated on the basis of international reference prices for imported drugs, as Vaitsos (1974) and others have done, but instead takes the minimum price at which a specified product was imported into Mexico and deems any excess over this minimum price to be an overprice. Since low prices may sometimes result from large bulk purchases of drugs, the minimum or reference prices are based on small annual orders (five kilograms or less) whose volume is always below, and usually far below, the other import sources used in the comparison. If anything, then, this method understates the overpricing in the industry.

The findings from table 4–2 indicate that the overpricing of imports in the Mexican steroid hormone industry was widespread and economically very significant. The rate of overpricing is more than 1,000 percent in several cases, reaching a high of 5,650 percent for progesterone imported from the Netherlands. In relatively few instances is the rate of overpricing less than 300 percent. For all five of the products considered, the highest rate of overpricing is linked to one of the European home countries of Mexico's steroid hormone TNCs (the Netherlands, the Federal Republic of Germany, or Switzerland). Overpricing of imports, in other words, in all likelihood was one of the main mechanisms used to transfer undeclared profits from Mexican subsidiaries to TNC parent companies in Europe. Potentially large amounts of tax-

Table 4–2

Overpricing of Imports in the Mexican Steroid Hormone Industry, 1974

Product	Country of Origin	Kilograms	Pesos	Unit Price	Rate of Overpricing[a] (percentage)	Amount o Overpricin (pesos)
Progesterone	Federal Republic of Germany	2	1,032	516	c	
	France	35	67,745	1,936	375	49,68
	Spain	5	32,060	6,412	1,243	29,48
	Netherlands	37	1,078,620	29,152	5,650	1,059,52
Total		79	1,179,457	14,930	2,893	1,138,69
Prednisone	Italy	3	6,026	2,009	c	
	France	137	1,037,565	7,573	377	762,33
	Brazil	10	102,660	10,266	511	82,57
	Netherlands	20	350,365	17,518	872	310,18
Total		170	1,496,616	8,804	438	1,155,08
Prednisolone	United Kingdom	5	31,250	6,250	c	
	Panama	29	292,750	10,095	162	111,50
	France	21	246,150	11,721	188	114,90
	Federal Republic of Germany	11	171,725	15,611	250	102,97
	Italy	6	118,063	19,677	315	80,56
	Netherlands	23	620,223	26,966	431	476,47
Total		95	1,480,161	15,581	249	886,41
Estradiol	France	5	56,999	11,400	c	
	Federal Republic of Germany	10	309,466	30,947	271	195,46
Total		15	366,465	24,431	214	195,46
Hydrocortisone	Netherlands	5	35,919	7,184	c	
	Federal Republic of Germany	7	68,330	9,761	136	18,04
	Bermuda	9	601,020	66,780	930	563,36
	Switzerland	13	1,006,355	77,412	1,078	912,96
Total		34	1,711,624	50,342	701	1,467,36

Source: Mexico, Secretaria de Industria y Comercio, 1975, pp. 166–168.

[a]The rate of overpricing is based on a minimum price at which a selected steroid hormone product was import into Mexico in 1974. Any excess over this minimum price is considered to be an overprice. To reduce the poss bility of bias from low discount prices for bulk purchases, the selected minimum (or reference) price for ea product is derived from import totals whose volume is always lower than that of any of the other import sourc used in the comparison.

[b]The amount of overpricing is calculated by multiplying the minimum unit price by the number of kilograms receiv from each importing country and then subtracting this result from each country's actual import total in pesos.

[c]The unit price from this import source is the minimum, or reference, price.

able income were lost to Mexico in this way. The total amount of overpricing for the five products listed in table 4–2 is almost P $5 million. When you consider that there are sixty-five different import codes for steroid hormone products entering Mexico and that there is evidence of overpricing in almost every one the concerns about fraud expressed by Proquivemex certainly appear justified.

The *derechos de monte* and tax fraud charges led the TNCs to realize that their original defense of not buying barbasco was insufficient since they were exposing themselves to political attacks that could allow the mass pressure for nationalization to become overwhelming. Thus, the transnationals decided to try to obtain a broader base of support among the main private sector business groupings in Mexico. In order to do this the foreign firms had to successfully redefine the nature of their battle with Proquivemex from a foreign/national conflict between six TNCs and the Mexican nation over peasant welfare and natural resources to a generalized struggle between the private sector in Mexico (national and foreign) and an increasingly interventionist Mexican state. This is exactly what happened.

After the mass meetings and charges made by Proquivemex in August 1976, the president of Concamin (the mandatory confederation of all industrialists in Mexico) denounced the state firm on two grounds. First, he claimed its charges were without legal basis. Concamin's president affirmed that he was not trying to defend the TNCs per se but rather a principle of law. In a very able move he pointed out that either the accusations made by Proquivemex were false or Proquivemex was implicating the corresponding federal authorities for corruption since the TNCs had never before been informed by either the Secretary of Agrarian Reform (with respect to *derechos de monte*) or the Secretary of the Treasury (with respect to the alleged tax fraud) that they were committing any offenses. Concamin's second, and principal, complaint with Proquivemex was that its directors were trying to agitate the peasants and create conflict in the countryside, which would be to the detriment of the private sector as a whole (*El sol de México,* Aug. 18, 1976). The president of Concamin claimed that the problem was particularly grave because "it puts social tranquility in danger since the peasant problem is the most serious that exists in the country; the businessmen do not want these irregular situations to be started and fomented, only to be blamed later for what is happening" (*Novedades,* Aug. 18, 1976).

The president of the National Chamber of Chemical-Pharmaceutical Laboratories in Mexico also spoke out sharply against Proquivemex. Again the main concern was not with the charges made against the TNCs per se. Rather, it was a more general problem: the danger that Proquivemex, with its production of finished pharmaceuticals,[24] would displace privately owned Mexican laboratories from the big government market for pharmaceutical purchases in Mexico.[25] The criticism leveled against Proquivemex was that it was guilty of "disloyal competition" vis-à-vis the private Mexican labs since the state firm had access to credit at lower rates of interest than the private firms did and it was exempt from taxes that the private companies had to pay (*El heraldo,* Aug. 19, 1976).

The government quickly took heed of this new situation. The direct negotiations that followed were placed in the hands of the Secretary of National

Patrimony rather than the three ministries that were represented on the study commission. The government claimed the price of barbasco could be lowered considerably if the TNCs "toll manufactured" for Proquivemex. The government also made known its desire to have the TNC subsidiaries "Mexicanize" by selling part of their stock to local partners. Somewhat ironically, it is clear that not having acquired local partners before Proquivemex was created was a big tactical error by the TNCs. Mexicanization may serve very conservative ends. By becoming "partly Mexican" a TNC becomes much less vulnerable politically without being required to improve its performance in Mexico, either with respect to the internal or the external (i.e., export) market.

Negotiations continued through the sexennial change of government at the end of 1976 in which José López Portillo replaced Echeverría. The devaluation of the Mexican peso (beginning August 31, 1976) helped the TNCs considerably in their bargaining with the government, however. By November 1976, for instance, the government price for barbasco had dropped from P $70 to P $55 a kilogram, with the TNCs offering to pay P $25 (*El sol de México*, Nov. 4, 1976). The value of the Mexican peso at the time, however, was only *one-half* what it had been before the devaluation in comparison with the U.S. dollar (P $25 to $1.00 U.S. after the devaluation, as compared with P $12.50 to $1.00 U.S. before). Thus, the dollar value of the TNCs' offer for dry barbasco at the end of 1976 was the same as what they were originally paying for the raw material in 1974, before Proquivemex had been created.

A workable agreement between the two sides was not reached until April 1977, at which time the TNCs consented to pay P $60 per kilogram for dry barbasco (approximately P $30 at predevaluation exchange rates). Proquivemex's total payment to the peasants was also raised, from P $2.10 during 1975 and 1976 (see note 14) to P $4.50 (*El día*, April 14, 1977). In the agreement no mention was made of the government's previously stipulated conditions that 1) the TNC subsidiaries "Mexicanize," and that 2) they "toll manufacture" finished products for Proquivemex. Thus, the government finally got the TNCs to pay a higher price for processed barbasco, but in so doing it dropped its demands for related industry change.

From 1977 to 1980 Mexico's position in the world industry continued to deteriorate. Whereas Mexican diosgenin accounted for 75 percent of the world supply of steroid raw materials in 1963 and nearly 40 percent in 1973 (see table 4–1), by 1980 this percentage had dropped to 10 percent. Several of the TNCs with subsidiaries in Mexico began switching to alternative raw materials and to processes that did not require barbasco; thus, the total amount of barbasco purchased from Proquivemex by the six TNCs dropped from 6,800 tons in 1977 to 2,800 tons in 1978. Proquivemex's primary response was to try to increase at all costs the vertical integration of the industry within Mexico (*El universal,* Oct. 18, 1978). This vertical integration was to proceed in three main directions: 1) the production from barbasco of all the diosgenin used in Mexico, 2) the production of intermediate steroids, in particular 16-D, hydrocortisone, and eventually the diuretic spironolactone, and 3) the production of fermented steroids in Mexico. Mexico also planned to use hecogenin from the sisal plant grown locally to manufacture without fermentation some steroid products that would require fermentation if barbasco were used as the starting material. Transnationals thus became increasingly marginal to the development of the steroid industry in Mexico.

Overall there are three principal reasons why Proquivemex was unable to impose its program of reforms on the TNCs in the Mexican steroid hormone industry. The first is economic. Mexico's overall plan for development continued giving an extremely high priority to exports, which began to fall off sharply as of 1975 (see table 4–3). It was apparently felt that the TNCs could stave off Mexico's deteriorating position in the world industry better than a newly created state firm could. The second reason is political. Proquivemex did not have the support it needed at the top levels of government to carry through its reforms. One clear demonstration of this in 1975 is the fact that the Mexican government allowed the TNCs to import diosgenin from the People's Republic of China, thereby directly undermining Proquivemex's pricing policy with respect to barbasco. In addition, by mid-1976 the state

Table 4–3
The Mexican Steroid Hormone Industry: Exports and Imports, 1965–1976

Year	Exports* Pesos[a]	Exports* Kilos[b]	Imports* Pesos[a]	Imports* Kilos[b]	Percentage of Total Production Exported**
1965	173	156	39	12	97
1966	205	179	51	7	97
1967	214	186	51	11	88
1968	208	199	89	3	80
1969	234	247	46	5	92
1970	224	208	58	11	93
1971	262	235	83	6	94
1972	217	227	111	117	94
1973	372	250	117	6	95
1974	448	236	140	8	98
1975	380	161	147	11	NA
1976	291	119	100	5	NA

Sources: * Mexico, Secretaria de Industria y Comercio, 1966–1977.
         ** Olizar, 1975–1976:155.

Note: NA = not available.
[a]Expressed in millions of pesos.
[b]Expressed in thousands of kilograms.

firm had been replaced as the chief negotiator with the TNCs in the industry by members of the state bureaucracy. The third reason is technological. Mexico's "technological dependence" in the steroid hormone industry is still very real. Mexico imports the vast majority of the active ingredients used in steroids and in the other pharmaceutical products consumed nationally. Had nationalization occurred, it would have seriously jeopardized the stream of technologically sophisticated pharmaceutical products controlled by foreign manufacturers.

State Autonomy and Its Limits vis-à-vis TNCs

A brief recapitulation of my conclusions about the Mexican steroid hormone industry as a crucial-case test of dependency theory is in order. Whereas most dependent countries are prevented from attaining integrated and relatively autonomous national industries by the absence of one or more critical factors of production, Mexico by the early 1950s could boast of possessing all that it needed to be the world leader in a dynamic and technologically sophisticated segment of the pharmaceutical industry: it had exclusive access to the most efficient and versatile raw material, barbasco; a local firm, Syntex, led the world industry in both output and steroid technology; and the Mexican state had taken an active role in supporting established local producers. Given these advantages, why was Mexico unable to develop a fully integrated steroid hormone industry that could make finished as well as intermediate steroid products? From Mexico's point of view, this forward integration would have been highly desirable. It would have 1) increased the value and diversity of the country's steroid exports, 2) had a positive impact on manufacturing value-added and local employment opportunities, and 3) reduced the prices of finished drugs to Mexican consumers.

The reason why Mexico was unable to obtain the benefits of full industrial development in steroid hormones, I have argued, stems from the multifaceted dependency relations in which the country was enmeshed. "Dependency," as the concept has been used in this study, is not implied by capitalism per se, as some Marxists would have it, but rather refers to the pattern of foreign-controlled capitalist development that is so common in many third world nations. This foreign control was manifested not only by the wholly owned TNC subsidiaries that took over the Mexican industry in the late 1950s and early 1960s and whose global strategies often conflicted with the country's national and social priorities; foreign control was also an inherent part of the structure of the international industry. Mexico's steroid hormone output had to be sold in mass markets abroad and the most important market of all was the United States. This fact allowed the U.S. government to play a key role in forcing the Mexican state to stop protecting domestic producers of steroid intermediates prior to the entry by U.S. and European TNCs. The dependency represented by this foreign control led to an inequitable distribution of industry benefits favoring the central capitalistic economies and the TNCs more than Mexico and to a restriction of Mexico's choices in pursuing its development options.

The structural power of the TNCs clearly limited the bargaining power of the Mexican state in the steroid hormone industry, although state inaction at certain junctures could also be explained at least in part by conflicting priorities within the state bureaucracy, inadequate administrative capabilities for monitoring and regulating the activities of TNCs, and corruption. When the state in Mexico did begin to act against the foreign firms in 1975, this new-found political will appeared to be sparked by alleged abuses involving the peasants; later the state's initiatives, embodied in Proquivemex, were tempered when the local private sector sided with the TNCs to protest the growing peasant mobilization that accompanied the state's involvement. Thus an understanding of the dynamics of dependency and Mexico's attempts to reverse it involves not just the issue of foreign control but also an analysis of the social class relations that made this control possible. This raises the general questions of how third world states use their autonomy to try to control TNCs and what factors increase the state's probability of success.

The relationship between the state and foreign capital in third world countries is complex and has changed rapidly in recent years. In his book *The State and Society,* Alfred Stepan (1978: Chapter 7) reviews some of these changes and, more generally, attempts to assess the capability of the state to control foreign capital. One of the most interesting features of his analysis is Stepan's identification of a bargaining cycle relating the potential power of the state to its ability to control foreign capital, with particular emphasis given to the case of Peru since 1968. This bargaining power model is considered applicable to manufacturing as well as extractive industries (Stepan, 1978:242) and thus might provide a useful framework for drawing some conclusions from the Mexican steroid hormone case.

There are two main dimensions to Stepan's bargaining cycle model: the importance to the state of attracting foreign investment in a particular economic sector (low priority or high priority), and the status of foreign investment prior to bargaining with the state (uncommitted or "sunken"). In table 4–4 this model is adapted to the case of Mexico's steroid hormone industry. According to Stepan's formulation, the state is in the *strongest)* position to control or exclude foreign capital at a minimal economic and political cost if the proposed investment involves an area of the economy given a low priority by the state and there is no existing foreign investment in the sector (cell 1). The state is in the *weakest* position to control foreign capital, on the other hand, in those sectors where foreign investment has a high priority in the state's development plan and foreign investment is still uncommitted to

Table 4–4
The State-Foreign Capital Bargaining Cycle, Adapted to the Case of Mexico's Steroid Hormone Industry, 1944–1982

Previous Status of Foreign Investment	Importance to the State of Attracting Foreign Investment	
	Low Priority	*High Priority*
	1	4
Uncommitted	State can bar entry of foreign capital at almost no economic or political cost	State has to offer incentives to attract foreign capital
	1944–1955: Local private capital phase	Not applicable
	2	3
"Sunken"	State can control or even eliminate foreign capital but at some economic and political cost	State cannot eliminate foreign capital but has some capacity to impose greater controls and exact greater rents
	1956–1974: Transnational corporation phase	1975–1982: State enterprise phase

Source: Stepan, 1978:244. The dates refer to the three phases of dependency in Mexico's steroid hormone industry.
Note: Scale of state potential to control foreign capital:
  1 = highest
  4 = lowest

the sector (cell 4); in these circumstances the state may have to forgo exacting conditions for entry and may even have to extend special subsidies to attract foreign capital. Between these extremes fall two intermediate positions of potential state power. When foreign investment is "sunken," Stepan argues, it is vulnerable to the broad range of control measures the state can apply. The state is in a stronger position in cell 2 (low priority) than in cell 3 (high priority), however, because in the former situation local factors of production are available that can adequately meet planned investment targets in the sector.

When these phases of the state-foreign capital bargaining cycle are related to the case of Mexico's steroid hormone industry, it can be seen that the Mexican state's power should have been greatest at the beginning of the industry's growth (cell 1) and weakest at the end (cell 3). In fact, my analysis of the industry does not fully support the predictions of Stepan's bargaining cycle model. The power of the Mexican state was probably weakest, or least in evidence, during the middle period when the TNCs' domination of Mexico's steroid hormone industry was greatest (cell 2). The state's role in the industry is most prominent, on the other hand, in the era of Proquivemex, when the bargaining cycle model predicts the state to be weakest (cell 3). And when the state should have been strongest (cell 1), local private capital enjoyed its only real moment of glory in the industry, with the state playing a supporting but definitely subordinate role. To explain these apparent inconsistencies, a closer look at the assumptions underlying Stepan's model is called for.

First of all, the notion of high or low priority of foreign investment to the state is more complicated than the bargaining schema implies. "Priority" has both an economic and a political dimension, and these need not coincide. Steroid hormone exports gave the industry a high *economic* priority in Mexico in phases 2 (1956–1974) and 3 (1975–1982). What changed over this period, however, was the industry's *political* priority to the state, which went from low in phase 2 to high in phase 3. The issue of alleged exploitation of the peasants by the steroid hormone TNCs first surfaced in Mexican newspapers at the end of 1974. It was this politically volatile peasant issue, more than economic issues, that prompted an expanded role for the state through the creation of Proquivemex in early 1975.

The ties of foreign capital to the prospective host country point to another aspect of Stepan's model in need of further refinement if it is to help explain what happened in Mexico's steroid hormone industry. "Uncommitted" foreign investment, as used in Stepan's bargaining framework, implicitly refers to TNCs only in their capacity as potential local producers. It is clear from the steroid hormone case, however, that TNCs may be linked to a host country in at least two separate ways: as producers and as foreign buyers.[26] In phase 1 (1944–1955), TNCs as producers were essentially uncommitted to Mexico (with the sole exception of the Schering Corporation's subsidiary, Beisa, which operated as a pilot plant). United States TNC buyers of Mexican steroid hormone exports in this period, on the other hand, were heavily committed to Mexico for their raw material supplies. Because their reliance on Mexico was so great, these TNC buyers helped pressure the U.S. government to break Syntex's virtual monopoly in Mexico. This opened the floodgates to the direct foreign investment that led in phase 2 to the denationalization of the Mexican steroid hormone industry. Transnational commitment, like state priority, is thus not a unidimensional concept. The high degree of commitment by TNC buyers limited the options of the Mexican state prior to the influx of TNC producers.

Finally, Stepan's model assumes that in manufacturing industries, as in extractive ones, the moment of new investment is the company's moment of greatest bargaining strength (Stepan, 1978:242). As time passes, "sunken" foreign investment is likely to become increasingly vulnerable to host country demands. The experience of TNCs in steroid hormones and other manufacturing industries does not seem to support this generalization, however.[27] Unlike industries in the extractive sector, manufacturing industries are not characterized by the reductions in uncertainty and the host country "learning curves" that cause shifts in bargaining power from companies to the host government after the initial investment is made and that frequently lead to the nationalization of extractive industries (see Moran, 1974a). In the manufacturing sector nationalizations are rare because, for one thing, rapidly changing technology is a continuing source of corporate strength and this technology is beyond the reach of most host governments. Even more important is the fact that over time manufacturing TNCs tend to forge domestic alliances with local suppliers, distributors, and creditors, among others. What this means for the manufacturing TNC is that the moment of initial entry may be its *weakest* bargaining point because the government controls the terms of access to the local market. Once established, however, manufacturing TNCs begin to acquire domestic allies and their bargaining position vis-à-vis the government improves. This ability to count on help from the local private sector explains why the steroid hormone TNCs in Mexico remained largely unscathed in phase 3 (1975–1982) even though the government directed an intense assault against them.

This study, then, tells not just of the exercise of state autonomy in Mexico but also of its limits. One should not infer from this account that the Mexican state fully and straightforwardly represented the interests of all the Mexican people. Although acting in the name of the nation, the state's development plan favored certain groups in the population over others. What greater state autonomy vis-à-vis TNCs in Mexico really represents is a shift in the locus of responsibility for development decisions: along with other national actors, the state now plays a larger role in setting development goals and also in establishing the means to reach these goals.

Transnational corporations, on the other hand, claim that they more than anyone else have promoted development in Mexico's steroid hormone industry. If so, it is development as defined by an international strategy rather than a national one. This international strategy has had some clear costs. Exports have been generated, but they are of intermediate products rather than finished drugs. The finishing continues to be done in the home countries of the TNCs where the big industry profits are made. Taxes have been paid in Mexico by the transnationals, but their amount has been reduced to a minimum through the use of tax havens and transfer pricing. And knowledge creation, the most valued resource of private drug companies, has remained tightly controlled near the center of each transnational organization.

Nor is there much solace for Mexico in the belief that these costs are inextricably bound into the industrialization process itself. [Counterfactual analyses indicate] that national alternatives—i.e., both private and state-owned firms—are likely to have been at least as beneficial as the TNCs, and perhaps more so, with respect to national welfare (as defined by local industry growth) and consumer welfare (as defined by lower drug prices) [see Gereffi, 1983:ch. 4].

Mexico's options in the steroid hormone industry have been narrowing. Mexico has access to raw material supply, and the TNCs have patents, technology, and marketing networks. Unfortunately for Mexico, its basis of strength has been weakened due to the development of substitute sources of supply and to the decline of raw material costs as part of the final sales price of steroid drugs. On the other hand, the TNCs still have a vested interest in maintaining their local subsidiaries' direct access to the Mexican source of supply since this has long been part of their strategy to gain a competitive edge internationally. Bargaining, therefore, continues to be viable.

What is good public policy for Mexico under these conditions? In a vertically integrated industry such as steroid hormones, one national strategy is for Mexico to get as much of the oligopoly profits and the value added as possible at the stage it controls. More specifically, it can follow any combination of policy measures, such as: 1) formulating an optimal excise tax on exports; 2) demanding a percentage of the final product price; 3) policing transfer pricing closely; and 4) demanding more local processing (fermentation, toll manufacturing, etc.). Again, however, Mexico's bargaining power in each area is constrained because technology is controlled and there are alternative sources of supply. The TNCs' threat that "they can go elsewhere" is credible.

At present Mexico has opted for a second national strategy: the use of a state-owned enterprise as a flexible policy instrument for dealing with both national development goals and TNCs.[28] Such a strategy has a number of advantages. First, it still allows bargaining with TNCs to be carried on for limited gains in which neither side feels it is in an all or nothing situation. Second, state resources can be used more directly to promote welfare goals that private firms, national or transnational, would ignore. In steroid hormones the state firm tried to eliminate exploitative middlemen, to lower the price of basic goods to the peasants, and to develop new rural industries to stabilize the peasant economy should demand for barbasco decline. A third advantage in using state firms as a policy instrument is that the state need not represent a direct threat to the private firms in the industry, thus lessening the chance of mutually destructive opposition. A good example of this is Central de Medicamentos (CEME), a state pharmaceutical company in Brazil created in 1971. The objective of CEME is to produce and distribute basic, generic name drugs without charge to that part of the population which receives the official minimum wage or less. This is exactly that sector of the population which is normally excluded from the commercial market for medicines. Thus, CEME is not likely to take any customers away from private firms. Furthermore, a large part of the medications distributed by CEME are purchased from the private sector, which probably hopes that its own market will be expanded someday as members of this poorer group acquire additional income (Evans, 1976:133–136).

A national strategy based on state enterprises as a policy instrument has disadvantages also. First of all, state firms may grow to a size where they are beyond the control of normal bureaucratic measures. Implementing a flexible state policy may be further complicated by the fact that an in-grown cadre of technical experts develops in these larger enterprises (a form of "state bourgeoisie") that gives them a life of their own. Second, formulation of the policy that these firms should follow may become tangled in a maze of bureaucratic politics at the middle levels of government as groups representing different interests all try to bring their weight to bear. A third problem is that publicly owned enterprises may greatly increase the state's political risk in an industry. Especially in cases where a particular *stage* of the industry is monopolized, like Proquivemex is attempting to do in steroid hormones, the state may often be called to bear the brunt of the responsibility for employment or price fluctuations caused by external or internal supply and demand changes completely beyond the state's control.

Evidence regarding the role and performance of state-owned enterprises in Mexico and other third world countries is sparse. It appears, however, that many of the larger nations are beginning to increase their use of state firms as a key element in national strategies for development. . . .

For their part, TNCs will continue to challenge the state in defining development priorities. Their global spread means their control in industries is not easily broken, especially where it rests with technology and marketing expertise. Until the developing countries gain their own control over knowledge creation, they will be forced to try to shape the contribution of foreign firms to national needs. This will require that national sovereignty and state autonomy be flexed, not buried. The challenge for nations will be to combine the elements of a strong state with those of a just society.

Notes

1. Eighty percent of Proquivemex's capital stock of 15 million Mexican pesos is owned by the government, with the remaining 20 percent divided equally among the six TNCs in the industry. See *El mercado de valores,* Nov. 17, 1975.

2. The diosgenin produced by China also comes from the barbasco plant. Internationally it is an unstable source of supply, however, since China only exports diosgenin if there is an excess after its own huge internal demand for steroids has been satisfied.

3. The data come from a study conducted by Mexico's Instituto Nacional de Investigaciones Forestales and were cited in *Excelsior,* Oct. 30, 1974.

4. Proquivemex claims this is due to an irrational exploitation of barbasco by the TNCs, who have been harvesting immature plants. The foreign companies don't deny they have been gathering immature barbasco, but they claim these plants are taken from land soon to be cleared for other purposes. Thus, they say, their collection policy is rational since the alternative would be to let this source material go to waste.

5. This fear is certainly not allayed by comments such as the following made by Syntex's General Manager in Mexico: "If [the foreign firms in Mexico's steroid hormone industry] have the possibility of obtaining their raw material at more convenient prices elsewhere, then naturally they will not need to keep their local facilities operating in the country. If they buy in other nations, logically the local plants will disappear" (*El sol de México*, Aug. 21, 1976).

6. Mexico had already suffered several major setbacks in rural industries due to the arrival of synthetic substitutes that largely displaced the demand for the natural products. When plastics, for example, greatly decreased the demand for the henequen fibers cultivated in Mexico, government subsidies to the unemployed peasants rose to P $2 million a day (*El universal*, Mar. 13, 1976). Similar problems have shaken Mexico's cotton and natural rubber industries as a result of the rapidly growing demand for synthetic fibers and synthetic rubber. Mexico is thus quite sensitive to the internal disturbances that could result if the world demand for barbasco drops because of external substitutes.

7. A similar situation exists in Brazil with respect to insulin. The raw material for insulin comes in the form of insulin "crystals" manufactured from the pancreas of cattle and hogs. In Latin America the only place where this raw material is produced is Eli Lilly's plant in Argentina. Between 1945 and 1960 insulin had been manufactured in Brazil by a local firm called Laboterápica. But in 1957 Laboterápica was bought out by Bristol-Myers, which decided that the Brazilian market for insulin was unsatisfactory and therefore ceased production. Brazil, with one of the largest cattle populations in the world, now exports some four hundred tons of pancreas a year. Yet the country pays about eleven thousand dollars per kilogram to import insulin, which it already possesses the know-how and resources to manufacture (Ledogar, 1975: 65–67). In case of a shortage that might affect the lives of many citizens, such as occurred in Brazil in April and May of 1975, the country is completely at the mercy of a foreign supplier.

8. The government wanted at least some part of the stock in these companies to be sold to Mexican partners. It did not specifically request that Mexicans be given a majority share, however, nor that this share be sold to the government.

9. Unless otherwise noted, all figures in pesos refer to an exchange rate of 12.50 Mexican pesos to one U.S. dollar.

10. The proposed arrangement was that Proquivemex would choose from among those products that each TNC had been producing in Mexico or elsewhere in its corporate family. Proquivemex would supply free barbasco and then pay the foreign subsidiary its processing costs plus a reasonable profit. The supply of barbasco to be "toll manufactured" would be additional to that which the TNCs contracted to buy for their own use. According to Proquivemex (1976:46–47), the TNCs in the industry were only operating at 67 percent of their installed capacity in the early 1970s.

11. According to one major study, the objectives of the TNCs can be characterized as private, simple, well-defined, and permanent: namely, "profitability and growth, evaluated for the integrated whole of their operations at the level of the world market and in a long-range perspective" (Fajnzylber and Martínez Tarragó, 1976:131).

12. The first sustained criticism of alleged TNC exploitation in the industry came out in a series of three newspaper articles published in *Excelsior* on October 30

and 31 and November 1, of 1974. The government immediately proclaimed that the TNCs would, in the future, be granted no more permits to extract barbasco (thus breaking with the policy that had been in force since the 1950s); only peasants organized in *ejidos* would henceforth be eligible to receive permits (*Excelsior*, Nov. 2, 1974).

13. In 1970 the five states where barbasco is gathered had the following average daily incomes: Oaxaca, P $14; Chiapas, P $17; Puebla, P $21; Tabasco, P $27; and Veracruz, P $28 (*IX Censo General de Poblacíon 1970,* Dirección General de Estadística, Secretaría de Industria y Comercio, cited in Proquivemex, 1976: Table 5.8). A peasant can gather, on the average, fifty kilograms of barbasco daily. At a price of P $0.60 per kilo, this means a daily income of P $30, which is above the average of the most prosperous barbasco-producing state (Veracruz) and more than double the normal daily income in the poorest state (Oaxaca).

14. The peasants received P $1.50 to $2.00 per kilogram of "green" barbasco from the TNCs in 1974. The Proquivemex pricing policy was to pay the peasant gatherer P $1.50 per kilogram of unprocessed barbasco for his labor, with P $0.50 going to the *ejido* from which the plant was uprooted for *derechos de monte* (see note 22) and a remaining P $0.10 going to a common *ejidal* fund managed by the Fondo Nacional de Fomento Ejidal. Thus, Proquivemex's total payment to the peasants was P $2.10 for each kilo of "green" barbasco they collected.

15. Both the TNCs and the Mexican government have made attempts to cultivate barbasco in Mexico. So far the method has proven too costly and the returns too limited for cultivated barbasco to be internationally competitive.

16. Proquivemex calculated its price for barbasco by working backwards from the price of the finished steroid hormone products to the raw material cost, subtracting the costs of transformation and overhead. The sample of final products on which this calculation was based ranged from the most advanced to the most elementary.

17. An economic study commissioned by the six TNCs concluded that at a price of P $12 per kilogram of dry barbasco the TNCs could export P $612 million of steroid hormones, at a price of P $20 exports would drop to P $548 million, and at the P $70 price the value of Mexico's steroid exports would plummet to P $30 million (Bremer et al., 1976:28).

18. Ironically, this report was first published by the *Wall Street Journal* (Mar. 8, 1976); it was quickly picked up by a major Mexico City newspaper (*El sol de México*, Mar. 9, 1976). The TNCs tried to recoup their prestige by placing full-page ads in all of Mexico City's main dailies denying the veracity of the story and making counter-charges of their own. (This ad, dated Mar. 11, 1976, appeared in most papers the following day.)

19. Newspaper accounts of this meeting were printed on March 13, 1976. The peasant unions formally published their demands for nationalization a few days later. See *Excelsior*, Mar. 15, 1976.

20. The meeting was held on August 15 and 16.

21. The one exception was Diosynth, which ran out of its barbasco reserves in May and agreed to "toll manufacture" 160 tons of dry barbasco into intermediate products for Proquivemex in June. Diosynth later discontinued its operations for the state firm, however.

22. *Derechos de monte* refer to the Mexican law stating that in order to exploit natural resources lying on the surface of the land—such as trees for lumber or surface mining to get at ore deposits—one must pay the owner of the land for the resource used. This law thus separates payment for the natural resource (e.g., to the *ejidos*) from payment to those who gather the material. The TNCs claim this charge is without any legal basis since no government authority had ever previously requested that such a payment be made for the *Dioscorea* plants. See *Excelsior*, Aug. 17 and 19, 1976.

23. See Proquivemex (1976:43–44). The estradiol example is also mentioned in *Excelsior*, Mar. 20, 1976. For more information on transfer pricing in the pharmaceutical industry in Latin America see Vaitsos (1974) on Colombia and Katz (1974: 33–34) on Argentina.

24. The Proquivemex product that seemed to worry the national laboratories most was the antibiotic ampicillin (the second-generation penicillin). Many firms knew how to make it and it was bought in large quantities by the government.

25. The government market accounts for about 25 percent of all pharmaceutical sales in Mexico. It was estimated to be worth $240 million (U.S.) in 1976 (*Business Latin America,* Mar. 24, 1976, p. 90).

26. A third role, applicable to transnational banks, is that of financier.

27. See Bennett and Sharpe's (1979) analysis of Mexico's automobile industry, which shows how and why TNCs increased their bargaining power with the state over time.

28. Under Echeverría this strategy was particularly prominent in major rural industries such as tobacco, coffee, sugar, and barbasco. Each of these four industries employs large numbers of peasants: sugar, about 300,000; coffee, 95,000; tobacco, 45,000; and barbasco, 25,000. In each of these industries a major state-owned firm was either created or revitalized during the Echeverría administration as part of its rural development program. In the sugar industry a decentralized agency called the National Commission on the Sugar Industry was created in 1970. The tobacco state-owned enterprise, Tabacos Mexicanos (Tabamex), was created in 1972. In the coffee industry an existing firm called the Mexican National Coffee Institute (Inmecafe) was revitalized. Finally, in the case of barbasco there was the creation of Proquivemex in 1975. Although these industries are quite diverse in their overall structure, it appears that the function of state-owned firms in each was similar: 1) to increase the economic strength and stability of these industries and of the rural areas depending on them, 2) to reduce the exploitation of the peasants, particularly by rural middlemen, and 3) stemming from the above, to increase the regime's legitimacy and political support in the countryside.

References

Bennett, Douglas, and Sharpe, Kenneth. 1979. "Agenda Setting and Bargaining Power: The Mexican State Versus Transnational Automobile Corporations." *World Politics,* 32, no. 1 (October):57–89.

Bremer, Quintana, Vaca, Rocha, Obregon y Mancera (law firm). 1976. "El problema del precio del barbasco en la industria mexicana de productos esteroides." Mimeograph. 37 pp. Mexico, D.F.: February 25.

Fajnzylber, Fernando, and Martínez Tarragó, Trinidad. 1976. *Las empresas transnacionales: expansión a nivel mundial y proyección en la industria mexicana.* Mexico, D.F.: Fondo de Cultura Económica.

Gereffi, Gary. 1983. *The Pharmaceutical Industry and Dependency in the Third World.* Princeton, N.J.: Princeton University Press.

Hansen, Roger D. 1971. *The Politics of Mexican Development.* Baltimore, Md.: Johns Hopkins Press.

Katz, Jorge M. 1974. *Oligopolio, firmas nacionales y empresas multinacionales: la industria farmacéutica argentina.* Buenos Aires: Siglo XXI.

Labastida M. del Campo, Julio. 1975. "Nacionalismo reformista en México." *Cuadernos políticos,* no. 3 (January–March):33–51.

Moran, Theodore H. 1974. *Multinational Corporations and the Politics of Dependence: Copper in Chile.* N.J.: Princeton University Press.

Productos Químicos Vegetales Mexicanos, S.A. de C.V. (Proquivemex). 1976. "Informe al honorable consejo de administracíon." Mexico, D.F.: January 16.

Stepan, Alfred. 1978. *The State and Society: Peru in Comparative Perspective.* Princeton, N.J.: Princeton University Press.

Vaitsos, Constantine. 1974. *Intercountry Income Distribution and Transnational Enterprises.* Oxford: Clarendon Press.

5
International Political Risk Assessment, Corporate Planning, and Strategies to Offset Political Risk

Theodore H. Moran

The attempt to use local political influence to bolster their position in the face of nationalistic demands is not the only strategy multinationals have adopted. They have also been experimenting with other tools and techniques to spread, minimize, and offset political risk in the Third World.

This study points out that the field of political risk analysis has expanded from a narrow focus on the attempt to predict social revolution (like the fall of the shah of Iran) to a broader preoccupation with threats that may be much less cataclysmic but no less damaging to corporate profitability. The majority of nationalistic pressures emerge in situations in which there is neither revolution nor (necessarily) nationalization on the horizon. As a consequence, multinational corporations have begun to include project vulnerability assessments as part of their political risk analysis. These assessments examine the characteristics of the investment that lead to strength or weakness in the Third World setting, not only at the initiation of the project but over the entire life cycle.

Beyond project vulnerability assessments, international investors have been reshaping corporate strategy to reduce their exposure, share their risk with others, and create deterrent structures designed to decrease the likelihood of threats to their operations. This study looks at the use of vertical integration, the arrangement of sourcing and disposition of product, the sequencing of investments, and the construction of financial networks as elements of corporate strategy aimed at continuing operations in the face of political risk.

Introduction

The growing discipline of political risk analysis has focused predominantly on the problem of predicting broad social revolution in Third World countries. There is sound justification for this preoccupation. Broad social revolution as occurred in Iran, or Cuba, constitutes the greatest single source of damage to the international investment community. To cope with such contingencies, the conventional wisdom of political risk management is probably the best advice available: in the face of high risk, the parent corporation should not invest in the first place; or, it should disinvest and reduce exposure; or, it should demand a higher premium for any new investments. To protect itself, the home company should buy insurance and/or establish a reserve.

But broad social revolution, while the greatest single source of injury to international investors, still accounts for much less than half and perhaps as low as thirty percent of the losses due to the deliberate political actions of host authorities. Much greater damage in the aggregate comes from business-as-usual economic nationalism in the Third World that does not involve fundamental indigenous upheaval but is rather a more rational (or quasi-rational) attempt by host authorities, to paraphrase Samuel Gompers, "to get more."

In these latter settings, new techniques of political risk assessment are necessary, moving beyond country assessments focusing on socioeconomic and political variables, toward a focus on the vulnerabilities associated with specific types of projects. And the management of political risk in such settings requires experimental corporate strategies that do qualify, in fact as well as in rhetoric, as global strategic planning.[1]

Project Vulnerability and Strategic Planning for Political Risk

Project vulnerability analysis has been derived from case studies to elucidate what factors determine the bargaining strength between multinational enterprises and local authorities in the less developed countries (plus Canada and Australia), and how the foreign investment-host government relationship is likely to evolve over time. In contrast to the perspective of country assessment studies, these vulnerability appraisals suggest an important and somewhat counterintuitive finding, namely, that project characteristics lead to certain likely outcomes independent of the ideology or socio-political make-up of the host regimes. Moreover, the evolution of business-government relations over the lifetime of a project is more predictable, in the aggregate of cases, on the basis of project-specific variables than on the basis of information about social institutions, political changes, or government ideologies in the recipient country.

Four project characteristics have emerged as having primary importance in determining whether an investment is particularly vulnerable, or invulnerable, in its relations with host authorities.

To summarize a literature that is now familiar:

The *first* is the size of the required fixed investment. Projects that cannot be brought on-line with investments less than multiples of hundreds of million dollars typically gain entry terms that are very favorable to the foreign investor. But, six to eight years after the project is successfully in operation, the large fixed investment becomes a hostage to host authorities with the parent unable to bargain flexibly.[2] In the case of smaller fixed investments, the parent can resist nationalistic demands by threatening to withdraw as IBM did in India or GM did in Peru.

The *second* project variable is the extent of competition (or potential competition) among investors. Here the strongest evidence comes from the petroleum industry where the dialectic between independents and majors improved the terms even relatively weak host governments could achieve.[3] There is impressive evidence, however, from the manufacturing sector as well; indeed, Knickerbocker has found a statistically significant "burst" phenomenon in the foreign investment decision process, with multiple companies following close behind after the first investor makes a commitment.[4] More investors mean more alternatives for host authorities to choose from and more rivals to play off against one another, increasing the strength of the local government.

Conversely, lack of competition strengthens the position of the foreigner. Fagre and Wells have found that in sixteen of eighteen industries in Latin America in which all foreign investments were wholly owned (one measure of a strong bargaining position), only one international corporation was present.[5]

The *third* determinant of the strength or weakness of a foreign investor is played by the technology associated with the project. Rather than the intuitively appealing separation into high technology and low technology, however, the contribution of technology to the bargaining equation appears to be more complex. Kobrin has found that the maturity of the technology has an impact on the vulnerability of the investor to nationalization.[6] In our work, the stability of the technology, as opposed to its changeableness or dynamism, is what imparts bargaining power to one side or the other in the business-government relationship.[7]

The *fourth* variable is marketing, or the importance of product differentiation via advertising. Companies whose sales are determined by a large degree of brand identification and consumer loyalty occupy a strong position vis-à-vis host authorities. Companies whose sales are made according to standardized specifications and price advantage are weaker. Fagre and Wells, for example, have found that international companies that spend more than seven percent of total sales revenues on advertising are particularly successful in resisting pressures for local ownership.[8] In the pharmaceutical and cosmetic industries where the highest advertising expenditures take place, ninety-five percent of 202 foreign operations were wholly owned, a finding that holds true even in a country like Mexico where local participation is strongly preferred.

These four project variables are coming to be accepted as tools in forecasting the bargaining position of an international company in the face of aggressive economic nationalism. This is especially true when all four characteristics point in the same direction, as they do in many natural resource industries (copper, nickel, petroleum, natural gas, iron ore, coal): large fixed investments, active competition, stable technology, and low product differentiation.

But they are useful in probing into new areas as well. Consider the question, will the petrochemical sector evolve in the same way in the Third World in the next decade that the petroleum sector has in the last decade?

On the one hand, a strong case can be made that it will not. Petrochemicals are, after all, different from petroleum. They utilize sophisticated process technology. They incorporate a great deal of value added. They create an advanced industrial product. They are downstream from the precious national patrimony. They do not require host authorities to concede long term concessions over sub-soil rights.

On the other hand, however, petrochemicals are like petroleum investments in combining large fixed investments with growing competition, stable technology (for basic feedstocks), and undifferentiated product marketing. From this perspective, the petrochemical investor would be well advised to be particularly wary about the vulnerability his operations will face six to eight years after they come on-line. (The petrochemical investor would also be well advised to look closely at possible strategies to offset political risks, especially investment sequencing, project financing, and joint partner selection.)

In addition to being useful in their application to new sectors, these variables remind all investors of lessons that should be commonplace to international corporations but are not: in particular (a) when an investor has a successful operation that is vulnerable to nationalistic pressures for increased revenues, more jobs, or greater exports, there is a high probability that he will find himself coming face-to-face with those pressures independent of the ideological composition of the host country government; and (b) depending on the above project characteristics, the investor should not be misled by his success in gaining generous terms at the outset so as to overlook an evolution toward increasing vulnerability over a long pay-back period.

A New Variable: Vertical Integration

To the four project characteristics enumerated above, a *fifth* variable is beginning to assume greater importance in the area of investment vulnerability analysis: vertical integration.

The dynamics of vertical integration as a component of corporate strategic planning are not very well developed. Most economic analysis focuses on economies of scale. In metal-working industries, extension plants, rolling mills, and blast furnaces are owned by the same parent to ensure contiguous operations and avoid reheating. Financial institutions yearn to combine lending, insurance underwriting, and other related activities that can exploit a common intelligence-gathering operation.

A second strand in the analysis of vertical integration focuses on the idea of bilateral monopoly, or oligopolistic-oligopsonistic bargaining. Beneath the jargon is a common-sense notion, the desire to avoid being at the mercy of an external agent during any particular part of the economic cycle. A buyer does not want to face high spot prices, discrimination, or rationing during scarcity; a seller does not want to have to sell in a distress market, or sell below average cost during abundance. These "wants" are reinforced in industries where there is a high ratio of fixed to variable costs, in which high constant volume of throughput is important. They give operational meaning to the notoriously slippery concept of "access" to markets or to outlets in the literature on corporate strategy. They have led not only to formal vertical integration via common ownership, but also to empirically verifiable patterns of informal vertical integration as well.[9]

This emphasis on bilateral bargaining to avoid a position of weakness contributes directly to the understanding of vertical integration as an element in corporate strategy in the face of political risk. In the aluminum industry, for example, the major international companies have consistently dragged their heels in building smelter capacity in bauxite producing countries despite the allure of cheap natural gas prices or the promise of subsidized hydroelectric rates. In the vertical chain from bauxite mining to the extrusion of aluminum wire and sheet, the smelter stage has the highest capital costs; it constitutes the stage with the highest barriers to entry.[10] Control over this stage gives the companies a hold over the narrow neck of the funnel between the bauxite fields and the final buyer. Despite the appeal of cheap energy input costs, the international companies have for strategic reasons resisted the call of host countries to construct this stage within the nationalistic reach of the latter.

The agribusiness sector provides a second case that illustrates the role of vertical integration in the face of economic nationalism in the Third World. In the 1950s and early 1960s, the then-famous banana companies, led by United Fruit, were convinced that ownership of the plantations was crucial for their successful operations. The overthrow of Arbenz in Guatemala in 1954 was, at least in part, related to this conviction.

From the mid-1960s through the mid-1970s, however, the strategic evaluation of the companies changed dramatically.[11] They began to divest themselves systematically of a large fraction (not all) of their plantation holdings. In the banana industry, the point in the vertical chain from tree to supermarket that is hardest to duplicate is the transportation-and-distribution stage. Here the key barrier to entry is not the amount of capital that figured prominently in the aluminum case but rather the speed and efficiency of operations. A time savings of four or five days in transportation can be translated into extra ripening on the tree that improves the meat-to-skin ratio in the final product dramatically. Sellers that cannot match the meat-to-skin ratio in freshly ripe bananas are unable to compete.

Thus, the banana companies, like the aluminum companies, began to focus their strategy on maintaining control over the stage in the vertical chain where the greatest barriers to entry lay. To be sure, they kept a fraction of plantation capacity under their own control and provided disease-resistant seeds and technical help to preferred suppliers. But they let the production stage become more competitive, buying their marginal demand from an array of suppliers at a good price. At the same time they shifted onto the producers the burden of fluctuations in supply and demand.

It is clear that vertical integration as an element of corporate adjustment to political risk is at an early stage of understanding. The implications for multinational investors, however, seem straightforward: corporate strategic planners must identify the stage where the greatest barriers to entry lie and determine whether that stage is likely to remain outside the control of host governments or not. Is the vertical structure of the petrochemical industry more like bauxite-aluminum, or more like petroleum? And who will control the stage where the greatest barriers to entry lie? There are tens of billions of dollars riding on the answer to this question.

Corporate Strategies to Offset Political Risk

The development of strategies to offset political risk may constitute the cutting-edge of corporate planning, but progress in this area has not been rapid. Previous studies[12] have identified three distinct elements that might be used separately or in combination to provide protection against political risk: (1) the sourcing of inputs to local operations and the disposition of the output of local operations elsewhere in the corporate system; (2) the sequencing of the investment process so as to dispel nationalistic pressures over time; and (3) the construction of project financing with the objective of raising the cost of irresponsible economic nationalism.

Subsequent investigations have suggested that modifications are needed.

First, early optimism about the construction of international patterns of sourcing and exporting to limit nationalistic actions against a local subsidiary may have to be tempered. As automotive and machinery companies with operations in the ASEAN or Andrean Pact regions have demonstrated, the geographic dispersion of component plants constitutes a double-edged sword: on the one hand, a host government cannot take over a complete facility; on the other hand, the shut-down of any single plant can cripple the output for an entire region. Thus, there are double dependencies, with the international corporation often in the weaker position. One solution, of course, is the construction of spare or redundant capacity. With interest rates and the opportunity-cost of capital as high as they are currently, however, this does not offer an easy or inexpensive tactic for corporate strategists.

Nevertheless, the fact remains that strategies of internal sourcing do appear to have an impressive aggregate impact on the ability of the parent corporation to avoid expropriation and/or demands for host country ownership. Bradley points out that not one of the 114 U.S. manufacturing affiliates that have been expropriated since 1960 sold more than 10 percent of its output to affiliates.[13] Similarly, Fagre and Wells show that of 54 subsidiaries that sell 50 percent or more of their output to the parent system, fifty-one have maintained a position of complete foreign ownership.[14]

Second, on the sequencing of investments to maximize the cards the parent corporation has to play in the face of nationalistic pressures, the prospects are both broader and more constrained than initial examination suggested. Early evidence came largely from case studies in the chemical and petrochemical industries in which corporate strategists deviated from both engineering and economic optimality to stage investments in a series that would provide them something new to offer when host authorities pressed in.

Across a wider spectrum of manufacturing industries, it is now clear that international companies can reduce host country fiscal demands if they agree to meet certain "performance requirements" for more value-added or for greater exports. One study has identified more than forty countries that levy significant performance requirements of this sort.[15]

Clearly there are opportunities to allay nationalistic pressures by participating ever more vigorously in host country industrial development plans. The idea of having corporate headquarters design an industrial expansion strategy in key Third World countries timed with the conscious objective of offsetting political risk, however, has produced difficulties on the homefront directly in proportion to its success abroad. The adoption of performance requirements as part of the standard arsenal of economic nationalism, and the acquiescence by multinational investors as a way of maintaining or enhancing overseas profitability has produced strong reactions on the part of organized labor in the home countries of the investors. In the United States the Labor-Industry Coalition on International Trade has demanded strong countermeasures via the GATT.[16] Other groups have sought reciprocity legislation, or American-imposed local content requirements, in the Congress. In the European community, the Vredeling Proposal would require consultations with the local groups where plants were located in the EC before the international investment plans of the parent corporation could proceed.

Thus, the future may hold new restrictions on the freedom of international corporations to try to use the sequencing of investment as a strategy to offset the pressures of economic nationalism.

Third, the use of project finance as a method of reducing the exposure of direct investors in activities that require a large lump-sum capital outlay while ensuring some rules of behavior across successive host country administrations has become more widely accepted over the past few years.[17] Until about ten years ago, international corporations combined retained earnings with their own reputation in international bond markets to raise the capital needed for large new investments. They then provided the capital to overseas branches or subsidiaries in the (predominant) form of equity. In mining, for example, prior to 1970 approximately ninety percent of the financial commitments for new operations or the expansion of existing operations in the less developed countries were made through equity investments or the use of cash from ongoing operations.[18] In the second half of the 1970s, however, there was a marked shift from equity to debt for the construction of new facilities. Between 1975 and 1980, Eurodollar markets provided at least $30 billion in loans for Third World extractive operations.

Most such loans now take the form of project finance. The idea of project finance, of course, is to use the stream of sales from a future operation as an asset that can be used (mortgaged, in effect) to raise the capital to bring the project into existence in the first place. Increasingly, the construction of the project finance package is designed to offset political as well as commercial risk. Woven in among the financial institutions participating in the syndication are banks located in all of the countries that are aid givers, military suppliers, trading partners and public creditors of the host government. Investment insurance and supplier credits are obtained from a diversity of developed country governments. Usually the lead bank in the syndication requires a trust account (or escrow account) held in New York or Frankfurt or London, subject to the laws of the local municipality, that can be frozen or attached in the case of an investment crisis. Finally, financial participation by a multilateral financial institution such as the World Bank or the Inter-American Development Bank provides an umbrella of legitimacy (and cross-default clauses) over the entire project. The objective, clearly, is to construct a transnational web of financial ties that will raise the price of irresponsible nationalistic behavior on the part of the host country for the life of the project. It is a strategy of spreading risk among a large group of institutions that provide capital for the project, and at the same time a strategy of deterrence to ensure that host obligations will be fulfilled.

Curiously, however, progress in developing this tool to offset political risks has been threatened by the Reagan Administration on programs like the energy facility of the World Bank. In general, World Bank participation in cofinancing or consortium lending provides stability to the entire project through the prevention of selective defaults to particular lenders (including the foreign direct investor himself). The Reagan Administration has taken the position, however, that Bank participation tends to crowd out private lenders and substitute for foreign direct investment. When subjected to empirical analysis, this contention is difficult to support on the basis of the empirical record. While there have been notable instances of misallocations of public funds by the IBRD since 1977 and cases of World Bank substitution for private sector investment, the majority of the cases, at least in the energy sector, support the opposite proposition, namely, that the Bank acts as a catalyst to private sector investment and provides an umbrella against political risk to investors and lenders alike.[19] If anything, World Bank programs should be expanded, not constrained, and risk-offset mechanisms strengthened, e.g., through making cross-default provisions mandatory rather than optional.

Finally, a new element is gaining prominence in corporate strategies to protect against political risk, the selection of local private partners. Since the mid-1960s conventional wisdom has suggested that companies that shared ownership with host government agencies (i.e., companies that submitted to Mexicanization, Zambianization, or Koreanization with public sector institutions) were safer than those that did not. Recent data show that this has not, in fact been the case.[20] Such Mexicanized, Zambianized, or Koreanized investors constitute a universe *more* likely to be nationalized than those who remain one hundred percent foreign owned. *Least* likely to be nationalized are those with local private partners. The implication is that corporate strategists should rethink the appeal of joint-ventures, especially with public agencies as local partners. Instead they should focus more exclusively on building alliances in the local private sector, moving beyond the traditional selection of partners on the basis of whom they happen to know best or who happens to have the best credit ratings, to those who can provide political protection under the broadest array of contingencies.

Conclusion

In summary, project vulnerability assessment is establishing itself as an important complement to country studies. The analysis of project characteristics does not supplant the need to examine political-social variables; but it does provide an important additional, independent perspective on how foreign company–host government relations are likely to evolve over the life cycle of any particular investment.

The development of possible methods to offset political risk remains the frontier of corporate strategic planning. Progress in this area is slow, however, and continues to constitute the greatest challenge to international companies trying to operate in environments where economic opportunity is great and economic nationalism inevitable.

Notes

1. These arguments draw on work previously contained in Theodore H. Moran, ed., *International Political Risk Assessment: The State of the Art* (Washington, D.C.: Georgetown University School of Foreign Service, 1980); and "International Political Risk Assessment: An Update on the State of the Art," a presentation before the Conference on Trade, Investment, and Public Policy in Latin America, sponsored by the American Enterprise Institute, September 9–10, 1982.

2. On the "obsolescing bargain" in such situations, see Raymond Vernon, *Sovereignty at Bay: The Multinational Spread of U.S. Enterprises* (New York: Basic Books, 1971); Theodore H. Moran, *Multinational Corporations and the Politics of Dependence: Copper in Chile* (Princeton University Press, 1974); Franklin Tugwell, *The Politics of Oil in Venezuela* (Stanford, Calif.: Stanford University Press, 1975); Richard L. Sklar, *Corporate Power in an African State: The Political Impact of Multinational Mining Companies in Zambia* (Berkeley: University of California Press, 1975).

3. For evidence from both petroleum and hard minerals, see Theodore H. Moran, "The International Political Economy of Cuban Nickel Development," in Cole Blasier and Carmelo Mesa-Largo, eds., *Cuba in the World* (Pittsburgh, Pa.: University of Pittsburgh Press, 1979).

4. Frederick T. Knickerbocker, *Oligopolistic Reaction and Multinational Enterprise* (Cambridge, Mass.: Harvard University Press, 1973).

5. Nathan Fagre and Louis T. Wells, Jr., "Bargaining Power of Multinationals and Host Governments," *Journal of International Business Studies,* Fall 1982.

6. Stephen J. Kobrin, "The Forced Divestment of Foreign Enterprise in the LDCs," *International Organization,* Winter 1980.

7. Focusing only on the level of R&D expenditures to distinguish high versus low technology industries (and not only the changeableness of the technology employed in the host country), Bradley has found that middle-range technology firms have been quite vulnerable to expropriation. David G. Bradley, "Managing Against Expropriation," *Harvard Business Review,* July-August 1977.

8. Fagre and Wells, *op. cit.*

9. For a classic work in this field, see John E. Tilton, "The Choice of Trading Partners: An Analysis of International Trade in Aluminum, Bauxite, Copper, Lead, Manganese, Tin and Zinc," *Yale Economic Essays,* Vol. VI (Fall 1966).

10. *Structure and Strategy in the International Aluminum Industry* (New York: United Nations Centre on Transnational Corporations, 1980); I.A. Litvak and C.J. Maule, *Transnational Corporations in the Bauxite-Aluminum Industry: With Special Reference to the Caribbean* (New York: United Nations Economic Commission for Latin America, 1977), working paper no. 2.

11. I.A. Litvak and C.J. Maule, *Transnational Corporations in the Banana Industry: With Special Reference to Central America and Panama* (New York: United Nations Economic Commission for Latin America, 1977), 1977. For a structural analysis including both bauxite and bananas, see Theodore H. Moran, "New Deal or Raw Deal in Raw Materials," *Foreign Policy,* Winter 1971–72.

12. Theodore H. Moran, *International Political Risk Assessment: The State of the Art, op. cit.*

13. Bradley, *op. cit.*

14. Fagre and Wells, *op cit.*

15. LICIT, *Performance Requirements* (Washington, D.C.: Labor-Industry Coalition for International Trade, 1981). LICIT asserts that performance requirements are ipso facto distortions of trade. The extent to which such local content or export rules are or are not economically rational is debatable, however. If they were consistent with international comparative advantage, it can be argued, the companies would have adopted them on their own so as to maximize profits. Yet, in some areas of the Mexican automotive industry, for example, host country pressures have pushed international car companies along an infant industry path (or up a learning curve) that has led them to discover a new dimension of comparative advantage. (Interviews with U.S. company representatives, Mexico, November 1981.)

16. LICIT, *op. cit.*

17. For an analysis of project finance in reducing political risk, see Theodore H. Moran with Debbie Havens Maddox, *Transnational Corporations in the Copper Industry* (New York: U.N. Centre on Transnational Corporations, 1981).

18. M. Radetski and S. Zorn, *Financing Mining Projects in Developing Countries: A United Nations Study* (London: Mining Journal Books, 1979).

19. For an anlaysis of the role of World Bank participation in thirty-seven energy projects in twenty countries, 1977–1982, see Theodore H. Moran, "Does the World Bank Have a Role in the Oil and Gas Business?" Columbia Journal of World Business, Summer 1982.

20. Stephen J. Kobrin, *op cit.*

6
Small-Scale Manufacturing as a Competitive Advantage

Louis T. Wells, Jr.

The question of whether foreign investors employ technology that suits the factor proportions of the host country has always aroused special controversy. It has also been particularly perplexing since one would assume that international companies could maximize profits in the Third World by utilizing the most labor-intensive techniques available.

Although Wells reviews the general issue of appropriate technology and what policies local governments can adopt to encourage its use, he approaches the subject from a new direction. He finds that foreign investors from the Third World may employ labor-intensive processes more readily than other international corporations. In general, small-scale manufacturing industries provide special opportunities for LDC investors because economies of scale and capital-intensive technology, which are the predominant feature of multinationals, from the developed economies are less often necessary. The advantages to Third World economies of choosing an LDC investor usually outweigh the disadvantages and contribute more fully to economic development. The LDC multinational may offer not only more appropriate technology but also smaller, more efficient operations and greater attention to price competitiveness.

Since much of the research on multinationals from the advanced countries has emphasized their technological advantages, it should not be surprising to discover that technical know-how also provides many foreign investors from the developing countries with competitive advantages that enable them to survive abroad. The latter's technological advantages are of a very special kind; they reflect the investors' home markets and give the firms considerable potential for contributing to the development process in the poorer countries.

Reprinted from Louis T. Wells, Jr., *Third World Multinationals*, published by The MIT Press. © 1983 by The Massachusetts Institute of Technology.

Table 6–1
Sources of Technology of Indian Parent Firms and Their Foreign
Manufacturing Subsidiaries (1977)

| Sector | India | *Source of Parents' Original Technology* | |
		Foreign Collaboration	Imports of Foreign Machinery
Paper and cardboard	1	2	2
Chemicals, soaps, and drugs	2	1	3
Edible oils	1	2	1
Automobile ancillary	1	5	3
Foods, beverages, and confectionary	1	3	1
Construction			3
Miscellaneous light ancillary	1	5	3
Heavy industry			3
Textiles	3	2	3
Total	10	20	22

Source: Interviews conducted by Carlos Cordeiro.

Small-Scale Markets

One particular feature in developing countries that gives firms in this study an edge abroad is the small size of the markets for most manufactured goods. Entrepreneurs in developing countries have a special propensity to respond to that characteristic.

If firms in the developing countries simply import manufacturing technology commonly used in the industrialized countries, the factories are likely to be too large for their market. In 1959, for instance, Sri Lanka turned to the Soviet Union for help in establishing iron and steel works. The first plant was to be a rolling mill. The smallest rolling mill the Russians had built had a capacity of 60,000 tons of steel per year. (Even this plant was very small by the standards of industrialized countries; the average steel mill elsewhere produced some one million tons per year.) But total Sri Lankan demand was only 35,000 tons. Moreover, this demand was for a wider variety of products than the Russian mill could supply and the export potential was poor. In spite of the scale problem, the Sri Lankans, like many other developing countries, acquired the large-scale technology instead of turning to, say, India for small, manually operated rolling mills.[1] As a result, Sri Lanka utilized only about a quarter of its installed capacity for rolled steel products in 1973 and continued to import rolled steel products, largely of kinds not produced by the existing plant.

Faced with small markets for many products, entrepreneurs in developing countries can increase profits if they can adapt technology to small-scale

Source of Foreign Subsidiaries' Technology			Source of Parents' 1977 Technology	
India	Japan	Other Foreign Countries	At Least 50 Percent Indigenous	Mostly Imported
7			5	
8	1		4	2
9			4	
7	1	1	8	1
5		3	3	2
3			3	
12		1	9	
4			3	
4	1	3	8	
59	2	9	47	5

manufacture. In most cases, they start with technology from an industrialized country and adapt it later. Of 52 Indian parent firms interviewed, 42 reported that they obtained their original technology abroad, but 47 also reported that over half of their technology was "indigenous" by the time of the interview (table 6–1). One Indian firm that processes edible oil illustrates the pattern. It began operations in India in 1917 with copra crushing equipment imported from the United States. By 1976, it was using entirely Indian equipment. The local equipment was not slavishly copied from the earlier imported machinery; it was changed in response to Indian conditions. In many cases, locally adapted technology was eventually exported to foreign subsidiaries, as is apparent from the fact that "Indian machinery" was the source of know-how in most of the foreign investments for which data were available.

A manufacturing process might be scaled down in various ways. When larger plants consist primarily of duplicate pieces of equipment, such as spinning and weaving plants, little innovation is required. Some of the small-scale plants observed in this study simply used fewer pieces of equipment than large-scale plants. In other cases, adaptation to small scale means the substitution of batch processing for mass production. Packages Limited of Pakistan manufactures paper containers in short runs, and a Philippine firm manufactures pharmaceutical products in batches. Sometimes assembly lines are dropped and semifinished products are moved in batches from work station to work station, such as in several flashlight battery manufacturers in Indonesia. On occasion, labor may be substituted directly for machines. Thus, steel auto bodies may be fashioned by hand to avoid the high fixed cost of dies. To facilitate manual work, some products are redesigned. Jeepney bodies in the Philippines, for example, were designed with simple bends instead of the curves typical of auto bodies in richer countries. Similarly, a Hong Kong firm redesigned appliances to use fewer molded plastic parts. The adaptation of the manufacturing process to small scale may sometimes involve a completely different technology, such as the use of fiberglass instead of steel for auto bodies. In some cases, factories for small-scale manufacture use machinery that has been especially designed for lower output levels. A carpet maker in the Philippines uses 16-inch looms; many U.S. firms use 200-inch looms. Some factories rely on multipurpose machines to manufacture at small volumes. Thus, parts for various products may be made on standard lathes or bent with simple equipment. One firm planning for a capacity of 20,000 refrigerators per year chose multipurpose equipment for the production of cabinets. The machines could be adjusted for various models of refrigerators and for other appliances. Sometimes workers may be used, much like multipurpose machines, for a number of tasks in the production process.[2]

It is exactly these kinds of small-scale technology that were exported by many of the firms in this study. Information from Lecraw's work in Thailand bears out the point.[3] Capacity utilization is one way to confirm the small scale of developing country firms. Multinationals from the advanced countries on the average operated at only 26 percent of their capacity, whereas foreign investors from other developing countries operated at 48 percent. The role of scale is verified when the outputs of the plants of various nationalities are compared. The size of an average plant owned by an industrialized country parent was more than twice the size of an average plant owned by a developing country parent within the same industry.

In another study, Lecraw compared a group of foreign investors from Southeast Asian countries with multinationals from wealthy countries. He calculated index numbers to measure relative size for each industry, with the largest firm in the industry assigned the number 100. The size of the subsidiaries from Southeast Asian parents averaged 46; the counterparts from the industrialized countries averaged 109.[4]

A study of Taiwan's exports of capital equipment provided additional support for the contention that firms in developing countries innovate small-scale technology.[5] It demonstrated that Taiwan's advantage in such exports appears in the sale of equipment for small-scale plants.

In the interviews for this study, managers were asked how the sizes of their home plant and their subsidiaries would compare to the size of typical plants in an industrialized country. The typical answer was "smaller." The following data illustrate the sizes of the subsidiaries of firms that were interviewed. Hong Kong managers reported, as evidence, the number of looms for five overseas subsidiaries to be 3,000, 1,920, 440, 250, and 200. One Argentine firm indicated that it had 169, 240 and 168 looms in its three Brazilian mills.[6] Hong Kong firms reported the number of spindles for seven spinning subsidiaries to be 110,000, 100,000, 40,000, 23,000, 16,000, 14,000, 10,000, 10,000.[7] Two Indian firms reported 30,000 and 20,160 spindles in their subsidiaries. The Argentine firm had 14,700, 29,800, and 11,500 spindles in its foreign factories.[8] By the standards of the industrialized countries, these are almost all small plants.[9]

More evidence of the comparatively small size of factories owned by foreign investors from developing countries was provided by foreign investors in Nigeria and Indonesia. In Nigeria, textile plants owned by nationals from other developing countries were, in most cases, smaller than the subsidiaries owned by European, American, or Japanese parents.[10] In Indonesia, factories for flashlight batteries show a similar pattern. A Singapore-owned factory (with Taiwanese technicians) had a capacity of 12 million batteries per year on a one-shift basis. In contrast, an American-owned factory in Indonesia could produce more than 65 million batteries in the same period.[11]

Aggregate data are more difficult to analyze but tend to support the same conclusions. Consider Indonesia, for which a great deal of information was available about investors of various national origins. The Indonesian data suggest that there might not be any consistent differences between the subsidiaries of parents from developing countries and those from advanced countries (table 6–2). However, the overall figures are misleading. A disproportionate number of developing country subsidiaries are for food processing, and they are among the largest projects of developing countries. When one examines the capital investment by industry, a more consistent pattern emerges. Out of 8 two-digit SIC (Standard Industrial Classification) industries with both developing country and industrialized country investors, the average developing country subsidiary has a smaller investment in 6 industries. (The exceptions are in "food, beverages, and tobacco" and in "stone,

Table 6–2
Average Investment in Manufacturing Subsidiaries in Indonesia (1967–1976)

Home of Investor	Average Total Investment (× $1,000)
Chinese in Hong Kong, Singapore, and Taiwan	2,722
Other Southeast Asian countries	960
Other developing countries	3,935
Japan	5,687
United States	2,403
United Kingdom	1,189
Other industrialized countries	2,063

Source: Calculated from data on realized projects from the Indonesian Investment Board.

glass and similar products," which contain only 2 developing country projects.) In the textile and paper products industries, the average developing country subsidiary is considerably less than half the size of its competitors from industrialized countries. In the remaining cases, the difference is at least 30 percent. When the industries are broken down to the three-digit level, the results are similar. Out of 14 industries with 2 or more subsidiaries of each type of parent, the average subsidiary of a parent from another developing country is smaller in 11 cases. The exceptions are all in food and beverages, where market size is probably not a major constraint in the choice of technology.

There is a substantial risk that differences in capital-labor ratios of the two types of investors could cause the figures to be misleading, as factories with smaller total investment may actually have larger output. To account for this possibility, the plants were compared in terms of capacity of production. Unfortunately, output data were not available for Indonesia. If the employment figures were also smaller for the developing country subsidiaries, then one could feel confident in claiming that the plants were indeed smaller. Unfortunately, the data are not thoroughly convincing. In 15 of the 22 three-digit SIC industries, firms from other developing countries had fewer employees than their advanced country competitors; but the remaining 7 had more.

Although the analysis of such data lends some support to the contention that foreign investors from developing countries have smaller subsidiaries than advanced country firms, a completely convincing case cannot be built without output data. Fortunately, data reported from other countries and the interviews provided strong support for the contention that the two types of investors do build plants of very different sizes.

To be sure, the small-scale technologies used in the foreign subsidiaries of developing country parents were not always those in use in the home plants at the time the investments were made. As wage rates have risen in Hong Kong, for example, labor-intensive machinery appropriate to conditions in Hong Kong a few years earlier has been replaced with more automated equipment, and some of the old machinery has been exported to various affiliates. A complete plant was, for instance, moved to Ghana for textile manufacture. In 1979, a Brazilian bicycle manufacturer had a large-scale factory at home but established a small-scale subsidiary in Bolivia. Managers pointed out that the capacity of the new Bolivian plant was comparable to that of the parent company in Brazil only ten years earlier. Although the Brazilian firm's small-scale technology was outdated at home, in the small Bolivian market it was quite appropriate[12] and not easily available from the advanced countries where such techniques had been long forgotten.

Characteristics of Small-Scale Technology

The most striking characteristic of the technology developed by firms in response to small markets is its labor intensity. India's small-scale sugar mills, for example, employ about three times the workers and a half or a third the capital for the same volume as a mill from an advanced country.[13]

The pattern is similar for the firms examined in this study. Capital-labor ratios for subsidiaries of parents from developing countries with those of subsidiaries of parents from industrialized countries offer the simplest kind of comparison.[14] In Indonesia, the first group uses, on average, only $8,500 of capital for each worker employed; the second group uses $16,300. (Table 6–3 breaks down the data further by nationality of investor.) The striking differences do not result from any special characteristics of Chinese firms, which are very important in Indonesia. It is apparent that investors from developing countries, Chinese or not, use more labor-intensive techniques than do investors from the advanced countries.

Such gross comparisons of capital-labor ratios are quite dangerous, as the observed differences could result from differences in industries in which the various investors are found. Developing country firms might be attracted to industries that are inherently more labor-intensive than those that attract firms from the advanced countries. A breakdown of investment by industry, therefore, allows a more careful comparison of firms originating from different countries. When the original Indonesian industry classifications are used, eight two-digit industries contain subsidiaries of parents from both developing and industrialized countries, and in all eight, the capital-labor ratios of the plants with parents from other developing countries are lower than those of their counterparts from the industrialized countries. In only one case (food and beverages) was the ratio for developing country firms more than 65 percent of the ratio for subsidiaries of firms from the industrialized countries. At the three-digit level, the average investors from other developing countries are more labor-intensive in 13 out of the 14 industries that have

Table 6–3
Capital-Labor Ratios in Manufacturing Subsidiaries in Indonesia (1967–1976)

Home of Investor	Average Capital-Labor Ratios (× $1,000/Worker)	Median Capital-Labor Ratios (× $1,000/Worker)
Chinese in Hong Kong, Singapore, and Taiwan	8.3	4.9
Other Southeast Asian countries	8.2	4.5
Other developing countries	10.4	9.4
Japan	18.8	14.1
United States	16.9	10.5
United Kingdom	19.9	10.6
Other industrialized countries	13.2	8.6

Source: Calculated from data on realized projects from the Indonesian Investment Board.

two or more of each group of firms. The exception again is in food products, where market size provides little constraint on scale.

The results might not arise from differences in technology but from differences in investments for building, working capital, or other assets. The figures for investment in machinery per employee, however, show a pattern similar to that for total investment per worker. The developing country firms invest less in machinery for each job created (table 6–4). These differences are only slightly less striking than the differences in overall capital-labor figures. In five of the eight industries, a comparison of the value of machinery per worker for the firms from other developing countries and the firms from industrialized countries indicates less difference than do the figures for total capital invested per worker.

An understanding of why the two measures differ slightly is not critical at this point, but the differences should not be surprising. Total investment reflects building and working capital as well as machinery. One might argue that a labor-intensive factory would require a larger building to house the greater number of workers. The observed results could arise from either of two sources. One possibility is that investors from developing countries spend less on building than do their industrialized counterparts. Another possible explanation of the pattern is that the developing country firms invest less in working capital. The fact that the Indonesian data show fixed assets as a slightly higher percentage of total investment for the investors from developing countries suggests that this might indeed be the case. One could argue that labor-intensive factories need more working capital than would capital-intensive plants because of the need to meet regular wage bills. One could also argue that such factories can run with smaller inventories and thus need less working capital. On this point, one can only speculate, particularly since the Indonesian data come from official application forms in which

Table 6–4
Machinery Investment per Worker in Manufacturing Subsidiaries in Indonesia (1967–1976)

Home of Investor	Average Machinery Investment (× $1,000/Worker)
Chinese in Hong Kong, Singapore, and Taiwan	4.42
Other Southeast Asian countries	2.92
Other developing countries	4.89
Japan	8.14
United States	5.37
United Kingdom	5.34
Other industrialized countries	7.14

Source: Calculated from data on realized projects from the Indonesian Investment Board.

working capital could only be estimated. My own guess is that firms from developing countries invest less in buildings and have a slight tendency to underestimate the required working capital when they apply for investment permits.

The main point, that the labor intensity of technology used by foreign investors from developing countries is high, is strongly supported by rather sophisticated analysis of Thai data.[15] Since output data were available for that country, Lecraw was able to estimate production functions for 12 four-digit industries. The results effectively demonstrate that foreign investors from other developing countries use more labor-intensive technology than either Thai firms or foreign investors from industrialized countries.

Another major difference that distinguishes the projects of foreign investors from developing countries from those of local firms in their host countries and those of the multinationals from the industrialized countries is flexibility. Flexibility was emphasized quite explicitly by the manager of a Hong Kong textile firm with subsidiaries in Indonesia and Malaysia, who said that the operations "have to be flexible to weave many kinds of textiles and spin many kinds of yarn. We don't make something and then sell it." The implication was that advanced country multinationals make a small variety of products and then devote their efforts to convincing consumers to accept the standardized versions, while his firm responds to market niches by providing a wide range of products.

Since one specialized model or version of a product is unlikely to have a sufficiently large market in developing countries to keep typical machines fully occupied, machines are designed or chosen for their flexibility. Thus, Packages Limited of Pakistan carefully studied the downtime involved in product changeovers for various kinds of European machinery used for making paper packages and used these studies to select equipment that minimizes the costs of short runs of many products. Similarly, a Hong Kong appliance maker selected sheet metal working equipment that can be used to produce various models of both stoves and refrigerators. The manager of a Hong Kong textile firm with spinning facilities in Indonesia explained that using "small package spindles" was more labor-intensive than the usual spindles, requiring more loading and unloading, but was "more flexible." A manager from a Southeast Asian pharmaceutical firm that makes as many as 400 products at home and 50–100 products in the company's foreign subsidiaries reported that the plants "must use the same equipment for many products."

In their efforts to design flexible plants, firms from developing countries occasionally build a special kind of excess capacity into their factories. The plant design includes extra machines required to produce special models or versions of the basic products, even though those machines may stay idle much of the year. The Hong Kong textile manager just quoted explained that he did "not expect every piece of equipment to be used all the time." Packages

Limited had a simple machine for making paper cups that was used only occasionally, since the principal customer for paper cups, the Pakistani national airline, did not order enough to keep the machine fully occupied. Nevertheless, paper cups and similar products were needed to fill out the company's line and keep other machinery busy.

In some cases, the design of a flexible, small-scale plant depends largely on knowing well equipment available from a large number of suppliers in the industrialized countries. A German machine for one step may be combined with an Italian one for the next operation. A few firms in the developing countries have made the large investment required to learn about a wide range of such equipment. They not only have collected specifications but have tried the equipment for reliability and know the availability of spare parts. Once acquired, such knowledge is useful in other small markets.

The special knowledge possessed by some companies from developing countries is quite extensive. One firm I interviewed had drawn up a list of suppliers for various pieces of equipment. The list covered a wide range of European suppliers and included the capacity and cost of the equipment and the set-up time required to adjust the equipment to other kinds of output. The supplying firms were evaluated according to their delivery and service records; the machines, according to their needs for maintenance. This was invaluable information for competition with firms in other countries.

To meet the special needs of small-scale manufacture, a number of developing countries have manufactured their own machinery. When special machinery from the home country was used by the firms interviewed, it was usually made by the firm that operated it, not by specialist machinery manufacturers. Typically, a firm started at home with all, or almost all, imported equipment. As the company replaced imported machinery or expanded, the experience gained by its technicians enabled it to supply more of the technology and machinery internally.[16] Eventually, some of this machinery was used abroad. For instance, the original plant of Packages Limited in Pakistan began with equipment acquired in Europe. Spare parts, however, were expensive by the time they reached Pakistan, and lead times in acquiring them were such that repairs could not be made quickly. Moreover, some of the original European equipment was second-hand and quite old; parts for this machinery were not easily available even in Europe. Since local shops were unable to make needed parts quickly and reliably, the firm established its own machine shop and foundry. The shop had excess capacity as long as it supplied only spares, so the shop operators began to experiment with modifications to the original machinery that might improve its performance. Such modifications in some cases increased flexibility by generally decreasing set-up time. Gradually, the shop began to copy the imported machines, but with modifications that were useful for short runs of many products. Eventually, the shop was producing a number of machines largely of its own design, with special features in response to local problems. As Packages Limited ventured outside of Pakistan, it provided its foreign affiliates with machinery of its own manufacture.[17]

Since U.S. studies have discovered the importance of a close link between the use of capital equipment and the supplier for successful innovation,[18] it should perhaps not be surprising that the adapted equipment in developing countries is so often made "in-house." If innovations were undertaken by firms that are first and foremost machinery manufacturers, they would probably be involved in some of the investments uncovered in this study. To sell innovative machines abroad, little-known machinery manufacturers from developing countries might well have to take equity positions in facilities that would use the machinery. The infrequency of foreign investments by firms that were primarily machinery manufacturers suggests that they have not been as innovative as some of the equipment users who felt pressing needs for changes in the machinery.

Investors from developing countries obtain a considerable amount of their equipment from their home nations. For this study, data were available on the source of machinery for 151 subsidiaries; 122 subsidiaries imported machinery from their home country (or, occasionally, another developing country). A study of Taiwanese firms found that more than 30 percent of their foreign investment in nontrade activities was made up of Taiwanese machinery.[19] The Indians are particularly likely to use equipment from home. Given the Indian government requirements that Indian firms use Indian machinery overseas, the finding is not surprising. Firms from other developing countries bring a quarter of their machinery from their home countries. Although this fraction is smaller than the fraction of home machinery used by investors from the advanced countries, it is still a large number given the small amount of machinery manufactured and exported by developing countries. Table 6–5 shows the sources of various foreign investors in Thailand.

A striking fact that appears in table 6–5 is that a quarter of the machinery of developing country investors is made in Thailand, which is more than even local investors use. Thus, the foreign investors have a high propensity to use local machinery as well as local materials in Thailand. My impression from interviews is that locally produced machinery is usually made to order to designs supplied by the parent.

Machines newly manufactured at home or in the host country and carefully selected new machinery from the industrialized countries do not exhaust the sources of small-scale equipment for foreign investment by firms from the developing countries. Second-hand machinery provides an important alternative.[20] In most cases, such machinery was produced in an industrialized country, but when the market there was smaller or before technological change had increased the optimal scale for the high-wage country.[21]

Table 6–5
Source of Machinery in Manufacturing Firms in Thailand (1962–1974)

| | Source of Machinery (%) | | | | | |
| | United States | Europe | Japan | India | Other Developing Countries | Thailand | Total (%) |
Home of Investor							
United States	51	25	16	0	0	8	100
Europe	20	57	13	0	0	10	100
Japan	6	4	80	0	0	10	100
India	4	10	8	45	8	25	100
Other developing countries	7	8	30	5	25	25	100
Thailand	30	27	26	2	25	13	100

Source: Donald Lecraw, "Choice of Technology in Low-Wage Countries," unpublished doctoral dissertation in business economics, Harvard University, 1976. Original data from Thai Investment Board and interviews.

The interviews for this study identified a large number of subsidiaries that operated some second-hand machinery. Machinery formerly used in Hong Kong, for example, has been located all over Southeast Asia and as far away as West Africa.

In most cases, old machinery is more labor-intensive and flexible than new equipment. In the textile industry, for instance, spinning equipment of 1950 vintage has roughly half the output per man-hour of 1968 equipment.[22] To be sure, occasionally newer machinery is more flexible; recent innovations in electronic controls for carpet weaving have increased flexibility, according to the manager of one firm interviewed. Although applications of electronics to machinery may make this kind of case more common, in the late 1970s it seemed that "old" usually implied "flexible."

In sum, foreign investors from developing countries obtain their equipment from a range of sources, but regardless of the source, the machinery that is selected is usually flexible, labor-intensive, and suited for relatively small-scale manufacture.

Low Overheads

Low overheads give many developing country firms a strength that supports their ability to manufacture at small volumes with low unit costs. The savings in overhead costs derive largely from the low salaries that such firms pay to managers and technicians and partly from the small expenditures on buildings.

Hong Kong-based foreign investors in one study reported that they consider lower costs for managerial and technical staff as their most important advantage over other multinationals.[23] The possible contribution to competitive position of low expatriate salaries is suggested by a study of U.S.-based multinationals that reported that expatriate costs represented 4 to 20 percent of the pretax profits of all international operations.[24] Since the number of expatriates in a subsidiary is not proportional to the size of sales, the costs would be an even larger percentage of profits for small operations in developing countries.

The salaries paid to managers and technicians of the foreign subsidiaries of firms from developing countries appear strikingly low compared to those paid by a multinational from an industrialized country. An Indian firm reported paying a department head between $350 and $700 a month at home, with no significant premiums for overseas assignments. A Hong Kong textile firm reported salaries for its engineers in Indonesia of about $1,000 to $1,200 per month, considerably less than that of a U.S. or European engineer stationed in Southeast Asia. Many of the managers and technicians from developing countries do not take their families with them on overseas assignments, even when the assignment is a year or more. This is especially true for Pakistani and Taiwanese firms. The result is more savings for the firm.

Two additional characteristics of compensation for managers are, in some cases, important in saving overheads for the firms in this study. In a number of Hong Kong enterprises, managers receive a significant part of their income in the form of a bonus, which is large only if the subsidiary does well. For such firms, the fixed costs associated with expatriate managers are comparatively low. In addition, the managers are, in many cases, relatives of the owners of the parent firm. For Chinese firms particularly, the relatives would be drawing a certain amount of income out of the enterprise even if they were not managing a foreign subsidiary. Thus, their incremental cost to the enterprise is small.

Why developing country investors spend less than multinationals from advanced countries on building and operate in more cramped quarters is less apparent, but this fact has been observed before.[25] The traveler in the developing world can hardly avoid being struck by the attractive, modern buildings of the advanced country multinationals. In many cases, they are virtual carbon copies of plants at home. In Indonesia, the Jakarta Coca-Cola bottling plant is, for example, hardly distinguishable from a Coca-Cola bottling plant in a medium-size U.S. city, even down to having windows for pedestrians to watch the automatic bottling equipment.[26] The plant is spacious and attractive and expensive. On the other hand, the Singapore-based F&N bottling plant in Jakarta is clean, sturdy, and seemingly quite adequate to the task but simple and somewhat crowded. Some of the Chinese-owned plastic sandal factories in Indonesia are more austere. Many operate from little more than rudimentary sheds, jammed with workers, inventory, and equipment. The manager may have only a tiny cubicle in a corner, filled with files and papers. Data on buildings in Mauritius and the Philippines indicate the same pattern.

The reasons for the different approaches to buildings probably lie in the role that image plays in the marketing strategies of firms from different areas. For certain multinationals from rich countries, such as Coca-Cola, image is important, and buildings play at least some part in maintaining that image. . . . Image is second to price and cost in the strategies of most foreign investors from developing countries.

The savings that can accrue from low overhead add up. The Thai data show administrative expenses to be only 5 percent of sales for foreign investors from developing countries. For the traditional multinationals, they amount to 14 percent.[28]

Exploiting the Advantage

The firm that ventures abroad from a developing country has two principal types of competition: firms indigenous to the country in which they are investing and multinationals from the industrialized nations. If the advantage of the firm from another developing country lies in small-scale manufacture, a potential indigenous competitor would have to develop similar skills or work out some kind of arrangement to obtain the skills from a foreign enterprise. To develop the skills at home, the potential competitor must incur costs similar to those already incurred by the foreign firm. If the equipment is designed and produced by the firm, the development costs are likely to be high. If the technology involves the gathering of machinery from a number of countries, the expenses involved in searching out such sources will be significant. If the machinery is second-hand, the task is to find reliable sources. Even when the potential competitor is knowledgeable about suppliers, the risks associated with purchase appear great, and the variance in performance of second-hand equipment is large.[29] The search for a reliable dealer is likely to involve some costly mistakes. Moreover, in most cases, the firm that has experience with small-scale technology has lower costs that have resulted from using technology over a period of time. A potential competitor must incur the costs of acquiring experience before it can be on equal footing with the foreign firm. Whatever the nature of the costs required of the potential indigenous competitor, they are almost certainly greater than those involved in transferring the foreign firm's skills to the potential competitor's country.

A multinational from the United States, Europe, or Japan could, it would seem, apply its formidable skills to scale down production and develop technology that is most suitable for developing countries. Through its large network, the multinational enterprise could spread the development costs over many plants. In fact, multinationals have usually not devoted their resources to down-scaling. Rather, they have preferred to concentrate on advanced technology or on marketing skills that enable them to avoid worrying about production costs. Most see their comparative advantages in fields other than small-scale manufacture. Even if they were to develop the know-how and experience, as some have attempted (such as Philips of The Netherlands),[30] they would still be saddled with high overhead costs not assumed by the investor from a developing country.

The strategies of a number of multinationals from the advanced countries have been just the opposite. Some familiar firms have built or preserved a competitive advantage in their international businesses by integrating operations across national boundaries. In some cases, such integration has allowed the enterprises to obtain low production costs through sheer scale of manufacture. In Europe, Ford Motor Company has, since the 1960s, designed its automobiles so that certain components are common to models offered in different markets. Common components are produced for all of Europe in large, specialized plants in one or two places. The German and British operations, for example, trade certain engines and transmissions that they produce in large volumes. Another approach in the search for economies of scale is to specialize plants by models of the final product rather than by parts. Volkswagen, for example, has produced the "Safari" in Mexico ("The Thing" in the U.S. market) for several of its overseas markets, even though some of those markets have plants that produce other models of Volkswagen.

In some truly exceptional cases, similar integration strategies appear from time to time among firms from the developing countries. A Peruvian firm, Pan Americana, produced television programs in several countries. The same programs could be used in different markets; moreover, there were opportunities to obtain certain kinds of talent cheaply in one country and other kinds in other countries. To take advantage of the opportunities, Pan Americana operated in Argentina, Puerto Rico, Venezuela, and cities of the continental United States with a large Spanish-speaking population. The international business ground to a halt only when the Peruvian government restricted the firm's activities and eventually acquired control. Similarly, Televisa, a large Mexican television firm, established operations in Los Angeles and elsewhere in the United States.[31] The firm is able to use the same programs in Mexico and for the Latin American community in Los Angeles.

In conventional manufacturing, no developing country firms were encountered that had integrated operations across borders. Rather than attempting to emulate firms from the richer countries, the developing country investors stuck by their skill in small-scale manufacture. The reader should not, however, be misled. The factories are neither primitive nor tiny. They are not the rural, almost handicraft industries of Ghandi. And . . . running them demands a great deal of management and technical skills.

Notes

1. P.T. Sirisena, "An Evaluation of the Efficiency, Foreign Exchange Savings and the Welfare Impact of the Steel Industry in Sri Lanka," *Staff Studies 5* (September 1975), pp. 15–32. For evidence that the socialist suppliers provided technology of a scale similar to that of capitalist suppliers, see UNCTAD, "Major Issues Arising from the Transfer of Technology: A Case Study of Sri Lanka," TD/B/C.6/6, 35, October 7, 1975.

2. For a summary of approaches to down-scaling, see R.B. McKern, "Working Paper," for Experts Meeting on Down-scaling and Adaptation of Industrial Technology, Paris, OECD, June 27–29, 1977.

3. These and other results are reported in Donald Lecraw, "Direct Investment by Firms from Less Developed Countries," *Oxford Economic Papers,* November 1977, pp. 442–457.

4. Donald Lecraw, "The Internationalization of Firms from LDC's: Evidence from the ASEAN Region," in Krishna Kumar and Maxwell McLeod, eds., *Multinationals from Developing Countries* (Lexington, Mass.: Lexington Books, 1981).

5. Yung W. Rhee and Larry E. Westphal, "A Note on Exports of Technology from the Republics of China and Korea," mimeograph, 1978, p. 10.

6. See 1973 annual report of Santista Textiles.

7. The two largest weaving factories and the two largest spinning facilities of the Hong Kong firms belonged to "Textile Alliance, Ltd." a firm 45 percent owned by Toray of Japan and highly integrated into the international network of that parent. Because of its ownership, Textile Alliance was included in the study with some hesitancy.

8. See 1973 annual report of Santista Textiles.

9. Lest the reader conclude from these figures that Hong Kong firms are especially large, the average annual sales for different groups of firms were compared, where data were available. The figures for Hong Kong firms were smaller than those for Argentine firms. The average Hong Kong firm is almost exactly the same size as the average foreign investor from all developing countries.

10. C.N.S. Nambudiri et al., in Kumar and McLeod, eds., *Multinationals from Developing Countries.* The study did not clearly distinguish operations owned by foreign firms from operations owned by entrepreneurs of foreign ethnic stock.

11. Louis T. Wells, Jr., "Economic Man and Engineering Man," *Public Policy,* Summer 1973, pp. 319–342.

12. For a number of examples of small-scale technologies that have generated foreign investment in Latin America, see Eduardo White, "The International Projection of Firms from Latin American Countries," in Kumar and McLeod, eds., *Multinationals from Developing Countries.*

13. C.G. Baron, "Sugar Processing Techniques in India," mimeograph from International Labour Office, Geneva, January 1973; and M.K. Garg, "The Scaling-Power of Modern Technology: Crystal Sugar Manufacturing in India," in Nicolas Jequier, ed., *Appropriate Technology Problems and Promises* (Paris: Development Centre of the OECD, 1976). In the case of sugar, the small-scale technology uses more sugar cane.

14. UNCTAD, "Major Issues Arising from the Transfer of Technology," table 13 presents comparable data for a few firms in Sri Lanka. The developing country investors are the most labor-intensive of the group.

15. See Donald Lecraw, "Choice of Technology in Low-Wage Countries: The Case of Thailand," doctoral dissertation in business economics, Harvard University, 1976; and Donald Lecraw, "Direct Investment by Firms from Less Developed Countries."

16. See Ashok Desai, "Research and Development in India," *Margin*, January 1975, p. 90.

17. Note that in many poorer countries, machinery may be imported with little or no duty, while final products face heavy import barriers.

18. See Nathan Rosenberg, Alexander Thompson, and Steven E. Belsley, "Technology Change and Productivity in the Air Transport Industry," NASA *Technical Memorandum 78505,* Moffett Field, Calif., September 1978; Nathan Rosenberg, "Learning by Using," mimeograph, Stanford University, n.d. See also Henry J. Bruton, "On the Production of Appropriate Technology," Research Memorandum Series, No. 13, The Center for Development Economics, Williams College, December 1979, pp. 42–48; and Eric von Hippel, "Users as Innovators," *Technology Review,* January 1978, pp. 31–39.

19. Wen-Lee Ting and Chi Schive, "Direct Investment and Technology Transfer from Taiwan," in Kumar and McLeod, eds., *Multinationals from Developing Countries.*

20. The relation of scale to used equipment is explored in Dilmus James, "Used Automated Plants in Less Developed Countries: A Case Study of a Mexican Firm," *Interamerican Economic Affairs*, vol. 27, no. 1, Summer 1973.

21. The characteristics of second-hand machinery are complex. An interesting study of second-hand jute processing equipment points out that such equipment appears on the market at various times for a number of reasons: changes may occur in machinery technology, product demand may shift, maintenance costs may become too high for a high-wage country, and so on. See Charles Cooper and Raphael Kaplinksy, "Second-hand Equipment in a Developing Country: Jute Processing in Kenya." Discussion Paper No. 37, Institute for Development Studies, University of Sussex, December 1973. See also Howard Pack, "The Optimality of Used Equipment: Calculations for the Cotton Textile Industry," *Economic Development and Cultural Change,* January 1978, pp. 307–324.

22. See R.B. McKern, Working Paper for the OECD Development Centre Experts Meeting on Down-Scaling and Adaptation of Industrial Technology, Paris, April 1977.

23. Edward K.Y. Chen, "Hong Kong Multinationals in Asia," in Kumar and McLeod, eds., *Multinationals from Developing Countries.*

24. Marion R. Foote, "Controlling the Cost of International Compensation," *Harvard Business Review,* November-December 1977, p. 124. See also Nambudiri et al., "Third World Investors in Nigeria," in Kumar and McLeod, eds., *Multinationals from Developing Countries.*

25. See, for example, R. Hal Mason, "The Transfer of Technology and the Factor Proportions Problem: The Philippines and Mexico," *UNITAR Research Report No. 10,* U.N. Institute for Training and Research, New York, n.d.

26. The operation is a Japanese investment operating under U.S. license.

27. Reported in Vinod Busjeet, "Foreign Investors from Less-Developed Countries: A Strategic Profile," unpublished doctoral dissertation, Harvard Business School, 1980.

28. See Donald Lecraw, "Choice of Technology in Low-Wage Countries: The Case of Thailand," unpublished doctoral dissertation in business economics, Harvard University, 1976.

29. See, for example, Cooper and Kaplinsky, "Second-hand Equipment in a Developing Country."

30. See the description in R.B. McKern, Working Paper for the OECD Development Centre Experts Meeting on Down-Scaling and Adaptation of Industrial Technology, pp. 29–35. See also Thomas G. Parry, "The Multinational Enterprise and Two-Stage Technology Transfer to Developing Countries," in Robert G. Hawkins and A.J. Prasad, eds., *Research in International Business and Finance* (Greenwich, Conn.: JAI Press, Inc., 1981), vol. 2, pp. 175–192.

31. For a brief description, see Jorge Casta Castaneda, "La Exportación de Capitales como Inversión," *Uno Mas Uno*, August 13, 1980.

Part II
Multinational Corporations and the Developed World

7

Multinational Corporations and the Developed World: An Analytical Overview

Theodore H. Moran

The evidence of growing power on the part of host governments in the Third World presented in part I of this book has been accompanied by mirror-image concerns about the impact of outward investment on the economy of the home countries. Such concerns have a long legacy, with controversies about whether overseas investment flows drain resources from the domestic industrial base being a perennial subject, for example, among British writers.[1] In the United States, Robert Gilpin has drawn an analogy between the British historical experience and the contemporary period in the United States, warning that although foreign investment can benefit the owners of capital, it may do so at a cost to the economic position of the mother country. From his geopolitical perspective, outward investment "contributes to an international redistribution of power to the disadvantage of the core."[2]

Following in this same tradition, critics from organized labor in the United States charge that U.S. multinationals ship capital rather than goods abroad, export jobs, and undermine the U.S. industrial base. The overseas operations of U.S. firms constitute an international version of the runaway plant, moving abroad to escape the burden of higher wages and better standards that workers in the home country have struggled for decades to achieve. If U.S. companies were forced to keep more of their operations at home, in this view, they would make a larger contribution to U.S. economic strength and welfare.[3] Moving beyond mere trade protectionism, union representatives combine a plea for restraints on imported products with more sophisticated proposals for controls on outward investment as well. They advocate changes in tax policy to make foreign operations less attractive and/or direct restraints on the freedom of U.S. companies to move abroad.

Multinational Investment, Deindustrialization, and Trade Protectionism

Sol Chaikin, vice-president of the AFL-CIO and president of the International Ladies' Garment Workers' Union, presents in chapter 8 a historical overview of the postwar commitment of the United States to unrestricted trade and outward investment. He points out that the liberal approach to international economic policy grew up during the emergence of the United States after World War II as the dominant economy in the world, possessing more than half of global industrial production. With an unchallenged position in world markets and seemingly unlimited industrial potential, the United States supplied Europe and Japan with the financial assistance, technological know-how, and direct investment necessary to rebuild their own industrial base.

Although this approach did confer some political and strategic benefits, Chaikin argues that there was a long-term cost as well: U.S. postwar economic predominance could not continue indefinitely. Once Europe and Japan were launched on the road to recovery, they devoted increasing attention to exports. The result was steadily climbing import penetration ratios for the United States in the 1960s in selected labor-intensive manufacturing industries such as textiles and electronics. In the 1970s, the challenge to U.S. industry broadened, affecting capital-intensive sectors such as automobiles and steel as well.

Chaikin suggests that these rising import penetration ratios cause a cycle of damage in the U.S. economy that is self-perpetuating. The decline in demand for U.S. products in the face of increasing imports results in excess domestic capacity. This leads to both lower profit margins and higher prices because the same fixed overhead costs must be amortized over fewer units of production. Overall labor productivity goes down since many managerial, technical, and clerical functions must be performed regardless of lower output levels. There is lower activity in supplier industries as well. The most harmful long-term effect is the decline in the level of domestic investment.

Unrestricted outward investment compounds the problem of deindustrialization in the United States, according to Chaikin. Once a sector in the United States is penetrated by imports, investment incentives for domestic expansion and modernization weaken. Rather than sinking additional resources into domestic plant and equipment, corporations judge that it may make more sense to seek greater profits abroad where the return on investment is higher. This profit advantage occurs because labor is the most variable cost of production in the international economy. With lower wage rates and inadequate employment practices, there is a permanent incentive for international investment in the developing economies. No one benefits but the multinationals, according to Chaikin.

What does contemporary research have to say about Chaikin's argument? Clearly, as the United States has become more interdependent with the rest of the world, the pressure from imports has played a growing role in forcing the rest of the economy to adjust. From the early 1950s to the early 1980s, the share of GNP represented by imports of goods and services has tripled, from 4 percent to 12 percent.[4]

Conventional trade theory holds that this growing interdependence has a beneficial impact for all economies. (Even with the rapidly rising levels of imports into the United States, the percentage of Japanese GNP represented by imports is still one-and-a-half times as large as the U.S. GNP; the percentage of the GNPs of Great Britain, France, and Germany represented by imports is twice as large as that of the United States.) Greater flows of goods, services, and capital maximize comparative advantage and leave every economy better off.[5] Nations with growing comparative advantages will gain from doing more of what they do best. Nations with declining comparative advantages will gain by doing less of what they do least well. Consumers have more choice, better products, and lower prices.

Moreover, there is a stimulative interaction between trade and economic growth, what William Cline has described as a "virtuous circle": economic growth leads to an even faster expansion of trade, which leads to greater economic growth, and so on.[6] From 1950 to 1975, the merchandise trade of the developed states experienced a rise of 8 percent per year, helping to support historically high economic growth rates of more than 4 percent per year. Without the stimulus of trade, those growth rates would have been substantially lower. Conversely, the restriction of trade produces a negative impact on economic activity. This leads to greater pressures for protection and steepens the downward spiral.

But what about the longer-run evolution of comparative advantage? Is the liberal approach to international economic relations espoused by the United States resulting, as Chaikin hypothesizes, in a fundamental process of deindustrialization?

The evidence thus far does not support Chaikin's argument about deindustrialization. It is true, as Robert Lawrence has pointed out, that the share of manufactured output has declined over the past three decades (largely in response to changing patterns of demand as U.S. incomes have risen), but the volume of output in the manufacturing sector has grown steadily throughout the period.[7] Value-added in manufacturing in 1982 was 17 percent higher than in 1975. In terms of domestic investment, the capital stock in manufacturing rose at a rate of 3.3 percent per year from 1960 to 1973 and at a higher 4.5 percent per year from 1973 to 1980.[8] Real research and development (R&D) spending did decline from an average annual rate of 3.1 percent between 1960 and 1973 to 2.5 percent between 1973 and 1980 but not the component devoted to U.S. industry. In the earlier period, real R&D expenditures in manufacturing grew 1.9 percent per year; in the latter period, it accelerated to 2.4 percent per year. Moreover, the private sector component of

R&D spending has been stronger, and steadier, than government-financed R&D, growing from 1.2 percent of GNP in 1961 to 1.4 percent in 1973 to 1.6 percent in 1980.

With regard to jobs, employment in U.S. manufacturing has risen from 15.2 million in 1950 to 16.8 million in 1960, 19.4 million in 1970, to 20.3 million in 1980. True, the capital-labor ratio in manufacturing grew more rapidly over the same period, supporting the view that automation has been taking place. But automation has not come at the expense of an absolute shrinkage in the manufacturing labor force.

Beyond the question of deindustrialization, how has international competition affected the structure of U.S. economy? Besides more products and lower prices for consumers, conventional economic theory also predicts that trade will speed the shift from less efficient to more efficient sectors. Does this mean the United States will merely become a nation of service activities, car washes, and fast food restaurants, or will it remain a preeminent industrial power?

In general, it is true that there has been a growth in the demand for services as Americans have spent more of their income on such items as education, medical care, government programs, and finance. This has meant a greater share of inputs going into the service sector and a smaller share of inputs going into manufacturing. In terms of output, however, the ratio of manufactured goods to GNP has stayed constant over the period 1960–1980 at approximately 45 percent of GNP, and the ratio of value-added in manufacturing to GNP has actually grown. This is because productivity has risen more rapidly in manufacturing than elsewhere in the economy.

Within the manufacturing sector itself, some of the shift produced by international competition has been intersectoral, from low technology to high technology. Industries with rapid rates of technological innovation (industrial chemicals, plastic products, machinery, electrical machinery, and professional goods) increased their employment share by 9 percent from 1973 to 1979. Industries with more mature technology (such as textiles, apparel, leather, footware, furniture, metals, shipbuilding) decreased their employment share by 6 percent from 1973 to 1978.

Some of the shift produced by international competition has also been intrasectoral, from less effective to more effective use of resources within the same industry. The latter has produced benefits even in sectors where competitive advantage appears to be weakening. In the United States, the cases of textiles, footware, and steel are instructive.[9] Despite efforts to slow the evolution of the international industry, change has had a favorable impact on the more efficient producers, as well as on consumers in all three. In textiles, the United States actually exports more than it imports (albeit not finished apparel; the U.S. advantage is in high-speed looms). In footwear, the industry has evolved to the point where there are several segments in which no other country can match the United States (long production run, injection molded shoes). In steel, the greatest market expansion at the expense of giants like Bethlehem and U.S. Steel has come not from foreign producers but from more advanced and efficient minimills.

What about the question of jobs? The absolute number of manufacturing jobs has risen by 5 million since 1950. Within the manufacturing sector, the sum of jobs created minus jobs destroyed by trade has been positive; that is, trade has provided a net addition to U.S. employment in manufacturing.

Looking behind this net effect, do policies of protectionism actually increase the size of the work force? Clearly specific protectionist actions may be able to protect specific jobs, albeit at a high price for society. The voluntary restraint agreement for automobiles with Japan did save some employment for U.S. workers in 1983–1984, for example, but it did so at a cost of approximately $160,000 per job.[10] In the aggregate, however, the search for a solution of the problem of unemployment by restrictions on trade frequently has a counterproductive result.[11] Limitations on copper imports proposed in 1984 to help save miners' jobs in Arizona and Montana would have produced even greater numbers of unemployed among copper fabricators in Indiana, Pennsylvania, and New Jersey whose products could not compete with rivals that had access to cheap foreign copper. Protection for U.S. steel has stunted the growth of the work force across the spectrum of U.S. equipment manufacturers, which are stuck with high-cost steel inputs.

Given the fact that restrictions lead to higher prices for consumers, losses in real income for society, and declines in the number of jobs for workers, Bruno Frey has advanced the proposition that democratic governments ought to be expected to win votes by supporting measures that lead to greater openness for the international economic system.[12] Instead, popularly chosen governments regularly turn to protectionist and restrictionist policies. Why?

Public choice theorists offer three principal kinds of explanations. First, there is an organizational explanation.[13] The costs of adjustment to those hurt by a more open system are concentrated while the benefits are dispersed. The losers have a direct interest in trying to protect themselves; they are more visible; they can organize themselves more easily; and they cause more concern to locally elected political representatives. The gainers are affected much less as individuals; they extend over society as a whole; they suffer from the free rider problem (a member of a large group may not bestir himself to participate in struggling for a goal whose benefits he will enjoy anyway if other members of the group achieve it).

Second, there is a payoff explanation.[14] Restrictions on trade and investment generate rents. Seeking protection is one of the most lucrative activities a firm, and its associated labor, can undertake, producing by some estimates an average of more than 200 percent on investment (legal fees) per year, with the U.S. government picking up almost 90 percent of the costs no matter what the outcome.[15] And success gives the protection seekers new resources to influence the political process in their favor.

Third, there is a lack-of-compensation-for-adjustment explanation.[16] Society should in principle be willing to buy off those who bear the brunt of the adjustment burden. From the point of view of gains versus expenditures, this would be one of the most cost-effective social programs in existence, with benefits averaging from fifty to one hundred times full compensation for adjustment costs.[17] But adjustment assistance programs in general have been both miserly and ill designed. They have not provided enough resources for uprooting a family, sending a middle-aged adult to college, or launching a new career. Instead they have tended to prolong the resistance to change.[18]

In addition to these explanations is the fact that the jobs created in the adjustment process are likely to be nonunion, leaving leaders of organized labor open to the charge that they do not fight politically for jobs in general; they only fight for unionized jobs.

As a consequence of all these factors, the pressures for limitations on the flows of goods and capital are strong. Since 1977 there has been a wave of new protectionism concentrated not in a demand for tariffs but in pressures for orderly marketing agreements and voluntary export restraints on supplier governments. Bela Belassa and Carol Belassa estimate that in 1980 20 percent of the total U.S. consumption of manufactured goods had been covered by major nontariff barriers. By 1983, this had grown to 35 percent, including textiles, apparel, automobiles, steel, footware, and televisions.[19] In short, the mere calculation of comparative costs and benefits, however persuasive in the abstract, is not at all certain to produce the most desirable public policy outcomes. Instead, democratic systems are likely to be biased on behalf of favoring protection for workers, industries, and communities.

Multinational Investment and Other Concerns of Organized Labor: The Question of Whether Multinationals Export Jobs

The issue of whether restrictions on outward investment might stimulate exports and save jobs in the home country is more complex than trade protectionism toward imports. It is one of several questions taken up in chapter 9 by Richard Caves.

Chapter 8 focused on the broad concern that pressures from international competition may be spurring a process of deindustrialization in the United States. There are other more specific issues of interest to labor as well. Caves addresses three of them: (1) whether foreign investment alters the pattern of income distribution within the home country, (2) whether foreign investment leads to decreased employment in the home country (that is, not whether jobs are lost in the aggregate to international competition but whether more jobs could be saved if multinational corporations were kept at home); and (3) whether foreign investment affects the welfare of workers through its impact on collective bargaining and labor-management relations.

With regard to income distribution, Caves points out that simple models of international trade suggest that outward investment lowers the marginal product of labor in the home market while raising the earnings of the owners of capital, thus worsening the relative position of workers in the country where the outward investment occurred. Within a more sophisticated Heckscher-Ohlin framework, however, in which each nation produces many goods and the ratios of capital to labor vary widely, much of the adjustment to factor migrations will be accommodated by changes in the structure of imports and exports. In other words, a shift in factor proportions will reduce export potential and boost industries that compete with imports, offsetting the negative impact on the labor of the home country. In the limiting case, changes in the composition of output, including traded goods, could completely offset the impact of factor movements in a way that returns to workers and owners of capital would be unaffected.

In his survey of the literature, Caves notes that several of the principal efforts to test the impact of foreign investment on U.S. income distribution, such as Musgrave and Thurow, suffer by ignoring the effect of trade adjustments.[20] Musgrave and Thurow concluded on the bases of simulating the consequences of repatriating the stock of overseas investment held by U.S. companies that outward investment decreases the returns to U.S. labor, but their conclusions would have to be changed substantially if they used the more complicated Heckscher-Ohlin framework. Studies that do, such as Frank and Freeman, Bergsten, Horst and Moran, and Koizumi and Kopecky, suggest that the impact of foreign investment on income distribution in the home country is much more ambiguous.[21] Finally, cross-investment by different firms on both sides of a border simultaneously clouds the issue of income distribution as a result of multinational corporate activity even further.

Turning to the question of whether foreign investment undermines the domestic economy by exporting jobs, Caves picks up a theme that was central to Chaikin's point of view. Caves begins by suggesting that the examination of the relationship between outward investment and domestic unemployment can be treated as a short-term aspect of the distribution of income problem, with the export of capital possibly resulting in surplus labor at the going wage. The longer-term question of whether multinational corporations export jobs, however, rests on the issue of how much discretion multinationals enjoy in choosing either to produce at home or to move their operations offshore. If firms have great leeway in making the choice about where to locate their plants, it opens them to the charge that their overseas operations are runaway plants that cost U.S. workers their jobs. Then a change in tax laws (or other home country policies) to keep the multinationals at home, as advocated by organized labor, might redirect their activities in a way that helped revitalize the local economy.

The defenders of an unrestricted approach to outward investment by U.S. companies point out, in contrast, that firms that do have overseas operations have a superior record in the home market in terms of job creation, export performance, and technological innovation. The finger should not be pointed at them, they argue, in ascribing blame for low levels of domestic activity; if they were prevented from responding when worldwide opportunities presented themselves, their contribution to national growth and welfare would be lowered, not raised.

Besides, they contend, most direct foreign investment is defensive in nature, taking place to preserve markets originally established through exports but subsequently threatened with local products (whether supplied by host country companies or by rival multinationals). If the market can no longer be served by exports from the home country, a policy of keeping the firms at home would deny them profits from overseas operations and preserve no jobs in the domestic economy. Unless the foreign investment is made, then, both exports and overseas earnings will be lost, leaving the home economy in the worst of all possible worlds.

How much discretion do international firms actually have? Are their foreign investments mostly defensive, aimed at keeping themselves in markets they can no longer export to from the home country? Or do they represent runaway plants, which could be kept alive and well if the firms stayed at home?

Supporting the defensive perspective in a study of nine foreign investment cases in industries that account for much of U.S. overseas corporate operations (machinery, chemicals, food processing, paper manufacturing, petroleum, rubber products, primary and fabricated metals, electrical goods, and transportation), Robert Stobaugh found that only in two could the parent firm have chosen the alternative of U.S.-based production, and even there the option would have expired in five to ten years.[22] He concluded that as a rule, U.S. corporations have little choice but to invest abroad and that their investments make a net positive contribution to U.S. employment and the U.S. balance of payments.

How representative are these nine cases in the large universe of foreign operations by U.S. companies? Caves points out that the literature contains a heavy dose of simulated calculations that evade the question of discretion by making one extreme assumption or the other. For example, the U.S. Tariff Commission postulated in a prominent study that all offshore production could be replaced by increased output in the country where the multinational had its headquarters.[23]

The problem in resolving the controversy about the effect of outward investment by U.S. firms on the U.S. economy lies in determining across large bodies of data whether foreign investment substitutes for exports or complements them. As Caves makes clear, the goal for research must be to answer the question of what would have happened on balance if the investments had not been made in the first place. To try to come to grips with this, Thomas Horst examined the relative export performance of firms that did invest abroad with other firms of similar characteristics, such as large size, high R&D, and heavy advertising, that did not.[24] (To compare the export performance of firms that invest abroad with the national average for all manufacturing firms, as international corporate spokesmen often do, does not provide a good test, since other firms' characteristics, such as large size or high R&D, might account for export performance rather than the outward investment itself. What is needed is to isolate the contribution of foreign operations to the level of exports by the parent.)

Horst found that although the results were quite heterogeneous across industries and the relationship between outward investment and exports largely random, there seemed to be a small positive correlation between foreign investment and exports as firms began the process of investment and then a small negative correlation as the amount of outward investment by the firms increased. In other words, a little bit of foreign investment tended to stimulate firms' exports a little, and a lot of foreign investment tended to depress firms' exports a little, when compared to the record of similar firms that did not engage in foreign investment at all. Using a different methodology, Frank and Freeman attempted to determine what share of foreign markets would be lost by U.S. companies versus how many U.S. jobs could be saved if U.S. overseas production were kept at home.[25] With the most extreme assumptions, they found, like Horst, the net job displacement to be relatively small, between 120,000 and 160,000 jobs annually, with most workers finding new employment within eight weeks.

Thus, even under the worst conditions, the magnitude of the runaway plant phenomenon appears to be quite limited, and a policy designed to keep firms at home would be at least partially counterproductive in terms of preserving employment opportunities. An approach that tried to regulate outward investment by U.S. firms through constraints designed to maximize U.S. exports and U.S. jobs would produce at best slight rather than large gains, and to be successful the policy would have to be very selective and finely tuned. Finally, the policy could well produce results that were the opposite of what was intended.

But accepting the outside world as it is, including the practice by host governments in the Third World of trying to squeeze multinationals into creating more value-added and generating more exports, is not the only outcome that has been recommended. Labor groups (and some threatened corporations) in the developed world have launched a straightforward attack on the right of Third World governments to levy the performance requirements on multinationals recorded in part I of this book.

The Labor-Industry Coalition for International Trade (LICIT) in Washington, D.C., for example, has declared, that "trade-related performance requirements—requiring minimum local content or export levels—now constitute one of the most serious trade policy problems facing the international trading community."[26] They identified more than thirty-five countries (developed and developing) that engage in regulating the activities of foreign affiliates so as to shift investment, jobs, and production to the country that imposes them.

Following the same line, the U.S. trade representative in 1985 proposed that investment-related trade policies be made one of the highest priorities for GATT (General Agreement on Tariffs and Trade) negotiation in the post–Tokyo Round era. And under pressure from domestic labor and industry groups, the U.S. Congress has undertaken to consider a series of local content requirements of its own as a new cornerstone for U.S. trade policy. Finally, Congress and the executive branch have made the extension of trade preferences for developing countries contingent on reciprocity on the part of Third World countries in the area of abolishing performance requirements on U.S. investors.

The evidence suggests, however, that the intensity of the preoccupation with performance requirements has not been matched by a demonstration of a serious impact on trade patterns. In a World Bank study of seventy-four major investment decisions (the most comprehensive survey extant), about half (thirty-eight) were found to be subject to some form of foreign exchange balancing.[27] But in contradiction to the charge that performance requirements are inherently trade distorting, the World Bank study found that in a number of cases, the requirements merely accelerated the foreign firms' plans to develop local suppliers or to enter export markets, suggesting that the host country policies did not violate the broad long-term structure of comparative advantage. Only in four cases did the performance requirements determine the country in which the investment was located. And all of these four were defensive in nature; that is, the firms accepted performance requirements in order to maintain access to the local market. This would seem to indicate that the "problem" of performance requirements as a fundamental distortion of trade is of relatively limited scope and magnitude and that international firms have little flexibility except to respond to the demands or lose their position. But the "solution" is designed to turn back the clock substantially against the shift in bargaining power from multinationals to host governments that Chaikin examines in chapter 8. And to achieve this solution, the First World has threatened to wage war against the exports that the Third World needs to develop and to repay its debts.[28]

Finally, in the area of the impact of multinational corporations on labor-management relations and collective bargaining, Caves discusses numerous hypotheses, with a particular focus on two: that unions appropriate some of the rents that accrue to MNC's oligopolistic activities and that unions are attempting to coordinate their bargaining across national boundaries to offset the potential ability of MNCs to outmaneuver workers in any single country. With regard to the first, many international companies do pay higher-than-average wages. But when the analysts control for size of firm, sector, and region, many of these differentials wash out. The exception appears to be in LDCs where foreign investors pay higher wages to attract better-quality labor.

With regard to multinational union activity, the evidence suggests that national labor groups have been active in sharing information across borders, setting common termination dates for contracts, and even coordinating demands at the bargaining table or engaging in sympathy strikes (or sympathetic refusals to engage in overtime during a strike in progress elsewhere).[29] Moreover, attempts at international union coordination appear to be on the rise, with the expectation that they will continue.

Caves points out that the extent to which unions have been successful in raising wages through transnational labor activity is problematic. But there may be even more interesting implications resulting from the phenomenon of cross-border union coordination. A trend in this direction may, in fact, provide a force to offset the drive for protectionism and restrictionism in any single country. That is, the demand by unions in one nation for special measures to insulate their own society could begin to produce an automatic reaction from unions in other countries that would be hurt by such measures. Hence, the drive toward multinational unionism may paradoxically help buoy up the relative openness of the international economic system. This is a theme picked up from the corporate side by John Kline in chapter 10.

Multinational Corporate Strategies and the Policies of the Home Country: Neomercantilism or New Liberalism?

Going hand in hand with the thrust toward protectionism and restrictionism has been a popular revival of neomercantilism, the idea of the state using its own international companies as vehicles to achieve home country goals. In Europe this has taken the form of support for "national champions," corporations designated to carry the flag against other countries' international companies in oil, automobiles, telecommunications, computers, and the rest of the commanding heights of the European economies. In some sectors, such as aerospace, Concorde and Airbus have sprung from the desire to create not merely a national champion but a Pan-European competitor to do battle against foreigners at home and abroad.

In Japan, the impulse to neomercantilism is evident in a targeting policy designed to position Japanese companies at the forefront of microchip or other advanced technology industries. The image is caricatured as a monolithic Japan Inc. that scans the globe for opportunities, captures resources, and dominates markets around the world.

At the same time, recurrent calls for an *industrial policy* in the United States and for stricter control over the export of U.S. technology echo the neomercantilistic theme that a nation must nurture and protect corporations of the home country nationality for reasons of preserving the parent state's place in the international system.[30] This contrasts with the liberal idea of putting faith in markets that are competitive and nondiscriminatory and relying on the lowest-cost supplier, whatever the nationality of the firm, to meet the needs of the population.

In chapter 10, John Kline examines some of the background motivations for building national champion multinationals that could be used in neomercantilistic fashion. But even from the beginning, in Europe, there were practical difficulties of trying to rely on home country companies as chosen instruments of national policy. These difficulties sprang from the potential contradiction for corporations between being mandated to do the bidding of authorities in the home state and wanting to formulate a global strategy unfettered by home government directives. The European experience was filled with cases like the one in which Fiat, for example, was urged to fall in line with Italian plans for the *mezzogiorno* but chose to build new plants in Brazil instead, or Phillips shifted production of electronics to Asia while parliamentarians in Amsterdam complained of soaring unemployment rates in the Netherlands. These cases suggest that as companies seek to strengthen their competitive position worldwide, they become less subject to the control of home authorities.

Kline extends this argument to the area of building cross-border corporate alliances that enable would-be national champions to gain easier access to the finance, management, and technology of the other side. In the automotive sector, for example, he points to cases that emphasize "cross-national linking mechanisms" for codevelopment-coproduction (Fiat-Peugeot, Renault-Volvo, Nissan-Alfa Romeo), marketing and distribution agreements (British Leyland-Honda; VW-MAN; Renault-Mack), component agreements (Fiat-Ford, Renault-Alfa Romeo, Fiat-Saab), and stock ownership (Chrysler-Mitsubishi, Ford-Toyo Kogyo; AMC-Renault). In ventures formed since Kline's study was published, the evidence is multiplying: Westinghouse, Sanyo, and Nissho-Iwai, for example, are pooling their resources to produce modular parts for cable television; Sony and Bell and Howell for filmless cameras; ICL-Fujitsu, Bull-NEC, and BSF-Hitachi for computers; ITT, Sony, and Phillips for digital audio disks; and McDonnell-Douglas and Fokker, and British Aerospace and Avco, for midsize and smaller aircraft.

But Kline takes the analysis a step further. The emerging patterns of transatlantic and transpacific corporate alliances spring not merely from an economic motivation. Instead some of the corporate alliances have a quasi-political rationale as well: to create a web of interests carefully positioned to offset the political influence of more neomercantilistic forces. General Dynamics was a pioneer with this strategy through building a transnational network of supporters among suppliers in the NATO (North Atlantic Treaty Organization) countries where it hoped to market the F-16 fighter. The company dangled coproduction agreements for the aircraft in front of aerospace companies in Great Britain, France, Germany, Italy, and other nations, guaranteeing contracts to produce 40 percent of the European version, 10 percent of the U.S. model, and 15 percent of all other sales worldwide if the F-16 were chosen by their national military services. This gave European companies that signed on with General Dynamics access to U.S. technology and U.S. markets if they were successful in helping counter domestic political pressures to "buy European."

According to Kline, this may prove to be a more general model in which multinational companies consciously shape their corporate strategy so as to provide the political reinforcement they need to keep the international system relatively open. As evidence of this, Airbus has not limited itself, as Concorde did, to a European engine for its aircraft. Instead it offered the option of GE or Pratt and Whitney engines to throw the weight of these two companies, and their unions, behind keeping the U.S. market open to foreign competition. Boeing, for the same reason, offered the option of a Rolls Royce engine for the 757s and 767s sold in Europe "as insurance against a wider outbreak of economic nationalism that could inhibit its overseas sales."[31] The fear was that head-to-head competition between an "American plane" and a "European plane" would lead to protectionism. As the president of Boeing Airplane commented, "If we were to bleed off all of the aerospace production, we'd get a backlash that would cause more trouble than sharing to a degree."[32]

The emerging transnational alliances among corporations (like those among labor organizations) that can exercise political as well as economic clout across borders constitutes a force running contrary to the neomercantilistic idea and may provide new underpinning for a more liberal approach to trade and investment.

The Soviet Pipeline Case: Beginning or End of Neomercantilism for U.S. Companies?

The Soviet gas pipeline case of 1982–1983 gave the United States a taste of the indignation Europeans first experienced toward their carefully nurtured multinationals almost exactly a decade earlier. Like the Americans, European government officials always instinctively felt that their "own" companies should be able to be counted on to respond to national needs and defend the home government's interpretation of the national interest when called upon to do so. Yet during the oil embargo crisis of 1973, European oil companies refused to give preferential deliveries to their home markets, despite the commands and entreaties of home government authorities. Instead, like the other oil companies, they rationed available output so as to apportion the suffering equally among all their customers. British Petroleum, for example, told Prime Minister Edward Heath that despite 48 percent government ownership, it would adhere to contractual obligations rather than to "instructions from stockholders" for additional output.[33]

For the United States the pipeline case of 1982–1983 was no less seminal an event of conflicting directives, with U.S. multinationals caught in the middle and trying to proceed as far as possible with what served their own corporate interests best. There have long been, to be sure, episodic efforts by Washington to use directives to the parents of U.S. multinationals to affect the dealings of their affiliates with Soviet-bloc countries. The United States ordered Ford, GM, and Chrysler in 1974 not to deliver automobiles and trucks to Cuba, for example, even though their Argentine subsidiaries had already contracted to do so. The Argentine parliament protested U.S. "meddling in Argentina's internal affairs" and ordered the subsidiaries to proceed with the sale.[34] The subsidiaries obeyed the local sovereign rather than the United States, and the U.S. government finally permitted this "exception" to its ban.

What was new in the pipeline case, as the study in chapter 11 by Gary Hufbauer and Jeffrey Schott points out, is that President Ronald Reagan extended controls in 1982 to include licensees as well as subsidiaries of U.S. companies and attempted to make them stick. The order restricted the subsidiaries from exporting wholly foreign-origin equipment and technology to the Soviet Union, and it forbade unaffiliated non-U.S. companies from exporting goods that were produced with technology acquired under licensing agreements with U.S. companies, whether or not that technology had been subject to controls at the time the agreements were signed. The objective was to stop the sale of compressors built by European companies with valid licenses from U.S. companies irrespective of the fact that the technology had been purchased in good faith well before the imposition of controls.

In reaction, some European governments issued formal counterorders requiring resident companies to honor their contracts with the Soviet Union despite the U.S. ban.[35] Dresser-France, John Brown Engineering (a British licensee of General Electric), AEG-Kanis (a German licensee of GE), and Nuovo Pignone (an Italian state-owned company, also a licensee of GE) complied. Not to be outdone, the United States retaliated with penalties against these companies, including the revocation of all existing export licenses, whether or not the Soviet Union was the destination of the exports. This propelled the conflict to the highest political levels, where in 1983 face-saving diplomatic solutions were ultimately found as the sales themselves proceeded.

It has become clear, however, that the problem of conflicting sovereign demands on international companies has in no sense been put to rest. That is a dilemma Raymond Vernon addresses in chapter 12.

Sovereignty at Bay Today

The image of multinational corporations in the international system has gone through a complete cycle since Vernon's *Sovereignty at Bay* first appeared in 1971. At that time it was popular to assert that sovereignty was indeed at bay, that multinational corporations were above control, and that international companies were escaping beyond the reach of the national governments where they operated, although as Vernon points out, *Sovereignty at Bay* was only the title of his book, not its message. Instead he argued that the apparent power and extension of multinationals would produce a reaction on the part of authentic sovereign bodies, which would discover that to be effective, they would have to pool their authority to reestablish a framework for dealing with multinationals.

In almost Hegelian fashion, the idea of the supremacy of the multinationals soon began to undergo a dialectical reversal, pointing to an era of host country power, the flavor of which is represented in some of the earlier chapters of this book. Governmental demands were in the ascendancy, multinational corporations at bay.

Now, as Vernon points out, elements of both tendencies persist: corporations stretching beyond reach and governments extending their grasp. But, to pursue the Hegelian metaphor, the contradiction between multinational corporate strategies and local requirements in the countries where they operate requires resolution at a higher level. As the pipeline case shows, the struggle over the behavior of international companies has risen, as Vernon predicted, to the realm of high politics.

Vernon's other contributions to the study of multinational corporations have undergone their own evolutions as well. The obsolescing bargain still characterizes the pattern of foreign investor–host government relations in the Third World, but it has produced a reaction on the part of some of the more vulnerable corporations. As chapter 5 pointed out, the corporations have been experimenting with ways to protect themselves in advance against various forms of economic nationalism, to use their moment of strength to shield themselves against the more extreme degrees of exposure.

Vernon's ideas about the motivation for foreign investment have also undergone an evolution. His original product cycle idea had corporations chasing their ability to extract oligopoly rents from an innovation first developed in home country markets, to other countries with similar taste structures and factor proportions, to production in the less developed world for both internal consumption and export. Here, however, he has become more pessimistic. A narrowing of income differentials and equalizing of factor proportions among the developed countries may both weaken the impulse for direct foreign investment and eliminate the cash cows the corporations could draw on to finance their new innovations.[36]

This could reduce the dynamism of multinational corporate activities and constrict the contest for the benefits they produce into more of a zero-sum struggle. Thus Vernon concludes where he began, warning that the conflict between sovereigns trying to use multinationals for their own objectives may grow, not recede. This possibility inspires him once again to call for supranational agreement on the responsibilities as well as the rights of sovereign states in attempting to regulate international investment. Without this, he offers a somber vision of a future in which the struggle over multinational corporate operations becomes more bitter and more intense. Vernon warns that in the absence of supranational policy coordination toward multinationals, the world may have to "stagger on" with jurisdictional conflicts over their activities exacerbating political conflict among self-interested nation-states.

Notes

1. W.B. Reddaway, *Effects of U.K. Direct Investment Overseas* (London: Cambridge University Press, 1967).

2. Robert Gilpin, *U.S. Power and the Multinational Corporation* (New York: Basic Books, 1975).

3. Gus Tyler, "The Threat of a U.S. without Factories," AFL-CIO Reprint (February–April 1976); cf. also Peggy B. Musgrave, *United States Taxation of Foreign Investment Income: Issues and Arguments* (Cambridge, Mass.: International Tax Program, Harvard Law School, 1969).

4. In addition to greater interdependence for the United States, there has been a decline in the relative predominance of U.S. companies in the world economy with the reconstruction and growth of Europe and Japan. This "catching-up" process has been good for consumers and for industries that use imports as inputs in the United States, as well as for U.S. exporters. But it has been experienced as painful for those industries and workers who felt their quasi-monopoly position erode.

5. The question of the relationship between outward investment and the potential export of jobs will be dealt with in the next section. Greater openness to trade is not Pareto-optimal (welfare increasing) if it produces a deterioration in the terms of trade great enough to lead to a fall in real income. For small countries this is virtually impossible. Even for large countries such as the United States, the terms-of-trade loss is extremely unlikely to outweigh the gains in aggregate welfare. Protectionism may also be justified to allow for the development of infant industries. See Richard N. Cooper, "Economic Assumptions of the Case for Liberal Trade," in C. Fred Bergsten, ed., *Toward a New World Trade Policy: The Maidenhead Papers* (Lexington, Mass.: Lexington Books, 1975); and William R. Cline, ed., *Trade Policy in the 1980s, op. cit.*

6. Cline, *Trade Policy.*

7. The evidence in this section is drawn primarily from Robert Z. Lawrence, *Can America Compete?* (Washington, D.C.: Brookings, 1984). See also *Industrial Change and Public Policy* (Kansas City: Federal Reserve Bank of Kansas City, 1983).

8. In the latter period a larger proportion of capital investment had to be dedicated to meeting regulatory requirements for pollution control and safety. The subtraction of expenditures on air and water pollution equipment, however, reduces the growth rate for manufacturing investment only from 4.5 percent to 4.2 percent per year. Lawrence, *Can America Compete?*

9. U.S. International Trade Commission, *Emerging Textile-Exporting Countries* (Washington, D.C.: USITC Publication 1273, August 1982); U.S. International Trade Commission, *Non-Rubber Footware,* PA-201-50 (July 1984); Robert W. Crandall, *Competition and Trade Protection in the U.S. Steel Market* (Washington, D.C.: Brookings, 1985). For evidence that the textile and footware industries can adjust successfully in the face of competition but that orderly marketing agreements and other protectionist measures are not effective policy tools to stimulate adjustment, see Vinod Aggarwal with Stephen Haggard, "The Politics of Protection in U.S. Textile and Apparel Industries," and David Yoffie, "Adjustment in the Footware Industry: The Consequences of Orderly Marketing Agreements," in John Zysman and Laura Tyson, eds., *American Industry in International Competition: Government Policies and Corporate Strategies* (Ithaca: Cornell University Press, 1983).

10. Robert Crandall, "Import Quotas and the Automobile Industry: The Costs of Protectionism," *The Brookings Review* (Summer 1984). This is not exceptional. The average cost per job saved in specialty steel, television sets, and footware has been approximately $98,000 annually in 1984 dollars. Robert W. Crandall, "Federal Government Initiatives to Reduce the Price Level," *Brookings Papers on Economic Activity* (Washington, D.C.: Brookings, 1978).

11. U.S. International Trade Commission, *Likely Costs and Employment Effects of Import Relief to the Copper Industry* (Washington, D.C.: ITC, July 19, 1984). See also Alan V. Deardorff and Robert M. Stern, "American Labor's Stake in International Trade," in *Tariffs, Quotas, and Trade: The Politics of Protectionism* (San Francisco: Institute for Contemporary Studies, 1979).

12. Bruno S. Frey, "The Public Choice View of International Political Economy," *International Organization* (Winter 1984). In addition to the explanations below, tariffs provide revenues for governments, which, in the absence of an effective tax system, may be appealing to finance public expenditures.

13. Anthony Downs, *An Economic Theory of Democracy* (New York: Harper, 1957); Mancur Olson, *The Logic of Collective Actions: Public Goods and the Theory of Groups* (Cambridge: Harvard University Press, 1965).

14. A.O. Krueger, "The Political Economy of the Rent-Seeking Society," *American Economic Review* 64 (1974); Robert E. Baldwin, "Rent-Seeking and Trade Policy: An Industry Approach" (forthcoming, 1985); J.N. Bhagwati and T.N. Srinivasan, "Revenue Seeking: A Generalization of the Theory of Tariffs," *Journal of Political Economy* 88 (1980).

15. John H. Jackson, "Perspectives on the Jurisprudence of International Trade," *American Economic Review* (May 1984). Corporate legal fees to pursue protection are counted as business expenses for tax purposes.

16. George R. Newmann, "Adjustment Assistance for Trade-Displaced Workers," in David B.H. Denoon, ed., *The New International Economic Order* (New York: New York University Press, 1979); J. David Richardson, "Trade Adjustment Assistance under the Trade Act of 1974," in J.N. Bhagwati, ed., *Import Competition and Response* (Chicago: University of Chicago Press for the National Bureau of Economic Research, 1983).

17. W.R. Cline et al., *Trade Negotiations in the Tokyo Round* (Washington, D.C.: Brookings, 1978).

18. C. Michael Aho and Thomas O. Bayard, "American Trade Adjustment Assistance after Five Years," *World Economy* 3 (1980); J. David Richardson, "Trade Adjustment Assistance under the United States Trade Act of 1974: An Analytical Examination and Worker Survey," in Bhagwati, *Import Competition.*

19. Bela Belassa and Carol Belassa, "Industrial Protection in the Developed Countries" (John Hopkins University, March 1984). Cf. also I.M. Destler, "The American Trade Policymaking System: Is It Finally Unravelling?" (Washington, D.C.: Institutional Economics, 1983).

20. Cf. Peggy B. Musgrave, *United States Taxation of Foreign Investment Income: Issues and Arguments* (Cambridge, Mass.: International Tax Program, Harvard Law School, 1969); L.C. Thurow, "International Factor Movements and the American Distribution of Income," *Intermountain Economic Review* 2 (Spring 1976).

21. Richard T. Frank and Richard T. Freeman, *Distribution Consequences of Direct Foreign Investment* (New York: Academic Press, 1978). C. Fred Bergsten, Thomas Horst, and Theodore H. Moran, *American Multinationals and American Interests, op. cit.,* chaps. 3–4; T. Koizumi and K.J. Kopecky, "Economic Growth, Capital Movements and the International Transfer of Technical Knowledge," *Journal of International Economics* 7 (February 1977); See also R.E. Lipsey and M.Y. Weiss, "Foreign Production and Exports in Manufacturing Industries," *Review of Economics and Statistics* 63 (November 1981).

22. Robert Stobaugh et al., *Nine Investments Abroad and Their Impacts at Home* (Boston: Division of Research, Harvard Graduate School of Business Administration, 1976).

23. U.S. Tariff Commission, *Implications of Multinational Firms for World Trade and Investment and for U.S. Trade and Labor* (Washington, D.C.: Government Printing Office, 1973).

24. Bergsten, Horst, and Moran, *American Multinationals,* chap. 3.

25. Frank and Freeman, *Distribution Consequences.*

26. Labor-Industry Coalition for International Trade, *Performance Requirements* (Washington, D.C.: LICIT, March 1981).

27. Stephen Guisinger, *Investment Incentives and Performance Requirements: A Comparative Analysis of Country Foreign Investment Strategies* (Washington, D.C.: World Bank, July 1983). In another study, the Overseas Private Investment Corporation reviewed eighty-six investment projects in the period 1981–1982 with the finding that while 30 percent of the total (twenty-six projects) did have local content requirements, maximum import ceilings, and/or minimum export requirements, none was found to "reduce substantially the positive trade benefits likely to accrue to the United States from the investment." J.E. Gale, *OPIC Experience with Trade-Related Performance Requirements* (Washington, D.C.: Overseas Private Investment Corporation, May 1982).

28. The threat against the Third World does not emanate solely from the United States. Within the European community, the Vredeling Proposal would require international firms to provide local labor representatives with information from corporate headquarters about any action that could affect the local employment situation prior to taking the action. Some analysts, pro and con, see this as a first step toward a worker veto system over a firm's trade and investment decisions. Cf. John Robinson, *Multinationals and Political Control* (New York: St. Martin's Press, 1983).

29. H.R. Northrup and R.L. Rowan, *Multinational Collective Bargaining Attempts: The Record, the Cases, and the Prospects* (Philadelphia: Wharton School Industrial Research Unit, 1979).

30. *Report to the President on International Competitiveness* (Washington, D.C.: White House, 1985). See also David J. Sylvan, "The Newest Mercantilism," *International Organization* (Spring 1981).

31. Louis Kraar, "Boeing Takes a Bold Plunge to Keep Flying High," *Fortune*, September 25, 1980.

32. Ibid. From the European side there is evidence of a similar corporate dilemma. A typical example may be the case of Scania: whether to produce an all-Swedish product and try to market it in head-on competition with planes of other nationalities or to gain technological and marketing allies through transatlantic joint ventures. For Scania, the Viggen II fighter (where parliamentary considerations are greatest) will be all-Swedish; the new generation of commuter aircraft (where marketing considerations are greatest) will be a fifty-fifty venture with Fairchild, powered by GE engines. One will have to wait to see which does better in the future. "Saab-Scania Kicks into High Gear," *Fortune*, November 26, 1984.

33. Robert B. Stobaugh, "The Oil Companies in Crisis," *Daedalus* (Fall 1975):189.

34. Cf. Thomas N. Gladwin and Ingo Walter, *Multinationals under Fire* (New York: John Wiley, 1980), pp. 242–243.

35. See Homer E. Moyer, Jr., and Linda Mabry, "Export Controls as Instruments of Foreign Policy: The History, Legal Issues and Policy Lessons of Three Recent Cases," *Law and Policy in International Business* 15 (1983).

36. Raymond Vernon, "The Product Cycle Hypothesis in a New International Environment," *Oxford Bulletin of Economics and Statistics*, 41, no. 4 (November 1979):225–267, and "Gone Are the Cash Cows of Yesteryear," *Harvard Business Review* (November 1980):150–155.

8
Trade, Investment, and Deindustrialization: Myth and Reality

Sol C. Chaikin

There is a long historical tradition of suspicion, in Great Britain as well as in the United States, that outward investment undermines the industrial base of the home country. Sol Chaikin offers a contemporary version of that argument. He asserts that the U.S. economy is threatened by deindustrialization, with high import penetration ratios in both mature technology and high technology industries. In his view, high import levels cause excess capacity, which in turn creates inflation, lower productivity, and depressed domestic investment. U.S. corporations have contributed to the displacement of U.S. manufacturing, Chaikin argues, by investing abroad rather than using their assets to stimulate domestic growth, improve productivity, and increase U.S. competitiveness. Free trade and unrestricted outward investment do not benefit the majority of American workers or the American people.

Chapter 7 examines the evidence of how international competition is forcing chances in the structure of the U.S. economy and within this context weighs Chaikin's thesis that the United States is undergoing a process of deindustrialization. Chapter 7 then turns to the politics of the policymaking process and analyzes the political economy of protectionist and restrictionist pressures.

The American labor movement has basically concentrated on domestic issues—with the notable exception of its vigorous efforts to further the cause of human rights, free trade unionism and political democracy throughout the world. This focus on the United States has been the result of both the sheer size of the American economy and work force and the specific circumstances which gave rise to the rapid growth of the labor movement in the 1930s.

The renaissance of organized labor in this country during the depression days was based mainly in the manufacturing sector. In those days, international trade accounted for a minute part of the nation's total output of goods and services. It was, therefore, manifest that the problems of the national economy that culminated in the Great Depression resulted from deficiencies in domestic policy. Gradual economic revitalization in the New Deal years reinforced the views of labor leaders that the viability of the American economy was inextricably and almost exclusively linked with the domestic scene.

In the early 1960s, workers in a number of labor-intensive industries, particularly the apparel industry, began to experience economic distress. For some, the problem was outright loss of jobs; for the majority, earnings failed to keep pace with average manufacturing wages. That this could occur during what was to become the longest period of sustained economic growth in American history was cause for consternation. What was happening compelled those affected to look beyond our borders.

It rapidly became obvious that the dilemma was due to market dislocations in the wake of a growing tide of imports. Unions might have been expected to respond by calling for a cessation of all labor-intensive imports. The International Ladies' Garment Workers' Union, however, did not follow that path. Unlike most unions in the United States, the ILGWU was founded by immigrants who arrived in this country with a firm commitment to the international solidarity of working people. The ILGWU leadership needed no lessons in the importance of international economic cooperation to maintain world peace. It rejected and continues to oppose a philosophy of extreme protectionism.

The threat to American jobs and living standards that had been limited to a few industries has now multiplied to the point where it affects workers—and many employers—in almost every industry. The issue is no longer the viability of entrepreneurial manufacturing. The specter of deindustrialization is not only apparent, but has continued to grow at a geometric pace.

In the course of more than 40 years as an officer of the ILGWU, I have been closely connected with the industrial scene. Especially since becoming the union's president in 1975, I have often discussed the loss of American manufacturing with my corporate counterparts. I have heard the concern of other union leaders in the highest councils of the labor movement and that of workers on the shop floor, along with the thinking of my opposite numbers in the developed and developing nations. Insights have also been gained in exchanges with government leaders in the United States and abroad and through participation in negotiations affecting both bilateral and multilateral trade.

The experiences of the apparel industry in particular and of the nation's manufacturing base in general have compelled me to think through more thoroughly the current implications of postwar national economic policy. I would like to share these explorations and some of the resulting conclusions.

II

By the end of the Second World War, U.S trade policy had shifted radically from the autarky of the 1930s to an ideology of "free trade." International cooperation created by the wartime alliance and the emergence of the United States as the dominant Western power were catalysts in this change. In the immediate postwar years, the output of the United States represented an unprecedented share of global industrial production. By 1948, three years after the end of the war, American output still represented more than half of the world's industrial product. America's newfound love affair with free trade was, consequently, solidly based upon a pragmatic assessment of domestic potential.

Prosecution of the war had brought important changes in the American economy. Fabrication of war material and the growth of the armed forces had reduced depression-related unemployment to a point where the dream of a full employment economy seemed possible. Capital outlays, encouraged by military needs, and research and development, both of which were underwritten by the government, had helped to modernize industry, yielding impressive gains in output and productivity.

Military expenditures declined sharply with the end of the war and millions of discharged servicemen reentered the domestic work force. The likelihood of a postwar slump was advanced by most economists, who foresaw a severe downturn once pent-up demand for consumer goods, created during the war years, was satisfied. The most effective way to avoid that prospect was to ensure new outlets for American industrial capacity.

If only in purely economic terms, the postwar U.S. commitment to a greater degree of unrestricted trade made a great deal of sense. Given the destruction of industrial plant in much of Europe and Japan and the time period they needed to rebuild, extraordinary advantages of the United States in capacity, technology and productivity permitted the economy to prosper. While Europe and Japan were rebuilding their industrial bases, American manufacturers enjoyed an unchallenged share of world markets which helped to facilitate rapid conversion of the economy to peacetime production and avert an economic downturn.

Postwar trade policy also enhanced opportunities to attain strategic political goals. The United States sought through the Marshall Plan to assist in the reconstruction of devastated European economies as an integral part of an effort to create and strengthen stable democracies. The Marshall Plan contributed significantly to Europe's recovery as did investment by American corporations, encouraged by government policy.

While the U.S. economy initially benefited from this policy, there were mid- and long-term costs associated with these efforts. In time, financial assistance, investment, shared industrial know-how and the rebirth of war-devastated economies began to diminish the advantage American manufacturing enjoyed in the period immediately following World War II.

As American investment in Europe continued to grow, the relative availability of capital for domestic investment declined. Earnings of European subsidiaries of U.S. corporations were not fully repatriated, further increasing the gap between potential and actual domestic capital formation. While overseas investments by U.S. corporations enhanced the profitability and competitiveness of these corporations, they restricted growth possibilities in the domestic economy.

The implicit restriction of domestic growth and the conscious sharing of the global market had aims which could not be calculated in purely economic terms. They were linked with efforts to avoid social unrest in Western Europe and to the establishment of a strong Western Alliance. The absence during the past 37 years of global military conflict, and especially of regional warfare in Europe, has been one outcome of U.S. policy. Its value is incalculable.

American policy toward postwar Japan had similar ramifications. Emergence of a stable, friendly and economically viable order in Japan was, as in Western Europe, a vital American concern. Japan, and Asia as a whole, however, did not readily offer as signficant a market in the immediate postwar years as did Europe. Nonetheless, for similar strategic reasons the United States provided aid and shared technology. The Korean War contributed to the rebirth and growth of basic Japanese industry as Japan became an important supply base for American and U.N. forces. Further substantial gains to the Japanese economy took place later, during the Vietnam War. The United States also provided an additional critical inducement to Japanese industries by establishing and helping to maintain until 1971 a foreign exchange rate favorable to the Japanese, even as that country pursued a highly protectionist trade policy.

America's postwar export predominance could not continue indefinitely, especially after Germany, France and Japan re-created and further developed their industries with the most advanced available technology. Throughout the 1950s and into the early 1960s, aided by the absence of large-scale military expenditures, both Japan and the principal countries of Western Europe enlarged plant and equipment and increased consumer output, thereby creating near full-employment economies and raising living standards. As their industrial plants grew, these nations devoted greater attention to increasing exports. American multinationals captured a share of the domestic and export markets in Western Europe and, to a far lesser extent, in Japan. Initially, the domestic economy in the United States was not as severely affected as had been anticipated earlier. The unbroken domestic growth of the 1960s made the markets of Western Europe and Japan relatively less important.

III

As a result of U.S. government policies and private encouragement, as well as the need to pay for raw material imports used in its growing industrial machine, Japan increasingly pursued a model of export-oriented development in a number of key industries. In this, of course, Japan was not alone. If Japan were an isolated case, perhaps trade policy would not bear so heavily on our current economic problems. But Japan is not an isolated case. Rather than acknowledging that there are limits to the American economy's ability to absorb imported goods, U.S. policy has been one of encouraging developed and developing nations to increase their exports to this country.

Continuation of a policy of relatively unrestricted trade without incurring disastrous internal results must be viewed both in the context of the domestic economic circumstance and, because the actions of the United States have international implications, in terms of foreign policy goals.

The consequences of this policy for domestic manufacturing have changed and intensified in the course of the last two decades. Yet, despite the growing importance of the problem, discussion of import-penetrated industries was, as recently as ten years ago, extremely narrow in scope and short in duration. The sectors concerned—primarily labor-intensive industries—were few, and, to most observers, imports did not appear to be a general threat to U.S. manufactures. Industries experiencing difficulty competing with foreign goods were viewed merely as isolated cases.

In the 1970s the nation came to learn that excessive import penetration was not peculiar to such labor-intensive industries as apparel, textiles or home electronics. The experience in these sectors was merely a preview of similar dislocations which have now affected almost every facet of American manufacturing.

Many nostrums have been suggested over the last 20 years. When the members of the ILGWU were first confronted with the rising tide of apparel imports from developing countries, we were advised that the solution in our labor-intensive industry was simple. Domestic industry, it was said, should become more competitive by improving worker productivity.

Even in the less-developed countries, however, apparel is manufactured with essentially the same state-of-the-art technology employed in the advanced nations. Frequently, manufacture abroad has been implanted by American corporations. Designs and production techniques created in the United States and supported by American merchandising skills are used in the developing countries. Capital, technology and managerial know-how have been internationalized, leaving no opportunity for domestic apparel manufacturers to obtain a meaningful edge in productivity. Consequently, wages represent the only area in which the domestic industry can compete in an open market with imports from the developing world.

By the standards of other manufacturing in the United States, wages in the domestic apparel industry are not high. Across the country, a sewing machine operator earns an average of $5.00 to $5.50 per hour. With benefits, this comes to total compensation of roughly $6.75 per hour. But workers in the major exporting countries earn a small fraction of this amount —less than $1.00 per hour in Hong Kong, less than 40 cents per hour in Taiwan, Korea or Singapore, about 20 cents per hour in India and even less in Sri Lanka and the People's Republic of China. For garment workers in the United States to compete with such wage levels, even taking into account shipping costs and applicable tariffs, would mean that they would have to accept total compensation of hardly more than $1.00 per hour.

When we brought this to the attention of the policymakers, they responded that additional constraints on apparel imports were still unwarranted. If the domestic apparel industry could not compete on a global basis, so be it. The displaced workers, they contended, would find other work in such industries as shoe production, novelties or plastics, where the skills were highly compatible. Yet these labor-intensive industries were afflicted with the same malady—they too were losing jobs in the wake of growing imports from low-wage areas.

Policymakers and corporate spokesmen then suggested that the loss of labor-intensive manufacturing jobs should not be cause for alarm. People displaced by imports, they maintained, could be retrained for better jobs in capital-intensive industries—autos, steel or, better yet, the technology-intensive growth industries. Such a strategem, however, had first to cope with limitations on upward or even horizontal job mobility.

IV

Even under the best of economic circumstances, occupational adaptability is far from perfect. As the shortcomings of the War on Poverty of the late 1960s clearly demonstrated, the American labor force has a broad spectrum of skills. High levels of employment and minimal unemployment, therefore, require a full spectrum of job opportunities—from the least skilled to the most advanced. Fitting people into job slots is a complex and frequently disheartening exercise, especially when an industry or a substantial fraction of it is phased out of existence. Limitations on occupational adaptability, which some economists slough off as "structural unemployment" (as though there are no human bodies behind that bland concept), are compounded by constraints on mobility created by family ties, inadequate financial resources, educational limitations, lack of access to information regarding available jobs, or de facto sex or racial discrimination.

In periods of economic stagnation or retrogression, it is difficult, if not impossible, to upgrade workers whose skills have become technologically or economically obsolete. Particular attention must, therefore, be paid to the availability of jobs in industries where skills are roughly compatible. Otherwise, massive sectoral unemployment results. Trends in several key industries thus have a critical bearing upon trade policies and, more broadly, upon industrial development and growth.

Between 1965 and 1981, the import share of developed countries in the domestic U.S. auto market grew from 6 percent to over 27 percent. Foreign-made trucks accounted in 1973 for only 5 percent of domestic purchases; in 1981, the figure had risen to 20 percent. The pattern in steel, the nation's backbone, parallels the auto industry's experience. From barely 5 percent in 1962, the import share of the developed countries in the domestic steel market increased nearly fivefold to almost 25 percent in 1981.

It is currently being said that the decline in the market share of domestic auto and steel output, as in many labor-intensive manufacturing industries, may well be an affordable price to pay for a productive restructuring of the American economy. This argument suggests that basic manufacturing is a drain on the resources available to technology-intensive industries. The latter, it is contended, should be the mainstay of an economically advanced nation. The proponents of this view concede that it will result in some permanent unemployment, but, they argue, the long-run result will be a more competitive economy. The problem presented by occupational adaptability is acknowledged, but subordinated to the conclusion that promotion of high-technology industries will ultimately produce the most effective means to secure real economic growth. Such growth, it is said, would in time provide for considerably lower levels of unemployment.

Even if the enormous problem of occupational adaptability is ignored, dependence upon technology-intensive industries as the primary source of manufacturing employment is conceptually flawed. It fails to take account of the small labor component in technology-intensive production, compared with either labor-intensive or even most capital-intensive manufacturing.

Thus, under the most ideal of circumstances, reliance on technology-intensive production could not support present levels of manufacturing employment, let alone reduce current high unemployment. The practical deficiencies of this development concept are underscored, moreover, by evidence that the market shares for domestically produced technology-intensive goods are themselves declining.

A case in point is the American electronics industry, a field that truly grew out of American ingenuity. The basic new discoveries in the industry were made in this country over past decades, with defense and space programs providing enormous resources for research and development and guaranteeing a market for innovation. America's infrastructure has been second to none, and our ability to provide industry with the best trained minds has been unparalleled. As recently as 15 years ago, the global preeminence of the

United States in electronics surpassed achievements in any other industry. Yet what should have been an enormous advantage has now dissolved.

The erosion began in consumer electronics. From negligible import penetration 20 years ago, we have moved to the opposite extreme. By 1978, the import share for videotape players and household radios was 100 percent. There was *no* domestic production in these products. In the same year, imports accounted for 90 percent of all domestic purchases of citizens band radios, 85 percent of all black and white television sets, 68 percent of all electronic watches and 64 percent of all stereo components. Even such sophisticated consumer electronics as color television sets and microwave ovens had large import shares. The figures (respectively 18 percent and 25 percent for 1978), however, do not tell the entire story; they understate the actual significance of import penetration because products assembled domestically and counted as American production include substantial overseas value-added in the form of foreign-produced components, sub-assemblies, circuit boards and complete chassis.

If the evaporation of American manufacturing leadership were limited solely to consumer electronics, perhaps we could console ourselves with the preeminence we have maintained in the most sophisticated areas of research. Even here, however, the outlook is increasingly distressing. Semiconductors, for example, represent literally the most home-grown U.S. industry, and epitomize the cutting edge of America's technological strength. Yet from a starting point of zero import penetration in 1975, Japanese firms alone have captured 40 percent of the U.S. semiconductor market and are rapidly moving into the international arena. Nor are the Japanese content merely to produce what has been created in this country. In less than a decade, they have made impressive progress in areas of high-technology research that were once the exclusive domain of American enterprise. The United States no longer holds the lead in such exotic processes as electron-beam lithography or memory circuit design. Rather, this country must now struggle to maintain parity in these and many other areas of high technology.

Even the computer, that great American technological achievement, is not safe from the mounting pressure of foreign competition. *U.S. Industrial Competitiveness,* a July 1981 publication of the Federal Office of Technology Assessment, concluded that, ". . . the Japanese have managed great strides since 1970. . . . hardware now seems largely competitive with American. . . . While . . . Japanese computer firms have yet to establish any real presence in the U.S. market, they clearly intend to try."

V

The demonstrated ability of foreign competitors to rapidly displace key American manufacturers in both the domestic and international markets suggests a fundamental weakening of the American economy. Lagging productivity is often cited as a cause. Yet, while the *rate* of productivity growth in the United States has been relatively low throughout the 1970s, the *absolute level* of American manufacturing productivity remains the highest in the world and the differential is substantial compared with that of our major trading partners. In absolute terms, Japanese and West German productivity levels in 1980 were respectively 66.3 percent and 88.3 percent of the American figure.[1]

Lagging productivity growth—from 1973 to 1980 it rose at an annual rate of only 1.7 percent—is itself symptomatic of a more profound malaise. Like any symptom, it raises a number of ancillary questions. Why has the American economy (not unlike that of Great Britain) increasingly failed to replace many of its worn-out, antiquated, uncompetitive factories? Why has plant capacity utilization been so low during most of the 1970s that it currently rests at one of the lowest levels since the Great Depression? Why have major American corporations been drawn increasingly toward acquisition of other large companies and toward continued high levels of foreign investment?

Broadly speaking, this country has been following policies which can only lead to intensified deindustrialization. Unrestricted import penetration (during more than a decade of economic stagnation and retrogression) and insufficient new investments have played a vital contributing role in this process.

To the extent that imports have captured significant shares of the American market, demand for domestically manufactured goods has declined and there has been a substantial drop in domestic output. The resulting excess of capacity requires fixed overhead to be amortized on the basis of fewer units of production. The consequently high capital consumption costs per unit represent an inflationary pressure which results in higher prices and lower profit margins. The former diminish the competitiveness of U.S.-based industry, and the latter decrease the attractiveness of new productive investment.

Another inflationary pressure which accompanies unused capacity is reduced labor productivity. Managerial and professional staff cannot always be reduced in proportion to cuts in output. The same is often true of technical, maintenance or clerical staff who must perform essential functions irrespective of the level of output. Increased unitized labor costs which accompany excess capacity place an added burden on import-penetrated industries. Additionally, layoffs of key managerial and professional personnel, now taking place at an increasing rate, lead to sizable losses in investment, both in skills and in special knowledge of the firm and industry.

The negative effects of high levels of unused capacity in key industries have become even more self-perpetuating for two reasons. First, in relatively short order, supplier industries are affected as demand for industrial commodities decreases substantially. The high and persistent unemployment caused by diminished output has a snowball effect, reducing consumption and restricting growth in nearly every economic sector. Second, excess capacity affects management investment decisions. In competitive, entrepreneurial industries such as, for example, apparel and consumer electronics, the general response to imports has been to shift further from manufacture to importation and distribution. Although the strategies vary among specific corporations, the major corporations in this country have dealt with unused capacity by increasing overseas investments, by mergers and acquisitions, or by speculation in currency, commodities and various financial instruments.

Finally, there is a propensity on the part of consumers who have altered their purchasing patterns in favor of imports to maintain that pattern. Irrespective of any future efforts by American producers to regain the market, a sizable residual level of demand for imports will remain.

VI

From 1950 to 1980, direct foreign investment by American companies expanded from $11.8 billion to $213 billion, an average annual growth rate in excess of 10 percent. The comparable average for domestic investment in the same years was less than 7 percent. This latter figure, however, is deceptively high, since in recent years massive amounts of money counted as productive investment have actually been used to finance corporate mergers and acquisitions.

Direct foreign investments divert assets which could stimulate domestic growth, improve productivity and increase American competitiveness in world markets. Tens of billions of dollars have been used to substitute foreign jobs for jobs in the United States. Mergers and acquisitions, which have dominated domestic corporate finance in recent years, have neither spurred growth nor created jobs. Resultant concentration of ownership, however, has contributed to the furtherance of oligopoly and with it increased levels of inflation.

The rationale behind U.S. Steel's acquisition of Marathon Oil is a case in point. At a time when the American share of both domestic and world steel output is shrinking and when mass layoffs have crippled entire communities, expending $6.4 billion to purchase a thriving energy company would not appear to be the best way to serve the interests of the nation. The motivating logic was, perhaps, best expressed by Thomas Graham, Chairman of Jones & Laughlin Steel Corporation, who, in a November 23, 1981 interview with *The New York Times,* stated: "There's too much capacity in the free world. We in the U.S. have been victimized by imports for 20 years. It would be an imprudent businessman who would expand until those problems are solved."

What he describes is part of a vicious cycle. Low levels of real domestic investment in past decades and excessive import penetration deprive American manufacturers of the incentive to expand. Plants become obsolete, further eroding competitiveness. Firms that lack resources die or are swallowed up. Those that have resources produce an increasing share of their output overseas, adding directly to domestic unemployment, diverting capital from domestic investment and making the United States even less competitive. Others engage in acquisitions which neither increase output nor cut costs. Those with adequate resources have engaged in speculation in the dollar, earning huge profits at the expense of price levels. Investment in financial instruments in lieu of productive outlays is yet another variation of the domestic deindustrialization process.

On January 29, 1982, *The Wall Street Journal* reported that, rather than expand its high-technology base, Bendix Corporation "may be content to keep its $500-million pool of cash in short-term investments." Citing a rate of return for its investment portfolio more than double that of its manufacturing equity, Bendix Chairman William M. Agee concluded: "We may be an investor of money for an extended period of time."

These alternative processes have renewed and intensified the cycle of deindustrialization; they are largely responsible for the loss of more than half of all the jobs in consumer electronics and large segments of steel, auto, home appliances, shoe production, tire and rubber output and apparel. There is no reason to believe that the trend will not continue to develop in every aspect of manufacture, simply because neither business nor government appears willing to do anything about it.

Since Japan has become the highly touted model of what to do, it is of interest that the Japanese have avoided this circular dilemma. As reported in *The Journal of Commerce* of November 6, 1981, Dr. Edwards Deming, often referred to as the prime architect of Japan's postwar boom, has observed:

> Management has failed in this country. The emphasis is on the quarterly dividend and the quick bucks, while the emphasis in Japan is to plan decades ahead. The next quarterly dividend is not as important as the existence of the company 5, 10 or 20 years from now. One requirement for innovation is faith that there will be a future.

Dr. Deming's last point should be emphasized in view of the apparent conclusion in some quarters that American manufacturing is expendable. Some of our economic pundits even suggest that industrialized countries, particularly the United States, abandon manufacturing and concentrate on service industries.

VII

The notion of an economy based entirely on services raises several distinct problems. Elimination of manufacturing jobs removes the usefulness of skills for which there is no analogue in the service sector, and creates insurmountable problems with respect to occupational adaptibility. Loss of investment in the training of literally millions of industrial workers represents an additional massive cost to the economy. Because there are relatively few well-paying jobs in the service sector, an economy devoid of manufacturing would also necessarily experience a general decline in living standards.

Aside from the direct economic effects, a pure service economy in the United States would diminish and ultimately eliminate the nation's capacity to provide the technological edge upon which American defense strategy rests. The viability of defense industry is inextricably linked with the highly diversified nature of American manufacturing. Equally essential is the ability to produce components to maintain and operate the defense apparatus. Forfeiture of America's industrial base would, in time, reduce the United States to the status of a client nation with respect to the purchase of arms.

Additionally, an economy which forfeits its right to produce for its own needs would also be unable to encourage general technological skill or innovation. Forfeiture of this country's goods-producing sector would compel the best technological minds to migrate.

Unrestricted trade and the investment practices of the multinationals, as I have contended throughout this article, can only lead to an America ultimately devoid of manufacturing. Nevertheless, present trade and investment policies must also be viewed in a broader context than just the domestic economy. The United States has responsibilities and strategic interests that must also be considered. They relate as well to nations seeking economic development.

VIII

Developing countries have been encouraged to adopt a rapid industrial development model, one that is heavily dependent upon export-oriented manufacture. However, the proposition that rapid industrialization of developing countries via exports contributes to the establishment of stable democracies is highly questionable. American trade policy toward Japan, for example, was only one component in a comprehensive plan that included genuine fostering of human rights and the establishment of institutions necessary to the existence of a participative democracy, including the creation of a national labor movement. The absence of similar efforts in the developing nations has severely limited the liberalizing role of trade. This is particularly clear with respect to those nations' chief resource—cheap labor.

In a world in which capital, technology, managerial skills and transportation techniques are largely internationalized, labor costs take on a special importance. Often labor represents the only meaningful variable in production costs. Consequently, rising wages make national economies that are dependent upon export income vulnerable to competition from other developing nations. This vulnerability is exacerbated by the difficulties associated with transition from export-oriented rapid development to an integrated industrial economy.

In those nations that have been characterized as new industrial countries, the policy has been to maintain artificially low wage rates and to permit unconscionable employment practices. These practices have resulted in economic polarization and repression of workers' rights—outcomes which perpetuate autocratic rule.

In short, unrestricted trade and investment do not benefit the majority of American workers or employers who depend upon the domestic market, nor do they benefit the majority of people in the developing nations. They serve neither American strategic nor political interests. Who, then, benefits from present policy?

The multinational corporations have the best of both worlds in developing nations. Their massive resources place them in an enviable position to negotiate with a prospective host country, enabling them to exact favorable conditions. Tax abatements, donations of land, site preparation, and waiver of requirements that they comply with government regulations are among the standard concessions made to global firms. Less publicized is the de facto subsidization of profits which occurs when the host country takes measures to keep wages artificially low. The incentive for repressive measures in developing countries comes, additionally, from the certain knowledge that there are other developing nations eager to host multinationals, nations where living standards are even lower.

How then should the United States deal equitably with assistance to developing nations, and, at the same time, maintain existing jobs, create additional employment, arrest the declining role of American industry and rebuild its industrial base?

IX

There are a number of specific measures that would facilitate reindustrialization in the United States and lead to positive development for both the United States and its trading partners. Implementation of a rational system of fair trade should certainly be a priority. Central to such a trade policy would be import quotas negotiated on a global basis in those sectors where import penetration has significantly diminished domestic employment and threatens to continue this process.

Increments in imports should be linked to the ability of the American economy to absorb them. Massive disruptions in domestic markets, the result of large increases in import levels from exporting countries, should be avoided. Negotiated import quotas would permit exporting nations to know in advance the potential size of the market in the United States and their share in it, and permit them to plan accordingly. Moreover, allocation on a global basis would prevent the rapid shift of market shares to nations where living standards are even lower than in the traditional exporting nations. A rational policy of fair trade can protect job opportunities in exporting as well as importing nations.

Let me emphasize that I am in no way advocating a revival of autarky. A return to the protectionism that characterized American trade policy in the 1920s and 1930s would be disastrous. I am just as convinced, however, that if we continue our present policy, mounting political pressure will make total protectionism unavoidable. Little time is available to begin corrective measures. The evident trend toward autarky is not likely to abate in the wake of anticipated levels of unemployment in excess of 10 percent and the fear of continued high levels of unemployment, even with economic recovery.

Profit-seeking, regardless of its costs to our nation and people, has been central to the process of deindustrialization. The rate of return on U.S. direct investments abroad is, as I have observed, significantly higher than profits on domestic investments. Many of the largest corporations and banks make 50 percent or more of their profits abroad, providing an irresistible incentive to those with enough resources to operate on a global basis. The allure also holds for diversification, via mergers and acquisitions.

Note

1. These estimates are those of the Bureau of Labor Statistics. The BLS data were cited before a congressional subcommittee by Under Secretary of Labor Malcolm R. Lovell, Jr., who noted that: "International comparisons of productivity are very difficult to make. The best available data [by the BLS] show that the United States has a higher output per employed person than other major developed countries, but that the gap is being narrowed." Statement of Mr. Lovell before the Subcommittee on Trade of the House Committee on Ways and Means, October 21, 1981, Xeroxed statement, p. 10. The relevant BLS table is unpublished but available on request under the title, "Real Gross Domestic Product . . . per Capita and . . . per Employed Person, 1950–1980." The figures presented by Mr. Lovell have since been slightly revised, to those given above.

9
Income Distribution and Labor Relations

Richard E. Caves

Besides the broad debate about international competition leading to a process of deindustrialization in the United States, there are other questions of specific concern to labor as well. Richard Caves addresses several of these, including income distribution, employment levels, and collective bargaining.

The export of capital by multinational corporations may, according to simple models, shift the distribution of income away from workers toward owners of capital. Within a more complicated Hickscher-Ohlin framework, however, Caves shows that international trade can perform all or part of the adjustment and eliminate the effect of outward investment on the returns to domestic factors of production. A short-term concern, however, is that foreign investment adds to unemployment by exporting jobs. Caves's survey of the evidence suggests that much outward investment is defensive, with no realistic possibility of continuing to serve foreign markets from the home country. The hypothesis that unions are able to appropriate for themselves a share of the multinationals' oligopoly rents is not, according to Caves, supported by data from firms of similar size, sector, and region. Transnational union activity is on the increase, but a positive impact on wage levels has not yet been clearly demonstrated.

The introduction to this selection in chapter 7 places Caves's survey within a more intensive examination of the runaway plant debate. It analyzes the question of how to measure whether outward investment exports jobs and what the results show.

T he MNE's relationship to wages and income distribution raises questions at two levels of analysis. In general equilibrium, the MNE reallocates capital between nations. That transfer may (or may not) alter the income distribution within the source and host countries. In the individual industry (partial-equilibrium analysis) the MNE affects the labor-management bargain just as it does the process of competition in the product market. . . .

Reprinted from "Income Distribution and Labor Relations," chapter 5 of *Multinational Enterprise and Economic Analysis*, by Richard E. Caves, published 1982 by the Cambridge University Press.

We shall take up these two levels of analysis in turn; the concluding section will suggest some propositions about the relationship between them.

9.1 Income Distribution in General Equilibrium

In the early 1970s the U.S. labor movement campaigned strenuously to restrict foreign investment by U.S. corporations, in the name of saving American jobs. Economic analysis does not buy the proposition that foreign investment permanently changes the level of unemployment, but it does affirm that short-run increases in unemployment and permanent declines in real wages can result. Neither prediction is categorical, and both depend sensitively on what we assume about the nature of direct investment and the structure of the economy. We shall start with the long-run effects on income distribution and wages, then treat employment effects as their short-run counterparts.

Theoretical Models

International-trade theory contains several models that relate international factor movements to the distribution of income. They abstract from a great deal, as do all tractable general-equilibrium models, but they offer an irreplaceable starting point for the analysis. Suppose we have two countries, Home and Foreign, each with a fixed factor endowment of (homogeneous) capital and labor. Each country produces a single good, and no commodity trade takes place between them. Suppose that (initially) the real return to capital is higher abroad, inducing some domestic capital to migrate to Foreign. In Home, each worker now is assisted by less capital in the production process; the marginal product of capital therefore rises, and that of labor falls. If all markets are competitive, including markets for factors of production, the wage falls. Home's national income rises because the capital that went abroad earns more for its owners than before. The returns to all units of Home's capital rise. Factor rewards go the opposite way in Foreign; the inflow of capital bids up the real wage and erodes the return to Foreign's native capital. Thus, self-interested labor opposes the emigration of domestic capital abroad but welcomes an influx of foreign MNEs.

This theoretical conclusion persists after we allow for commodity trade, so long as each country produces but a single commodity for domestic consumption and export, or all the commodities that each produces utilize capital and labor in the same proportions at any given set of factor prices.

The analysis does change substantially, however, if each nation produces more than one good, and the production functions differ in their factor intensities (proportions of capital to labor used at any given factor-price ratio). Then we are into the rich framework of the Heckscher-Ohlin model.[1] . . . The structure of the nation's trade does part of the adjusting to any international factor movements—an important new element in the model. Suppose that Home possesses more capital per worker than does Foreign, so that Home is well suited to produce capital-intensive goods. It tends to export capital-intensive goods, therefore, and import labor-intensive commodities; unless Home's citizens' tastes lean disproportionally toward capital-intensive goods, these will be cheap in Home in the absence of trade. Now suppose once again that some Home capital migrates to Foreign, leaving Home with a lowered level of capital per worker and Foreign with more than before. This shift in their factor endowments cuts into the international comparative advantage of Home and Foreign and generally predicts a reduced level of international trade between them.[2] Within each country the change in factor endowments induces a shift of the factor stock away from the exportables industry and into import-competing activities.

But that shift itself mitigates the negative effect of capital's emigration on the wage of Home's labor. That is because in *neither* Home's exporting industry nor its import-competing industry is the decline in the capital-labor ratio as large as it is for the country as a whole. That seeming impossibility results because the transfer of factors from Home's export-competing industry releases a lot of capital, and only a little labor, relative to the proportions called for in Home's import-competing industry. The interindustry shift of factors of production thereby does part of the job of adjusting to the economy's overall lower capital-labor ratio. Because the capital-labor ratio in each sector falls less, the wage falls less than it otherwise would.

In the extreme, the adjustment of Home's output pattern and international trade could account for the system's whole response to an outflow of capital, so that wages (and returns to capital) at Home would be unaffected by the capital outflow. This outcome is possible if Home is a small country whose exportable and import goods' prices are set competitively in a larger international market. Home's terms of trade then cannot be affected by the capital outflow. True, the outflow tends to cheapen Home labor and raise the return to Home capital, as before. But any such tendency generates profits for Home's import-competing industry (which uses relatively much labor) and makes Home's exportables industry (using more costly capital) run losses. Factors are shunted to the import-competing industry, as before. Indeed, because the terms of trade are given, this factor reallocation must go until the capital-labor proportions in all industries are back to their levels before the disturbing capital outflow. Then the old wage and capital-rental levels are consistent once more with equilibrium: Home's markets for labor and capital are cleared, and each of Home's commodity sectors earns normal profits.[3] This adjustment through the shifting of factors between industrial sectors will break down, of course, if Home's exportable industry is actually wiped out before the *ex ante* factor rewards are restored. Should that occur, Home would be back in the situation of the one-commodity model described earlier, and the direct connection between the economy's capital-labor endowment and the returns to its factors of production would again operate.

The preceding paragraph shows that real wages and capital rentals can be left quite undisturbed by exogenous international movements of capital or by other "quantity" disturbances such as shifts of demand between products. What the factor rewards in a country then depend on is the terms of trade, the price of the exported good relative to that of the good produced in competition with imports. International factor movements or demand shifts that leave the equilibrium terms of trade unchanged also leave relative factor rewards unchanged. But if Home's terms of trade should improve, for example, the rise in the price of its capital-intensive export good is associated with a rise in the rentals to capital and a fall in the real wage. This proposition is known as the Stolper-Samuelson theorem.

An important corollary of the Heckscher-Ohlin model is that a country's tariff policy affects international capital movements (Mundell, 1957). Suppose that Foreign wishes to adopt a policy that will provide higher rentals to its domestic capitalists. Aware of the Stolper-Samuelson theorem, it imposes a tariff on imports of capital-intensive goods, raising their domestic price and therefore tending to raise capital rentals. But suppose also that capital remains indifferent as to the country in which it "works." If Foreign is a small country, its tariff and the resulting rise in capital rentals set off unlimited capital inflows from abroad, which persist so long as the local reward to capital lies above the world level. The favor that Foreign's tariff does for its capitalists' income is therefore transitory, because the capital inflows from the rest of the world continue until its return is pushed back down to the world level. Foreign winds up with a larger capital stock in residence, but no permanent change in either capital rentals or wages.

[We have] developed a variant on the basic Heckscher-Ohlin model by assuming that capital is perfectly mobile between countries but not between industries. Then "food capital" earns the same rental everywhere in the world, as does "clothing capital," but the two rentals need not equal one another. The qualitative implications of that model for income distribution and real wages differ only in some respects from those of the simpler Heckscher-Ohlin model developed here. An outflow of either type of capital from home will lower Home's real wage, unless factor rewards are locked in to the terms of trade in the way described earlier. Assume an exogenous rise in the price of Home's import-competing good (i.e., a deterioration in Home's terms of trade). This terms-of-trade change affects the real wage in this specific-capital model in a different way than in the basic Heckscher-Ohlin model. Capital rentals rise in Home's labor-intensive clothing sector (clothing is assumed the labor-intensive good . . .) and they fall in Home's export-oriented food sector.

But now we cannot tell whether Home's real wage will rise or fall.[4] Somewhat in the same spirit is Hartman's (1980) model, in which MNE capital and Foreign's capital are complements in foreign-subsidiary production. Expansion of MNE capital in Foreign then raises the demand for Foreign capital and could lower Foreign wages.

Empirical Evidence

The only empirical estimates of the effect of foreign investment on U.S. income and its distribution have used a simple model that makes no allowance for the important role of international trade in curbing the redistributive effects of international capital movements—the one-commodity model described earlier. Musgrave (1975, Chapter 9) simulated the consequences of repatriating to the United States the stock of direct investments that it held abroad in 1968. Her results depend on the measure of capital used and the assumption made about the elasticity of substitution between capital and labor in U.S. production (the lower it is, the more does the repatriated capital drive down capital's share and raise labor's). But the basic story is simple: Although the repatriation does not change U.S. total income much,[5] it substantially increases labor's income (and share) and lowers the income flowing to capital. A study by Thurow (1976), using a similar model, came to the same qualitative conclusion. It is unfortunate that these studies neglected the influence of international trade on income distribution, because, as we have seen, their conclusions could be greatly altered if the Heckscher-Ohlin relationship between the terms of trade and the distribution of income holds empirically (Bergsten et al., 1978, p. 104–10).

Frank and Freeman (1978, Chapter 8) rested their estimates on a somewhat more ambitious model, although their efforts were addressed to taking account of saving behavior rather than international trade. In their model, Home is a single-product economy using labor and capital, but Foreign contains two sectors—one using only imported (MNE) capital, the other using only domestic capital, both employing domestic labor. Productivity may differ between Home's economy and Foreign's MNE sector: The higher is Foreign's relative productivity, the greater the incentive for Home's capital to go abroad. Similarly, MNE capital in Foreign may enjoy a capital-specific productivity advantage over domestic capital. At this stage the model yields the same conclusion as that of Musgrave and Thurow: Repatriating all of Home's exported capital will raise the real wage in Home, lowering the return to capital.[6] Home's saving rate is next made endogenous in the Frank-Freeman model. This change affects the results strongly. The chance to place capital abroad in high-productivity activities now increases Home's rate of saving. Conversely, requiring the repatriation of Home's MNE capital restricts saving in Home and cuts the capital stock, rather than providing more capital to work with Home's labor. Therefore, the action lowers Home's wages and national income. Thus, Frank and Freeman identified a second significant theoretical omission from those simulations that confidently predict that MNE's exports of capital lower the domestic wage: the adaptive adjustment of saving, as well as of international trade (also see Koizumi and Kopecky, 1980). The distributional consequences of foreign investment in the long run remain a strictly unsettled issue.

9.2 Employment and Wages: Short Run and Long Run

The late 1960s and early 1970s saw extensive controversies in the United States over whether or nor foreign investments by U.S. MNEs were reducing employment in America and worsening the balance of payments. These two short-run effects are related to each other as well as to the long-run analysis just set forth. Here we continue to focus the analysis on income distribution and employment. . . .

Under certain assumptions, the effect of foreign investment on employment is the short-run counterpart of its ultimate effect on real wages. If foreign investment reduces Home's real wage in the long run, then in the short run Home's export of capital brings labor into excess supply—increases unemployment—at the going wage rate. Some interesting analyses, however, deal with the short run directly, rather than borrowing from the long-run context. They lack standard names in the literature, but we shall call them the *investment-substitution* and *export-substitution* questions.

1. When a unit of capital is transferred from Home to Foreign, does it really add an extra unit to Foreign's capital stock and subtract one from Home's? This is the investment-substitution question.
2. When a unit of capital has been transferred from Home to Foreign *and* changed the two countries' capital stocks unit for unit, does it actually reduce the scope for commodity trade as the Heckscher-Ohlin model predicts? This is the export-substitution question.

Both questions turn on the behavior of variables other than employment and real wages. However, they certainly do affect those variables, and so they can usefully be considered here. . . .

Investment Substitution

What makes these short-run models differ from the long-run analysis of section 9.1 is their recognition of a direct administrative link between international capital movements and commodity-output decisions. This link, the essence of the MNE, is missing from the long-run general-equilibrium model. The long-run model is at least internally consistent, because in perfectly competitive markets the manufacturing firm plays no essential role as an owner or exporter of capital; capital exports affect firms' production decisions only by altering the prices of their factor inputs. If a competitive firm also runs a foreign subsidiary, it will see no connection between its decisions to place capital abroad and its decisions about what goods to produce at home or abroad; each decision depends solely on market prices.

The investment-substitution question arises from two properties of the firm as a microeconomic organization. First, MNEs and other firms compete directly in particular product markets. If a MNE spots an investment opportunity, it transfers a substantial sum of capital[7] and establishes a new subsidiary. This action preempts the investment opportunity for any local firms or other MNEs that have had their eyes on it, and they adjust their investment plans accordingly. Of course, in a neoclassical competitive model we expect the addition of some capital to a nation's stock to drive down capital's marginal product; the investment-substitution problem arises because large, lumpy investments may be involved, and the adversary relationship appears in particular product markets. The second property concerns the firm's ability to finance projects. The competitive model assumes that each firm can borrow (or lend) unlimited amounts of funds at "the" market rate of interest— a property preserved in sophisticated modern models of competitive capital markets. However, there are also good reasons why capital markets may be imperfect in the sense that the individual firm faces a rising marginal cost of borrowed funds; the more it borrows, the higher rate of interest it must pay. This constraint puts alternative uses of the firm's funds in competition with one another in a way not recognized in the purely competitive model. Internally generated funds (i.e., retained earnings) may be adequate to support an investment in a foreign subsidiary or an expansion of domestic capacity, but not both. If the less profitable opportunity cannot be justified at the higher interest rate demanded for funds borrowed on the capital market, another firm may grab the project.

The investment-substitution problem concerns the possibility that a dollar of capital transferred from Home to Foreign may not correspond to the change that actually occurs in the two countries' capital stocks. Hufbauer and Adler (1968), who explored the alternatives, described as *classical* the assumption that the amount of capital moved internationally corresponds to the change in each country's capital stock. The first alternative that they posed, the *reverse-classical* assumption, rests on product-market competition between the MNE and other firms. The MNE invests one dollar in Foreign. It preempts an investment opportunity that would otherwise have been taken by a domestic firm, which now cancels its investment plans. As a result, total investment in

Foreign does not increase. When our MNE invests abroad, we can imagine that it strains its investment capacity so that it must withdraw from some investment project in Home. But this abandoned project leaves an opening for some other Home firm, and as a result total investment in Home does not fall. The reverse-classical case leaves the world's capital stock unchanged, as does the classical case; unlike the classical case, it also leaves each country's capital stock unchanged.

To provide microeconomic underpinning for Hufbauer and Adler's third assumption, suppose that our MNE produces distinctive goods with no close substitutes either at home or abroad. It makes a foreign investment, but without reducing its capital expenditure in Home. No other firm in Foreign finds its market shriveled, and so no offsetting decline in expenditure occurs there. And no other Home firm perceives an investment opportunity left untended, and so Home's capital formation is not further affected. In this, the *anticlassical* case, Foreign's capital stock is expanded, but Home's remains unchanged.

These three alternative assumptions about international investments and capital stocks rest on conflicting views about the market context of foreign-investment decisions. Each is logical under some assumptions, and each can be spun into a consistent story about general-equilibrium adjustments in the economy.[8] They have quite different implications for employment in the short run and real wages in the long run. The reverse-classical version involves no change in nations' capital stocks, only in their ownership. Therefore, a capital transfer does not affect real wages. The classical assumption about transfers implies the real-wage effects outlined in Section 9.1. The anti-classical version entails an increase in Foreign's capital stock but no reduction in Home's; it cannot be analyzed simply, but its implications for real wages are likely to lie between those of the classical and reverse-classical cases.

Export Substitution

The export-substitution question stands forth most clearly if we make the classical assumption about capital transfers: Home's capital stock falls and Foreign's rises by the amount of the transfer. What happens to Home's equilibrium level of exports?[9] What does the effect on exports in turn imply for real wages and employment? In the long-run Heckscher-Ohlin model of Section 9.1, capital transfers, on certain assumptions, substitute for exports, reducing Home's equilibrium level of international trade (exports and imports) overall. The capital transfer also lowers Home's real wage under most assumptions. However, the shriveling of trade and the reduction of real wages are not inevitably connected, and indeed a capital transfer can lower wages without affecting trade, or vice versa.

Most discussion of export substitution, however, has taken place in a more microeconomic and political context: Are American MNEs "running away" from American labor to serve their foreign markets through plants abroad rather than by exports from the United States? The Heckscher-Ohlin model shows that this emotive charge could be theoretically well grounded. However, as with the investment-substitution question, the simple case ignores the MNE as an organization and the product-market setting in which it operates. One response to the runaway charge is that capital transfers from the United States are purely defensive, intended to preserve the U.S. company's stake in a market that it can no longer serve profitably via U.S. exports. This case is essentially Hufbauer and Adler's reverse-classical assumption: Somebody puts capital in place abroad to serve the foreign market and oust U.S. exports, and the only question is whether that export-displacing plant is owned by a U.S. MNE or by somebody else. This counter to the runaway charge, once again, can be made logically tight with a friendly set of assumptions. Give the U.S. exporter and potential MNE a goodwill asset resting on its past exporting and sales-promotion activities in the foreign market, but an asset that will crumble if product-market rivals increase their local capacity to supply competing goods. Impose some disturbance that shifts absolute advantage so as to favor serving the foreign market from a plant abroad. It then follows that the foreign market is lost to U.S. exports in any case, and the only question is whether or not the U.S. firm invests abroad—goes multinational—in order to defend the cash flow from its goodwill asset.

Another response to the runaway charge focuses not on whether or not exports fall without the foreign investment but rather on whether or not they rise subsequent to the foreign investment. In the extreme, exports and foreign investments may be complementary rather than substitutes. . . . Suppose that high costs of information about foreign markets can be greatly reduced if the MNE has a plant in the foreign market. Suppose that the plant's presence increases the firm's credibility as a reliable source of supply and reduces the cost of selling locally its full line of goods, including exports from the home base. Then the foreign investment might initially displace some of the firm's exports to a market, but ultimately these transactional factors could bring its exports to a higher equilibrium level than before the subsidiary was founded. The transactional approach to the MNE . . . shows that this outcome is possible, and some empirical evidence on the mixture of vertical and horizontal relationships lends its some plausibility.[10] However, the fact that it is possible does not make it inevitable for the individual firm.[11] Furthermore, the ultimately complementary relationship between exports and foreign investments runs into some trouble in general equilibrium. Firm *A* may profitably lay hands on the capital required both to found a plant abroad and to expand its export capacity at home. But the country's capital stock is ultimately limited by its savers' responsiveness to higher expected rates of return. Therefore, not every firm can tread the primrose path of export complementarity without the game being spoiled by overall resource constraints. Once again, the issue joins onto the investment-substitution question: Export complementarity has a close affinity for Hufbauer and Adler's anticlassical assumption that foreign investment actually raises the capital stock abroad without reducing it at home.[12]

In summary, we have suggested that the short-run and partial-equilibrium approaches to the effects of MNEs on real wages and income distribution lead into a messy array of considerations that can be grouped around the questions of investment substitution and export substitution. These questions substantially overlap each other and lead to the adduction of a series of models that one by one sound partial and arbitrary, but together provide some feeling for the array of possible outcomes. And they show how the transactional underpinnings of the MNE can be related to general-equilibrium models that emphasize the constraints on the economy's overall stock of resources and its influence on resource allocation and factor rewards.

Empirical Evidence

Empirical evidence relevant to these models takes several forms. One is simulated calculations that illustrate the consequences of these various models but do not help us to determine which is more nearly correct. Other approaches employ either case studies or statistical analysis to test the predictions directly.

One simulation that received much attention in the United States was prepared by the U.S. Tariff Commission under a Congressional charge. Concentrating on export substitution, it sought to determine the short-run effects of U.S. investments abroad on jobs provided by U.S. industry under various assumptions about export substitution or complementarity. The U.S. Tariff Commission (1973, pp. 651–72) concluded that all foreign investments that had occurred through 1970 had cost the United States 1.3 million jobs, on the assumption that all foreign production by MNEs (whether U.S.-based or foreign) could instead have been replaced by production at the MNE's national base—full export substitution. However, this large loss can be turned into a slight gain by shifting to the following assumption: If foreign production by U.S. MNEs were eliminated, U.S. exports would hang onto only that proportion of the displaced subsidiaries' market equal to the share that U.S. exports to that market held of all goods exported to that market. Also, an allowance was made for the increased jobs provided in the United States by investments from abroad associated with the gain that had occurred in foreign countries' share of world exports. This case can be described either as limited export substitution or as a partial embrace of the reverse-classical assumption about investment substitution. Frank and Freeman (1978) attempted to get somewhat further, estimating what share of foreign markets would be lost if U.S. companies had to serve them from higher-cost domestic production facilities (1978, Chapter 3), and they also pursued domestic job losses due to foreign investment by means of the input-output structure of the economy (1978, Chapter 5). Useful though they are, these calculations still pursue the implications of their own assumptions, rather than discriminating among the competing models.

That brings us to the case studies and statistical analyses. The case studies, in the nature of things, are of limited value because they represent small and nonrandom samples. In a collection of nine cases, Stobaugh et al. (1976) concluded that foreign investment by U.S. MNEs is not generally hostile to jobs in the United States. Some foreign investments had little to do with American exports or imports; others allowed the investing firm to avoid losing its foreign market entirely. The only foreign investments deemed to displace U.S. exports served markets that would have grown noncompetitive for U.S. exports anyhow. Critics have not been won over by Stobaugh's cases. Some of them can be read to yield different conclusions. Case studies from other sources support no clear-cut conclusions.[13]

Statistical approaches have also been rather diverse in their results, but together they do leave a fairly clear set of conclusions. They have, one way or another, sought to determine whether exports and foreign investments of the United States are substitutes for one another or complements. Several studies, such as that of the U.S. Tariff Commission (1973, pp. 334–41), noted that exports and imports undertaken by U.S. MNEs were growing faster than other U.S. trade or that U.S. domestic output and employment were growing faster in industries with more foreign investment. But neither finding really bears on the question of what would happen to exports or employment if the industries making foreign investments made fewer of them. Several cross-sectional statistical studies . . . concluded that tariffs raised around a national market promote an inflow of foreign investment and can be presumed to reduce imports. That result suggests that exports and foreign investments are substitutes, but it does not preclude the possibility that the foreign subsidiaries, having taken root, can *later* draw in enough complementary imports to offset the initial substitution.[14]

The most revealing statistical analyses are those that examine the net relationship between exports of U.S. companies and the sales of their foreign subsidiaries after controlling for as many as possible of the variables that should affect both (such as the advertising and research activities of the U.S. industry, scale economies in production, and various other factors relating to U.S. comparative advantage in international trade). Bergsten et al. (1978, pp. 73–96) concluded that investment abroad is complementary with U.S. exports up to a point: U.S. exports increase with net local sales of U.S. subsidiaries until the latter reach a certain level, but the further overseas capacity starts to displace exports.[15] This conclusion accords well with the organizational model of the MNE that has emerged . . . : Foreign subsidiaries' role in promoting exports should depend on the subsidiaries' existence, but not especially on their size.

Lipsey and Weiss (1981) undertook an analysis similar to that of Bergsten et al. and reached similar conclusions about the general complementarity between U.S. exports and the net sales of overseas affiliates. But some additional findings also turned up: The complementarity relationship holds for most major commodity groups, and it holds for both developed-country markets and LDCs. The sales of U.S. subsidiaries abroad prove to be substitutes for exports to their local markets coming from industrial countries other than the United States. There is also weak evidence that the subsidiaries of foreign MNEs are hostile to the performance of U.S. exports (Glejser, 1976). The Lipsey-Weiss study thus suggests that the complementary export and subsidiary sales by U.S. MNEs are both in a competitive relationship with sales by other exporting countries and their MNEs.

Neither of these statistical inquiries into export substitution addressed the general-equilibrium problem, and thus they cannot be generalized to the overall effect of foreign investment on real wages. For example, if foreign investments and exports are complementary up to a point, that could merely mean that the U.S. capital stock is diverted toward industries that undertake foreign investments (which place it partly at home, partly abroad) and away from those uninvolved in foreign investment. Whether real wages rise or fall will then depend in part on the relative capital intensities of the two sectors, a question with no obvious empirical answer. Furthermore, we should recall that the investment-substitution issue has been left unenlightened by empirical evidence. Some macroeconomic studies (Lubitz, 1971*a*; Van Loo, 1977) have supported the classical assumption, finding that capital formation in Canada expands by at least one dollar when a dollar inflow of foreign investment is received. But the experiences of other countries have not been studied.

9.3 Labor-Management Relations and Collective Bargaining

Beyond its effects on overall wages and income distribution, the MNE may change the welfare of workers through its employment policies and its stance in collective bargaining. Recent research (Pugel, 1980*a*) has confirmed that trade unions capture some fraction of the monopoly rents available to employers, and thus firms' multinational status may affect the wage bargain by placing rents imputed to the MNE within the union's reach. Or the MNE may curb wage demands by means of bargaining tactics not available to single-market rivals. The MNE's influence on the labor bargain may devolve simply from its large size or the size of its plants, not its international operations. For example, recent research suggests that workers' pay and their discontent with the job both increase with the size of the plant that employs them.

Study of this subject is complicated by the diversity of objectives that trade unions may pursue and differences among countries in collective-bargaining practices. For example, in West Germany, labor possesses important statutory rights of codetermination—to be represented in decisions concerning the enterprise. American unions, although they may try to block some decisions of MNE managers, persist in the tradition of confrontational relationships between labor and management and show interest in codetermination only in special situations.

Organization of Labor Relations within the MNE

How far the MNE decentralizes its labor-relations activities provides useful background evidence to the analysis. The large differences between countries in terms of the legal and cultural environment of labor relations predict that MNEs will choose a substantial degree of decentralization. So do the patterns of organization typically found in MNEs. . . . Because labor markets are, at most, national in scope, and because the firm's labor-market decisions are largely, if not entirely, tactical and short-run decisions, most decision-making responsibility should devolve to the national subsidiary or even to the plant. The empirical evidence clearly supports this prediction. A Conference Board survey (Hershfield, 1975) of both U.S. MNEs and foreign companies operating in the United States found that subsidiary managers in nearly three-fourths of the companies could conclude formal labor agreements without seeking parental approval.[16] The independence increases with the physical and cultural distance of the subsidiary from its parent: Only the labor relations of U.S. MNE's Canadian subsidiaries are closely integrated with those of their nearby parents. Most large British MNEs similarly stay out of actual collective bargaining by their subsidiaries (Roberts and May, 1974). The more countries in which the MNE operates, the more likely is a hands-off policy. But 63 percent of the U.K. firms occasionally advise subsidiaries on labor-relations matters and four-fifths are at least sometimes involved with subsidiaries' changes in pensions and other investment-type decisions.[17]

This evidence of decentralization need not imply that the MNE's labor relations are indistinguishable from those of a neighboring national enterprise. Rather, the pattern simply accords with the evidence that labor markets are nationally distinctive and independent of one another, so that MNEs typically see little advantage in the transnational coordination of their collective-bargaining activities. But bargainers on labor's side may nonetheless find it useful to recognize and exploit the MNE's international affiliations. Furthermore, labor relations are a "latently transnational" issue (Kujawa, 1975, Chapter 7), because they may involve investment-type commitments that significantly affect the expected future cash flow of the subsidiary and thereby trespass on the MNE's centralized financial functions.

Hypotheses about MNEs

The descriptive literature on MNE's labor relations suggests a number of hypotheses about how a company's MNE status might affect the outcome of collective bargaining. The following are representative:

1. The successful MNE generally holds some firm-specific rent-yielding assets. The more closely does the cash flow approximate a pure rent, the more attractive a target it is for trade-union bargaining efforts. To the extent that national wage-setting processes permit bargaining at the level of the firm (rather than industrywide or economywide), employee-compensation levels should be elevated where such rents can be appropriated.
2. Multinational status may carry a variety of advantages in the bargaining process that counter the MNE's attractiveness as a target. Transfer pricing can serve to obscure the appropriable cash flow of any one subsidiary and thus frustrate the appropriation effort. The MNE enjoys bargaining ploys that national firms lack. If the MNE maintains capacity to produce the same goods in different national markets, output curtailed by a strike in one market can be replaced from another subsidiary's plant. The cash flows of corporate affiliates permit a given subsidiary greater discretion in taking a strike. The MNE can credibly threaten to close down a given plant, or shelve any expansion plans there, and choose another national market for any additions to output. These ploys can be used either to forestall assaults on the MNE's rent stream or to take bargaining advantage of any inelasticity in the labor supply that it faces.
3. Apart from the substance of the labor bargain, the MNE's presence as bargainer may wield qualitative effects on labor relations and productivity. These effects also run in various directions. The MNE's management comes equipped with an inventory of labor-relations practices that, at least initially, reflect conditions in its national base and harmonize poorly with those in the host nation. Even without foreign gaucherie, long lines of bureaucratic communication may impair the MNE's responsiveness to local labor problems (to the extent that the delegation of authority to subsidiaries is incomplete). And the universal suspicion of foreigners can afflict any of the MNE's transactions in the host economy. Counter to these disadvantages, the MNE may arbitrage successful practices and innovations from one labor market to another.

These hypotheses lead to diverse predictions about the wage levels that MNEs will pay, the harmony of their labor relations, and the plant productivity that they will attain. One can only turn to the empirical evidence to let the data sort out these diverse possibilities.

Evidence on Labor Relations

The available studies of MNE's wages and working conditions have controlled for far too few extraneous influences to shed much light on these hypotheses, but they are worth a brief review.[18] United States affiliates of foreign companies pay compensation per employee 7 percent higher than that for all U.S. companies. However, nearly all the difference can be explained by differences in the industrial and regional distributions of the subsidiaries; with these controlled, no clear difference remains.[19] Outside the United States, the only systematic study of other industrial countries has been that of the U.S. Tariff Commission (1973, Chapter 7), which provides data on the wages of U.S. MNEs and national enterprises in the United States and in six other countries. The data come from diverse sources and may not be comparable. Overall, the MNE's wages exceed those of indigenous firms in the United States and Canada, are about the same in Belgium-Luxembourg, France, and West Germany, and are a little lower in the United Kingdom. These comparisons did not control for industry mix, region, or other variables. Dunning and Morgan (1980) added controls for differences in the industry mix between MNEs and indigenous firms—a desirable step, because high technology and product differentiation as bases for foreign investment bias the MNE's distribution toward high-wage industries. They found that control for industry mix halves the excess of MNE parents' wages in the United States but still leaves them significantly above national firms; the same holds for Canada. In the European countries, however, control for industry mix pushes the U.S. MNE's wages significantly below those of national firms. Company size differences may explain the pattern. United States MNEs are the largest firms (and often operate the largest plants) in the United States and Canada, whereas on average they are smaller than the leading national firms in the European countries. Considerable evidence suggests that wages tend to increase with size of plant and company within national labor markets. Unfortunately, no studies have controlled for both industry mix and company (or plant) size (not to mention region), and so we do not know the size or sign of any residual difference that could be attributed to MNE status per se.[20]

Casual evidence that MNEs pay higher wages than national firms is fairly abundant for LDCs. The pattern held for Mexico in the U.S. Tariff Commission study, for example, and Reuber et al. (1973, pp. 175–6) found quite a strong effect on wages of skilled and semiskilled labor. This difference in the setting of LDC labor markets suggests another feature that often is not controlled in comparisons between MNEs and other firms. One reason suggested why large plants and companies pay higher wages is to secure "better" workers, meaning those more congenial to accepting responsibility or direction and thus cooperating harmoniously in a large and complex organization. In

LDC labor markets there is probably great variance in individual experience with the discipline of a complex organization. This would increase the differential advantageously paid by large companies, especially those with alien management, to buy improved supervision at the plant level. Taira and Standing (1973) tested this hypothesis by inquiring whether or not the wage differentials paid by MNEs are proportionally greater in LDCs where quality differentials in the worker population . . . are greater—indicated by low literacy rates and average income per capita. The hypothesis was confirmed.

Overall, the evidence on wages paid by MNEs does not affirm any pervasive differences due strictly to their transnational status, once we take account of their industry mix, size, and so forth. Most of the case studies (comparisons made within one industry or a single country) have shown no appreciable difference (International Labour Organization, 1976b, pp. 4–18). Nonetheless, the organizational models of the MNE do lead us to expect some differences in other aspects of the MNE's labor relations. One promising avenue is the incidence of labor disputes. This performance dimension has been studied particularly in the United Kingdom, where the issue is frequently to the fore. Steuer and Gennard (1971) investigated differences in the frequencies of strikes affecting foreign subsidiaries and their industrial competitors in Britain. For two years in the 1960s they found the MNEs to experience fewer strikes. The distribution of strikes by duration indicated that the MNEs in particular incur fewer of the short, unpredictable strikes that seem so costly to industrial productivity in Britain. However, Forsyth (1972, Chapter 7, 1973) examined the pattern for U.S. MNEs in Scotland over the 1960s decade and failed to confirm the overall pattern found by Steuer and Gennard. The difference may be due to different size distributions of foreign-controlled and domestic plants, or to the particular traits of a somewhat backward industrial region. Creigh and Makeham (1978) employed a statistical procedure that allowed them to control for at least two relevant variables—the labor intensity of the industry and the average size of its plants. Both should be positively related to the incidence of strikes, and in fact they are. With these variables controlled, no relationship exists between strike-proneness and foreign ownership among British manufacturing industries.

A certain amount of anecdotal evidence supports the proposition that MNEs make some innovations in labor relations as one aspect of the international arbitrage of skills and intangible assets.[21] An important example is the introduction into British labor relations of productivity bargaining—negotiations to remove work rules that drain productivity in exchange for higher wages. Gunter (1975, pp. 150–1) noted that MNE's innovations sometimes have far-reaching effects on the organization of labor relations. In Europe, the presence of MNEs accelerates a trend toward more labor bargaining at the plant level rather than at industry and national levels. This occurs partly at the urging of MNE managers and partly because of the opportunity MNEs offer for trade unions to gain a share of higher productivity levels (alternatively, to evade the downward pull on industry-determined wages of marginal producers' ability to pay). In LDCs, the foreign subsidiaries sometimes prove more adept at dealing with trade unions than do inexperienced domestic companies (Kassalow, 1978). Another effect of the MNE is to complicate the legal arrangements for worker participation in management that prevail in a number of European countries, because the centralization in the parent of certain important decisions on finance, investment, and employment puts them outside the reach of workers' representatives in the subsidiary. Still, the overall judgment holds that MNEs have not worked any transforming effects on national systems of labor relations (Banks and Stieber, 1977, pp. 6–9, 120–34).

Multinational Union Activity

We noticed that MNEs often enjoy rents to their specialized assets—rents that present an attractive target to trade unions or others whose bargaining power might give access to a slice. Yet there is no broad-based evidence that MNEs pay above-market wages in the industrial countries where trade unions' bargaining power is most likely to count. Unions' efforts may not have been crowned with success, but have efforts been made at all? Hostility toward the MNE has been in good supply among industrial-country trade unions. In this section we shall explore their bargaining relationship to the MNEs, emphasizing the effort to coalesce labor's bargaining power across national boundaries. The view taken of trade unions here is a narrowly economic one that assumes the exertion of monopoly power in the labor market to be one of their functions. Would labor gain from extending the bargaining process across national boundaries? If so, are transnational union coalitions an actuality or a likely prospect?

First, some analytical points. In the case of the horizontal MNE—actual or potential—a monopolistic seller of labor clearly gains from a bargaining coalition across national boundaries. If the firm can (actually or potentially) serve a given market from plants in several countries, its demand for labor is more elastic in any one country than in the whole set, and so monopolizing its labor supply internationally should yield larger rents than would monopolizing it country by country. But the gains to unions from international bargaining with MNEs should not be oversold. The monopoly power of internationally coordinated labor actually does not depend on transnational ownership links among companies. Unions that coalesce to force up widget-industry wages in both Home and Foreign will find themselves facing a less elastic derived demand for labor whatever the organization of the industry. Also, the short-run situation with established horizontal MNEs differs from that in an industry of non-MNE national producers only if the MNEs can juggle their market supply patterns in the short run but independent firms cannot work out equivalent arm's-length transactions among themselves.

Nonetheless, let us put aside these doubts and assume that MNEs do in fact increase the rents unions can expect from transnational bargaining. How likely, then are the necessary coalitions of unions across national boundaries? The theoretical models set forth in Section 9.1 make the point that sellers of labor in different countries face the same plight as any potentially colluding sellers: Although they benefit from acting jointly, each has an incentive to cheat on the coalition and free-ride on the price increases exacted by the others. In the general-equilibrium model, capital transfers from Home to Foreign lower Home's real wage (under some conditions) and raise that in Foreign. The same proposition holds for the single industry: If Home's union demands a higher wage but Foreign's does not, the MNE shifts to Foreign and increases the demand for labor there. In short, the international solidarity of union bargaining has the same built-in tendency to self-destruct as does any collusive arrangement.

Discussions of transnational bargaining in the field of labor economics stress not this theoretical stumbling block but rather the national labor markets' differing institutions and legal systems. National unions differ in their goals. Some are concerned with the paycheck and immediate working conditions, others with broader social and political goals. Bargaining takes place at different points in the market—the individual plant or company, across a whole industry, or indeed for the whole national labor force. There is obviously little room for international cooperation in bargaining when labor's claims are targeted to an industry that contains assorted MNEs and also a roster of national firms. Labor-relations systems differ on the issues bargained over. Fringe benefits central to one country's bargaining arena may be mandated by legislation in another, and thus removed from contention. These points are merely examples, but they serve to establish the general point that differences among countries in general and specific objectives, labor-market structures, and legal frameworks are formidable deterrents to the international coordination of labor's bargaining power.[22]

With the dice loaded against transnational coordination of labor's demands, how far has the process actually gone? These coordination efforts cost real resources for the unions involved. Like other rational economic actors, unions can be expected to make only modest investments in games that are unlikely to be worth the effort. That simple prediction seems well supported. American unions have been active in a general way in encouraging labor organization in other countries, but not with specific coordination in mind. They have urged their counterparts abroad to demand U.S.-level wages and working conditions in the overseas plants of U.S. MNEs, but in light of the generally higher levels of real productivity prevailing in the United States, that posture is surely intended more to deter foreign investment than to maximize labor's income internationally once the foreign investment is in place. American labor has also tried to use the machinery regulating labor-management relations to wield some influence on companies' decisions to invest abroad (Kujawa, 1973, pp. 253–8). This strategy joins with complaints over the centralization in MNEs of authority for decisions that affect jobs and the employment bargain in local labor markets. However, neutral observers have concluded that the issue in the United States is strictly the substance of the decisions, not a desire for codetermination.

What international coordination does take place adds up to much less than internationally coordinated bargaining. There may be exchanges of information designed, say, to determine the joint profitability of a MNE's various arms and the effects of a strike in one country on its operations in another. There may be gestures of sympathy in one country over a labor dispute taking place in another. There may be efforts to get a MNE's labor contracts to expire at the same time in several countries, to pave the way for parallel international wage demands. But actual successes in bringing about international collective bargaining with a single MNE seem essentially nonexistent.[23]

These generalizations have been confirmed by survey evidence for the United States (Hershfield, 1975) and the United Kingdom (Roberts and May, 1974). The U.S. survey determined that 10 percent of U.S.-based MNEs had been contacted by unions on a transnational basis. These contacts had not actually led to transnational bargaining, only to union representations on transnational issues. Another 10 percent of companies knew of union efforts to undertake international coordination but had not yet been confronted with the results. Of non-U.S. MNEs contacted in the U.S. survey, somewhat larger proportions had encountered international union activity—one-fifth being contacted about transnational issues, another one-quarter aware of coordination efforts. In the survey of British MNEs, 10 percent indicated some international coordinating mechanism in place among their unions, and another 10 percent expected to face this prospect in a few years.

These surveys also provided some evidence that transnational efforts at labor coordination take place where the expected rewards are highest. Hershfield (1975, pp. 10–11) found that target companies tend to be larger and more involved internationally, which would increase the return expected of unions' investment in coordination efforts. Target companies also are much more centralized in their labor-relations policies, so that unions might find it easier to hammer out coordinated demands with some hope of their acceptance. Those areas of the industrial nations where international unionism has made some headway also match one's economic predictions. They are the United States and Canada, with similar language, culture, and productivity levels (Crispo, 1967), and the European Community, with its rapid expansion of international business (Gunter, 1975, pp. 151–7).

Despite the modest headway made in transnational union activity, the general expectation seems to be that it will increase. This prospect points to some scope for research on whether or not MNEs have in fact tended to make movements of money wages—as the outcome of the labor bargain—behave more similarly among countries. Dunning and Morgan (1980) found no evidence in a crude test, but more remains to be done.

9.4 Summary

The effects of MNEs on real wages and income distribution can be examined in both general equilibrium and the partial-equilibrium context of the individual industry. In the simplest version of general equilibrium, capital export by MNEs reduces the real wage, and capital import increases it. In the Heckscher-Ohlin model, however, international trade does part of the adjusting to an international capital flow, and, in the limit, it can do all the adjusting and eliminate any effect of capital flows on real rewards to factors of production. Simulation studies that have neglected this trade-adjustment effect have shown, not surprisingly, that repatriation of the stock of capital invested abroad by U.S. MNEs will redistribute income substantially toward labor.

These general-equilibrium models can be given a short-run content by supposing simply that any change that lowers real wages in the long run lowers employment in the short run. However, empirical controversies over the effects of foreign investment on employment and the balance of payments have flushed out some additional theoretical considerations. The investment-substitution question addresses the possibility that a transfer of capital does not actually lower the sending country's stock or raise the recipient's by the full amount. If it does not reduce the domestic capital stock, then the adverse effect on wages should not arise. The export-substitution question asks whether or not, in the MNE's own sourcing decisions, its foreign investment necessarily substitutes for exports sales. The nature of the MNE's activities suggests that a complementary relationship might prevail—up to a point, and in some settings. The statistical evidence gives appreciable support to the complementary relationship (with its "up to a point" qualification attached), and that mitigates the theoretical likelihood that investing abroad will be adverse to real wages in the home country.

The effect of MNEs on wages can also be analyzed in the partial-equilibrium context of the MNE's bargaining with its own employees. MNE's access to alternative overseas production sites may make their demand for labor more elastic than other companies' and thus more resistant to unions' wage demands. Or the MNE's rents may themselves be subject to capture by labor. As background evidence, it is useful to note that MNEs decentralize their wage and employee-relations decisions because labor markets are local and highly institutional. Studies of wages paid by MNEs have suggested that they are generally neither above nor below those of comparable local firms, once other factors are controlled, except that in LDCs the MNE is likely to pay higher wages to acquire better "quality" labor. MNE's foreignness is a disadvantage and might be expected to render MNE's employee relations less tranquil than those of local firms; on the other hand, they may also be able to arbitrage innovations in labor relations across national boundaries. Empirically, the MNEs seem to suffer no serious disadvantage in handling labor relations. They are responsible for some innovations, but their presence has not transformed national labor-relations systems. Potentially, trade unions can gain from international coalitions to bargain with MNEs, and they have made some efforts along this line, but there are strong reasons why such coalitions are unlikely to succeed.

Notes

1. We now make the assumptions, necessary for most propositions deduced in that model, that all product and factor markets are purely competitive, that labor is completely immobile internationally, but that capital moves internationally so long as any differential exists in capital rentals.

2. . . . In alternative versions of this model, trade and international factors movements are complementary rather than substitutes. Purvis (1972) showed that a flow of capital from Home to Foreign can expand the trade between them if production functions differ in the two countries so that Foreign's import-competing industry has a relative productivity advantage (even though it has been "disadvantaged" by Foreign's small endowment of capital). . . .

3. Chipman (1971) generalized this situation to the world economy. He provided conditions under which, with labor immobile but capital freely mobile internationally, the terms of trade in the world economy are unaffected by shifts in demand among products. Capital rentals are also unaffected, as is the distribution of income. The transformation curve for the world economy as a whole (transformation curves for individual countries were represented in Figures 2.2 to 2.4 in Chapter 2) must have a "flat spot" on it—meaning that various quantities of food and clothing can be obtained from the world's factor endowment at given terms of trade. However, shifts in world demand from one of these combinations to another may require the reallocation of capital between countries, as described in the text.

4. The marginal product of Home's labor falls in terms of food but rises in terms of clothing. Whether or not labor is better off in real terms therefore depends on workers' preferences for food relative to clothing.

5. The repatriation is actually estimated to increase the nation's total income. . . .

6. As in Musgrave's analysis, Home's national income actually expands when all foreign investment is repatriated, because of the effect of the corporation income tax.

7. We neglect for now the possibility that the firm borrows an appreciable proportion of its investment in the country where the project is installed.

8. The chief problem concerns the behavior of saving, if saving and investment decisions are to be in equilibrium. The reverse-classical case requires that supplies

of saving in each country be highly elastic in response to expected rates of return. Otherwise, when Home's MNE borrows to invest abroad *and* its rival borrows to finance the domestic investment that the MNE passes up, the rate of return in Home's capital market will be driven up, and one or another firm will be discouraged from its plans. Similarly, the depressed profit expectations in Foreign must reduce saving there, or otherwise the rate of return will fall and tempt *some* Foreign firm to make an investment. The anticlassical case requires the same assumption about an elastic supply of saving in Home, but in Foreign either the available investment opportunities (the marginal efficiency of investment) must be quite elastic or the supply of saving must be inelastic.

9. The qualification for "equilibrium level" puts aside a problem of short-run adjustment associated with the capital transfer itself. When Home transfers capital to Foreign, the financial consequence is an increase of total spending in Foreign and a decrease in Home. That change by itself raises Foreign's imports and reduces Home's. But the change in trade is merely transitional, and it dies away once the capital transfer ceases. . . .

10. This discussion has followed the literature in assuming that the MNE under study is horizontal, producing the same line of goods abroad as at home. Other types give different results. Forward vertical integration in the foreign investment can prove complementary with exports if the subsidiary secures inputs from its parent for further processing. On the other hand, a backward integration to secure an input from abroad can expand imports and reduce the demand for labor at home. Finally, a diversified foreign investment is unlikely to affect the investing firm's trade activities directly.

11. Not even all transactional considerations point toward complementarity. For instance, the subsidiary goes through a learning process in its production activities such that it grows able to self-supply more and more components, rather than importing them from the parent. This import-displacing effect was noted by Safarian (1966, p. 158) and Brash (1966, p. 206).

12. Detailed literature references are not provided on the export-substitution question because much of the discussion has been diffuse and casual, and the more cogent contributions have also been concerned with empirical evidence and therefore will be mentioned later. For critical surveys, see Bergsten et al. (1978, Chapter 3 and 4) and Frank and Freeman (1978, Chapter 2).

13. For critical surveys, see Bergsten et al. (1978, pp. 59–65) and Frank and Freeman (1978, Chapter 2).

14. Adler and Stevens (1974) tried to estimate cross-elasticities of demand between American exports and the output of foreign subsidiaries that would directly reveal complementarity or substitution by their signs, but no significant results emerged pointing in either direction.

15. This conclusion holds both for exports of U.S. multinationals to their own foreign affiliates (where the complementary relationship is especially likely) and for the total exports of U.S. manufacturing industries, whether sold to affiliates or sold at arm's length. Also see Swedenborg (1979, Chapter 7) on Sweden and Reddaway (1968, pp. 282–97) on the United Kingdom.

16. Jedel and Kujawa (1976, pp. 32–41) reported similar conclusions for foreign subsidiaries in the United States. For a description of the decentralized system of a major U.S. MNE, see Kujawa (1975, Chapter 6).

17. Apparently, there is not much evidence on why some companies decentralize more than do others (see Roberts, 1972). Kassalow (1978) pointed out a key trade-off at issue: the company can sustain the communications costs of a centralized system or the employee costs of staffing the subsidiaries with high-quality labor-relations personnel.

18. The numerous fragmentary studies of wages have been summarized by the Internatinal Labour Organization (1976b).

19. Whichard (1978) showed that the subsidiaries tend to be located in higher-wage industries but lower-wage regions than in all U.S. business. The analysis-of-variance method that he used does not drop out a pure residual imputable to foreign ownership per se.

20. Dunning and Morgan (1980) employed a crude test of association between the wages paid by U.S. multinationals and their profitability. A positive association would confirm the hypothesis that unions intercept some of the rents accruing to MNEs. No association was found—which may mean either there is no association or the data are inadequate.

21. For evidence, see Steuer and Gennard (1971), Gunter (1975), and International Labour Organization (1976b, especially p. 50). Foreign subsidiaries in the United States seem at least to have integrated themselves successfully into the American labor-relations system (Jedel and Kujawa, 1976, pp. 49–56).

22. Among the many authors discussing this issue have been Kujawa (1971), Roberts (1973), Curtin (1973), Flanagan and Weber (1974), Gunter (1975), Banks and Stieber (1977, Introduction), Bergsten et al. (1978, pp. 110–18), Kujawa (1979), and Northrup and Rowan (1979, pp. 535–44). All reached essentially the same conclusion.

23. For descriptions of coordination efforts in the labor movement, see Blake (1972), Roberts (1973), Curtin (1973), Kujawa (1975, Chapter 5, 1979), Weinberg (1978, especially Chapter 3), and the exhaustive investigation of Northrup and Rowan (1979).

References

Adler, M., and G.V.G. Stevens (1974). "The Trade Effects of Direct Investment," *J. Finance,* 29 (May), 655–76.

Banks, R.F., and J. Stieber (eds.) (1977). *Multinationals, Unions, and Labor Relations in Industrialized Countries.* Cornell International Industrial and Labor Relations Report No. 9. Ithaca, N.Y.: New York State School of Industrial and Labor Relations, Cornell University.

Bergsten, C.F., T. Horst, and T.H. Moran (1978). *American Multinationals and American Interests.* Washington: Brookings Institution.

Brash, D.T. (1966). *American Investment in Australian Industry.* Cambridge, MA: Harvard University Press.

Chipman, J.S. (1971). "International Trade with Capital Mobility: A Substitution Theorem." In J.N. Bhagwati et al. (eds.), *Trade, Balance of Payments and Growth: Papers in International Economics in Honor of Charles P. Kindleberger,* pp. 201–37. Amsterdam: North-Holland.

Creigh, S.W., and P. Makeham (1978). "Foreign Ownership and Strike-Proneness: A Research Note," *Brit. J. Ind. Relat.,* 16 (November), 369–72.

Crispo, J. (1967). *International Unionism: A Study in Canadian-American Relations.* Toronto: McGraw-Hill.

Curtin, W.J. (1973). "The Multinational Corporation and Transnational Collective Bargaining." In D. Kujawa (ed.), *American Labor and the Multinationals,* Chapter 9. New York: Praeger.

Dunning, J.H., and E.J. Morgan (1980), "Employee Compensation in U.S. Multinationals and Indigenous Firms: An Exploratory Micro/Macro Analysis," *Brit. J. Ind. Relat.,* 18 (July), 179–201.

Flanagan, R.J., and A.R. Weber (eds.) (1974). *Bargaining without Boundaries: The Multinational Corporation and Internatinal Labor Relations.* Chicago: University of Chicago Press.

Forsyth, D.J.C. (1972). *U.S. Investment in Scotland.* New York: Praeger.

Forsyth, D.J.C. (1973). "Foreign-owned Firms and Labour Relations: A Regional Perspective," *Brit. J. Ind. Relat.,* 11 (March), 20–8.

Frank, R.H., and R.T. Freeman (1978). *Distributional Consequences of Direct Foreign Investment.* New York: Academic Press.

Gunter, H. (1975). "Labor and Multinational Corporations in Western Europe: Some Problems and Prospects." In D. Kujawa (ed.), *International Labor and the Multinational Enterprise,* Chapter 7. New York: Praeger.

Hartman, D.G. (1980). "The Effects of Taxing Foreign Investment Income." *J. Publ. Econ.,* 13 (April), 213–30.

Hershfield, D.C. (1975). *The Multinational Union Faces the Multinational Company.* Conference Board Report No. 658. New York: Conference Board.

Hufbauer, G.C., and F.M. Adler (1968). *Overseas Manufacturing Investment and the Balance of Payments.* Tax Policy Research Study No. 1. Washington: U.S. Treasury Department.

International Labour Organization (1976). *Wages and Working Conditions in Multinational Enterprises.* Geneva: International Labour Organization.

Kassalow, E.M. (1978). "Aspects of Labour Relations in Multinational Companies: An Overview of Three Asian Countries," *Int. Lab. Rev.,* 117 (May/June), 273–87.

Koizumi, T., and K.J. Kopecky (1980). "Foreign Direct Investment, Technology Transfer and Domestic Employment Effects." *J. Int. Econ.,* 10 (February), 1–20.

Kujawa, D. (1971). *International Labor Relations Management in the Automotive Industry: A Comparative Study of Chrysler, Ford, and General Motors.* New York: Praeger.

———. (ed.) (1973). *American Labor and the Multinationals.* New York: Praeger.

———. (ed.) (1975). *International Labor and the Multinational Enterprise.* New York: Praeger.

———. (1979). "Collective Bargaining and Labor Relations in Multinational Enterprise: A U.S. Public Policy Perspective." In R.G. Hawkins (ed.), *Research in International Business and Finance: An Annual Compilation of Research. Vol. I. The Economic Effects of Multinational Corporations,* Chapter 2. Greenwich, CT: JAI Press.

Lubitz, R. (1971*a*). "Direct Investment and Capital Formation." In R.E. Caves and G.L. Reuber, *Capital Transfer and Economic Policy: Canada 1951–62*, Chapter 4. Cambridge, MA: Harvard University Press.

Mundell, R.A. (1957). "International Trade and Factor Mobility," *Amer. Econ. Rev.*, 47 (June), 321–35.

Musgrave, P.B. (1975). *Direct Investment Abroad and the Multinationals: Effects on the United States Economy.* U.S. Senate, Committee on Foreign Relations, Subcommittee on Multinational Corporations, Committee Print, 94th Congress, first session. Washington: U.S. Government Printing Office.

Northrup, H.R., and R.L. Rowan (1979). *Multinational Collective Bargaining Attempts: The Record, the Cases, and the Prospects.* Multinational Industrial Relations Series No. 6. Philadelphia: Industrial Research Unit, The Wharton School, University of Pennsylvania.

Pugel, T.A. (1980). "Profitability, Concentration and the Interindustry Variation in Wages," *Rev. Econ. Statist.*, 62 (May), 248–53.

Purvis, D.D. (1972). "Technology, Trade and Factor Mobility," *Econ. J.,* 82 (September), 991–9.

Reddaway, W.B. (1968). *Effects of U.K. Direct Investment Overseas: Final Report.* University of Cambridge, Department of Applied Economies, Occasional Papers No. 15. Cambridge University Press.

Reuber, G.L., with H. Crookell, M. Emerson, and G. Gallais-Hamonno (1973). *Private Foreign Investment in Development.* Oxford: Clarendon Press.

Roberts, B.C. (1972). "Factors Influencing the Organization and Style of Management and Their Effect on the Pattern of Industrial Relations in Multi-national Corporations." In H. Günther (ed.), *Transnational Industrial Relations,* Chapter 6. London: Macmillan.

——— . (1973). "Multinational Collective Bargaining: A European Prospect?" *Brit. J. Ind. Relat.,* 11 (March), 1–19.

Roberts, B.C., and J. May (1974). "The Response of Multi-National Enterprises to International Trade Union Pressures," *Brit. J. Ind. Relat.,* 12 (November), 403–16.

Safarian, A.E. (1966). *Foreign Ownership of Canadian Industry.* Toronto: McGraw-Hill.

Steuer, M., and J. Gennard. (1971). "Industrial Relations, Labour Disputes and Labour Utilization in Foreign-Owned Firms in the United Kingdom." In J.H. Dunning (ed.), *The Multinational Enterprise,* Chapter 4. London: George Allen & Unwin.

Stobaugh, R.B., et al. (1976). *Nine Investments Abroad and Their Impact at Home: Case Studies on Multinational Enterprises and the U.S. Economy.* Boston: Division of Research, Harvard Business School.

Swedenborg, B. (1979). *The Multinational Operations of Swedish Firms: An Analysis of Determinants and Effects.* Stockholm: Industrial Institute for Economic and Social Research.

Taira, K., and G. Standing (1973). "Labor Market Effects of Multinational Enterprises in Latin America," *Nebr. J. Econ. Bus.,* 12 (Autumn), 103–17.

Thurow, L.C. (1976). "International Factor Movements and the American Distribution of Income," *Intermountain Econ. Rev.,* 2 (Spring), 13–24.

U.S. Tariff Commission (1973). *Implications of Multinational Firms for World Trade and Investment and for U.S. Trade and Labor.* Washington: U.S. Government Printing Office.

Van Loo, F. (1977). "The Effect of Foreign Direct Investment on Investment in Canada," *Rev. Econ. Statist.*, 59 (November), 474–81.

Weinberg, P.J. (1978). *European Labor and Multinationals.* New York: Praeger.

Whichard, O.G. (1978). "Employment and Employee Compensation of U.S. Affiliates of Foreign Companies, 1974," *Surv. Curr. Bus.*, 58 (December), 23–24, 58.

10

Multinational Corporations in Euro-American Trade: Crucial Linking Mechanisms in an Evolving Trade Structure

John M. Kline

What kinds of transnational corporate alliances have multinational enterprises been building among the developed countries? And what is the impact of these alliances on the domestic policies of the individual states?

Kline argues that growing domestic pressures are moving the United States away from support for traditional free trade principles to more direct national interest calculations of production-oriented benefits. Government-negotiated production-sharing arrangements have set a precedent in the Atlantic area for a nationalistic structuring of trade patterns based on political determinations of domestic employment and public revenue needs rather than on price or other market-based principles. At the same time, multinational corporations are expanding the number and variety of their intercorporate business ties, thereby blurring national corporate identities while establishing a broader presence within foreign markets.

Kline suggests that the expanding linkages among multinational corporations may provide a mechanism that can help check the swing of the pendulum away from broad free trade principles and instead reinforce the political and economic constituency for freer flows of trade, technology, and investment.

S torm flags are flying in Euro-American trade relations at the beginning of the 1980s. The major Western industrialized nations are making painful adjustments to spiraling energy costs, recurring inflation, sluggish productivity and slower overall economic growth projections. These troubles manifest themselves in renewed protectionist tendencies, as multilaterally incompatible policies of national export stimulation and import restriction are debated. In the United States, important aspects of foreign investment policies—both inward and outward—are also on the public agenda along with more traditional import/export issues. The challenge of resolving these interlinked policy issues in a manner consistent with multilateral accommodation and cooperation will require a careful new analysis and approach to defining the role of multinational corporations (MNCs) in Euro-American trade.

For three decades MNCs have been perceived as challengers to governmental economic policy control, first in Europe and now more recently in the United States. Past MNC growth sometimes failed to provide the type of national benefits needed to assuage certain domestic political concerns. While offering many market-oriented benefits in terms of product choice, availability and price, the inherent "foreignness" of MNCs seemed to increase risk and uncertainty on more politically sensitive production issues of plant ownership, employment and expansion. These concerns naturally appeared first on the European side of the Atlantic during the early postwar years, stimulating the development of European MNCs to counter American influence and carry forward national interest objectives. Many of these concerns are evident now in the U.S. debate over the reformulation of current national trade and investment policies.

The different bases for U.S. and European policy development stemming from the postwar period can explain much of both the cooperation and the conflict which has marked trans-Atlantic trade and investment relations. Even more important, the current evolution of national policies and attitudes toward foreign investment and MNCs may now hold important clues to the future development of general Euro-American trade relations.

Changes in the international economic equation, which have essentially equalized the competitive standing of the U.S. and European nations, also have begun to alter the political value base upon which many past policy differences were founded. These changes are especially likely to impact the United States, which emerged from the period of postwar economic dominance with a trade policy pegged to broad systemic concepts, an investment orientation adapted from free trade flow principles, and virtually nonexistent policy regarding the role of multinational corporations.

Economic pressures at home and tougher business competition abroad are now forcing the U.S. to reevaluate its trade and investment policies. At the same time, the expanding use of transnational business arrangements such as co-development, co-production, joint equity and joint marketing systems adds a new and challenging dimension to the task of defining a coherent government approach to the role of MNCs in national policy objectives.

A critical time is approaching in the United States where a broad array of policy issues are being reassessed, with most indications pointing toward a shift from broad international principles to more specific national interest applications. This change will involve a shift from primarily an overseas marketplace view of MNC importance to greater emphasis on home production political values, thereby bringing policy-makers on both sides of the Atlantic closer together than ever before in their basic orientation to international companies.

While these developments could enhance the prospects for nationalistic, beggar-thy-neighbor competition, they might just as well lay the basis for a more realistic and equitable trading relationship in the Atlantic area. The renewed protectionist pressures which so concern current analysis could prove to be a temporary transition phase in a broadly evolving trade structure. Multinational corporations can play a key role in determining the direction of this evolution through their cross-national linking mechanisms which now may be more capable of meeting both economic marketplace and production oriented political needs. Governmental policy-makers, on the other hand, must face up to the central challenge of developing national and multilateral policy positions which will encourage a positive and reinforcing use of MNC linkages within a cooperative Euro-American trading system.

An Historical Perspective

Traditional views on the role of multinational corporations in Euro-American relations were formulated during the first two decades following World War II. This period was distinguished by unbalanced relationships in many areas, including the perception of MNCs as synonymous with dominant American influence. While there is much valuable literature already documenting the nature of postwar economic relations, a brief review of these years is advisable to provide the historical perspective necessary to more accurately evaluate the role of MNCs in current trade policy developments. In particular, it is important to focus in on the different origins of American and European policies toward foreign investment and MNCs as they bear on trade policy values.

United States attitudes toward MNCs developed over the years through an *ad hoc* decision-making process that applied broad economic standards in piecemeal fashion to functionally related MNC issues. Although there are many components to this patchwork pattern, the most important early standards involved non-discriminatory (MFN) free trade; national treatment for foreign investors; tax neutrality (foreign tax credit and "deferral"); and the extra-territorial application of antitrust and export control regulations.

The first three policy areas of trade, investor treatment and taxation all reflected an emphasis on macro-level, market-oriented principles within which MNC operations were to fit. This approach also implicitly assumed an overall identity between corporate and U.S. national interests. The extra-territorial enforcement principle established a functional check on that identity of interests to make certain that U.S. domestic principles did not get distorted by the vagaries of foreign influences and temptations.

Some accounts offer a sinister or at least more economically aggressive interpretation of U.S. intentions toward postwar Europe. While one would assume that U.S. corporate motivations were not altogether altruistic, a persuasive case can be made that official U.S. policy at the time stemmed from a more benign extension abroad of a domestic U.S. policy consensus based on economic growth, productivity and efficiency objectives.[1] Thus the fundamental thrust of U.S. policy decisions relating to MNCs simply sought to apply abroad the market-oriented value standards which seemed to work so well at home, essentially treating overseas business activities as if they were an extension of the U.S. domestic market.

Decision-makers in the U.S. could afford to focus on this macro outreach area of MNC policy because in-place domestic productive capacity was booming and both export sales and U.S. investment abroad seemed to further establish postwar reconstruction goals. The possible impact of trade and investment policies on the American home economy was of much less concern since the trade component of GNP was relatively small, import dislocation was minimal, the dollar was strong and foreign investment in the U.S. consisted mainly of companies which had long ago blended into the American economic scene.

United States trade values were therefore systemic in nature and their application to MNCs was primarily determined by functional responses to conditions encountered abroad rather than a directed policy based on domestic economic necessities. This approach to international economic policy tended to obscure rather than define the interaction between foreign trade and investment, submerging them under broad free market principles in a way that the specific role of MNCs as linking mechanisms embodying both trade and investment activities was never sufficiently addressed. In terms of the approach and objectives of U.S. policy, there was essentially no difference between domestic and foreign market activities.

The roots of a divergent perspective on MNCs in relation to trade and investment policy took hold in Europe during this same time period. At first European policy options were severely constrained by the physical demands of reconstruction and the policy thrust contained within U.S. assistance mechanisms. Both public and private economic resources were needed to meet first-line necessities of the populace and to stave off the threat of further communist penetration.

As recovery progressed and a bi-polar military stand-off developed, European leaders began to perceive policy choices rather than political or economic imperatives. Galvanized by Jean-Jacques Servan-Schreiber's popular description of *The American Challenge,* their concerns shifted from the political threat from the East to the actual economic penetration from the West. This reaction to the continental spread of U.S. MNCs helped determine European policy not only to foreign investment at home, but also to the development and expected role of their own MNCs in world commerce.

It is dangerous to over-generalize about a "European" policy during this period of time—or perhaps during any time period. Certainly there were important distinctions between national policy approaches and even different policy stages within a given country. For example, France generally was more restrictive than Germany in its control over foreign investment, but even French policy shifted from broad investment denials to individually bargained access. Nevertheless, some policy generalizations may be risked if structured as broad contrasts with American policy development.

First, European motivations focused more on home-based production-end issues. Concern over the spread of U.S. MNCs stemmed not from an analysis of their influence on market factors (product price, choice, service, etc.) but rather from political unease over who was to control European productive resources, both actual and potential. Heading the list of factors motivating the European policy response were several interrelated concerns: fear of U.S. industrial dominance as American investment tended to locate in the "commanding heights" of the economy; the threat of long-term technological dependence as the leading edge of key industrial sectors fell into foreign hands; and the loss of national control over the kind of economic planning deemed essential for domestic political stability and sociocultural integrity.[2] These types of concerns obviously relate to market-oriented factors further downstream in both a time and a process sense, but the origins of policy sprang more from dissatisfaction with the nature of the productive facilities rather than their actual market output.

The second significant difference in policy development was that this European reaction led to a more planned and directed policy response which incorporated an integrated view of trade and investment activities. While there were again differences in national application, most European nations gravitated toward the French planning mode and aimed at the promotion of corporate "national champions." To achieve the size and economies of scale thought necessary to compete successfully with American MNCs, these designated corporate challengers were slated to become trans-European from the start and globally competitive when mature. In short, governmental trade and investment tools involving import restraints, restricted investment sectors, mergers, subsidies, public procurement and other similar policies were consciously utilized to build European multinational corporations.

Viewed against this historical backdrop, European trade policy values can be seen to focus on home country conditions, where political control over domestic production factors was critically important and dictated a more purposeful and directed approach to the use of market forces both at home and in a broader trading system. Multinational corporations played a central role in both policy formulation and execution—the former aspect occurring when foreign MNC penetration stimulated countering trade and investment policy decisions and the latter when specific trade and investment tools were used in an interrelated fashion to encourage European MNC development and to define the national interest objectives these MNCs were to serve.

Rather different characterizations can be drawn regarding the wellsprings of American trade policy values. Possessing a prosperous domestic production base, trade policy objectives centered on responding to overseas conditions. Policies were pursued which sought to replicate abroad those domestic market principles which were seen to bring economic prosperity, political stability and a better standard of living. Multinational corporations were perceived as playing a generally beneficial but not central role in advancing these objectives. Little in the way of specific policy initiatives beyond verbal encouragement was taken to structure or integrate MNC trade and investment impacts within the broader operating construct of systemic free market forces.

These historically different foundations of postwar trade and investment policies established the basis for a divergent perspective on and application of trade policy values as they apply to MNC operations in the Atlantic area.

MNCs and Multilateralism

Developing from these divergent perceptual foundations, and considering in particular the early European reaction against U.S. MNC influence, it is perhaps surprising that the record of Euro-American trade relations involving MNCs has been one of general multilateral cooperation with confined specific conflict. A system of multilateral economic cooperation emerged early, primarily operating through the General Agreement on Tariffs and Trade (GATT) and the Organization for Economic Cooperation and Development (OECD). Most MNC-related conflicts tended to be limited to bilateral settings, primarily those involving the functional application of U.S. trade policy values to U.S. MNC operations.

The major threat of unilateralism involving MNCs at the systemic level was probably the European "national champion" policy, itself a response to the singular thrust of U.S. MNC penetration. The discriminatory potential of this approach was somewhat restrained, however, by multilateralizing influences stemming from the formation and growth of the European Economic Community (EEC). The EEC held forth broadening opportunities for national companies to organize for transnational markets. It also partially offset the restrictiveness of national actions taken against U.S. MNCs, since companies could usually avoid such measures by locating in a less restrictive country while still remaining within the Community Market system. In fact, American MNCs often proved to be more responsive to EEC integrative initiatives, such as regional investment measures, than many European national companies.

The United States government, in the meantime, also supported EEC development, primarily on the political-security grounds of building a strong contributive ally. It may be somewhat more problematic if such support would be as forthcoming today for what was an exclusionary trade device if viewed from the U.S. domestic perspective. The internal European position of many U.S. MNCs probably helped calm any such misgivings, however, and there was little offsetting U.S. domestic concern at that time regarding the effect of those MNC investments on the home country economy. Thus on balance, the role of MNCs during this period tended to support multilateral and integrative economic activities.

Serious trans-Atlantic friction involving MNCs did arise, however, from unilateral American application of extraterritorial antitrust and export control regulations. These actions became identified with the multinational corporate vehicle and served to reinforce European concerns regarding the national integrity of their economic institutions. Europeans found it particularly irritating when they were asked to treat U.S. MNC subsidiaries in a non-discriminatory, national treatment manner, only to be told that for certain issues that subsidiary must be considered a U.S. subject first rather than a French, German or British citizen. These cases were also the hardest to cope with for an MNC, which generally had little room for maneuver once the political battle lines had been drawn.

The logic of American extraterritorial law application is easier to understand within the context of a general systemic approach to trade and investment policy. These regulations were simply a functional application of the domestic policy values that the U.S. was seeking to replicate abroad. The absence of a specifically defined U.S. policy toward MNCs created no offsetting pressure to address subjects like differing jurisdictional claims which arise when trade and investment interaction occurs within an MNC business instrument.

Fortunately the occurrence of such conflicts, while still far from rare, has diminished in recent years. European political and economic strength has increased to the point where it can effectively counter U.S. initiatives in most individual cases. Nevertheless, the U.S. policy thrust has changed very little, as witnessed by the recent extraterritorial extension to U.S. subsidiaries of such items as the Foreign Corrupt Practices Act and regulations on compliance with international boycotts.

Euro-American relations have also been marked by a series of specific trade disputes, ranging from chicken wars to trigger price mechanisms. The role of MNCs has generally not been the central element in these conflicts, however. While they may defend particular advantages accruing from favored sectoral tariffs or government procurement policies, MNCs have been among the strongest political supporters of liberal trade policies. Within the U.S., MNCs have been particularly important since the Burke-Hartke legislation in the early 1970s in opposing unilateral restrictive measures which threaten established multilateral trade policies.

Overall the goal of cooperative Euro-American trade relations appears to have been aided during the postwar period by MNC activity, which can adapt to and benefit from a relatively open trading system. Multinational corporations are generally more supportive of multilateral cooperation than unilateral government action, if for no other reason than a desire to avoid being sandwiched between competing political sovereigns.

The last decade did mark the beginning point, however, for a reexamination of U.S. liberal trade policy values. When the MNC "export of jobs" argument gained prominence in the Burke-Hartke debate, it cast doubt on the previously assumed beneficial impact of overseas investment on the domestic U.S. economy. This issue then set the stage for a serious reassessment of U.S. policy as it relates to fundamental changes occurring in the international economic system.

The Current Policy Debate

Over the past decade there have been some important changes in the historical backdrop to Euro-American trade policy and its relationship to multinational corporations. The unbalanced Atlantic relationship is now more equal. European postwar recovery objectives have long since fallen before the onslaught of both national and European Community progress. With the recovery and growth of domestic industry and increasingly effective bargaining leverage over U.S. MNCs, the goal of reasserting control over national economic decison-making has been largely achieved. Most European nations even appear to have survived relatively well the energy price spirals which could have proven disastrous at an earlier time period.

The concept of national or trans-European corporate champions has met with mixed success in terms of both economic viability and national interest fulfillment. There can be no doubt, however, that in many major industries European corporations now compete on an equal basis with U.S. MNCs, as illustrated in the relative rankings [in table 10–1]. Finally, the spread of these European MNCs abroad has added a new dimension to Euro-American relations, even to the extent of posing a "European Challenge" in the U.S.[3]

The United States, on the other hand, suffers from the shocks of the '70s. The phrase "sound as a dollar" took an ironic twist after August, 1971. Despite devaluations and floating exchange rates, the nation's trade deficit plummeted to over $30 billion annually toward the decade's end just as the trade component of U.S. GNP was doubling. Once-proud domestic industries face serious import dislocation while U.S. MNCs abroad encounter stiffer foreign competition and more leveraged governmental demands. To add

Table 10–1
European and U.S. MNCs in Selected Sectors

Rand Company	Country	Total Revenue
Automotive		
1. General Motors	United States	$66,311
2. Ford Motor Co.	United States	43,514
3. Fiat Group	Italy	18,121
4. PSA Peugeot-Citroen	France	17,114
5. Volkswagen Group	West Germany	16,753
6. Renault	France	16,101
7. Daimler-Benz AG	West Germany	14,931
8. Chrysler	United States	12,002
Chemicals		
1. Hoechst Group	West Germany	$14,774
2. Bayer Group	West Germany	14,186
3. BASF Group	West Germany	14,128
4. EI du Pont de Nemours	United States	12,572
5. Imperial Chemicals Inds. Ltd.	United Kingdom	11,389
6. Dow Chemical	United States	9,255
7. Union Carbide	United States	9,177
8. Montedison Group	Italy	8,224
9. Rhône-Poulenc Group	France	7,940
10. Naamloze Vennootschap DSM	Netherlands	6,356
Electrical Equipment		
1. General Electric	United States	$22,980
2. N.V. Philips Lamp	Netherlands	16,568
3. Siemens Group	West Germany	15,065
4. Cie Générale d'Électricité	France	8,310
5. AEG-Telefunken Group	West Germany	7,752
6. R.C.A.	United States	7,455
7. Westinghouse	United States	7,332
8. Thompson-Brandt Group	France	7,052
9. Texas Instruments	United States	3,224
10. Singer	United States	2,598
Banking		
1. Citicorp	United States	$10,904
2. Bank of America	United States	9,450
3. Banque Nationale de Paris	France	7,241
4. Barclays Bank Group	United Kingdom	7,173
5. Crédit Lyonnais Group	France	6,964
6. Deutsche Bank Group	West Germany	6,634
7. National Westminster Bank	United Kingdom	6,496
8. Crédit Agricole	France	6,307
9. Chase Manhattan	United States	6,079
10. Sociéte Générale Group	France	5,600

Note: Information for the ranking drawn from listings of the 100 largest U.S. MNCs and the 100 largest foreign companies, *Forbes* (July 7, 1980):99–108; *Business Week,* March 17, 1980, pp. 84–116.

seeming insult to injury, Arab, Japanese, and European interests also appeared to be using the devalued American dollars to buy up undervalued U.S. productive resources.

This somewhat exaggerated picture is actually a rather accurate reflection of U.S. public perceptions which frame the current policy debate. Within the pending U.S. policy agenda, there is real potential for a value role reversal in Euro-American trade relations, with the U.S. becoming home production oriented, utilizing its MNCs as more specific national interest sales leaders. Europe, on the other hand, may be pulled away somewhat from MNC production end goals by the global market imperatives now facing its own MNCs.

The growing tension between old trade policy values and current economic pressures appears greatest in the United States, which is the primary focus of this analysis. Generalized systemic trade principles are under challenge as they appear increasingly insufficient to either safeguard or advance U.S. domestic interests. This change is most evident in the expression of nationalistic sentiments which fuel protectionist trade fears. The same attitude is also causing a new look at foreign investment policy, where a reassessment of inward investment flows may ultimately affect U.S. policy toward outward investment as well. Overall, there is less of a "fit" between the traditional, generalized U.S. policy approach and specific trade problems now facing the country.

Evidence for these developing U.S. policy changes can be garnered from diverse sources, including public opinion surveys, congressional activities, governmental program initiatives and interest group position-taking. Since the mid-1970s the proportion of Americans perceiving the U.S. as becoming more economically dependent on other countries has grown to nearly two-thirds of the population. Over this same time frame, there has been an increase in the percentage of Americans favoring restrictions on imported goods, ranging between 68 percent to 81 percent.[4] Taking these two changes together, one could interpret the growing protectionist sentiment as a reaction against interdependence and a reassertion of historical American withdrawal policies which favor national self-sufficiency. A further analysis of the data, however, suggests that this time around there is something more at work than simple isolationist tendencies.

Mr. Alvin Richman, a Senior Public Opinion Analyst of the U.S. Department of State, found that: "The desire to increase import restrictions does not necessarily connote opposition to foreign trade per se. The groups most desirous of tighter restrictions are also among those most favorably disposed toward the idea of trade—executives/professionals, those earning $25,000 or more annually, males and Westerners."[5] Thus some of the change in U.S. trade sentiments may come not from isolationism, but from a more directed and activist desire to achieve a "better trade deal." Certainly the group favoring this posture would probably have a different orientation than isolationists to the role of MNCs in trade relations, although both groups will seek a change in broad U.S. free trade policies.

Public attitudes toward foreign investment also appear at odds with official U.S. policy positions. In June, 1979 the following question was asked in a Roper poll:

> Foreign companies can invest in the United States, and American companies can invest in foreign countries in a number of ways—by buying up companies, by buying stock in companies and by building and operating plants. This benefits the companies that invest in other countries by expanding their business, and benefits the countries they invest in by providing greater production and more jobs in those countries.
>
> We'd like to know whether you are in favor of or opposed to foreign companies investing in the United States . . . or don't you have any feelings one way or the other about it?

Even with such a beneficially worded preface, the question elicited a plurality of respondents opposed to foreign investments in the U.S. (44 percent opposed; 34 percent favor, 17 percent no feelings one way or the other; 5 percent don't know). An earlier Harris poll also documented similar attitudes, revealing a pattern of public opposition to different forms of inward investment which parallels historical reaction in other countries—the greatest opposition to natural resource investments and corporate acquisitions, with less (although still a majority) of those surveyed opposed to new productive investments by foreign MNCs.[6]

The public mood is complicated further by the ambivalent reaction to U.S. investment abroad, the measurement most closely associated with attitudes toward U.S. MNCs. A June, 1979 Roper poll found the public evenly divided on U.S. investments overseas (38 percent opposed; 38 percent favor; 18 percent no feeling one way or the other; 6 percent don't know).[7]

None of these surveys provide much support for traditional U.S. free trade and investment principles. There does appear to be some room for influencing public sentiment, since there is a steady proportion of nearly one-fourth of those questioned who have no set opinions of these issues. However, to either capture the support of this segment, or to pacify the groups pushing for a better U.S. deal, it will be necessary for the government to address a range of specific domestic impact issues. U.S. trade policies, and even inward investments, are now being measured against a rough, home-oriented benefit standard. "When the public evaluates arguments in favor of free trade or protectionism, the most persuasive argument for either policy is that it results in more—or fewer—jobs for Americans." The consumer price impact of imports is another top-rated factor which proved important to respondents.[8] Concerns such as these are not easily reached by appeals to international trade principles said to operate for the greatest good for all nations.

These broader value changes mirror the critical public evaluations of U.S. MNC impacts, begun in the early 1970s, which sought to measure MNC benefits in relation to specific U.S. economic sectors. That debate is still going on, as evidenced by the public's ambivalent feelings toward U.S. overseas investment and the continuing opposition of organized labor and certain other interest groups to MNC operations in general. The connecting link between the debate over U.S. MNC actions and the future course of more generalized trade policy is drawing tighter, and may now turn on the same U.S.-centered cost/benefit calculations.

While national interest considerations were undoubtedly a part of earlier policy decisions, the period of postwar economic dominance allowed U.S. policy-makers greater latitude regarding official support for broader trade benefit considerations. The tenor of domestic debate at that time was rather constrained and even somewhat altruistic. Changed world economic conditions have removed this luxury from the U.S. government shelf and dumped the country into a period where more sharply drawn self-interest distinctions will be both common and necessary.

Recent congressional activities reinforce the impression that the persuasive power of broad international economic principles is on the demise while stricter national benefit determinations are gaining prominence. A sampling of trade and investment actions turns up the following examples:

> While Congress turned away the Burke-Hartke bill in the early 1970s in favor of new multilateral trade expansion talks, it is generally accepted that such an effort to reduce global trade barriers would not be reauthorized today. Even though Congress recently approved a package of agreements resulting from the Multilateral Trade Negotiations (MTN), the clear emphasis in congressional hearings was on the need for vigorous enforcement of U.S. rights and aggressive pursuit of potential U.S. trade gains, rather than the need for further systemic trade reform—a topic still officially on the GATT agenda.

> Two U.S. programs which have been challenged, in the U.S. as well as elsewhere, as antithetical to U.S. support for free market trade principles are the Domestic International Sales Corporation (DISC) and Webb-Pomerene Export Associations. While Congress cut back the DISC, it refused to heed Administration calls for its elimination and is now moving to expand Webb Act authority into more widely applicable export trading company legislation.

> Numerous bills to restrict foreign investment in the U.S. have been discussed in Congress, ranging from moratoriums to outright bans on new investment. Certain limited restrictions have already been added on foreign banks by national legislation while state actions affect several

types of inward investment. The concept of a cost-benefit review determination or other similar screening process is gaining new credence despite its obvious clash with the official U.S. "open door" position regarding both inward and outward foreign investment.

The Senate rejected a U.S.-U.K. Tax Treaty provision which would have restricted U.S. state use of a unitary tax formula in favor of a more internationally accepted approach. Similarly, while the U.S. has pressed for a multilateral agreement to limit investment incentives and disincentives, it is far from certain that such an agreement would be approved by Congress if it limited the states' rights to either entice a foreign plant or discourage a corporate takeover bid.

A number of governmental programs and interest group actions also portend a more nationalistic economic posture. The Commerce Department's new International Trade Administration and Foreign Commercial Service boast that for the first time, the U.S. Government is acting as an American business advocate in specific projects abroad. This approach contrasts with the arms-length formality traditionally observed between U.S. business and government where it was the latter's job only to assure a fair international trading environment within which the former would compete for business strictly on its own initiative and merits. Now the Commerce program has adopted a stance which is not based on some reference to implementing broad international trade principles, but rather justifies governmental involvement more simply as a want to improve the U.S. trade account.

The evidence stemming from interest group positions probably needs the least explanation. Organized labor support for a more restrictionist trade policy has grown even stronger with the new posture of the United Auto Workers, just as several automobile companies now feel compelled to back national necessity arguments over strict adherence to international free trade principles. While most business groups would not endorse protectionist trade policies, there is widespread backing for more aggressive U.S. trade action. For example, the "Gentlemen's Agreement" on export credit financing was perceived as the type of multilateral accord which only disadvantages the U.S., thereby occasioning wide business support for a "meet and beat" approach by Eximbank to competition in this field.

International economic changes during the 1970s have thus created pressures in the U.S. for a more specifically directed foreign economic policy. In some respects this situation has parallels in the period when European policies were formulated, at least regarding the diminished power of international policy themes like anti-communism or free world trade expansion. The impression arising from the evidence of U.S. attitude changes clearly seems to point in the direction of a more nationalistic policy, politically premised on the importance of such factors as domestic employment, retention in the U.S.

of leading-edge technological advances, suspicion of incoming foreign investment and the need to "reindustrialize" the home economy. Whether these pressures evolve into a negative, protectionist trade posture or more outwardly aggressive but positive trade competition could be strongly influenced by the role multinational corporations will play in linking the trans-Atlantic community together by addressing both its economic and political needs.

MNCs as Linking Mechanisms

Some potentially important but as yet unmeasured changes are underway which add a new dimension to the role of MNCs as transnational linking mechanisms. A series of governmentally directed or inspired inter-MNC business arrangements are being forged in areas such as military armaments, civil aviation and motor vehicles through devices like co-development, co-production, joint equity and joint marketing agreements. Many of these changes relate specifically to the altered trade policy conditions described above. The future development of these arrangements and specifically their relationship to governmental policy could have significant impact upon the trans-Atlantic trading structure and the role of MNCs as a supportive element behind multilateral cooperation.

Research studies, public debates and very often governmental policies have addressed MNCs primarily from a narrowly defined, national gain-or-loss perspective. This approach focuses on the organization concept of an MNC parent firm headquartered in one country with subsidiaries abroad that function simply as directed arms of the parent—ready, willing and able to do its bidding.

It is, of course, but a short step from this perception to the analogous view of MNCs acting as arms of the home country, doing that nation's bidding abroad. As we have seen, such a view both underlay European perceptions of U.S. MNCs and led them to structure a "national champion" policy based on precisely the same assumptions. This type of conceptualization tends to cast MNCs as biased actors in a trading relationship between nations where everything is played out as a zero-sum game. Integrative and linking aspects of MNC activities, both actual and potential, are thereby minimized or even discouraged.

In reality, of course, MNCs have never been limited to unidimensional parent-subsidiary ownership, although early American patterns were heavily weighted in this direction. There are a wide variety of business patterns to choose from, ranging from branches and wholly owned subsidiaries to licensing and franchise agreements. Recently a new dimension has been added to some of these devices through the more direct involvement of governments in structuring co-development/co-production arrangements and the broader response of other private sector business schemes to changes in governmental trade policy values. The direction and utilization of these inter-MNC linkages as they relate to political trade pressures could help determine whether trans-Atlantic relations will move toward competitive trading blocks or a more progressive economic relationship.

One of the most obvious growth areas for these new arrangements is the field of military armaments, particularly the production of aircraft. Naturally this area exhibits more direct and influential governmental involvement than most economic sectors, but for that very reason it may allow a clearer look at these linkages and the public considerations they involve. Developments in this area have an important carry-over impact as well on related production outside of the defense field.

The early record in NATO military aircraft evidences reliance upon rather straight-forward national development and direct purchase agreements. This approach became increasingly unsatisfactory, however, for many of the same reasons that led to the general European reaction against U.S. MNCs, i.e. concerns about industrial dominance, technological dependence and control over national political/economic decision-making. [See figure 10–1.]

Direct international purchase of nationally developed aircraft is probably the most economically efficient method of production which also meets the military goal of NATO standardization and interoperability. National development activities, however, became concentrated mainly in the U.S. and, to a lesser extent, the U.K. and France. This production distribution pattern relegated most countries to only a buyer status, making direct purchase agreements more politically unpopular in these countries due to its negative impact on domestic employment, balance of payments and foreign industrial/technological dependence. Alternative options were then explored to essentially compromise market-end goals of final price and NATO standardization with these more home production-oriented considerations.

A relatively recent innovation in this direction has been the use of cooperative development schemes between two or more countries, with at least eleven such instances occurring since 1962. These arrangements have linked the U.S./France, France/FRG; Canada/U.S.; Italy/U.S.; U.K./France; U.K./FRG/Italy; and FRG/Netherlands/Belgium. The trend in European military aircraft procurement programs over the last three decades demonstrates the growing importance of cooperative developed projects at the expense of national development programs. The utilization of co-development and co-production programs to give more countries a "piece of the pie" became especially critical as the pie grew smaller (fewer procurement programs) but more expensive (higher development costs).

While having important implications within the military field, these changes both symbolize and reinforce the importance of domestic-based

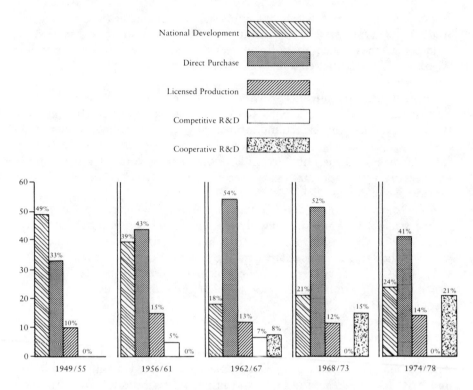

Source: Adapted from data in Norman Asher and Janice Lilly, "Types of Weapon Programs and Their Implications for NATO Standardization on Interoperability," Institute for Defense Analysis, July, 1978.

Figure 10–1. Aircraft Procurement Programs by Type

economic factors in broader Euro-American trade values. The cooperative schemes also provide a pattern for more direct governmental involvement in transnational business, since these production arrangements are pieced together through intergovernmental negotiations and many of the contracting corporations are owned or heavily supported by their national governments. This increased government participation in business can in turn impact on the nature of MNC linkages, leaving less room for MNC maneuver and action—except where the MNCs may be governmentally connected entities.

The nature of trade in military aircraft can also carry over more broadly to other economic sectors through commercial product spin-offs and the impact that success or failure in this area may have on corporate strength needed to remain competitive in other product sectors. One of the clearest examples of carry-over influence occurs in the closely related civil aviation industry. While the governmental role is not quite as dominant as in military aircraft, many of the lessons learned there are being used now to structure trade competition in civil aviation.

In order to mount a challenge to U.S. domination of the civil aircraft market (for all the employment, technology, balance of payments, etc., factors discussed before), several European nations formed new transnational business alliances to produce first the Concorde and now the more highly successful Airbus. Having been burned by management problems raised by excessive political direction in the Concorde project, participating governments sponsored the creation of a separate new company to handle Airbus production once the officially determined national roles had been agreed upon. Thus this co-development/co-production venture established linkages involving a full range of private, government-sponsored and government-owned entities.

In a related development, even industry leader Boeing, now faced with a challenger capable of offering a "family" of competitive aircraft models, is apparently ready to explore new transnational linking mechanisms. For the first time the company has tied itself through risk-sharing sub-contracting arrangements to aerospace companies in Italy and Japan. This development seems to involve not only economic development considerations, however, but perhaps even more importantly the changing climate concerning trade policy values. "Boeing seeks insurance against a wider outbreak of economic nationalism that could inhibit its overseas sales. As (President of Boeing Airplane Co.) Ernest Boullioun says, "If we were to bleed off all of the aerospace production, we'd get a backlash that would cause more trouble than sharing to a degree."[9] These new co-production links, reportedly totaling up to 30 percent of 767 and 777 airframe components, are designed to help head off such a trade policy "backlash." Thus governmentally sponsored business arrangements are being matched by private company initiatives, with both developments being tied to the pressures of political trade policy values.

Another industry experimenting with new transnational business arrangements is motor vehicles, most specifically automobiles. Some linkages follow the simple parent-subsidiary straight-line relationship, like the establishment of Volkswagen of America, Inc. Other developments introduce more complicated arrangements, such as Renault's expanding interest in American Motors Corporation, where assemblage, distributorship marketing, financial and technological support and future co-development projects all appear to be involved.

Many other transnational schemes are appearing within Europe, between Europe and the U.S., and also with Japan. Some of these linkages have provided for co-development/co-production (Fiat-Peugeot, Renault-Volvo, Nissan-Alfa Romeo); marketing and distribution agreements (British Leyland-Honda; VW-MAN; Renault-Mack); component agreements (Fiat-Ford, Renault-Alfa Romeo, Fiat-Saab) and stock ownership (Chrysler-Mitsubishi, Ford-Toyo Kogyo; AMC-Renault).[10]

The presence of these arrangements can add a new dimension to MNC linking mechanisms in the automobile industry. As political pressures push companies from traditional import strategies toward full subsidiary establishment, these mechanisms can provide many more economically sound stopping points along the way, while maintaining the benefits of international flows of components and technology. Much as Boeing's "sharing-out" of production is aimed at maintaining market access so the utilization of various levels of joint production or marketing arrangements could hold the potential for ameliorating if not altogether avoiding political objections to foreign import patterns.

A recent letter from Japan's Minister of International Trade and Industry to the U.S. Trade Representative demonstrates how these ideas relate to current political difficulties in the U.S. automobile industry. While noting the recent U.S. International Trade Commission ruling refused to recommend action against auto imports, Minister Rokusuke Tanaka pledged:

> Japan also tends to play a responsible role in maintaining the world free trade system and at the same time we remain sensitive to the problems the U.S. auto industry is facing, particularly the problem of unemployment.
>
> The Japanese government will continue its effort to encourage the Japanese auto industry to make economically viable investment in the U.S. and realize economically viable co-production activities with the U.S. auto industry.
>
> The Japanese auto industry will expand the planned purchases of U.S. automotive parts in order to help create future job opportunities in the U.S.[11]

These three industry examples are meant to stimulate debate in this area rather than offer any hard and fast conclusions as to their more general representative nature. It is difficult to evaluate just how widely such inter-MNC connections may be spreading in various industries because data is not centrally collected or analyzed on such a basis. A careful gleaning of reports in trade journals and specific industry newsletters allows one to draw a general picture, but it will only reflect at best a rough snapshot in time whose images are blurred by unsystematic collection methods and the unavailability of much commercially sensitive information. An orderly system to gather and evaluate this type of information, perhaps through a centralized OECD office, would give public policy-makers a valuable tool for their upcoming trade policy decisions.

It is nevertheless apparent that MNCs are fully capable of playing an increasingly varied role in trans-Atlantic trade relations—through direct foreign establishment or a variety of cooperative business arrangements; subsequent to or in advance of specific intergovernmental agreements; and with private, governmentally connected or state-owned participants. The choice between various MNC forms of business can sharply affect physical trade flows and trade balance measures which are central to changing political values. Thus the nature of these MNC linkage patterns could play an important role in determining the future of Euro-American trade relations.

Evolving Policy Choices

The challenge for Euro-American relations during the 1980s will be to structure a mature trading system which meets both political and economic needs through an integrated approach to trade and investment policy issues. There is no turning back the clock to earlier days when broad free trade principles provided a satisfactory framework for European recovery and a sufficient guide to U.S. economic power. National and international economic changes have altered this relationship in a way which demands a more specific and equitable trading structure in terms of both opportunities and responsibilities.

The interrelationship between foreign trade and investment forces has never been closer, largely due to the linking mechanisms of multinational corporations. Europe has had experience dealing with all different sides of these forces and has developed an integrated view of foreign policy objectives as they relate to national economies. Both large trade adjustments and inward investment issues are relatively new for the U.S. A satisfactory response to these developments will require a level of policy integration and specificity very different from traditionally broad U.S. trade principles. The most immediate challenge then is probably to U.S. foreign economic policy, which must evolve a more refined and defined approach to advancing U.S. national interests, without allowing the pendulum to swing once again to the extremes of protectionist trade measures.

There should not be undue hesitancy on either side of the Atlantic about U.S. movement toward more specific and even outwardly aggressive policy positions. Measurement of U.S. trade and investment policies against a more explicit self-interest standard is probably overdue in international terms; it is also a necessary move to respond to domestic concerns which, if ignored, will turn U.S. policies much more surely toward an inwardly directed, protectionist trade posture.

Trans-Atlantic attention should focus instead on forging new Euro-American understandings on trade and investment policies as they relate to the role of national governments in transnational business arrangements. While in the past MNCs have been perceived as placing national "sovereignty-at-bay," the danger now is more that governments have gained too much explicit control over MNCs. Through governmentally negotiated production and marketing arrangements, public ownership or susidization, as well as trade and investment policy tools, national governments can directly structure MNC economic activities far more specifically than was previously possible.

Multinational corporations could play a crucial role in supporting multilateral cooperation if policy-makers on both sides of the Atlantic encourage the integrative, linking aspects of MNC activities, rather than focusing primarily on their utility as instruments of unilateral national gain.

Notes

1. See Charles S. Maier, The Politics of Productivity: Foundations of American International Economic Policy after World War II, in: Peter J. Katzenstein, *Between Power and Plenty*, 1978.

2. See Jack N. Behrman, *National Interests and the Multinational Enterprise*, 1970 and Raymond Vernon, *Big Business and the State*, 1974.

3. See: The European Challenge, in: *European Community*, July–August 1978, and Roy Eales, Challenge in Reverse, in: *The Economist*, October 1978.

4. The difference depends upon whether the survey question indicates that import restrictions would increase prices paid by consumers, with knowledge of the price impact lowering support for restrictions. For the poll data, see: Alvin Richman, *Public Preservations of World Trade*, a report prepared for the League of Women Voters Education Fund, 1980.

5. Richman, *Public Perceptions of World Trade*, p. 10.

6. U.S. Department of State, *Public Is Wary of Foreign Investment in the U.S.*, a Briefing Memorandum, September 6, 1979.

7. Ibid.

8. U.S. Department of State, *Public Attitudes Toward Foreign Trade*, a Briefing Memorandum, August 27, 1980.

9. Louis Kraar, Boeing Takes a Bold Plunge to Keep Flying High, in: *Fortune*, 25 September 1980.

10. Information gathered from a variety of news accounts, industry publications and other public sources.

11. Letter from Japanese Minister of International Trade and Industry, Rokusuke Tanaka to U.S. Trade Representative Reubin Askew, November 23, 1980.

11

The Soviet-European Gas Pipeline: A Case of Failed Sanction

Gary Clyde Hufbauer
Jeffrey J. Schott

U.S. governments have a less prominent tradition than the Europeans or the Japanese of trying to utilize their own multinationals, in mercantilistic fashion, as instruments of home country foreign policy. They have even less experience in being rebuffed when they make the attempt. The pipeline case was a notable exception and could represent a new impetus toward neomercantilism in the United States, or it could constitute a turning point in U.S. awareness of the difficulties of pursuing a mercantilistic approach toward its multinationals in the modern era.

In an attempt to retard the construction of a Soviet pipeline to supply gas to Western Europe, the Reagan administration prohibited U.S. companies from carrying out contracts to supply components and technology. In addition, it restricted the foreign subsidies and foreign licensees of U.S. firms from proceeding with their contracts as well. In reaction, European governments issued counterorders demanding that the sales of equipment and technology proceed, escalating the conflict to the policy level between heads of state.

Chapter 7 discusses the denouement of this episode in terms of the dilemma for international firms when confronted by conflicting sovereign directives.

Economic sanctions have played a major role in East-West rivalry throughout the postwar period. The most recent episode involved U.S. opposition to the construction of a natural gas pipeline from the Soviet Union to several European countries. At issue was European participation in a long-term supply agreement with the Soviet Union for up to 40 billion cubic meters (BCM) a year of natural gas to be channeled to Western Europe through a new 4,500 kilometer pipeline. European firms offered to provide steel pipe, gas turbines, and other equipment needed for the construction of the pipeline in return for future deliveries of natural gas.[1]

Negotiations on the pipeline were already well advanced by the time the Reagan administration took office in 1981. In fact, in his role as NATO commander during the Carter administration, Alexander Haig had registered no objection to the pipeline. By the time President Reagan asked European leaders to reconsider the prospective deal with the Soviet Union during the Ottawa summit in July 1981, the financing package for the construction of the pipeline was being wrapped up. A few months later, despite strong U.S. pressure to defer plans, Ruhrgas, which led the consortium of gas companies in Europe, signed an agreement for delivery of Soviet gas starting in 1984.

The Reagan administration opposed the pipeline for two main reasons: to deny the Soviet Union hard currency receipts, which could be used to strengthen the Soviet economy, and to prevent Europe from becoming overly dependent on supplies of Soviet gas. The European attitude to these concerns was colored by two factors. First, because of falling demand, the Europeans were not contracting for the full 40 BCM of gas—indeed, initial contracts were for little over half that amount—and thus the ratio of Soviet gas to total supplies was not so high. Second, the Europeans found the expansion of U.S. grain exports to the Soviet Union hard to reconcile with U.S. demands to limit European exports of other products. It particularly irked the Europeans to be asked to forgo lucrative export contracts, crucial for their recession-plagued industries, while U.S. farmers continued to sell grain to the Soviet Union. The fact that the United States offered to sell the Soviet Union an additional 15 million metric tons of grain on October 1, 1981, just as U.S. officials were lobbying European governments to cancel plans for the gas pipeline, added to the discord among the Western allies.[2]

The first specific actions against the pipeline were taken on December 29, 1981, as part of the trade sanctions imposed by the United States against the Soviet Union for its complicity in the decision to impose martial law in Poland. Export licenses for a wide range of high technology goods, and for oil and gas field technology and equipment, were suspended. This suspension had an immediate effect on the shipment of rotors by General Electric to various European firms under contract to supply turbines for the pipeline. At a NATO Council meeting in early January 1982, the Europeans hesitated to support U.S. sanctions against the Soviet Union (although they endorsed sanctions taken against Poland), but they agreed to consider measures that would affect trade with the Soviet Union (including civil aviation and maritime agreements and the terms of official export credits).[3]

In addition to the sanctions, the Reagan administration sought to restrict the amount of subsidized credit available to finance the construction of the pipeline, thereby making the project less attractive economically. This was done in conjunction with efforts to increase the minimum lending rates permissible under the OECD (Organization for Economic Cooperation and Development) International Arrangement on Official Export Credits to a level closer to current market rates. The arrangement had previously allowed credits for medium-income countries (such as the Soviet Union and Poland) at a rate of 8.5 percent. The United States argued that this rate was excessively generous, especially in the light of prevailing market rates of over 15 percent. As a result, the United States pushed for an increase in the minimum rate to 11.35 percent for medium-income countries and an upgrading of the Soviet Union to the class of developed countries (effectively raising the interest costs another percentage point).[4] These changes were accepted, but it was not clear whether they were prospective only or also covered existing credit lines.

The Versailles summit communiqué reflected some degree of consensus on export credit restrictions. The summit participants "agreed to handle cautiously financial relations with the USSR and other Eastern European countries in such a way as to ensure that they are conducted on a sound economic basis, including also the need for commercial prudence in limiting export credits."[5] After the meeting, however, the United States and the Europeans came back home with widely divergent views of what this commitment meant. U.S. Treasury Secretary Donald Regan hailed it as "a major step toward cutting off imprudent credit" and argued, "What we are saying here about credit—no expansion of credits; stop where you are."[6] The Europeans, however, felt the agreement referred only to prospective credits, not those already in the pipeline and already negotiated by European bankers. This disagreement precipitated a major crisis within the Atlantic alliance less than two weeks after the summit.

On June 18, 1982, President Reagan announced that the sanctions on oil and gas field equipment would be amended, effective June 22, 1982, to include "equipment produced by subsidiaries of U.S. companies abroad as well as equipment produced abroad under licenses issued by U.S. companies."[7] The administration justified extraterritorial application of the pipeline sanctions on the grounds that a wider reach was simply an elaboration of measures announced on December 29, 1981, and therefore was part of the considered response of the United States and its NATO allies to Soviet interference in Poland. However, the new measures were regarded by the Europeans in a totally different light: as a dramatic shift in administration policy, one effected without consultation with the allies and quite possibly undertaken in a fit of pique.[8]

The European reaction to the extension of the Soviet trade sanctions was vocal and harsh. A meeting of the leaders of the Common Market on June 29 charged that "the open world trade system will be seriously jeopardized by unilateral and retroactive decisions on international trade, attempts to exercise extraterritorial legal powers, and measures which prevent the fulfillment of existing trade contracts."[9] By attempting to void existing contracts, the extraterritorial controls would subject about twenty European companies to various nonperformance penalties and result in job losses in many areas that already suffered from severe unemployment. Governments of the United Kingdom, France, West Germany, and Italy objected to the new sanctions and either urged or ordered their domestic companies not to comply with the U.S. measures, even if contract clauses mandated compliance. The firms were thus placed in the unhappy position of being liable to prosecution at home if they abided by the sanctions or to penalties in the United States if they did not.

The United States acted swiftly when the first shipments for the pipeline left European ports in late August. Dresser (France) S.A., a fully owned U.S. subsidiary, and Creusot-Loire were immediately slapped with a ban on all imports from the United States. These measures were tempered a week later when a "clarification" was issued by Secretary Regan limiting the coverage of the restrictions to oil and gas field equipment and technology. Limited sanctions were also imposed on the Italian and British pipeline suppliers when their turbines left port in early September. U.S. Secretary of State George Shultz began a quiet campaign in the Reagan administration to heal the breach in the alliance, but the internecine dispute was not resolved until two days after the death of Leonid Brezhnev (on November 11, 1982), when President Reagan lifted most sanctions against the export of oil and gas field equipment and dropped enforcement actions against the European firms.

Policy Lessons

The pipeline case is only one of the many instances of economic sanctions deployed over the years in pursuit of a host of national security and foreign policy goals, among them, nuclear nonproliferation, human rights, and anti-apartheid. These goals are often laudable; however, an extensive review of U.S. sanctions imposed since World War I shows that sanctions more often than not fail to change the policy of foreign countries.[10] Several general lessons of particular relevance to the pipeline case can be learned from this historical experience.

1. Policymakers need to take a close look at both the political and economic aspects of sanctions when designing foreign policy strategy. As in the pipeline case, political costs can decisively undermine a sanctions strategy.

2. Success depends on the type of goal sought. In some instances—particularly situations involving small target countries and modest policy goals—sanctions have helped to alter foreign behavior. But attempts to disrupt military adventures, to impair a foreign adversary's military potential, or otherwise to change its policies in a major way generally fail.

3. Countries often have inflated expectations of what sanctions can accomplish. Sanctions cannot move mountains or force strong target countries into making fundamental changes. At most, there is a weak correlation between

economic deprivation and political willingness to change. The economic impact of sanctions may be pronounced, both on the sender and the target country, but other factors in the situational context almost always overshadow the impact of sanctions in determining the political outcome.

4. Economic sanctions seem most effective when aimed against erstwhile friends and close trading partners. By contrast, sanctions directed against countries that have long been adversaries of the sender country or against countries that have little trade with the sender country are generally less successful. The Soviet Union has been the target of Western economic sanctions since the 1920s and has developed a remarkable resistance to this tool of foreign policy. The higher compliance with sanctions by allies and trading partners reflects their willingness to bend on specific issues in deference to an overall relationship with the sender country. Such considerations may not be decisive in the calculus of an antagonistic target country or a target country that has little economic contact with the sender.

5. A country should shy away from deploying sanctions when the economic costs to itself or its allies are high. Although popular opinion at home may welcome the introduction of sanctions, public support for sanctions often dissipates over time, especially from sectors that bear the brunt of the costs of the sanctions. In this regard, governments should design sanctions so as not to impose unduly concentrated costs on particular domestic groups. In the pipeline case, the costs were clearly focused on a very few U.S. and European industries.

6. International cooperation does not guarantee success, as evidenced by the long history of the U.S. and COCOM strategic controls against the Soviet Union and the Council for Mutual Economic Assistance. Basically, a country looks to its allies for help because its goals are ambitious; in cases with more modest goals, such cooperation is not needed. Sanctions should either be deployed unilaterally—because the impact on one's allies is slight—or designed in cooperation with allies in order to reduce backlash and evasion.

Conclusion

The United States has imposed sanctions for both national security and foreign policy reasons. The line between the two is not always clear, as the pipeline episode demonstrates.

Throughout the postwar period, the United States has sought to restrict strategic sales to the Soviet Union to curb the flow of sensitive technologies and prevent or delay advances in weaponry. These, by definition, are national security controls. No one disagrees with the need to stem the flow of sensitive goods and technologies to the Soviet Union; however, the United States and its allies agree on only a limited list of products and technologies that should be subject to such controls.

Problems have arisen, as in the pipeline case, when the United States restricted sales of goods and technology—especially dual-use items, with both military and commercial applications—not deemed sensitive by the other Western allies. Such controls presumably have been taken in pursuit of national foreign policy rather than joint security goals. In those instances, European trade interests clashed with U.S. trade controls. In some cases, the United States has sought European compliance with its sanctions through the extraterritorial application of U.S. law. Such actions have been criticized by both the U.S. business community, which has lost export sales of goods readily available from foreign suppliers, and by the Europeans, who often sensed they were targets of U.S. controls, along with the Eastern bloc nations.

Instead, U.S. export control policy should limit national security controls to narrowly defined strategic exports (such as those on the COCOM list) and be predisposed against the use of controls in pursuit of foreign policy goals if alliance cooperation is a necessary ingredient of a successful outcome. This simple, commonsense approach would be warmly embraced by U.S. business and U.S. allies. Almost certainly it would have avoided the pipeline fiasco.

Notes

1. An abstract of this case, excerpted from our recent book, *Economic Sanctions Reconsidered: History and Current Policy* (Washington, D.C.: Institute for International Relations, June 1985), is appended at the end of this chapter.

2. U.S. grain sales to the Soviet Union almost doubled from 8 million tons to 15.3 million tons in the year after President Reagan lifted the partial grain embargo. Cf. *New York Times,* August 5, 1982, D10.

3. See *Department of State Bulletin* (February 1982):19–20 for the text of the NATO Council Declaration.

4. Department of the Treasury, "New International Arrangement on Export Credits" (July 1, 1982).

5. *New York Times,* June 7, 1982, p. D6.

6. *Wall Street Journal,* June 15, 1982, p. 26.

7. Statement by the President, White House Press Release, June 18, 1982.

8. At the time, there were several press reports that the president was annoyed by public statements by Mitterand and Schmidt that the Versailles Summit communiqué language on export credits to the Soviet Union would not, as a practical matter, affect their current government policies.

9. *Declaration of the European Council on European Community-United States Relations* (Brussels, June 29, 1982).

10. Hufbauer and Schott, *Economic Sanctions Reconsidered.*

Appendix 11A
Case: U.S. versus U.S.S.R.
(1981–82: Poland)

Chronology of Key Events

12 December 1980

NATO ministers issue communiqué warning Soviets that: "Any intervention [in Poland] would fundamentally alter the entire situation. The Allies would be compelled to react in the manner which the gravity of this development would require." (Marantz 1)

24 April 1981

President Ronald Reagan lifts grain embargo imposed by President Jimmy Carter in retaliation for USSR invasion of Afghanistan (*New York Times,* 25 April 1981, A1)

Late July 1981

At Ottawa summit, Reagan presses European and Japanese leaders for tighter restrictions by Coordinating Committee for Multilateral Export Controls (COCOM). He also urges reconsideration of Yamal pipeline deal in which Western European firms provide pipeline equipment in return for gas deliveries later. Europeans agree to review COCOM but refuse to drop pipeline. (*Journal of Commerce,* 21 January 1982, 2A)

24 July 1981

USSR, Germany conclude outline agreement for financing pipeline. (*Business Week,* 10 August 1981, 36)

1 October 1981

US extends existing grain agreement for one year, will allow USSR to buy up to 15 million metric tons (mmt) above 8 mmt allowed without consultation under old agreement. (*New York Times,* 2 October 1981, A1)

6 October 1981

Italy announces signing of agreement in principle to buy USSR natural gas, first firm commitment by West European country. (*New York Times,* 19 October 1981, D8)

20 November 1981

FRG, USSR sign agreement for delivery of gas, clearing way for pipeline to go forward. (*Washington Post,* 21 November 1981, A1)

13 December 1981

Martial law is declared in Poland; USSR rushes to nail down contracts for pipeline equipment. (*Washington Post,* 14 December 1981, A1)

23 December 1981

Reagan's Christmas address to nation announces sanctions against Poland. (*Washington Post,* 24 December 1981, A1)

29 December 1981

US sanctions imposed on USSR for role in declaration of martial law in Poland are characterized by US Secretary of State Alexander M. Haig, Jr., as "interim step that hardly exhausts the list of potential actions." Actions taken include: suspension of Aeroflot flights; suspension of export licenses for high tech items including oil, gas equipment; closing of Soviet Purchasing Commission office in New York; suspension of negotiations on new long-term grain agreement; suspension of new maritime agreement; allowing technical exchange agreements to lapse—energy, space in May, science, technology in July. (*Washington Post,* 30 December 1981, A1)

11 January 1982

NATO Council condemns Soviet interference in Poland, agrees to: restrictions on activities of Soviet, Polish diplomats; reduction of scientific and technical exchanges with USSR. (*Department of State Bulletin,* February 1982, 19)

Early January 1982

US refuses to grant export licenses to General Electric to ship $175 million worth of components for gas compressor turbines to be built for pipeline by Nuovo Pignone of Italy. AEG Telefunken of West Germany, John Brown Engineers, Ltd., of Great Britain. (*New York Times,* 11 January 1982, A1)

23 January 1982

France concludes 25-year contract with USSR for 280 billion cubic feet of gas per year, one-third of France's gas imports. (*Washington Post,* 24 January 1982, A1)

28 January 1982

Italy reaches tentative agreement with USSR on price, volume of gas shipments. (*Wall Street Journal,* 29 January 1982, 33)

Early June 1982

Participants at Versailles economic summit discuss subsidized export credits to USSR. Reagan pressures Western Europe to charge market interest rates on such credits. Final summit communiqué calls for "prudent and diversified economic approach to the Soviet bloc and to take into account a need for 'commercial prudence' in limiting export credits to the Soviet Union and its allies." However, "conflicting statements from US and European officials in the week following the summit indicated that the communiqué did not reflect a consensus on the subject of export credits." (Moyer 81)

18 June 1982

Reportedly in response to reluctance of West European allies, particularly France, to limit export credits to Soviet bloc, US extends ban on sale of oil, gas equipment to foreign subsidiaries of US companies and foreign companies producing equipment under US license, effective 22 June 1982. (*Washington Post,* 19 June 1982, A1)

Late June 1982

"European governments promptly denounced the extraterritorial extension of U.S. regulation as violative of their sovereignty, contrary to international law, inconsistent with the understandings purportedly reached at the Versailles Summit, and insensitive to their commercial interests." (Moyer 81–82)

22 July 1982

France orders French companies to honor their contracts and supply equipment for pipeline despite Reagan's ban. (*Washington Post,* 23 July 1982, A1)

OECD officials announce agreement on new arrangement for export credits. Included is reclassification of USSR, other East European countries from intermediate to "relatively rich" category, which increases minimum allowable rate for USSR from 10.5 percent to a range of 12.15 percent to 12.40 percent. (*Keesing's* 31639)

25 July 1982

Italy announces "signed agreements will be honored" but stops short of ordering its companies to fulfill contracts associated with pipeline. (*Wall Street Journal,* 26 July 1982, 21)

26 July 1982

Belgium postpones signing of contract with USSR for gas. (*Financial Times* [London], 27 July 1982, 4)

28 July 1982

UK announces it will not order British companies to defy US sanctions but that British government will defend firms from US retaliation if they choose to go ahead with pipeline deals. (*Washington Post,* 29 July 1982, A30)

30 July 1982

Reagan announces one-year extension of grain agreement with USSR but refuses to negotiate new long-term agreement because the Soviet Union "should not be afforded the additional security of a new long-term grain agreement as long as repression continues in Poland." (*Department of State Bulletin,* October 1982, 40–41)

2 August 1982

UK reverses policy, orders British companies to fulfill contracts for pipeline equipment. Trade Secretary Lord Cockfield invokes Protection of Trading Interests Act in issuing the order. In preelection speech to National Corn Growers Association, Reagan says Russians can buy as much grain as they want if they pay cash. (*Washington Post,* 3 August 1982, A4, A11)

11 August 1982

House Foreign Affairs Committee votes 22 to 12 to rescind administration's pipeline sanctions. (*Washington Post,* 12 August 1982, A1)

23 August 1982

France orders Dresser-France to deliver 21 pipeline booster compressors already on order. Dresser industries orders its French subsidiary to comply with French order, files suit in US federal court to block implementation of US penalties for violating sanctions. (*Wall Street Journal,* 26 August 1982, 4; *New York Times,* 24 August 1982, D1)

25 August 1982

Germany informs its firms that US sanctions are illegal under international law, violate German sovereignty. (*Washington Post,* 26 August 1982, A1)

26 August 1982

Three compressors leave French port of Le Havre bound for USSR. US bans Dresser-France, Creusot-Loire from importing any US goods, services, or technology until further notice. (*Financial Times,* 27 August 1982, 14)

27 August 1982

Senior administration officials say sanctions could be lifted "if other means could be found to keep equivalent economic pressure on Moscow." Goal still is said to be end to repression in Poland; desired means are said to include: limiting export credits; tightening technology transfer controls; withholding exports of other oil, gas technology and equipment; canceling second strand of gas pipeline. (*New York Times,* 28 August 1982, A1)

1 September 1982

US Treasury Secretary Donald T. Regan announces sanctions on French firms will be lessened to restrict only imports of US oil, gas equipment. (*New York Times,* 2 September 1982, A1)

6 September 1982

US imposes sanctions on Nuovo Pignone of Italy for shipping three pipeline turbines with US parts to USSR. (*Wall Street Journal,* 7 September 1982, 3)

10 September 1982

US imposes sanctions against British firm, John Brown Engineers, Ltd. (*Wall Street Journal,* 10 September 1982, 5)

16 September 1982

European nations say it is US responsibility to resolve dispute caused by its unilateral action. (*Financial Times,* 16 September 1982, 3)

5 October 1982

US imposes sanctions against AEG-Kanis and Mannesmann of Germany for shipping two turbines for pipeline to USSR. AEG-Kanis announces it was not certain it would fulfill rest of its contract for pipeline turbines. (*Washington Post,* 6 October 1982, A20; 7 October 1982, A37)

15 October 1982

Reagan says USSR can buy up to 23 mmt of grain in 1982, guarantees contract sanctity if orders are placed before November 30; USSR does not oblige. (*Weekly Compilation of Presidential Documents,* 18 October 1982; *Financial Times,* 20 October 1982, 19)

16 October 1982

Administration officials announce they have provided British, French, Italian, West German officials with draft proposal that could lead to lifting of sanctions. (*New York Times,* 17 October 1982, A1)

18 October 1982

Reagan publicly states willingness to consider lifting sanctions. (*Wall Street Journal,* 19 October 1982, 3)

11 November 1982

Leonid Brezhnev, Soviet president and Communist party general secretary, dies. (*New York Times,* 12 November 1982, A1)

13 November 1982

Reagan announces lifting of sanctions, saying US, West European allies have reached "substantial agreement" on overall economic strategy with East. France immediately announces it is not party to agreement. Reagan's announcement pertains only to restrictions on sales of oil, gas equipment, does not affect curbs on airlines or other sanctions imposed on Poland, Russia for martial law in Poland. Main elements of agreement are as follows: not to engage in trade agreements that "contribute to the military or strategic advantage of the USSR," particularly high tech goods and oil, gas equipment; not to give preferential aid; not to sign new gas agreements pending completion of energy alternative study by allies; to strengthen COCOM controls; to monitor financial relations with view to harmonizing credit policies. (*Congressional Quarterly*, 20 November 1982, 2883; *Department of State Bulletin*, January 1983, 28)

In practice, new policy means that validated export licenses will be required only for oil, gas exploration, production equipment, no longer for oil and gas transmission and refining equipment exported by domestic US companies and their overseas subsidiaries. In addition, all enforcement actions against these subsidiaries are dropped. (*New York Times*, 14 November 1982, A1; Moyer 83–85)

6 January 1983

USSR announces completion of 2,000-mile trunk gas pipeline linking Siberia with Ukraine, expects completion of Siberian–West European pipeline by end of 1983. (*Journal of Commerce*, 6 January 1983, 1A)

11 January 1983

Reagan announces he will sign legislation "that substantially restricts the power of the president to limit grain sales abroad as an instrument of foreign policy." Under new legislation, restrictions will not affect "agricultural exports covered by contracts calling for delivery within 270 days of an embargo announcement." However, president still will have authority to restrict foreign grain sales in declared national emergencies. (*New York Times*, 12 January 1983, A1)

22 April 1983

Reagan lifts ban on negotiations for a long-term grain agreement with Soviet Union; stated reason is "to reaffirm our reliability as a supplier of grain" to USSR. In July 1982, president had said ban would continue "until the Soviet Union indicates that it is prepared to permit the process of reconciliation in Poland to go forward and demonstrates this desire with deeds and not just words." On 22 April 1983, Mark Palmer, acting assistant secretary of state for European affairs, states, "It's not linked to the situation in Poland. We continue to be deeply concerned about developments in Poland." US Trade Representative William Brock adds that ban on negotiations "simply had no validity as a tool in that capacity anymore . . . we believe this sanction has made its political point." (*New York Times*, 23 April 1983, A1)

8 May 1983

US and Europe, negotiating in context of International Energy Agency (IEA), agree on pledge to avoid "undue dependence" by Europe on Soviet energy. Agreement falls short of European commitment to abandon planned second strand of USSR-European gas pipeline. (*Wall Street Journal,* 9 May 1983, 37; *Washington Post,* 10 May 1983, A12)

20 August 1983

Following policy battle between Defense Secretary Caspar W. Weinberger on one side and Commerce Secretary Malcolm Baldridge and Secretary of State George P. Shultz on other, Reagan lifts export controls on sale of Caterpillar Tractor pipelayers to USSR. Controls had been imposed in July 1978 by Carter in response to jailing of dissidents Anatoly B. Shcharansky and Aleksandr Ginzburg, and continued by Reagan as part of pipeline embargo. While Commerce Department had approved licenses for sale of 200 pipelayers costing $90 million, USSR diverted its orders to Komatsu of Japan as long as vestigial US export controls remained in place. Lifting all controls is said to represent "a major policy shift by the administration because pipelayers have become the touchstone of East-West trade policy." (*New York Times,* 21 August 1983, A1; *Washington Post,* 20 August 1983, A1)

25 August 1983

US, USSR sign five-year grain agreement, raising minimum annual Soviet purchases from 6 mmt to 9 mmt and containing a "no-export-control" clause. (*Washington Post,* 26 August 1983, A19)

January 1984

Fire reportedly destroys imported electronic equipment at pumping station at Urengoy, largest of 41 such stations on pipeline. Western sources estimate damage could delay Urengoy commissioning six months or more. Soviet sources had claimed pipeline had been completed months ahead of schedule despite sanctions and that gas shipments to France through it had begun. One Western diplomatic source expressed skepticism that pipeline would be completed before 1985 or even 1986. (*New York Times,* 11 January 1984, A1)

Goals of Sender Country

29 December 1981

Reagan: "The repression in Poland continues and President Brezhnev has responded in a manner which makes it clear the Soviet Union does not understand the seriousness of our concern and its obligations under the Helsinki Final Act and the UN Charter.

"By our actions we expect to put powerful doubts in the minds of the Soviet and Polish leaders about this continued repression. . . . The whole purpose of our actions is to speak for those who have been silenced and to help those who have been rendered helpless."

Secretary of State Haig: Sanctions are needed because "we just could not go on doing business as usual while freedom is being trampled in Poland." He lists US goals as: lifting of martial law in Poland, freeing of Solidarity leaders, opening of dialogue with Solidarity. (*Washington Post*, 30 December 1981, A1)

31 January 1982

"One month after President Reagan announced economic sanctions against the Soviet Union for its 'heavy and direct responsibility for the repression in Poland' the administration is studying new steps that could delay if not block the completion of the largest single East-West project: the $25 billion natural gas pipeline from Western Siberia to Europe." (*Washington Post*, 31 January 1982, A1)

10 February 1982

It is believed that delaying or blocking pipeline could significantly affect Soviet economy, which needs revenues from gas sales to replace hard currency lost from declines in oil exports as reserves are depleted. Pipeline also has raised concern because of potential leverage it could provide USSR over Western Europe if Soviet Union threatened to cut off gas supplies, or did so. (*New York Times*, 10 February 1982, D1)

18 June 1982

Reagan, announcing extension of pipeline sanctions to US subsidiaries and licensees abroad: "The objective of the United States in imposing the sanctions has been and continues to be to advance reconciliation in Poland. Since December 30, 1981, little has changed concerning the situation in Poland; there has been no movement that would enable us to undertake positive reciprocal measures." (*Washington Post*, 19 June 1982, A1)

23 July 1982

Assistant Secretary of Commerce for Trade Administration Lawrence J. Brady: "There is little question that if the West exercises its collective will to enforce these sanctions, the entire Soviet bloc will find itself in very difficult straits throughout the rest of the decade." (*Washington Post*, 24 July 1982, A1)

30 July 1982

Under Secretary of State James L. Buckley: "Above all, we seek an end to the repression of the Polish people. The sanctions imposed against the sale of oil and gas equipment increase the internal costs to the Soviet Union of the project and cause an additional strain on already thinly stretched Soviet resources." (*Department of State Bulletin,* September 1982, 38)

September 1982

US Trade Representative Brock: "We cannot continue to provide subsidized export credits to the Soviets which they can then use to strengthen their military capacity, further threaten us—because it forces us to respond, and it costs everybody in any number of ways." (*US News & World Report,* 13 September 1982, 27–29)

21 September 1982

Secretary of Defense Weinberger: "In recent weeks the evidence has been mounting that the Soviet Union may be using slave labor" to build pipeline. Weinberger concedes "the evidence is not conclusive" but is "profoundly troubling." He also reiterates administration's other fears: ". . . it is a little hard to see how trade of this kind, that has such an obvious military advantage in providing this much [hard currency earnings] most of which would go into military spending, can do anything but increase the danger to all of us." (*Washington Post,* 22 September 1982, A14)

27 September 1982

Secretary of State Shultz, in New York for opening of UN General Assembly, meets with French, West German representatives but avoids discussion of pipeline sanctions because of divisiveness of issue.

The previous week, "a senior administration official, speaking with reporters on background, [had] warned that unless the allies agree on measures even tougher than the US strategy on the pipeline, President Reagan intends to keep pursuing his current strategy." (*Washington Post,* 28 September 1982, A20)

13 November 1982

Reagan's radio address announcing lifting of sanctions: "The understanding we and our partners have reached and the actions we are taking reflect our mutual determination to overcome differences and strengthen our cohesion. I believe this new agreement is a victory for all the allies. It puts in place a much-needed policy in the economic area to complement our policies in the security area." (*New York Times,* 14 November 1982, A1)

Response of Target Country

19 November 1981

Vladimir Filanovsky, chief of oil and gas industry department of USSR state planning committee: "The USSR has never used its gas supplies as a lever to pressure its partners, nor is it going to. Also, it has always honored scrupulously its commitments." (*Journal of Commerce,* 20, November 1981, 1A)

30 December 1981

Tass: "The Soviet Union is a great power which has never allowed and will never allow anyone to speak to it in the language of blackmail and diktat. . . . [President Reagan is trying] to hurl the world back to the dark times of the cold war." (*Washington Post,* 31 December 1981, A1)

Mid-July 1982

From Soviet journal, *Literaturnaya Gazeta:* "The master of the White House wanted to disrupt or slow down the construction of the gas pipeline but he achieved quite an opposite effect: the embargo only piqued the pride of the Soviet people and worked up the workers' enthusiasm. In this sense, Reagan's embargo has boomeranged against him" (*New York Times,* 20 July 1982, D1)

14 November 1982

Tass: The sanctions have failed. "By means of those measures, Washington unsuccessfully tried to frustrate the construction of the Siberian–Western European gas pipeline." (*Washington Post,* 15 November 1982, A15)

16 November 1982

USSR Minister of Foreign Trade Nikolai Patolichev says US-Soviet trade would increase only after Soviets had "regained complete confidence that agreements will not be broken. It is necessary for the US to renounce once and for all the doctrine of using trade as a weapon against our country." (*Financial Times,* 17 November 1982, 1)

Spring 1983

"In order to speed the completion of the export line the Ministry of Gas and Oil Construction seems likely to opt for its own Soviet built compressors rather than wait for the delivery of all the import compressor units ordered from Western European manufacturers." (*Financial Times,* 5 April 1983, 14)

Attitude of Other Countries

North Atlantic Treaty Organization and
European Community

30 December 1981: In meetings of EC officials in London and NATO ambassadors in Brussels, Allies are reluctant to follow US lead: "agreed only to continue consultations at a special meeting of their foreign ministers in Brussels Monday." (*Washington Post,* 31 December 1981, A1)

NATO Council Declaration

11 January 1982: "Recognizing that each of the Allies will act in accordance with its own situation and laws, they will examine measures which could involve arrangements regarding imports from the Soviet Union, maritime agreements, air service agreements, the size of Soviet commercial representation and the conditions surrounding export credits." (*Department of State Bulletin,* February 1982, 20)

NATO

January 1982: Allies pledge not to "undermine" US-imposed sanctions but do not commit themselves to taking any specific trade actions. Compliance is uncertain as FRG goes ahead with sale of turbines for pipeline to USSR despite US ban on US components. (*Washington Post,* 15 January 1982, A1; Moyer 80)

European Community

12 August 1982: EC issues formal protest against pipeline sanctions, saying they violate both international, American law. Protest note also states: "The recent US measures provide the Soviets with a strong inducement to enlarge their own manufacturing capacity and to accelerate their own turbine and compressor developments, thus becoming independent of Western sources." (*Washington Post,* 13 August 1982, A12)

September 1982: "The Europeans have opposed the US tactics as interference in their internal affairs, as a contributor to unemployment at a time when their economies are in recession, and as an ineffective and potentially dangerous way to deal with Moscow." (*Washington Post*, 28 September 1982, A20)

NATO and EC

November 1982: Sources say November agreement entails little in way of new commitments by Allies, "with one apparent exception, an undertaking not to sign or approve new contracts for the purchase of Soviet natural gas while a series of studies are under way. The agreement covers areas where attempts have been made for years to coordinate Western policy." These sources say Europeans made no concessions and elements announced by Reagan "represented studies rather than concessions to harder trade policies with the Soviet Union." Oil glut, they say, makes new gas contracts with Soviets a dead letter in any event. (*New York Times*, 14 November 1982, A1)

"All European sources concur that the 'substantial agreement' is so vague that 'it doesn't mean anything,' in the words of one German official, but most of the Europeans accepted it as a means for Reagan to get off a hook that was causing trouble at home as well as abroad." (*Journal of Commerce*, 29 December 1982, 1A)

Italy

29 December 1981: Prime Minister Giovanni Spadolini of Italy says his country is reconsidering participation in the Soviet gas pipeline deal. (*New York Times*, 30 December 1981, A6)

7 July 1982: Spadolini announces that Italy will fulfill its commitment to provide turbines (produced under GE license) for pipeline despite US embargo. (*New York Times*, 8 July 1982, A1)

West Germany

29 December 1981: "Although the West Germans have not ruled out the theoretical possibility of participating in sanctions—they seemed relieved that the Reagan administration's first package of measures involving the Polish military regime was essentially mild—their attitude in the past about the use of such pressures has been both negative and contradictory." (*New York Times*, 30 December 1981, A6)

9 July 1982: Chancellor Helmut Schmidt: "We will stick to the agreements our firms made with the Soviet Union and so will France and Britain. . . . This will create some irritation in our relations with the United States but that will have to be overcome." (*Washington Post*, 10 July 1982, A24)

29 July 1982: Minister of Economics Otto Graf Lambsdorff: "The West Europeans are in agreement: the application of the principle of extraterritoriality in US government decisions is unacceptable to us. It violates our sovereignty. Therefore, we have to reject it . . . we have no differences of opinion on the events in Poland. The declaration of NATO in January 1982 was unanimous. But we do doubt that embargoes are an adequate answer. In my opinion, this applies to both the pipeline and the grain!" (*Washington Post*, 28 July 1982, A21)

Horst Keren, vice president of AEG-Kanis: "There is a doubt, a lack of trust, a feeling against the United States, that is the worst thing to come out of this affair. We have to be very cautious now about any new contracts that would bind us so totally to the United States." (*Journal of Commerce*, 29 December 1982, 1A)

United Kingdom

30 June 1982: Britain's Trade Ministry "issued an order under the Protection of Trading Interests Act of 1980, asserting that the US move was damaging to British trading interests. This enables Britain to take whatever legal steps are available to overturn the embargo." (*Washington Post*, 1 July 1982, A1)

14 November 1982: UK Foreign Secretary Francis Pym: "We now have a broad measure of agreement to guide the West's economic approach to the East. More work remains to be done but a good start has been made." (*Washington Post*, 14 November 1982, A9)

France

4 July 1982: "French President François Mitterand, who feels he was duped by Reagan at the Versailles Summit into believing that such an extension of the pipeline equipment ban—already in force for American firms—would not take place, said publicly last week that Reagan had exhibited 'a grave lack of solidarity with his allies.' " (*Washington Post*, 4 July 1982, F1)

13 November 1982: Mitterand says sanctions had been directed against Allies rather than USSR and no concessions would be connected to their removal. France, however, is expected to accede to agreement later. (*New York Times*, 14 November 1982, A1)

14 November 1982: "It was the joining of the East-West trade agreement and the lifting of the sanctions in the same public announcement that left the French 'very disappointed, very surprised,' the sources said." (*Washington Post*, 15 November 1982, A15)

"True, after dinner at the Quai d'Orsay, Mr. Shultz and French Foreign Minister Claude Cheysson, both dressed in dinner jackets, sipping drinks, and speaking English—a sign. I suppose of the Frenchman's extraordinary willingness to please—jointly briefed a few reporters. That hardly amounted to a joint statement, much less a formal agreement. . . .

". . . all future efforts to broaden the studies into a general economic strategy will be met by the French with at best delaying tactics—and at worst, with open opposition." (*New York Times*, 4 January 1983, A19)

Legal Notes

West German Minister of Economics

"The West Europeans are in agreement: the application of the principle of extraterritoriality in US government decisions is unacceptable to us. It violates our sovereignty. Therefore, we have to reject it. This is the unanimous position in Bonn, London, Paris and Rome—despite the content and clauses in civil law contracts between European and US companies. Such private agreements, the concrete content of which still would have to be examined carefully, cannot and must not alter the legal basis of international relations between states. Above all, they must not retroactively block execution of contracts that were concluded between the European companies and the Soviet Union long before the events in Poland." (Senate, Trowbridge 10)

Duane D. Morse and Joan S. Powers

"The novel question raised but not resolved in the pipeline controversy is whether the Act [EAA] authorizes the president to impose new restrictions on foreign use of commodities or technical data that have *previously* been exported from the United States and punish foreign nationals who refuse to observe these new restrictions. . . .

The pipeline controversy marked the first time wholly foreign nationals faced the denial of export privileges for reexporting previously exported commodities or foreign-produced products of previously exported technical data to newly forbidden destinations. . . .

"Recognizing . . . the possibility that trade restrictions may prompt international resentment and retaliatory measures against the United States, Congress has confined the president's delegated power to apply export control restrictions to persons or property 'subject to the jurisdiction of the United States.' The pipeline controversy illustrates quite clearly the dangers of ignoring that limitation. Once goods and technical data have left U.S. shores and reached foreign hands, the United States must relinquish jurisdiction to regulate, at least absent a direct threat to our national security. That international and domestic furor that surrounded the United States' largely unsuccessful attempt to impede construction of the Soviet pipeline provides an important lesson as to the limits of U.S. regulatory power." (Morse 545, 553, 567)

Economic Impact

Observed Economic Statistics

Initial press reports indicate pipeline will be installed at expected capital cost of $10 billion to $15 billion; that total USSR hard currency earnings in 1981 from oil and gas were $17 billion; earnings from new gas flow could be as much as $6.5 billion. (*Washington Post,* 21 November 1981, A1; Hewett 15–18)

However, primarily because of estimates of declining demand and, secondarily, warnings from US about dependence on Soviet energy, project is scaled back. Under agreements as signed, Soviets are committed to gradually increasing existing gas exports, if demanded by buyers, up to approximately 60 billion cubic meters (BCM) annually. USSR currently is delivering 27 BCM of gas to Europe. "The FRG has signed a contract for 10.5 BCM, with an additional 0.7 BCM for West Berlin; France for 8 BCM; Austria for 1.5 BCM, with an option on an additional 1 BCM; and Switzerland for 0.36 BCM. There is a strong indication that Italy will eventually sign for 8 BCM; Belgium, the Netherlands, Spain and Greece may be interested in small volumes at some later date." (Stern 22; also see *The German Tribune* [Hamburg], 8 May 1983, 6)

Contract for new USSR gas has floor price, rising at 3 percent per year in real terms, to reach $5.70 per million BTUs in 1990 (1981 dollars), plus base price indexed to oil prices. (*Wall Street Journal,* 15 March 1983, 26)

". . . only some 21 BCM have thus far been firmly contracted. . . . At a level of 21 BCM, Soviet hard currency earnings from Urengoy sales will amount to $3.8 billion per year in 1982 dollars, considerably less than the often quoted sum of $10 billion per year." (Stern 23; also see *New York Times,* 29 July 1983, D1)

"A total of 45,000 people now work on the 7.5 billion roubles (£ 6.8 billion) export line. So far they have been laid over three-quarters of the 4,500km pipeline. The export line is but one of six being laid along the 'energy corridor' from Urengoi. Some 25 billion roubles (£ 22.7 billion) is being invested during the 1980–85 period on these pipelines which total 20,000 kilometres in length." (*Financial Times,* 5 April 1983, 14)

Imports account for about 30 percent of pipelaying machinery used on export line. Another $3.5 billion has been spent on imported pipe, turbines, ancillary equipment. (*Financial Times,* 5 April 1983, 14)

Under Secretary of State James Buckley: "US firms have lost at least $800 million worth of potential business with the Soviet Union. . . ." Press report cites US, West European, Japanese sources as saying US lost at least $1 billion in contracts related to pipeline. (*Department of State Bulletin,* September 1982, 38; *Journal of Commerce;* 16 September 1982, 1A)

Washington Post estimates loss to US companies, subsidiaries from sanctions at $2.2 billion. Under Secretary of Commerce Lionel H. Olmer says that $2.2 billion estimate covers three-year period, feels most of it could be recouped. (*Washington Post*, 14 November 1982, A1; *New York Times*, 15 November 1982, A10)

Wharton Econometrics estimates that, by importing 1 mmt of grain at cost of $160 million, USSR can free sufficient resources to produce 2.8 mmt of oil, worth $700 million on world market. (*Financial Times*, 20 October 1982, 19)

State Department estimates Soviets lost $122 million in exports of furs, diamonds, caviar, salmon, other products to EC because of their ban on imports of 56 Soviet products. (House, Wallis 10)

Calculated Economic Impact

	Annual cost to target country
Delay in construction of pipeline; welfare loss estimated at 15 percent of value of reduced gas production (assumes either deferred export earnings or diversion of domestic gas supplies to export sales).	$190 million
Increased construction cost of pipeline caused by unavailability of US equipment and technology; welfare loss estimated at 25 percent of value of cancelled US purchases ($800 million).	200 million
Suspension of export licenses for oil, gas field equipment, high technology exports; welfare loss estimated at 60 percent of reduced US exports ($150 million).	90 million
Total	$480 million

Relative Magnitudes

Gross indicators of USSR economy	
USSR GNP (1981)	$1,587 billion
USSR population (1981)	268 million
Annual effect of sanctions related to gross indicators	
Percentage of GNP	negl.
Per capita	$1.79

USSR trade with US as percentage of total trade
  Exports (1981)   0.3
  Imports (1981)   3

Ratio of US GNP (1981: $2,958 billion) to USSR
GNP (1981: $1,587 billion)   2

Assessment

Homer E. Moyer, Jr., and Linda A. Mabry

"The effects of the pipeline controls on the Soviet Union appear to have been negligible. Even advocates of the controls admitted that the sanctions would only cause approximately a two-year delay in the completion of the project. This projection assumed, of course, that the controls would remain in place. . . . The pipeline controls, in fact, remained in place only five months, and were generally disregarded by foreign subsidiaries of US companies under contract to supply pipeline equipment to the Soviets. As a result, it appears that the sanctions neither thwarted nor appreciably delayed construction of the Yamal pipeline." (Moyer 88–89)

" . . . it is not too harsh to characterize the pipeline controls as perhaps the least effective and most costly controls in U.S. history." (Moyer 91)

Congressional Quarterly

"Reagan initially imposed the sanctions in December 1981 as a protest against Soviet pressure on the Communist government of Poland, which had imposed martial law and imprisoned leaders of the independent Solidarity trade union. But as it became increasingly clear that the sanctions were having no effect on Soviet behavior, Reagan shifted their focus to disrupting construction of a 2,600-mile natural gas pipeline from Siberia to Western Europe." (*Congressional Quarterly*, 20 November 1982, 2882)

"The reaction from US allies was less than enthusiastic. Although praising Reagan's decision to lift the sanctions, allied leaders made it clear that they had agreed only to study future limits on trade with the Soviet Union and had not committed themselves in advance to take specific actions." (*Congressional Quarterly*, 20 November 1982, 2883–84)

Paul Marantz

"Moscow was informed that should its troops be sent into Poland, the West would respond with a broad range of economic sanctions. Although little is known about Kremlin decision-making during the Polish crisis, it may well be that Soviet concern about the effect of an invasion on East-West economic relations was one of the factors that caused the Soviet leadership to temporize for so long and ultimately to choose a more indirect and less provocative means of crushing Solidarity." (Marantz 1)

"If anything Moscow was probably sorry to see US Secretary of State George Shultz succeed in negotiating a face-saving compromise that enabled the United States to abandon its ill-fated attempt to stop the pipeline. From the Soviet perspective, the minor economic inconvenience caused by having to shift to European suppliers was far outweighed by the political benefits resulting from the deep cleavage in the Western alliance that was provoked by American attempts to limit the activities of European companies." (Marantz 1)

". . . perhaps we should be thankful that the attempt to apply sanctions against Poland and the Soviet Union was anemic and half-hearted. Had Western nations moved more forcefully, in all likelihood they would have done more damage to their own economies and alliance structure, without in any way loosening the cruel repression that has been inflicted upon the Polish people." (Marantz 25)

"The unwillingness of the Europeans to impose stronger sanctions meant that the Soviet Union was made to pay only a minor economic penalty for its actions in Poland, a penalty which indeed was insufficient to alter Soviet conduct." (Marantz 9)

". . . rather than limit their exports which would directly affect employment in their own industries, they [the Europeans] curtailed imports from the Soviet Union. . . . The truly significant commodities such as oil, natural gas, and raw materials were never even considered for restrictions, and as a result, it was estimated that the measures adopted would affect no more than 1.5 percent of the $10 billion in goods that the nations of the EEC import annually from the Soviet Union." (Marantz 12)

Journal of Commerce

"While the measures may have slowed pipeline progress somewhat, they did not stop the project. They did cost American companies hundreds of millions of dollars. They also showed the world that the United States does not fully respect contracts and is prone to the use of trade sanctions as foreign policy weapons." (*Journal of Commerce*, 9 May 1983, 4A)

Gordon Crovitz

"President Reagan did not adequately emphasize the credits and hard currency issues and instead cited the Soviet role in Poland's martial law as the reason for the sanctions. Although in the end the sanctions were lifted without any firm agreement on future trade, it is doubtful that there would even now be any debate about East-West trade if the United States had not applied its temporary sanctions against the pipeline." (Crovitz 407)

Richard Pipes, former Soviet Expert on
National Security Council

"It is an open secret that the Reagan Administration is not of one mind on the issue of trade with the Communist bloc. . . . One school of thought, strongly represented in the Departments of Commerce and State, regards embargoes on energy equipment as not only futile but also counterproductive. . . . The other school, forcefully championed by the Department of Defense, views all commerce with the Communist bloc in the context of 'Grand Strategy.' It wishes to deny the Soviet Union the opportunity to earn additional hard currency from energy exports on the grounds that such money would be used to bolster Soviet military capabilities and to make Western Europe dependent on Soviet goodwill. Rather than give up on embargoes as unenforceable, we should agree with our Allies on a coordinated policy of economic containment. . . . The Soviet Union is one giant war machine. . . . Thus, Western energy assistance helps the USSR to build up its military and to avoid shifts in budgetary allocations that now favor the military. . . ." (*New York Times*, 21 August 1983, F2)

Under Secretary of State for Economic Affairs
Allen W. Wallis

"[T]he Soviets completed the pipelaying phase of this project last year [1983], installed a small number of compressor sets, and have transported relatively small amounts of gas over the line. . . . However, we should recall that the Soviets originally planned to complete the project, including both laying the pipe and installing all associated compressor stations, by 1984. We now estimate that this task will not be finished until 1986. We believe that much of this delay can be attributed to our sanctions. Moreover, in evaluating the effectiveness of our sanctions, it is impossible for us to ascertain to what extent the Soviets have been forced to divert resources from other priority projects simply to meet this delayed target for pipeline completion." (House, Wallis 6)

Authors' Summary

Overall assessment	Assigned Scores
• Policy result, scaled from 1 (failed) to 4 (success)	1
• Sanctions contribution, scaled from 1 (none) to 4 (significant)	1

- Success score (policy result *times* sanctions contribution), scaled from 1 (outright failure) to 16 (significant success)   1

Political and economic variables

- Companion policies: J (covert), Q (quasi-military), or R (regular military)   —
- International cooperation with sender, scaled from 1 (none) to 4 (significant)   2
- International assistance to target: A (if present)   —
- Sanctions period (years)   1
- Economic health and political stability of target, scaled from 1 (distressed) to 3 (strong)   3
- Presanction relations between sender and target, scaled from 1 (antagonistic) to 3 (cordial)   1
- Type of sanction: X (export), M (import), F (financial)   X
- Cost to sender, scaled from 1 (net gain) to 4 (major loss)   3

Bibliography

Crovitz, Gordon. 1982. "The Soviet Gas Pipeline: A Bad Idea Made Worse," 5 *World Economy* (December):407–13.

Drabek, Zdenek. 1983. "The Impact of Technological Differences on East-West Trade." 119 *Weltwirtschaftliches Archiv*. 630–48.

Hewett, Edward A. 1982. "The Pipeline Connection: Issues for the Alliance." *The Brookings Review* (Fall):15–20.

Marantz, Paul. 1985. "Economic Sanctions in the Polish Crisis." In *The Utility of Economic Sanctions,* ed. David Leyton-Brown. London: Croom Helm. Forthcoming.

Morse, Duane D., and Joan S. Powers. 1983. "U.S. Export Controls & Foreign Entities: The Unanswered Questions of Pipeline Diplomacy." 23 *Virginia Journal of International Law* 537–67.

Moyer, Homer E., Jr. and Linda A. Mabry. 1983. "Export Controls as Instruments of Foreign Policy: The History, Legal Issues, and Policy Lessons of Three Recent Cases." 15 *Law and Policy in International Business* 1–171.

Stern, Jonathan. P. 1982. "Specters and Pipe Dreams." 48 *Foreign Policy* (Fall):21–36.

US Congress, House Committee on Foreign Affairs. Subcommittee on Europe and the Middle East. 1984. *Hearings on East-West Economic Issues: Sanctions Policy and the Formulation of International Economic Policy.* Statement by Under Secretary of State for Economic Affairs Allen W. Wallis. 98 Cong., 2 sess., 29 March.

——— . Senate Committee on Foreign Relations. Subcommittee on International Economic Policy. 1982. *Hearings on Economic Relations with the Soviet Union.* 97 Cong., 2 sess., July 30, August 12–13.

——— . 1982. Statement by Alexander B. Trowbridge, president, National Association of Manufacturers. August 13.

12
Sovereignty at Bay:
Ten Years After

Raymond Vernon

Raymond Vernon reexamines the major assumptions underlying the analysis in *Sovereignty at Bay* in the light of developments of the last decade.

The idea of sovereignty at bay emerged in a period when the spread of multinational corporations seemed to surpass the domain of the nation-state. Such a situation, according to Vernon's seminal work, could not persist. The attempts of sovereigns to capture the benefits, avoid the costs, and harness the operations of multinationals, documented in this book, represent the reaction.

In attempting to predict the behavior of U.S.-based multinationals in the coming decade, Vernon suggests that the product-cycle hypothesis has stood up well in numerous tests but may have to be modified substantially for the future as the innovational lead of U.S. firms declines in relation to the Europeans and Japanese. Despite multiple challenges, international corporations have proved to be flexible and resilient in their ability to operate in developed and developing countries. While the evidence of whether they are maintaining centralized or more decentralized control is mixed, the prognosis for the future is a continued reliance on adhering to a common global corporate strategy.

For the future, Vernon warns that problems of multiple jurisdiction will likely intensify as diverse governments try to use multinationals as instruments for the projection of their own sovereign will.

The author of *Sovereignty at Bay,* musing in public about his opus after ten long years, faces one very special difficulty. Practically every reader remembers the title of the book; but scarcely anyone will accurately recall its contents. For after its publication, like Aspirin and Frigidaire, the label (but not the contents) became generic. Robert Gilpin identified a "Sovereignty at Bay model," subscribed to by visionaries devoted to the proposition that the nation-state was done for, finished off by the multinational enterprise.[1] Seymour J. Rubin lustily attacked the visionaries;

Reprinted from *International Organization*, summer 1981, Raymond Vernon, "Sovereignty at Bay: Ten Years After," by permission of The MIT Press, Cambridge, Massachusetts. © 1981 by the Board of Regents of the University of Wisconsin System.

Lincoln Gordon ably provided supporting fire; C. Fred Bergsten was only a step behind. Even Walter B. Wriston turned briefly from his labors at building one of the world's biggest banks to cast a few stones in the same general direction.

Meanwhile, the themes of *Sovereignty at Bay,* if they were ever learned, were half-forgotten in the heady pursuit of more vulnerable quarry. Only the author and a few of his more attentive students would remember the argument of his final chapter, which concluded somewhat lugubriously:

> The basic asymmetry between multinational enterprises and national governments [that is, the capacity of the enterprises to shift some of their activities from one location to another, as compared with the commitment of the government to a fixed piece of national turf] may be tolerable up to a point, but beyond that point there is a need to reestablish balance. . . . If this does not happen, some of the apocalyptic projections of the future of multinational enterprise will grow more plausible.

Roots of the Multinationals

Because *Sovereignty at Bay* was one of the earlier works in a stream that would soon become a torrent, much of the book was devoted to chronicling and describing the phenomenal growth and spread of multinational enterprises. Interwoven in the history and the description, however, were inevitably some hypotheses about causes. Some of these, although still bearing a touch of novelty in 1971, seem hackneyed today—suggestive, I suppose, of their validity and durability. The increased efficiencies of communication and transportation, which had been reducing the costs of learning and the costs of control, were given appropriate credit as expeditors of the multinationalizing process. Oligopoly was recognized as a near-necessary condition for breeding multinational enterprises, a conclusion that simply reaffirmed a point made ten years earlier by Stephen Hymer.[2]

Two kinds of oligopoly that seemed particularly relevant in explaining the spectacular growth of U.S.-based multinational enterprises in the postwar period were explored with special attention. (The subtitle of the book, after all, was "The Multinational Spread of *U.S.* Enterprise"). One was the oligopoly based upon the special technological capabilities of the participating firms, while the other was the oligopoly based on the sheer size and geographical spread of the operating firms concerned, as in the oil and metals industries. In that context, a number of hypotheses were elaborated, which later would be tested and retested in various contexts. The most widely known of these, particularly applicable to the technology-based oligopolies, came to be called the product-cycle hypothesis. I shall have more to say about that concept in a moment. But there were other propositions, which also were exposed to considerable testing in subsequent years, such as the follow-the-leader hypothesis.

These various concepts purporting to explain the growth and spread of multinational enterprises have stood up about as well as one could have hoped. The follow-the-leader hypothesis has been adequately confirmed in one or two solid studies.[3] As for the product-cycle hypothesis, there have been numerous confirming and elaborating studies,[4] as well as a few important qualifications, reservations, and demurrers.[5] On the whole, the concept seems to have had considerable utility in explaining past developments and predicting future ones.

However, what has changed—indeed, changed quite dramatically—is the applicability of the product-cycle hypothesis in explaining the present behavior and the likely future behavior of multinational enterprises based in the United States. As an explicator and predictor of U.S. performance, the product-cycle hypothesis had particular applicability to the conditions of, say, 1900 to 1970; this was a period in which the income levels of U.S. residents were higher than those in any other major market in the world, in which U.S. hourly labor costs were the highest in the world, and in which U.S. capital and raw materials were comparatively cheap. That set of unique conditions, it was posited, had been generating a stream of innovations on the part of U.S. firms responsive to their special environment. And as the income levels and relative labor costs in other countries tracked over the terrain previously traversed by the U.S. economy, U.S. innovations found a ready market in those other countries. These innovations were thought to provide an oligopolistic handhold that gave U.S. firms their dominant position in many markets of other countries.

But even as I went to press with *Sovereignty at Bay,* there were a few signs that the pattern might be losing its explanatory force for the United States. A section captioned "Toward Another Model" presented speculations about the consequences that might ensue as U.S. incomes and labor costs became more closely aligned with those of Europe and Japan. In that case, U.S.-based enterprises would no longer have the advantage of doing business in home markets under conditions that were precursors of those which eventually would appear in Europe and Japan. Accordingly, the innovational lead that the Americans had enjoyed in earlier decades could be expected to shrink.

I cannot say, however, that I had the prescience to realize how rapidly the factor cost configurations of the various national markets would be brought into alignment, speeded by the rise in raw material prices, by the increasing nominal cost of capital, and by the weakness of the U.S. dollar. In my speculation about the growth of European and Japanese investment in the United States, therefore, the tone was hypothetical; there was no sense of conviction that the trend would soon develop. Intellectually, readers were put on notice; glandularly, they were not forewarned.

It was only in the latter 1970s that the convergence in the factor costs of the principal exporting countries had developed sufficiently to prompt me to reappraise the relevance of the product-cycle concept as an explicator of U.S. behavior.[6] As a result of that reappraisal, I concluded that the product-cycle concept continued to have some utility, explaining some of the trade and investment patterns visible in various countries of the world; but its utility in explaining the behavior of the U.S. economy had measurably declined.

Effects of the Multinationals

When *Sovereignty at Bay* was published in 1971, the advocates and the opponents of multinational enterprises were already locked in furious combat. Several dozen propositions about the consequences of the operations of these enterprises had been advanced by both sides. One of the objectives of *Sovereignty at Bay* was to test the leading propositions of the opponents with such data as could be mustered for the purpose.

The issues involved were too numerous and too diverse to be effectively reviewed here. At the time when *Sovereignty at Bay* was published, however, it seemed clear that both sides were grossly overreaching in their arguments; some cases were consistent with their sweeping hypotheses, some were not. Even more often, the asserted effects of the operations of these enterprises, whether benign or destructive, could not be supported by the evidence. The classic Scotch verdict—not proven—seemed more justified than any.[7]

By 1977, however, numerous researchers all over the globe had published a great many additional studies of the multinational enterprise. Some of these studies cast new light on the issues that had been dealt with tentatively in *Sovereignty at Bay*: typical of such issues, for instance, were those relating to the technological transfer activities of the multinationals. The piling up of such evidence moved me to publish a second book on multinational enterprises, which appeared under the title of *Storm over the Multinationals*.

The added evidence reviewed in that book went some way to confirm the fact that simpleminded propositions about the effects of multinational enterprises were as a rule highly vulnerable. On the basis of the new work, it was possible to speak with somewhat greater assurance about some of the economic and political effects of multinational enterprises; but those effects were not simple. The caution with which I had approached such questions as the balance-of-payment effects, income-distribution effects, and employment effects of multinational enterprises in *Sovereignty at Bay* seemed justified by the conclusions of *Storm over the Multinationals*. Generalizations on some points are possible; but they must be framed with due regard for the vast differences in the activities of multinational enterprises. Numerous variables determine the economic effects of the operations of individual firms, including for instance, their innovative propensities and their marketing strategies. Both the uninhibited broadsides of writers such as Barnet and Müller and the more restrained generalizations of scholars such as Robert Gilpin suffer from this lack of differentiation.

Threats to the Multinationals

With the acuity that goes with hindsight, I might better have entitled my 1971 volume *Everyone at Bay,* in the spirit of its closing lines. But there would be some overreaching in such a title; I could hardly claim to have foreseen the spate of expropriations and nationalizations of the foreign properties of the multinational enterprises that occurred during the first half of the 1970s. My chapter on the raw materials industries, in fact, was written in a tone of complacency that must have been insufferable at the time to some of the worried managers of the international oil companies. The mood of that portion of *Sovereignty at Bay* is captured in the final paragraph of the raw materials chapter:

> Strong initiatives on the part of the governments of less developed countries to control the key factors in the exploitation of their raw materials are likely to continue. And as they do, the capacity of host governments to participate in management will increase. It is another question, however, whether the host countries will feel that their 'dependence' on the outside world has declined simply because their management role has increased. As long as the product requires marketing in foreign countries, dependence will presumably continue in some form.

Yet, as one reads the raw materials chapter with the hindsight of 1981, the argument for the increasing vulnerability of the oil companies is all there, carefully laid out under a heading dubbed "The Obsolescing Bargain." The oil-exporting countries, it was pointed out, no longer needed the oil companies as a source of capital; their taxes on the sale of crude oil were already providing a sense of independence on that score. Nor did the oil-exporting countries any longer feel shut away from access to the technology of oil exploration and exploitation; too many independent companies were bidding to provide that information and expertise. In the latter 1960s, the principal remaining source of vulnerability of the oil-exporting countries and the principal source of strength of the international oil companies was the companies' control over the channels of distribution.

What prevented me (and practically every other scholar at the time) from fully applying the lesson of the obsolescing bargain to the situation of the oil companies was our inability to appreciate that a profound shift in the supply-demand balance was taking place, which might reduce the need of the oil-exporting countries to rely on the marketing channels of the multinationals.

Most of us took the chronic weakness of oil prices during most of the 1960s to mean that supplies were more than adequate. Accordingly, it was hard to contemplate that demand would soon grow so rapidly that the oil-exporting countries would feel free to cut their umbilical cord to the international oil marketers. Nor do I think that many analysts in the oil industry itself were aware of the dangers of an oil shortage at the time.

To be sure, by the latter 1960s, some thoughtful executives in the industry were deeply worried. Some were expressing alarm over the deterioration in their negotiating position, as Libya and other countries gleefully used the independent oil companies to leapfrog over one another in a continuous escalation of their terms. But so far as I know, nobody in the 1960s foresaw the great bulge in the demand for Middle East oil that would soon undermine the majors' position.

Looking back at the text of *Sovereignty at Bay* after ten years, I am frustrated by the fact that the analysis comes so close, while not quite drawing the key conclusion. The weakening of the international oil oligopoly during the 1960s is accurately enough portrayed; the appearance of the state-owned oil companies and the emergence of OPEC are appropriately chronicled. But it was not until a year or two later that I fully appreciated the key role played by the independent oil companies in weakening the position of the majors and in strengthening the negotiating hand of the oil-exporting countries. And it was a few years after that before it became evident that the period of weakening prices in the 1960s had been masking a shift in the supply-demand balance.[8]

No two persons will draw quite the same lessons from the experiences of the oil market during the 1960s and 1970s. The lessons that I draw, I suspect, will not be widely shared.

One of these is that any five-year projection of the supply-demand balance for world oil is inherently subject to gross margins of error, margins so large as to encompass both the possibilities of painful shortage and the possibilities of disconcerning glut. The importers of oil, of course, are justified in acting as if they expected an acute shortage, simply because the consequences of a shortage are so much more painful than those of a glut; prudence, therefore, demands that we act as if a shortage were inevitable. But whenever I review the various projections of supply and demand in the world oil market that are being circulated today, I am persuaded that today's projections are just as vulnerable as those of fifteen years ago.

A second conclusion, based as much on other raw materials as on oil, is that the concept of the obsolescing bargain does have a certain utility in analyzing the changing position of the multinational enterprises engaged in any given product line. Accordingly, wherever the conventional wisdom of any market turns from an expectation of shortage to an expectation of glut, I anticipate in accordance with the obsolescing bargain concept that the position of the multinationals will be somewhat strengthened.

And a third conclusion is that, for phenomena as complex as the role of multinational enterprises, scholars may be as vulnerable as laymen in speculating about the shape of future events. If scholars do their work well, their predictive models may be better crafted than those of the layman—more fully articulated, internally more consistent, more firmly based on earlier events. But scholars, perhaps more than laymen, must live with the risk of neglecting or overlooking what may prove to be the controlling factor that determines those future events.

The Problem of Multiple Jurisdiction

As the title Sovereignty at Bay suggests, the book was much more concerned with the interests and attitudes of governments than with the aspirations and fears of the multinational enterprises themselves. Insofar as the title was justified, the justification rested on the validity of three propositions: that most governments, reluctant to give up the advantages they perceive in inviting multinational enterprises into their jurisdictions, will continue to permit a significant part of their national output to be accounted for by the affiliates of such enterprises; that the policies of any affiliate of a multinational enterprise are bound to reflect in some degree the global interests of the multinational network as a whole, and hence can never respond single-mindedly to the requirements of any one national jurisdiction; and that the network of any multinational enterprise cannot escape serving as a conduit through which sovereign states exert an influence on the economies of other sovereign states.

After ten years, I see no strong reason to modify any of these propositions. During those ten years, some foreign affiliates of multinational enterprises were nationalized, while other foreign affiliates were liquidated or sold on the initiative of their parents. But, all told, these withdrawals were only a minor fraction of the new advances that multinational enterprises were making all over the globe. In 1979 alone, for instance, U.S.-based multinationals increased their foreign investment stake by $25 billion, of which $18 billion was in developed nations and $7 billion in developing countries. Indicative of the resilience of such enterprises to the buffeting they had received only a few years earlier was the fact that nearly $4 billion of the $7 billion build-up in developing countries was in the form of fresh money remitted by the U.S. parent, while the remainder consisted of the reinvestment of past earnings.

To be sure, there have been some changes during these ten years in the identity of the world's multinational enterprises. Those based in Europe and Japan have gained a little in importance relative to those based in the United States. Moreover, the world is beginning to see enterprises of this sort that have their home bases in Spain, Brazil, Mexico, India, Hong Kong, and other such locations.[9] But these changes simply add to the sense of vitality and durability of the multinational structures.

At the same time as there have been some marginal shifts in the identity of the multinational enterprises, there have also been some marginal alterations in their business practices. U.S.-based enterprises as a class have grown somewhat less reluctant to enter into joint ventures with foreign partners than had been the case in earlier decades. Multinational enterprises from all countries have proved increasingly flexible in taking on management contracts, acceding to so-called fade-out clauses, entering into partnerships with state-owned enterprises, and involving themselves in other ambiguous arrangements.

The proliferation of such arrangements raises the question whether the various affiliates of multinational enterprises continue to respond to a common global strategy and to draw on a common pool of resources to the same degree as in the past. The available signs point in many directions. Some observers insist, for instance, that when the subsidiaries of multinational enterprises enter into partnerships with state-owned enterprises, they often manage to increase the degree of their control in the local market rather than to diminish it.[10] The increased prevalence of joint ventures and other ambiguous arrangements suggests that the authority of the parents of the multinational networks over their affiliates is being diluted. But other developments seem to be pushing in the opposite direction. For instance, there has been a constant improvement of software and communication systems for the command and control of distant subsidiaries, a trend that places new tools in the hands of headquarters staffs. In addition, the multinational enterprises in some industries, including automobiles and machinery, have been pushing toward the development of world models for their products, a trend that requires increasing integration among the production units of the multinational enterprises concerned.

I anticipate that, in the end, the generalizations will be exceedingly complex. We may well find, for instance, that in many firms control over the finance and production functions has increased, even though the physical location of these activities has been dispersed. We may find, too, that in the selection of business strategies some multinational enterprises have opted to develop maximum flexibility and adaptation toward local conditions while others in the same general product line have opted for the maximum exploitation of global economies of scale.[11]

Still, I would be surprised if on balance multinational enterprises had greatly reduced the degree of central control over their global operations. For insofar as multinational enterprises have any inherent advantages over national enterprises, those advantages must rest on the multinational character of their operations, that is to say, on their multinational strategies and their common resources. Multinational enterprises, therefore, may have no real option; by giving up their multinational advantages, they may be destroying the basis for their competitive survival.

If multinational enterprises continue to pursue some elements of a global strategy and to draw on a common pool of financial and human resources, then the problems of multiple jurisdiction will continue to play a considerable role in their operations. At times, affiliates of such enterprises will be marching to the tunes of a distant trumpet being played from the ministries of another government or from the offices of another affiliate. Some cases of this sort are well enough known; the occasional forays of the U.S. government's antitrust division in attempting to break up international restrictive business practices that affect the U.S. economy have received particular attention. But these well-publicized cases are on the whole less important than those that are less transparent. Multinational enterprises with an affiliate in Germany, for instance, will have to entertain the demand of German unions for more output and more jobs, expressed through the hard-won rights of *Mitbestimmungsrecht*; responding to such pressures, the parent enterprise may be obliged to reduce the output of its Brazilian subsidiary, thereby exporting Germany's unemployment to Brazil. For multinational enterprises with an affiliate in Mexico, the insistence of the Mexican government that the local affiliates must import less and export more may lower the output of these networks in Barcelona and Detroit. And India's insistence that foreign parents should charge their Indian subsidiaries nothing for their technology could lower the income taxes and export earnings of the parents of those subsidiaries operating from their bases in other countries.

Since 1971, the problems of multiple jurisdiction generated by the existence of multinational enterprises have grown. More than ever before, governments are telling the affiliates of multinational enterprises what they must do or not do as the price for their right to continue in business. As the world's overt trade barriers have diminished, these commands have become a principal weapon of many governments for pursuing a beggar-my-neighbor economic policy. Accordingly, when I published *Storm over the Multinationals* in 1977, I developed the jurisdictional issue in considerably greater depth than in *Sovereignty at Bay*. But the second book was launched under the shadow of the first; whatever the second book had to say, it was commonly assumed, had already been said in *Sovereignty at Bay*.[12] The heightened emphasis on the jurisdictional issue in the second book, however, seems appropriate to current circumstances.

So far, jurisdictional conflicts have been contained by the fact that not all governments are systematically playing the beggar-my-neighbor game, and by the added fact that multinational enterprises have a strong incentive for muffling the effects of the game within their respective networks. My assumption has been, however, that the number of players and the intensity of the game will gradually increase. In that case, if multinationals are to avoid being the instruments through which national jurisdictions are brought into repeated conflict, the sovereign states must be willing to agree on some international regime that can reconcile their interests. Any such agreed regime would presumbly do two things: it would specify the rights of multinational enterprises in and their obligations to the international community; and it would delineate and restrain the jurisdictional reach of the governments involved, wherever an important clash in national jurisdictions might be involved.

Since 1971, there have been dozens of projects for achieving international agreement with respect to the multinational enterprises. Most of them have included proposals to restrain the multinational enterprises in various ways; a few have proposed some guarantees for the multinational enterprises as well; but until very recently, most have neglected or avoided the pervasive problem of conflicting jurisdictions.

Indeed, some of the international actions and international proposals that have been launched since 1971 have seemed carefully designed to preserve the contradictions rather than to resolve them. The member countries of the OECD, for instance, have adopted a set of declarations proposing that each government should grant national treatment to foreign-owned subsidiaries in its jurisdictions, thus acknowledging the national character of such subsidiaries; at the same time, these governments have paid obeisance to the applicability of international law in the treatment of foreign-owned subsidiaries, whether or not such treatment conformed with national law, thus acknowledging the foreign element in the subsidiaries' identity. In a similar obfuscating mood, the developing countries, as a rule, have simultaneously insisted upon two propositions: that foreign-owned subsidiaries, being nationals of the host country, were subject to all the obligations of any other national; but that such subsidiaries, as the property of foreigners, could rightly be denied the privileges of other nationals.

I can find only one functional area in which governments have made a serious effort to reduce the conflicts or resolve the ambiguities that go with the operations of multinational enterprises.[13] The industrialized countries have managed to develop a rather extraordinary web of bilateral agreements among themselves that deal with conflicts in the application of national tax laws. Where such laws seemed to be biting twice into the same morsel of profit, governments have agreed on a division of the fare. Why governments have moved to solve the jurisdictional conflict in this field but not in others is an interesting question. Perhaps it was because, in the case of taxation, the multinational enterprises themselves had a major stake in seeing to the consummation of the necesssary agreements.

So far, the world has managed to stagger on without effectively addressing the many facets of jurisdictional conflict and without directly acknowledging the inescapable fact that the behavior of any affiliate is unavoidably influenced by external forces. The various sovereigns direct their commands at a unit in the multinational network; the unit responds as it can, giving ground to the sovereign if it must; the other units in the network adjust their operations to the new situation, spreading the adjustment cost through the global system. As long as there is no overt acknowledgment of what is going on all the parties can pretend that the jurisdiction of each sovereign is unimpaired.

The Future of the Multinationals

Lincoln Gordon would agree, I think, that his one-time proposal for a tract entitled "Multinationals at Bay" would not arouse much interest today. The tumult of the 1970s over the multinational issue has lost some of its stridence. The incidence of nationalizations in developing countries has declined dramatically. Kolko, Williams, Barnet, and Müller seem somehow out of date, while the various scholars of *dependista* theory seem a bit jaded. The U.N. Centre on Transnational Corporations has developed a businesslike air, more akin to the professionalism of the Securities and Exchange Commission than to the prosecuting fervor of the Church Committee.

In retrospect, it appears that the numerous threats to the multinationals that were launched in the 1970s—the spate of nationalizations, the codes of conduct, the U.S. legislation against bribery, the demands and resolutions of the General Assembly—were fueled by a number of different elements. One of these was a manifestation of a much larger phenomenon, namely a pervasive revulsion in much of the world against the effects of industrialization, against the symbols of entrenched authority, against the impersonal tyranny of big bureaucracies. Embodying all of these unfortunate attributes and burdened besides by the sin of being foreign, multinationals were inevitably a prime target of the period. A second factor that explained the attack on the multinationals, however, was the inexorable operation of the obsolescing bargain; as shortages appeared in various raw materials, multinationals lost the bargaining power that their marketing capabilities normally afforded.

The revulsion against bigness and bureaucracy that exploded in the late 1960s and early 1970s may have been ephemeral; but the process of the obsolescing bargain is not. From time to time, in the future as in the past, one foreign-owned industry or another will lose its defensive capabilities; and when that happens, some of those enterprises will be nationalized, joining the plantations, the power plants, and the oil wells that have been taken over by governments in years past.

But the future is no simple extrapolation of the past. Some forces seem to be speeding up the process by which the bargain between governments and foreign investors becomes obsolescent. At the same time, other forces seem to be diffusing and defusing the underlying hostility that gives the process of the obsolescing bargain some of its motive force.

The expectation that agreements between governments and investors will be breached even more quickly in the future than in the past is based on various factors. In reappraising their bargaining positions, governments are better informed and better equipped than they have ever been. Perhaps more to the point, opposition forces that are bent on embarrassing their governments have more information and more expertise. Besides, according to evidence presented in *Storm over the Multinationals,* governments are finding that in many lines of industry they have an increasing number of options for securing the capital, technology, or access to markets they require. Accordingly, although multinational enterprises taken as a class continue to account for a considerable share—even an increasing share—of the economies of most countries, individual multinationals have nothing like the bargaining position they sometimes held in the past.

Yet governments seem constrained to use their increased bargaining power in more ambiguous ways. Instead of outright nationalization, they seem disposed to settle for other arrangements, such as arrangements that make a gift of some of the equity to favored members of the local private sector or to an expanding state-owned enterprise, or contracts that allow the multinationals to manage their properties without formal ownership. Perhaps the increase in ambiguous arrangements is due to the decline in the power of the individual multinational enterprises; being less threatening, they are less to be feared. Perhaps, too, the ambiguity is due to the increasing power of the private industrialists in some countries who prefer to squeeze the foreign goose rather than to strangle it;[14] or to the unceasing struggle of the managers of some state-owned enterprises to weaken the control of their national ministries.[15] It may even be that the hostility of some countries to the multinational enterprises of others is being blunted by the growth of their own homegrown brand of multinationals.

Whatever the precise causes may be, I anticipate that business organizations with the attributes of multinational enterprises will not decline and may well grow in their relative importance in the world economy. Anticipating that development, I am brought back to what I regard as the central questions. How do the sovereign states propose to deal with the fact that so many of their enterprises are conduits through which other sovereigns exert their influence?

Perhaps they will not deal with the problem at all. There is plenty of evidence for the proposition that nations are capable of tolerating ambiguity on a massive scale for long periods of time. And there are numerous cases in which scholars, peering into the future, have mistaken bogey men for monsters. But I am betting that the problem is real and its emergence as a political issue close at hand. In any event, it is this problem that invests the title *Sovereignty at Bay* with its real meaning.

Notes

1. Robert Gilpin, *U.S. Power and the Multinational Corporation* (New York: Basic Books, 1975), p. 220. Be it said to Gilpin's credit that although he ascribes the

phrase to me, he does not list me as one who subscribes to the model. Others, however, have been less careful in their attributions.

2. S.H. Hymer, *The International Operations of National Firms: A Study of Direct Foreign Investment* (Cambridge: M.I.T. Press, 1976), based on his 1960 thesis.

3. See. F.T. Knickerbocker, *Oligopolistic Reaction and Multinational Enterprise* (Boston: Harvard Business School, 1973). His subsequent work on the hypothesis, unfortunately never fully published, went even further in confirming its utility.

4. The number of such studies by now is very large. Illustrations are: L.T. Wells Jr., ed., *The Product Life Cycle and International Trade* (Boston: Harvard Business School, 1972); J.M. Finger, "A New View of the Product Cycle Theory," *Weltwirtschaftliches Archiv* 3, 1, 1975; M.P. Claudon, *International Trade and Technology: Models of Dynamic Comparative Advantage* (Washington, D.C.: University Press of America, 1977); Seev Hirsch, "The Product Cycle Model of International Trade," *Oxford Bulletin of Economics and Statistics* 37, 4 (November 1975), pp. 305–17; Hiroki and Yoshi Tsumuri, "A Bayesian Test of the Product Life Cycle Hypothesis as Applied to the U.S. Demand for Color-TV Sets," *International Economic Review,* October 1980, pp. 581–95.

5. For instance: W.B. Walker, *Industrial Innovation and International Trading Performance* (Brighton, England: Sussex University, 1976); and Kiyoshi Kojima, "A Macroeconomic Theory of Foreign Direct Investment," *Hitotsubashi Journal of Economics* 14, 1 (June 1973).

6. Raymond Vernon, "The Product Cycle Hypothesis in a New International Environment," *Oxford Bulletin of Economics and Statistics* 41, 4 (November 1979), pp. 255–67; and Raymond Vernon, "Gone are the Cash Cows of Yesteryear," *Harvard Business Review,* November 1980, pp. 150–55.

7. For a review of many of these issues and a well-balanced critical appraisal of my views, see T.J. Bierstecker, *Distortion or Development? Contending Perspectives on the Multinational Corporation* (Cambridge: M.I.T. Press, 1979).

8. Those points are developed at some length in two later publications. See Edith Penrose, "The Development of Crisis" in Raymond Vernon, ed., *The Oil Crisis* (New York: W.W. Norton, 1976), pp. 39–57; and Raymond Vernon, *Storm over the Multinationals* (Cambridge: Harvard University Press, 1977), pp. 83–87.

9. A book on this subject will shortly appear under the authorship of Louis T. Wells, Jr.

10. This is a subject that is just beginning to be researched. For an analysis covering Brazil, see Peter Evans, *Dependent Development: The Alliance of Multinational, State, and Local Capital in Brazil* (Princeton: Princeton University Press, 1979).

11. Patterns of this sort are being researched by Yves Doz at INSEAD, Fontainebleau.

12. See for instance, C.P. Kindleberger's review of *Storm over the Multinationals* in *Business History Review* 51, 4 (Winter 1979), pp. 95–97.

13. Nevertheless, there are glimmerings of some additional action eventually on the subject. Reference to the problem appears in a composite working draft of a code of conduct for multinational enterprises, prepared for consideration of an intergovernmental working group under the sponsorship of the U.N. Centre on Transnational Corporations; see Working Paper no. 7, November 1979, paragraph 56. But the prospects for action are not very great.

14. See for instance Evans, *Dependent Development.*

15. Yair Aharoni, "Managerial Discretion," in Aharoni and Vernon, eds., *State-Owned Enterprises in the Western Economies* (London: Croom Helm, 1980).

Part III
Conclusions

13
Conclusions and Policy Implications

Theodore H. Moran

T he studies presented in this book raise important public policy questions. What are the implications for host states? For home states? How can Third World governments most effectively capture the benefits from multinational corporations and avoid unnecessary costs or distortions? How can home country authorities be most effective in serving their own national interests? Do Third World successes with multinational firms necessitate special measures on the part of developed country governments to protect against an ebbing of their industrial base?

Among the developed countries, what are the implications of the increasing efforts by many governments to alter the distribution of international economic activity in their favor, especially in high technology industries? Are U.S. corporations facing the prospect of steady retreat in the face of international competition from publicly nurtured companies in Japan and Europe? Does the United States need a special *industrial policy* to keep its high technology firms competitive on the new frontier of sunrise industries?

What are the implications of multinational corporate operations, and the policy responses to them, for the structure of the international system? Will the South gain at the expense of the North? Will the North shut off the prospects for an international redistribution of economic activity? Will both benefit together? Or might there be a new era of zero-sum struggles for multinational corporate activities and investment wars between home and host governments?

Can the nations of the North maintain a liberal international economic order? Or was the liberal order a product of U.S. postwar hegemony, which must inevitably decline as international competition erodes the preeminence of the United States? What might take the place of the liberal system of relatively free flows of goods and investment capital: a lethargic drift toward cloture or an energetic new structure of rival mercantilisms as developed and developing countries intervene in the market to create their own comparative advantage?

This concluding chapter will attempt to draw together the policy implications of the studies in this book for home and host countries and examine fundamental questions about the evolution of multinational corporate activity and the structure of the international economic system. In addition it will point out areas for new research and investigation.

Multinational Corporations and the Developing Countries

A decade of research has moved the representation of multinational corporations in the Third World from the simple—they are exploiters, or saviors—to the complex. The studies from which contemporary assessments emerge are more thorough and more solid, but also with more nuances, than those of ten years ago. On the one hand, foreign investors have scarce resources that less developed economies need, resources all the more scarce for countries burdened by debt and squeezed by domestic austerity requirements. On the other hand, given the oligopolistic structure of the industries in which foreign investment takes place, the potential for distortions in Third World development is and will be a regular part of the setting. In these circumstances, it is clear that the actual contribution of multinationals will vary greatly depending on the structure of the industry, the design of host government policies, and the evolution of the foreign investor–host relationship.

For those who wish to search among the studies in this book for confirmation of a *dependencia* or neo-Marxist perspective, there are numerous instances in which foreign investors are able to insist on an investment agreement that provides generous treatment for their projects. Indeed, the analysis of the role of risk and uncertainty in the studies here leads one to predict that such lopsided negotiations are inevitable, at least at the initiation of the foreign investment process for any one industry. Does this confirm the *dependencia* view of exploitation?

That would require a static perspective. The studies here emphasize the dynamism of negotiation and renegotiation of investment agreements. And as the determinants of bargaining power become clearer, it is evident that across broad sectors of manufacturing as well as extractive industries (those with some combination of large fixed investments, stable technology,[1] little product differentiation or non-brand-name marketing, and growing competition) there may be a steady increase in the potential strength of the host country. This puts the analysis in the studies here at odds with the *dependencia* perspective in that a greater number and greater spread of multinational corporations increases rather than decreases the options available to Third World governments, widens rather than narrows the margin for autonomous self-interested nationalistic actions, and improves rather than worsens the prospects for development over time.

This also puts the analysis in the studies here at odds with the laissez-faire approach of the Chicago school in that foreign private enterprise carries the potential for distortions as well as for benefits, requires careful governmental intervention rather than the mere withdrawal of governmental "interference," and necessitates the conscious harnessing of multinationals rather than merely giving market forces free reign.

Besides helping to improve the perspective for viewing the possible contribution of international corporate investment to Third World development, the studies here provide more specific assistance in assessing how best to design host country policies. A decade ago there was great appeal to the idea of cataloging every tough measure toward multinationals ever proposed throughout the Third World (perhaps documented by the United Nations) and constructing mandatory codes or regulations that embodied them all. Now, although there is still an ongoing need for LDCs to share experience about "what works" with multinationals (perhaps using the United Nations Centre on Transnational Corporations or the World Bank), it is clear that the approach of the host countries themselves must be more flexible, pragmatic, and balanced, with a place for both toughness and generosity. Moreover, the specific content of both tough and generous policies is crucial in determining how much the outcome will contribute to the recipient nation's development.

On the generous side of the host country–foreign investor interaction, the analysis here suggests the need for compensation high enough to reward the foreign investor for taking the initial risk, which in many cases is quite large. What form should the reward take? One of the easiest kinds of reward, market exclusivity, is unfortunately one of the potentially most damaging. Multinational investors like it because it shields them from competition; host authorities like it because it requires no fiscal expenditure.[2] But a theme running through the studies in this book is that market exclusivity cushions the choice of inappropriate technology, allows inefficiency, and makes it much more difficult for subsequent renegotiation of the opening investment agreement by the host government. Thus the counsel of "money, not monopoly" is probably good advice to Third World authorities, although the idea of initially low tax rates, lengthy tax holidays, guaranteed convertibility, and unhindered profit remittances is not appealing to nationalistic sentiments.

A more effective strategy combines fiscal generosity with the encouragement of competition. The evidence cited in this book suggests that fear of loss of market share is the most powerful motivator to multinational corporate risk taking and to the decision to undertake a new investment. The stimulation of competition may require the host to engage in an active search for an independent to play off against a major in natural resources or for the first manufacturing investor to produce a "burst phenomenon" among other manufacturers looking for a lower-cost export platform (see page 13). A strategy built around aggressive enticement of foreign companies (exhibited, for example, in the Indian computer case) runs counter to the conventional image of international corporations as being omnipotent, scanning the globe for every opportunity, which they then leap to take advantage of immediately. But the evidence suggests that active search, aggressive enticement, and the stimulation of competition are crucial elements in host country success.

Similarly, the use of the subsequent rivalry among foreign firms to renegotiate the award of benefits granted to the first investor runs counter to the advice of international business groups that stability be the principal feature of the model investment climate.[3] Surveys of corporate opinion frequently confuse the desire for profitability commensurate with risk with the demand for stability in the investment climate of the host country. The studies in this book have underscored the need for the former but not necessarily the latter.

Finally, there is an important role played by how host governments are organized to negotiate with multinational corporations. Those that can close a deal rapidly, with an authoritative negotiator and a united front among all the ministries involved, have a strong advantage in attracting foreign investors.[4]

On the tough side of the host government–foreign investor interaction, the structure and form of nationalistic demands are equally important. In the natural resource sector, Michael Shafer's analysis of the copper industry in Zambia and Zaire demonstrates the ability of even relatively weak states to hold the foreign companies' equity hostage to obtain greater managerial participation, expanded operations, more processing, and a larger share of total earnings. But the study also reveals the superiority of tax brinksmanship to actual nationalization in gaining benefits for the host.

Shafer's analysis in chapter 2 provides some additional insights on the issue of *control*. On one hand, control can be had without ownership, by requiring certain major decisions to have ministerial approval or placing a single government representative on the board of a foreign subsidiary and specifying that major decisions be approved unanimously (in essence giving the government veto power, without the expense of acquiring 51 percent equity).[5] These strategies offer the host the opportunity for supervision without destroying the insulation that Shafer's cases show to be so valuable.

On the other hand, ownership does not necessarily impart control, as the copper nationalization in Zambia and Zaire illustrates. Even worse, as the examination of the nationalization experiences in the bauxite-aluminum and the banana industries in this book reveal (see page 111), expropriation of the production stage when a choke point lies further downstream in the vertically integrated chain may leave the host government at the mercy of the foreign multinationals it has just alienated. These findings do not mean that nationalization should never be attempted or that nationalization can never be made to work, but they suggest caution, circumspection, and an evaluation of whether the same or greater benefits cannot be achieved through other means.

In manufacturing, the evidence shows a shift in Third World priorities away from tax or ownership issues that remain prominent in natural resources. Instead, the objectives of host authorities have been changing, from a narrow focus on greater revenues or possible nationalization to the active use of multinationals for job creation, industrial development, and export promotion. In these three areas, there has been demonstrable success. In others, such as the supervision of transfer pricing, there has been less progress (a fact that comes through clearly in Gereffi's study of steroids in Mexico in chapter 4).[6]

In high technology industries in the Third World, as the studies of the computer industry in India and the pharmaceutical industry in Mexico illustrate (chapters 3 and 4, respectively), the record is also mixed. Shielding high technology multinationals from being squeezed too hard is the need to maintain an organic link to the foreign parent, which provides what is required to keep a local plant supplied with new products and new processes.

Does the importance of such an organic link mean weakness and dependency for the host country? Here the contrast between the computer and the pharmaceutical cases is instructive. In the former, India played upon competition among foreign corporations (eight principal corporations) to its own advantage. In the latter, Mexico did not (despite the fact that there were six foreign multinationals involved). That constituted the difference between relative autonomy and relative dependency.

In the face of rising nationalistic demands, the chapters in this book show that multinational corporations have not been standing passively by. In many cases they have been hesitant to invest at all. Of more interest, perhaps, is the fact that for projects that do go forward, foreign investors have been beginning to experiment with countermeasures to reduce their vulnerability.

Do the corporate risk management strategies sketched out in this book in chapters 4 and 5 spell doom for Third World efforts to harness multinationals? A return to stasis for investment agreements? A new capability on the part of multinationals to freeze contracts when the bargaining relationship is most favorable to them? Or will the risk management counterstrategies of multinationals merely help ensure that the interaction between foreign firms and nationalistic pressures moves along a non-zero-sum course?

The experience in this area is too short to make a judgment, but some of the tools devised by corporate strategists to manage their exposure to risk may have a value to both sides. As game theory teaches, it can be a valuable asset to have a means of binding oneself in advance to ensure the credibility of one's own commitments when both foreign investors and host authorities know that whatever contracts they sign will be buffeted by demands for revision. To take one example (see page 114), for a multinational investor to create a financial network of lenders to act as a deterrent against fundamental abrogation of an investment agreement is unlikely to prevent some renegotiation in the case of a vastly successful project. But it may provide enough security to enable a risky project to go forward in the first place that otherwise could never be launched.

Such an outcome could be particularly valuable in the coming decade as developing country states try to grow out of the debt crisis. In an era in which

Third World societies need foreign direct investment more than ever to create jobs and generate exports to help relieve the pressures from paying off their loans, risk management tools could be a key to enabling good foreign investment projects to proceed with international commercial bank financing even though the lending institutions themselves are skittish about increasing their overseas exposure.

There remain large gaps in the research about multinational corporations and Third World development. Some sectors of foreign investment activity are simply not well studied—for example, agribusiness and services.[7] What has been, and what could be, the role of international agribusiness in Third World development? Can a concentration on cash crops and export products be reconciled with broad national development? Is the bias of foreign agribusiness investors toward capital intensity, fertilizers, and pesticides purely pernicious? Can their behavior be modified? What might be the role of international companies in local processing and international marketing? What are the implications for the policies of the developing countries?

And there are fundamental questions that have hardly been touched. Will the processes of multinational corporation–host country interaction examined here extend beyond the largest and richest Third World states to middle-range developing countries? What contribution can foreign direct investment make, if any, to the poorest countries that do not have natural resources? Are there lessons to be learned for the poorest countries from richer Third World nations that also have very poor regions, such as India, Brazil, and Indonesia?

Finally, a caution is in order: direct foreign investment is unlikely under even the most optimistic circumstances to be a deus ex machina for the development needs of the less developed countries. There is evidence for this at the microlevel; the total work force employed by multinational corporations in the most recent survey (1978) was 4 million persons; a hypothetical doubling of this stock of foreign investment, accompanied by an increase of labor-intensive process by 50 percent, would create no more than 6 million new jobs. Yet the unemployment estimates for the Third World run to hundreds of millions, and the underemployment estimates run to hundreds of millions more. There is also evidence for this at the microlevel: the most careful analyses of the impact of multinational corporate investment on the LDCs point to the fact that host country policies on economic and social issues *other than* direct foreign investment are the primary determinants of economic growth.[8]

Thus there is reason to conclude with a cautious appraisal of the potential contribution of multinational corporations to Third World development even if the process of foreign investment continues in robust fashion. But the converse is not true if the First World moves steadily away from a liberal posture; it is necessary to be pessimistic if developed countries adopt new measures to keep multinationals at home and Third World products away.[9]

In short, there is an asymmetrical relationship between the good the North can offer the South by access to its multinationals and the damage the North can inflict on the South if it turns more restrictionist and protectionist.

Multinational Corporations and the Developed World

What are the implications of the studies in this book for the policies of the developed countries, in particular the United States, and what are the implications for the changing structure of the international economic system? The liberal principles that have predominated in U.S. policy since the end of World War II, principles that combine greater openness for flows of goods and investment capital with nondiscrimination among firms or sectors, are being fundamentally challenged. Does the liberal approach still make sense? Can a liberal international economic system survive?

As this book has shown, the attack on openness and nondiscrimination is coming from two directions. First has been the attack from labor groups and companies threatened by international competition who want protection through slowing the pace of change. Their argument, as represented in chapter 8 by Sol Chaikin, has been that the liberal approach is leading to a process of deindustrialization that undermines the economic vitality of the United States. Their recommendation is not limited to protectionism against imports from abroad but also includes the proposal for restrictions on outward investment by U.S. firms.

Second has been an attack from the opposite direction: those threatened by international competition who want special help to meet it at home and abroad. Not only do firms in this category deny the charges of the first group (by pointing to their own superior domestic record of creating jobs, exporting goods, and carrying out R&D), but they argue that they need more assistance and stronger support, equal to what their counterparts in Europe and Japan receive from their governments, to meet competitive challenges wherever they occur around the world. It is time, in this view, for the U.S. government to adopt the approach of the European and Japanese governments and pursue an *industrial policy* that will ensure the superiority of its own national firms.[10] This position is buttressed by a newly emergent neomercantilistic impulse that sees the creation of a stronger U.S. corporate sector as a way of reasserting U.S. power in the international system.[11]

With regard to the first attack on the liberal approach, this book has documented the growing adjustment problems as the United States has become more interdependent with the global economy but rejected the thesis about deindustrialization. The evidence suggests that although the share of manufactured output in GNP has dropped, the volume of manufacturing output has been rising, value-added in manufacturing has been rising, domestic investment in manufacturing has been rising, and employment in manufacturing has been rising. The United States has a larger industrial sector today than it did a decade, or two decades, ago. Not only has a relatively liberal approach to trade benefited consumers, as economic theory would predict, it has had a net positive impact on job creation. And the stimulus of international competition has spurred U.S. companies to be more efficient through creating new processes and new technologies.

Moreover, with regard to the thesis that outward investment by U.S. multinationals is undermining the U.S. economy, the difficult test of what would have happened if the investment had been kept at home suggests that most foreign direct investment takes place to preserve markets that otherwise would be lost completely. The option of staying at home to serve the foreign market is no longer available. And for the cases in which the motivation for foreign investment is not defensive, the gain to the United States from hypothetically preventing the companies from moving abroad would be small. Thus, the best approach toward outward investment is what has been affirmed by every postwar administration: neutrality (capital export neutrality), or not trying to influence the location of investment by U.S. multinationals one way or another through U.S. public policy.[12] The losses from a policy of neutrality, if any, are not large. The gains from moving away from a policy of neutrality are at best slight. And the downside risk from retaliation if the United States deliberately were to try to keep its firms at home is great.

Thus, in the face of the protectionist (toward trade) and restrictionist (toward investment) challenge, the traditional liberal approach is vindicated, at least in analytic terms, and should be backed by a vigorous effort to push all developed countries in the direction of reaffirming it.

What about the challenge to the liberal approach from the other direction: the assertion that the United States must match the interventionist policies of Europe and Japan to nurture its own national champions? The appeal of this approach is buttressed by the assertion that the convergence of similar factor proportions and equal technological capabilities among the developed countries will make the evolution of comparative advantage among the developed countries more and more a function of deliberate government support.[13] Nation-states may find themselves in the position of having to create their own comparative advantage. They may be required to create a new *industrial policy* of sector-specific interventions or even firm-specific interventions, so this argument goes, to promote change and bolster national strength. Countries that ignore this requirement could fall behind.

The evidence for the United States does not support the need for this major deviation from the liberal approach to international economic relations either. Between 1973 and 1980 the share of employment in those parts of U.S. industry characterized by high R&D intensity and rapid rates of technological innovation rose 9 percent in the United States, far in advance of Germany (an increase of 3 percent) or Japan (an increase of 1 percent).[14] In terms of comparative R&D, the United States was spending about 1.5 times as much on manufacturing R&D as Japan, Germany, France, and the United Kingdom combined and employing about 1.3 times as many scientists and engineers. In fact, the pattern of industrial hiring runs contrary to the idea of U.S. scientific effort tapering off. The rate of growth in the number of scientists and engineers employed in industry has doubled, from 1.6 percent per year in the much celebrated post-Sputnik era (1960–1973) to 3.2 percent per year from 1973 to 1980. These data do not suggest that the United States is being left behind from policy neglect while others are surging ahead.

Moreover, there are dangers to this call for government intervention to support its firms as national champions. On the one hand, there is little support for the conclusion that the U.S. government can pick winners better than the market can. The U.S. experience with such attempts suggests not.[15] On the other hand, there is a great danger that control over a sector-specific industrial policy will be captured not by sunrise industries but by sunset industries.[16] The likelihood is that industry-specific policies will become dominated by those who are already hurting and not by those who may in some future time be able to take their place. The potential for capture, given the imperfections in the public policy formation process already examined here (see page 143), is not insubstantial.

In short, the evidence does not support the idea that the United States has to play catch-up in creating a new industrial policy to match European and Japanese efforts. Moreover, it does not make sense for the United States to take a vigorous new role in creating distortions that others will match. Since U.S. defense spending will always act as an artificial spur to commercial innovation, it is not realistic to suggest that the United States can ever characterize itself as having no industrial policy toward high technology industries. Other than the civilian spinoffs from defense expenditures, however, the best policy remains one of public sector neutrality toward all sectors and firms in the economy. Once again the traditional liberal approach is reaffirmed.

Thus, despite attacks from both directions, the evidence suggests that from the point of view of its own national interests, the United States is best served by continuing to support an approach of openness toward trade and investment and of nondiscrimination among firms or sectors as the fundamental principle of international economic relations.

But, as always, the best arguments may not dominate the policy result. Indeed, as the examination of the political economy of policy formation in chapter 7 has shown, there is likely to be a systematic bias toward slowing or stopping the process of change to protect those hurt by it. Within this setting, what are the prospects for the liberal international economic system?

A growing body of analytical work on the structure of the international system is skeptical about its survival. Charles Kindleberger, Robert Gilpin, and Stephen Krasner argue, for example, that the international liberalism of the post-World War II era was a product of U.S. hegemony.[17] As U.S. preponderance in the international system declines (in economic, political, and military terms), there will be no one to take the long-term perspective, bear a disproportionate share of the short-term costs, and tolerate free riders and cheaters that is needed to maintain an open economic order. In this view, in the absence of a hegemonic actor, the actions needed to sustain a liberal world economy, like other public goods, will be undersupplied, leading to competition for individual gain, to retaliation, and to the deterioration of the system itself. Domestic politics in each individual state will push the actors toward self-centered nationalism, not toward the common international good. The result will be a downward spiral, either toward cloture or toward a new system of rival mercantilisms.

The studies in this book point in a less pessimistic direction. First, the process of bias in policymaking can be improved to make it more resistant to pressures for protection. Robert Baldwin, for example, urges that the International Trade Commission be mandated to publicize not just whether a flow of goods and services causes injury but how much the costs of the proposed remedy are likely to be to the country at large.[18] Gary Hufbauer argues that any forms of relief should be made explicitly on budget (making the political system acknowledge at least some of the distortions it is creating as real expenditures) rather than off budget as protectionist and restrictionist measures are now.[19] John Jackson questions why the U.S. government should pay more than $200 million of the $240 million in legal costs on cases brought by firms seeking protection.[20] Remedies in these areas could help diffuse the pressures to halt the process of having to adapt to international competition.

Second, for governments facing an intensified struggle over the direction of national economic policies, this book points to new sources of support for the liberal approach. In chapter 10, John Kline shows multinationals building transnational corporate alliances to back their own interest in keeping markets for goods, investment capital, and technology open with the political clout of partners, suppliers, and subcontractors across the Atlantic and the Pacific. This phenomenon is not limited to the U.S. partner. From the opposite side of the corporate relationship, pressures are also being generated for greater market access. In Japan, for example, the principal thrust for greater openness, outside of the highest government circles, has come from the giant trading companies, almost all of which have growing foreign corporate alliances of the kind this book has described.[21]

Beyond these joint arrangements has been the rising flow of direct investment by foreign corporations in the United States (from approximately $25 billion in 1975 to $102 billion in 1983, with a sectoral growth from approximately 6 percent to 12 percent of total U.S. manufacturing assets over the period.)[22] Part of the strategy in making the investments has been to diffuse protectionist pressures. More broadly there may be a growing experimentation of non-U.S. firms with trying to influence the determination of U.S. economic policy through their U.S. subsidiaries.[23] Also, providing a possible counter to protectionism may be the trend toward multinational union coordination reported in Caves's survey in chapter 9. (Both of these two areas, however, need more extensive research and investigation.) Finally, the international financial community has a strong interest, more direct and intense than at any previous time in the postwar era, in ensuring that debtor countries can continue to earn foreign exchange from exports.

But neither of these (a search for new allies on the side of greater openness or a focus on techniques to improve the public policy process) should deflect attention from the real needs. First, there is a need for an effective adjustment assistance program. The cost-benefit ratio of such programs is extraordinary. In the Tokyo Round, for example, the benefits from tariff cuts ran from fifty to one hundred times the adjustment costs.[24] Instead the trend has been in the opposite direction. Rather than strengthening the program as adjustment pressures have risen, the United States has done just the reverse.[25] From 1975 through 1979, there were 6,118 petitions, of which 44 percent were certified for relief. From 1980 through 1984, there were 9,362 petitions, of which 25 percent were certified for relief. In 1985 the Office of Management and Budget began to target the entire adjustment assistance program for termination. Moreover, the structure of the program that remains exhibits large deficiencies. Instead of prompt lump-sum payments that would facilitate geographical mobility and reeducation, there is a lengthy certification process, followed by welfare-like monthly payments, that tend to delay adjustment and retard movement. Consequently, it is not surprising that workers characterize the program as burial insurance rather than the opportunity for a fresh start.[26]

Second, and more important, there is a need for more responsible macroeconomic management in the United States so that such a large penalty from fiscal and monetary misalignment is not placed on export-producing and import-competing industries. From 1980 to 1984, for example, relative price incompetitiveness due primarily to the high value of the dollar induced a fall of 33 percent in U.S. export volumes and a rise of 17 percent in U.S. import volumes. These accounted for approximately 42 percent of the total manufacturing unemployment during the period, far eclipsing the impact of foreign industrial and trade policies. In terms of investment, the strong dollar has led to the transfer of 1.5 million to 2.0 million jobs abroad.[27] The appropriate response to support U.S. industry is to reduce U.S. budget deficits and U.S. interest rates, allowing the exchange rate to move the current account toward equilibrium.

If measures are taken in these two areas, the outlook for defending a relatively open approach to trade and investment is not so bleak.[28] But the struggle for the shape of the international system in the coming decade will not take place solely in a dichotomy between liberal and protectionist-restrictionist approaches. This book also documents a resurgence of mercantilistic tendencies, or the attempt to support and favor one's "own" firms on a selective basis as a means of meeting national needs and bolstering national strength.

Here the evidence presented in this book is again modestly reassuring. The neomercantilistic approach, even if pursued vigorously, does not work very well. Certainly states can help launch high technology firms with the resources equal to their international counterparts. But as those high technology firms, like mature technology firms, set their sights on meeting international competition, they become less amenable to control by the home government. A hidden hand seems to lead them away from the possibility of neomercantilistic control, and they seek allies from among the ranks of international firms from other countries to ensure their access to markets and to external sources of technology.

Does this thrust of international companies to move beyond a purely national identity point in the direction of a new era of sovereignty at bay? Does it herald a restructuring of the international system in which multinational corporations rather than national governments exercise preponderant discretion in the conduct of international economic affairs? It is true that when the firms expand abroad their corporate strategies become more anational. But it is equally true, as the Soviet gas pipeline case demonstrates (chapter 11), that they do not become immune to sovereign directives from home authorities. Rather, with the multiplication of sovereign directives to them, multinationals become paralyzed. In a crunch, it is multinationals that are at bay, not national governments. This may lead to increased tension and acrimony in the international political system, but the potential for a positive impact is possible as well. The cases in this book show nation-states acknowledging a growing impotence as they match each other in the intensification of threats against multinationals that do not obey them. Ultimately, as the pipeline case demonstrated, on questions of high politics heads of state have no choice but to move in the direction of reaching agreement or at least finding some accommodation among themselves.

Thus the evidence suggests that the struggle to reaffirm traditional liberal principles as the basis for the international economic system still serves the best interests of the United States and of other developed countries. And as this book shows, it also serves the best interests of the Third World in the North-South relationship. Moreover, it is not impossible to see states mobilizing the forces of support needed to reverse the trend toward cloture. To do so, however, will require meeting and turning back some of the most severe challenges to the liberal system posed in the last half-century.

Notes

1. Or, as the case of computers in India points out, rapidly changing technology that acts as a stimulus for increasing competition.

2. Lall and Streetan found that 40 percent of the foreign investment projects they studied had net negative effects on the host country, but this was due not to their foreignness but to the extent of effective protection afforded them. Sanjaya Lall and Paul Streetan, *Foreign Investment, Transnationals and Developing Countries* (Boulder, Colo.: Westview Press, 1977).

3. OECD, *Investing in Developing Countries* (Paris: OECD, 1983).

4. Dennis J. Encarnation and Louis T. Wells, Jr., analyze a range of organizational approaches available to host governments. While their research generally supports a more centralized model, they point out that agencies bypassed in the effort to streamline the decision-making process may reassert their power or sabotage the agreement at a later stage. Encarnation and Wells, "Sovereignty en garde: Negotiating with Foreign Investors," *International Organization* (Winter 1985). See also Robert Hellawell and Don Wallace, Jr., ed., *Negotiating Foreign Investments: A Manual for the Third World*, 2 vols. (Washington, D.C.: International Law Institute, 1982).

5. Cf. David N. Smith and Louis T. Wells, Jr., *Negotiating Third-World Mineral Agreements: Promises as Prologue* (Cambridge, Mass.: Ballinger, 1975).

6. It appears that between 20 percent and 40 percent of world trade in manufacturers are intrafirm. On the transfer-pricing issue, see G.K. Helleiner, "Intrafirm Trade and the Developing Countries: An Assessment of the Data," *Journal of Development Economics* (1979); Sanjaya Lall, "Transfer Pricing and Developing Countries: Some Problems of Investigation," *World Development* 1, no. 7 (1979); Constantine Vaitsos, *Intercountry Income Distribution and Transnational Enterprises* (Oxford: Clarendon Press, 1974).

7. Cf. United Nations Centre on Transnational Corporations, *Transnational Corporations in Food and Beverage Processing* (U.N. Document ST/CTC/19, 1980); E. Feder, *Strawberry Imperialism: An Enquiry into the Mechanisms of Dependency in Mexican Agriculture* (Mexico City: Editorial Compesina, 1978); Van R. Whiting, Jr., "Transnational Enterprise in the Food Processing Industry," in Newfarmer, *op. cit.*, 1985.

8. Michael B. Dolan and Brian W. Tomlin, "First World-Third World Linkages: External Relations and Economic Development," *International Organization* (Winter 1980).

9. The assumption here is that a gradual realignment of developed country policies away from a liberal posture would not only restrict the offshore products of multinational corporations but also reinforce the process of slowing the importation of all products from the Third World.

10. Ira C. Magaziner and Robert B. Reich, *Minding America's Business: The Decline and Rise of the American Economy* (New York: Harcourt Brace Jovanovich, 1982); Felix Rohatyn, "Reconstructing America," *New York Review of Books,* March 5, 1981; Robert B. Reich, *The Next American Frontier* (New York: New York Times Books, 1983).

11. *Report to the President on International Competitiveness* (Washington, D.C.: White House, 1985). See also David J. Sylvan, "The Newest Mercantilism," *International Organization* (Spring 1981).

12. This should, in theory, include an effort to bring state, regional, and municipal policies to attract investment, as well as national policies, into a position of net neutrality. For a discussion of capital-export neutrality (taxes structured so as not

to distort the market choice between domestic or foreign investment for home countries) and capital-import neutrality (taxes structured so as not to distort the market choice between local or imported investment for host countries), see Richard E. Caves, *Multinational Enterprise and Economic Analysis* (Cambridge: Cambridge University Press, 1983), ch. 8.

13. In addition to the citations in note 10, see Bruce R. Scott and George C. Lodge, *U.S. Competitiveness in the World Economy* (Boston: Harvard Business School Press, 1985).

14. Robert Z. Lawrence, *Can America Compete?* (Washington, D.C.: Brookings, 1984). See also Federal Reserve Bank of Kansas City, *Industrial Change and Public Policy* (Kansas City: Federal Reserve Bank, 1983).

15. Richard R. Nelson and Richard N. Langlois, "Industrial Policy: Lessons from American History," *Science*, February 23, 1983. The evidence from Japan suggests that the government there does not have a good record in picking winners rather than losers either. The targeting of the 1970s included petrochemicals, aluminum, copper refining, and shipbuilding, all failures. Paul R. Krugman, "Targeted Industrial Policies: Theory and Evidence," in Federal Reserve Bank, *Industrial Change;* and Thomas Pepper and Merit Janow, "Troubled Industries in Japan" (Washington, D.C.: Institute for International Economics, forthcoming).

16. To be sure, it is possible, in theory, to combat this by making policies of protection self-liquidating and by insisting on a requirement that funds allocated to facilitate adjustment be linked to obligations to demonstrate actual change. See John Zysman and Laura Tyson, *American Industry in International Competition: Government Policies and Corporate Strategies* (Ithaca: Cornell University Press, 1983).

17. Charles Kindleberger, *The World in Depression, 1929–39* (Berkeley: University of California Press, 1974); Robert Gilpin, *U.S. Power and the Multinational Corporation* (New York: Basic Books, 1975); Stephen Krasner, "State Power and the Structure of International Trade," *World Politics* (April 1976). For Robert Keohane's modification of the hegemonic thesis, supported by evidence from this book, see his *After Hegemony: Cooperation and Discord in the World Political Economy* (Princeton: Princeton University Press, 1984).

18. Robert Baldwin, "Rent-Seeking and Trade Policy: An Industry Approach" (forthcoming). Baldwin has also suggested taxing industry expenditures on information or advertising aimed at securing protection. "The Political Economy of Protectionism," in Jagdish N. Bhagwati, ed., *Import Competition and Response* (Chicago: University of Chicago Press for the National Bureau of Economic Research, 1982).

19. Gary Clyde Hufbauer and Howard Rosen, *Trade Policy for Troubled Industries* (Washington, D.C.: Institute for International Economics, forthcoming).

20. John G. Jackson, "Perspectives on the Jurisprudence of International Trade," *American Economic Review* (May 1984).

21. Kent E. Calder, "Opening Japan," *Foreign Policy* (Summer 1982). A similar argument is made, in global terms, by Susan Strange, "Protectionism and World Politics," *International Organization* (Spring 1985).

22. U.S. Department of Commerce, *International Direct Investment: Global Trends and the U.S. Role* (Washington, D.C.: Government Printing Office, August 1984).

23. Cf. "Pressure Grows on States to Reject World-Wide Unitary Tax System," *Wall Street Journal*, December 28, 1984.

24. William R. Cline et al., *Trade Negotiation in the Tokyo Round* (Washington, D.C.: Brookings, 1978).

25. U.S. Trade Representative, *Annual Report of the President of the United States on the Trade Agreements Program* (Washington, D.C.: USTR, 1983).

26. J. David Richardson, "Trade Adjustment Assistance under the United States Trade Act of 1974: An Analytical Examination and Worker Survey," with comments by C. Michael Aho and Martin Wolf, in Jagdish N. Bhagwati, ed., *Import Competition and Response*.

27. Lawrence, *Can America Compete?*; "Strong Dollar Has Led U.S. Firms to Transfer Production Overseas," *Wall Street Journal*, April 9, 1985.

28. This analysis supports the position of Robert Keohane in the debate about whether the presence of a hegemonic power is necessary to sustain a liberal international economic regime. Keohane, *After Hegemony*, argues that a hegemon may help create and maintain an international regime, but the existence of a hegemon is not necessary for the continuation of such a regime if political actors within a group of nations perceive the common interest clearly enough and have the wherewithal to prevail over more parochial domestic influences. For accounts of international economic policymaking that stress the possibility of building coalitions to resist protectionism, see Robert A. Pastor, *Congress and the Politics of U.S. Foreign Economic Policy 1929–1976* (Berkeley: University of California Press, 1980), and I.M. Destler, *Making Foreign Economic Policy* (Washington, D.C.: Brookings, 1980).

Index

About the Contributors

Richard E. Caves is professor of economics at Harvard University. His principal books include *Trade and Economic Structure* (1960), *Air Transport and Its Regulators* (1962), *Competition in the Open Economy* (1980), and *Multinational Enterprise and Economic Analysis* (1982). Recently published articles include "From Entry Barriers to Mobility Barriers," *Quarterly Journal of Economics* (May 1977); "Industrial Organization, Corporate Strategy and Structure," *Journal of Economic Literature* (March 1980); and "Intraindustry Trade and Market Structure in the Industrial Countries, *Oxford Economic Papers* (July 1981).

Sol C. Chaikin is president of the International Ladies' Garment Workers' Union and vice-president of the AFL-CIO and member of its Executive Council. He attended the College of the City of New York and graduated from Booklyn Law School in 1940, immediately going to work as an organizer for the International Ladies' Garment Workers' Union. He has represented the AFL-CIO at the Labor summits held in London (1977) and in Tokyo (1979). He is the author of *A Labor Viewpoint: Another Opinion,* and articles on such diversified issues as immigration reform, the growing wage gap among industrial sectors, and international trade.

Gary Gereffi is associate professor of sociology at Duke University and a visiting research fellow at the Center for U.S.-Mexican Studies at the University of California. He received the Ph.D. in sociology from Yale University. His current work in the area of policies for the production and marketing of essential drugs focuses on Latin America and Asia.

Joseph M. Grieco is assistant professor of political science at Duke University. He received the Ph.D. in government from Cornell University and served as a predoctoral fellow at the Center for International Studies, Princeton University, and a postdoctoral fellow at the Graduate School of Business

Administration, Harvard University. He has also written "American Multinationals and International Order," in Kenneth Thompson (ed.), *Institutions for Projecting American Values Abroad* (1983).

Gary C. Hufbauer is a Marcus Wallenberg Professor of International Financial Diplomacy at Georgetown University. He was deputy assistant secretary for international trade and investment policy of the U.S. Treasury, director of the international tax staff at the Treasury, and professor of economics at the University of New Mexico. Dr. Hufbauer has published numerous studies on international trade, investment, and tax issues.

John M. Kline is deputy director of the Karl F. Landegger Program in International Business Diplomacy at the School of Foreign Service, Georgetown University. Previously he served as director of international economic policy at the National Association of Manufacturers. He received the Ph.D. from George Washington University. His recent publications include *State Government Influence in U.S. International Economic Policy* (1983), and *International Codes in Multinational Business* (1985).

Jeffrey J. Schott is a research associate at the Institute for International Economics and is associated with the Diebold Institute for Public Policy Studies in New York. He was formerly a senior associate at the Carnegie Endowment for International Peace, an international economist in the U.S. Treasury Department, and a member of the research staff at the Brookings Institution.

Michael Shafer is assistant professor of international relations at Rutgers University. He received the Ph.D. from Harvard University, where he was a teaching fellow in the Department of Government and an associate of the Center for International Affairs. Other publications include "Mineral Myths," *Foreign Policy* (Summer 1982).

Raymond Vernon is Clarence Dillon Professor of International Affairs, Harvard University. He has also been Herbert F. Johnson Professor of International Business Management at the Harvard Business School and director of the Harvard Center for International Affairs. Among his publications are, *Sovereignty at Bay: The Multinational Spread of the U.S. Enterprise* (1971); *Big Business and the State: Changing Relations in Western Europe* (1974); and *Storm over the Multinationals: The Real Issues* (1977). He is editor of the *Journal of Policy Analysis and Management*.

Louis T. Wells, Jr., is Herbert F. Johnson Professor of International Management at Harvard Graduate School of Business Administration. He received the D.B.A. degree from Harvard, where he has been teaching since. He is a faculty associate of Harvard's Center for International Affairs and a member of the faculty council of the Harvard Institute for International Development. Professor Wells's recent publications include (edited with Robert Stobaugh) *Technology Crossing Borders* (1984); *Third World Multinationals* (1983); and (with Raymond Vernon) *Manager in the International Economy* (1981).

About the Editor

Theodore H. Moran is Karl F. Landegger Professor and director of the program in International Business Diplomacy, School of Foreign Service, Georgetown University. His publications include *International Political Risk Management: New Dimensions* (with Fariborz Ghadar, 1984); *Managing International Political Risk: Strategies and Techniques* (with Fariborz Ghadar and Stephen Kobrin, 1983); *International Political Risk Assessment: The State of the Art* (1980); *American Multinationals and American Interests* (with C. Fred Bergsten and Thomas Horst; Brookings, 1978); *Oil Prices and the Future of OPEC: The Political Economy of Tension and Stability in the Organization of Petroleum Exporting Countries* (Resources for the Future, 1978); *Multinational Corporations and the Politics of Dependence: Copper in Chile* (Princeton University Press, 1974). He has been a member of the board or advisory committee of *International Organization, World Trade,* The Overseas Development Council, and the Americas Society. He is a member of the board of the Association of Political Risk Analysts.